The Political Economy of Nationalisation in Britain is the first modern analysis of the causes of the nationalisations of the 1940s. It analyses the economic and political arguments used by the advocates and the opponents of public ownership. Special attention is given to the widespread belief that nationalisation would lead to higher levels of industrial efficiency. After introductory chapters dealing with the background to industrial organisation and the political aspects of nationalisation, the remaining chapters examine the public ownership debates in particular industries. In some, such as motor vehicles and cotton textiles, the option of nationalisation was contemplated but ultimately rejected, and it is just as important to understand why these sectors were left in private hands, as it is to explain the nationalisations of coal and the railways. While the criteria for nationalisation were not identical in every case, the studies in this volume indicate that a crucial factor was a perceived need to improve the efficiency with which basic inputs were supplied to British industry.

The political economy of nationalisation in Britain 1920–1950

The political economy of nationalisation in Britain 1920–1950

EDITED BY

ROBERT MILLWARD

Professor of Economic History at the University of Manchester

AND

JOHN SINGLETON

Lecturer in Economic History at Victoria University of Wellington

CAMBRIDGE
UNIVERSITY PRESS

Published by the Press Syndicate of the University of Cambridge
The Pitt Building, Trumpington Street, Cambridge CB2 1RP
40 West 20th Street, New York, NY 10011–4211, USA
10 Stamford Road, Oakleigh, Melbourne 3166, Australia

First published 1995

Printed in Great Britain at the University Press, Cambridge

A catalogue record for this book is available from the British Library

Library of Congress cataloguing in publication data

The political economy of nationalisation in Britain 1920–1950 /
edited by Robert Millward and John Singleton.
    p.   cm.
Papers presented at a conference held at St Anselm's Hall, University
of Manchester, April 1993.
Includes index.
ISBN 0 521 45096 9
1. Government ownership – Great Britain – History – Congresses.
2. Government ownership – Great Britain – Case studies – Congresses.
3. Great Britain – Economic policy – 1918–1945 – Congresses.
4. Great Britain – Economic policy – 1945– – Congresses.
I. Millward, Robert.   II. Singleton, John.
HD4145.P65   1995
338.941–dc20   94–9879   CIP

ISBN 0 521 45096 9

CE

Contents

List of tables	*page*	ix
List of contributors		xi
Preface		xiii

I *Government and industry 1920–50*

1 Industrial organisation and economic factors in nationalisation
ROBERT MILLWARD — 3

2 Labour, the Conservatives and nationalisation
JOHN SINGLETON — 13

II *Case studies of industry organisation, performance and nationalisation*

3 The coal industry: images and realities on the road to nationalisation
DAVID GREASLEY — 37

4 The changing role of government in British civil air transport 1919–49
PETER J. LYTH — 65

5 The motor vehicle industry
SUE BOWDEN — 88

6 The railway companies and the nationalisation issue 1920–50
GERALD CROMPTON — 116

7 The motives for gas nationalisation: practicality or ideology?
JOHN F. WILSON — 144

8   Public ownership and the British arms industry 1920–50   164
    DAVID EDGERTON

9   The water industry 1900–51: a failure of public policy?   189
    JOHN A. HASSAN

10 Debating the nationalisation of the cotton industry, 1918–50   212
    JOHN SINGLETON

III *Government and the process of industrial change in the 1940s*

11 'The Thin Edge of the Wedge?': nationalisation and industrial
    structure during the Second World War   237
    PETER HOWLETT

12 The political economy of nationalisation: the electricity
    industry   257
    MARTIN CHICK

13 Partners and enemies: the government's decision to nation-
    alise steel 1944–8   275
    RUGGERO RANIERI

IV *Review and Conclusions*

14 The ownership of British industry in the post-war era: an
    explanation   309
    ROBERT MILLWARD AND JOHN SINGLETON

Index   321

List of tables

1.1 Establishment of major statutory public enterprises in British industry 1900–51   *page* 5

2.1 Nationalisation plans in Labour election manifestos 1918–51   16

2.2 Summary of Gallup polls on nationalisation March 1944–May 1945   22

2.3 Union sponsored members of Parliament 1918–50   28

3.1 British coalmining productivity in 1938   43

3.2 Output and productivity in north Derbyshire and Nottinghamshire   43

3.3 Mine size and productivity in 1944   45

4.1 Airline revenue, passengers and subsidies: Britain and Germany 1924–55   72

5.1 Production of motor vehicles 1924–48   90

5.2 Exports of motor vehicles 1924–48   90

5.3 The performance of Morris 1920–50   92

5.4 The performance of Austin 1922–38   92

5.5 British motor vehicle production by firms 1938 and 1947   103

5.6 Ford and Vauxhall's share of total 'Big Six' car production 1929–38   106

7.1 The British gas industry 1882–1937   146

7.2 The size distribution of gas undertakings in 1937   148

7.3 The ownership structure of statutory gas undertakings 1910–45   154

8.1 Expenditure on armaments and warlike stores 1923–33   168

8.2 Government actual expenditure on fixed capital for war production 1 April 1936–31 March 1945   180

8.3 Distribution of government financed fixed capital for war production 1 April 1936–31 March 1945   181

8.4 Employment in government-owned factories and plant June 1943   181

9.1   Estimate of numbers of undertakings in the water supply
       industry 1904–70   190
11.1   Estimated capital assistance to aircraft industry July 1939–
       September 1945   239
11.2   Summary of industrial panel investigations by topic July
       1942–April 1944   241
11.3   Shorts Group output of Stirling bombers: average weekly
       output per month November 1941–December 1943   246
11.4   The impact of the Concentration of Production Drive on
       four industries   251
11.5   Change in share of manufacturing employment (by percent-
       age point) 1924–38, 1938–45 and 1948–55   252
12.1   Total costs of distribution per unit of electricity sold 1933–4   259
13.1   Concentration in the steel industry: selected indicators
       1951–3   292

Figure 11.1   Stirling bomber output as percentage of programme   247

List of contributors

ROBERT MILLWARD is Professor of Economic History at the University of Manchester and has published articles and books about the economic history and economics of the British public sector.

JOHN SINGLETON is a Lecturer in Economic History, Victoria University of Wellington, New Zealand, and author of *Lancashire on the Scrapheap: The Cotton Industry, 1945–70*.

SUE BOWDEN is a Lecturer in Economic History in the School of Economics and Business Studies, University of Leeds and has published several journal articles on the motor industry in Britain.

MARTIN CHICK is a Lecturer in the Department of Economic and Social History, University of Edinburgh. He has written widely on nationalisation, privatisation and government–industry relations and he is currently writing a book on the economic planning of the Attlee governments.

GERALD CROMPTON is a Lecturer in Economic and Social History at the University of Kent at Canterbury. He has interests in business history and transport history, and has published several articles on the problems of the railways in the period between grouping and nationalisation.

DAVID EDGERTON is Head of the Department of History of Science and Technology at Imperial College, London. He is the author of *England and the Aeroplane: An Essay on an industrial and technological nation* and a number of papers on the industrial relations of technology and warfare in Britain.

DAVID GREASLEY is a Senior Lecturer in Economic and Social History at the University of Edinburgh. He has published several articles on the Economic History of the British coal industry.

JOHN HASSAN is a Lecturer in Economic History at the Manchester Metropolitan University. He has written a number of articles on the history of the water and energy industries.

PETER HOWLETT is a Lecturer in Economic History at the London School of Economics. He has published several articles on the British economy in the Second World War.

PETER LYTH is a Research Associate in the Business History Unit of the London School of Economics and teaches modern European history at the University of Tel-Aviv. He has published several articles on civil aviation and is currently working on a comparative history of the British and Dutch airline industry.

RUGGERO RANIERI teaches History and European Studies at the University of Essex. He has published several articles on the steel industry in western Europe after 1945. His latest work, published by Il Mulino, is a discussion of Italy's post-war industrial performance.

JOHN WILSON is a Lecturer in Economic History at the University of Manchester. He has published several books and articles on the development of Britain's energy industries, as well as working in the field of business history.

Preface

This book originated from a perception that the causes of the nationalisation of the 1940s in Britain were very thinly treated in the literature. John Singleton and I discussed this gap in industrial history and decided to organise a conference of those academics in Britain who had detailed knowledge of particular industries. We are grateful to the Nuffield Foundation for providing part of the finance for the conference which was held at St Anselm's Hall, University of Manchester in April 1993. The University also provided financial help from its Small Grants Fund and since altogether some forty people attended, the Conference was a great success. John Singleton was then a Lecturer at the University but was about to depart for a tenured post in New Zealand. Subsequently he and I have communicated regularly in editing the Conference papers. We are grateful for John Wilson's help with the organisation and finances of the Conference and we would like to thank Freda Diggle and Fran Morris of the History Department for help with the Conference and with the preparation of this book.

ROBERT MILLWARD

I

Government and industry 1920–50

1 Industrial organisation and economic factors in nationalisation

Robert Millward

The changes in the ownership of British industry in the 1940s were quite remarkable. Only fifty years before, at the end of the old century, the British government's disinclination to intervene in industrial matters was renowned. By the end of the 1940s government regulation and ownership of industry matched any country in the Western World. Nationalisation of transport and fuel by the 1945–51 Labour government was a major element in these changes: coal, railways, docks, inland waterways, road transport, gas, electricity, airlines, telecommunications, the Bank of England, iron and steel were all taken into public ownership. Only Supple (1986), Hannah (1979) and Edgerton (1984) have really tried to explain the reasons for this. The mainstream textbook explanations have involved two arguments (Aldcroft 1968, 1986, Alford 1988, Cairncross 1985). The first is that nationalisation was an inevitable outcome of long-standing problems especially in the ailing coal and railway industries. This however raises questions about why non-ailing industries like electricity, tele-communications and airlines were nationalised and why some ailing industries like cotton and shipbuilding were not. Why moreover was nationalisation the chosen form of public intervention for long-standing problems – what was inevitable about that? The second argument has been that the Labour government's nationalisations of the 1940s were the centrepiece of the socialist vision; they crystallised all that had been discussed and promised in the rise of socialism in the twentieth century. This raises the question of why socialism should have very restricted industrial boundaries with most of manufacturing left in private ownership.

These questions are addressed in this book and take on added significance from subsequent industrial developments in the UK including the 1980s privatisations. It will become clear from the rest of this book that the importance of sound finance and the promotion of efficiency were central elements in the push to nationalisation and in the minds of those who drafted the 1940s industrial legislation. The assets of the old private companies were vested in new bodies like the Iron and Steel Corporation, the British Transport Commission, the National Coal Board, all of which had a corporate status free from Treasury supervision of personnel and from day to day supervision by the Minister or Parliament. This was expected to promote initiative, enterprise and a basically commercial ambience. By the late 1970s and early 1980s questions of finance and efficiency were precisely, if not necessarily justifiably, at the front of the dissatisfaction with the nationalised industries. By the 1980s the absence of defenders of nationalisation was quite marked across much of the academic and political spectrum. A recent volume on the long-term features of the post-war British economy concludes that nationalisation, as a model, had had its day (Dunkerley and Hare 1991, p. 416). This critique has been buttressed by a new wave of literature on incentives and property rights. The seminal work was by Alchian and Demsetz (see for example Alchian 1965 and Demsetz 1983). Private ownership allows individual owners unilaterally to sell or exchange their shares in a firm. In public ownership individuals can exchange their set of rights only by migrating or by political action. Hence, so the argument goes, the pressure on management is so much less in public firms. These arguments raise very clear puzzles about the motives for nationalisation; how could anyone, one might ask, have thought it an appropriate instrument of industrial policy.

Let us start here by recalling the main elements of government industrial policy in the inter-war period and the main phases of public ownership of industry. For the latter, table 1.1 provides a chronological list of the major highlights. In the nineteenth century, British government intervention in manufacturing and mining was concerned mainly with questions of safety and was often triggered off by mine explosions and factory accidents. This was also important in railways, tramways, electricity, gas and water supply where in addition problems of granting rights of way, compulsory land purchases and monopolistic tendencies had drawn in both central and local government. Then there were the collective actions increasingly characterising the wage bargaining of both workers and employers with contingent threats to law and order. Finally the widening of the franchise from the 1860s meant that Members of Parliament were subject to a wider set of pressures many of which stemmed from economic, including industrial, issues. From the late nineteenth century, workers with complaints about wage and employment levels came increasingly to expect their MPs to press their case.

In the period 1914–40 three additional factors were at work. The First World War not only brought trade unions into national wage negotiations and introduced central planning in some sectors but it also revealed certain new techniques, technological gaps and weaknesses on

Table 1.1. *Establishment of major statutory public enterprises in British industry 1900–51*

1902	Metropolitan Water Board
1908	Port of London Authority
1926	Central Electricity Board
1926	British Broadcasting Corporation
1933	London Passenger Transport Board
1940	British Overseas Airways Corporation
1943	North of Scotland Hydro-Electric Board
1946	Bank of England
1946	British European Airways Corporation
1947	National Coal Board
1948	British Transport Commission
1948	British Electricity Authority and Area Electricity Boards
1949	Area Gas Boards and British Gas Council
1951	Iron and Steel Corporation of Great Britain

which government action was expected in peacetime – for example, airframes, dyestuffs and related chemical products leading to government involvement in the establishment of Imperial Chemical Industries (ICI) in 1926 and the development of the 'ring' of aircraft manufacturers (Fearon 1974, Reader 1977). Secondly the stagnant economic conditions of the inter-war period caused governments to be involved in industrial performance. The most dramatic output losses were in the export trades which had been central to the economy in the late nineteenth century and which were regionally concentrated. Given the widening electorate this carried political difficulties and in addition the output losses were seen, then and subsequently, as a manifestation of industrial decline. The third factor was that technological and administrative changes were making for larger sized industrial undertakings. Interest in this stemmed in part from the potential monopoly power of such large business units but also and (cf. Hannah 1976, p. 73), perhaps more important, British governments, conscious of the loss of export markets and apparent industrial decline, saw the move to large firms as typical of the USA and Germany, the pace-setters, and indeed of the 'new industries' (non-ferrous metals, telephone apparatus, tyres); hence the green light to push British industry along that path.

In the 1920s industrialists, politicians and civil servants clung to the pre-war world, which included an Empire bias, whilst the Treasury's classical view on crowding out and wage flexibility helped to erode some of the state intervention hanging over from the war (Lowe 1978). Unemployment persisted in certain regions where decline seemed to be reinforced. The establishment view that regional unemployment was essentially a symptom of the world depression and that the depressed areas were a social rather than an economic problem gave way by the 1930s to attempts, albeit half-hearted, to shift industry to the depressed areas (Parsons 1988, chapters 1 and 2). A product of this complex of forces was a government policy towards industry with two elements. First was a hesitant and often reluctant alleviation of key sectors from the full brunt of market forces. Short-term palliatives to cotton, iron, steel and other staples came from bank loans and overdrafts which by the end of the 1920s were drawing in the Bank of England, anxious to avoid financial disasters and to avoid embroiling the government (Kirby 1974, Heim 1983, 1986). The longer-term policy was to support the introduction of price-fixing schemes whose effectiveness has been much disputed except where foreign competition was excluded by protection as in the 33 per cent steel tariff of the 1930s.

In any case such price fixing came increasingly, as in the coal industry, to be seen as undermining the second element of policy, the elimination of excess capacity and promotion of amalgamation. For much of the period such promotional activity by the government was hesitant. Contraction and rationalisation occurred towards the end of the 1930s for the cotton industry but largely because demand never recovered; rationalisation through the 1930 Coal Mines Act was undermined by the lack of compulsory powers which again did not materialise until the end of the 1930s (Kirby 1973a, b). In the utilities field the major success was the Central Electricity Board which from 1926 centralised the high-tension transmission of electricity in a national grid and saw the gap with US technical efficiency eliminated by the end of the 1930s (Foreman-Peck 1991). Finally the generally protective and anti-competitive attitudes which inter-war governments displayed, especially towards large business units, carried over to transport. In a broad sense the main characteristic of the inter-war years was the emergence of the four railway companies under such tight regulation that they had difficulty in adapting to the new small highly competitive mode of transport. As a result government policy restricted road transport in such a way as to favour both the large railway companies and the larger business units emerging in both road freight and road passenger activities – Pickfords, Carter Paterson, Tilling, Scottish Electric Traction (Savage 1966, chapters 7 and 8).

Transport, communication and fuel are what one might call network industries, carrying classical market failure problems of natural monopoly and externalities. In the distribution networks of electricity, gas, railways and telecommunications it was often cheaper for one firm to supply the same service as two or more firms: natural monopoly. In addition the social benefit of investment in roads, railways and tele-communications may be expected to exceed private benefits through reductions in road congestion and pollution and through the opening up of new territories. The movement to larger business units in transport, communications and fuel was a central feature of the inter-war period. Several of the chapters which follow describe this in detail. They show how the optimal size of business organisation was extended beyond the local to a regional, sectoral and generally sub-national dimension. But the whole process of voluntary amalgamation proved to be very slow, and professional, official and political opinions were converging in a call for a more rapid movement to larger units of business organisation in gas supply, electricity retail distribution, airlines and coal. Thus in electricity supply, whereas the national grid was being developed from 1926 by the Central Electricity Board, retail distribution was in the hands of a vast number of private and local authority undertakings who were resistant to amalgamation and not thereby able to capture, as the McGowan Com-mittee (1936) pointed out, economies in marketing and finance. The same story applies to gas; there was no case here for a national grid but economies in distribution were possible from larger business units, as the Heyworth Report (1945) suggested. In domestic airlines up to twenty companies were operating in the 1930s in what was a small market and the private companies were disinclined to amalgamate and streamline operations; the Cadman Report (1938) was particularly critical of the Civil Aviation Authority in this respect. Finally official reports on the coal industry throughout the inter-war period pressed for larger business units to raise investment and productivity but by 1938 70 per cent of the industry's 1,034 companies still employed less than 6 per cent of the industry's labour force (Supple 1987, p. 303).

At the very minimum, government intervention to promote amalga-mation would necessitate legislation but it would have to be much stronger than the arms-length variety typical of the inter-war years. Indeed more generally, the perceived failure of inter-war arms-length regulation seems to be enough to explain the move in the 1940s to changing the *ownership* structure of many of the industries and in par-ticular to a shift to public boards of a regional or at least sub-national dimension. There is a further ingredient that was present. The concentra-tion in the railway industry was already sufficient to exploit any regional economies of scale, and economies on a national scale were, as in coal, not so obvious. Yet both finished up not with sets of regional boards but with centrally owned and organized enterprises – the Railway Executive, the National Coal Board. Moroever, whilst regional boards did emerge in the other utility sectors they were supervised by overarching bodies like the

British Gas Council and the British Electricity Authority as well as the British Transport Commision which came to own all the assets in railways, docks, harbours and significant sectors of road transport. There is little doubt that this outcome was a product of the particular historical circumstances. Railways and coal were ailing industries, with a run-down capital stock and the second half of the 1940s after the war was in general a reconstruction period and one with a Labour government committed to administrative planning. The overarching national bodies were an intrinsic part of the legislation which established the nationalised industries and the Acts of Parliament placed on them the obligation to develop investment and training programmes (cf. Foreman-Peck and Millward 1994, chapter 8).

This analysis of the existing literature provides then certain pointers to the links between industrial organisation and nationalisation. These links are explored in the following chapters which also deal with the many unresolved questions. Thus the arguments we have advanced so far do not apply readily to cotton, aircraft, armaments production and shipbuilding. Larger business units were seen as desirable, yet none of these industries were nationalised. Nor was the water industry which displayed all the problems of local gas and electricity supplies. Further the coal industry had all the properties of a classic competitive industry and industrial arguments for nationalisation based on natural monopoly or externality issues look rather weak here, yet coal was the first major industry to be nationalised.

These puzzles are addressed in the detailed industry chapters which follow and we draw the threads together in the concluding chapter of the book. When nationalisation occurred in the 1940s it invariably took the form of the 'public corporation' which had many similarities to the earlier public boards listed in table 1.1 and we can usefully conclude this introduction by showing why this came to be the chosen legal instrument of public ownership in Britain.

In the nineteenth century, public ownership and nationalisation had been invariably associated with an enterprise run by a government department. Where the municipal undertaking was the appropriate form for local government, the Post Office was a model for the nationalised industry. For many outside socialist circles this had generated a major fear, that of bureaucratic rigidities and political interference; the naval dockyards often being quoted as a classic example of poor performance (cf. W.S. Jevons 1867, 1874). This led several observers during the 1920s to favour the idea of a public board, taking the operations 'out of politics' (Ostergaard 1954, p. 206). For some, contemporary changes in the private sector appeared to point the way. The growing dominance of the joint stock company seemed to involve the divorce of ownership and control, with top management rewarded by salary rather profit. As one student of these views said: 'If it was not essential to good management for the directors to own some or all of the capital could there not be bodies without equity capital, that is without shareholders, but managed by a Board of Directors' (Chester 1979, p. 384). On the left there were also leanings towards public boards but for different reasons. Guild socialists and syndicalists envisaged them as Boards of Management with representatives from the work force and hence close to worker cooperatives. In the 1920s the Central Electricity Board and British Broadcasting Corporation were established without worker representatives, and some trade unionists – the Union of Postal Workers in particular – opposed the idea of a public corporation right through to the 1940s because it omitted representatives of what they conceived as the democratic elements, Parliament and the unions.

A crucial step in the development of the basis of ownership and control of the public corporation seems to have been a memo drawn up in 1928 in part as a response to the criticisms of the coal industry nationalisation proposals which the Labour Party had put to the 1925 Samuel Commission. The authors were Shinwell and Strachey who envisaged a 'public utility corporation' which would be vested with the assets of the industry and which would issue fixed interest stock held by the state in lieu of the compensation it, the state, had paid to former owners (Ostergaard 1954, pp. 209–10). There were to be no trade union representatives who would have conflicting interests and though many subsequently pressed for union representation it never emerged. In practice the Central Electricity Board stock and the London Passenger Transport Board stock were held by the former owners, a matter of concern to some who saw the industry as thereby reconstructed rather than brought under social ownership. These reservations disappeared once it had been made clear (by, amongst others, the Trade Union Congress in 1932; cf. Ostergaard 1954, p. 216) that the stockholders had no voting rights, did not own any equity and the government was the sole owner. In fact in one or two corporations, including the National Coal Board, the private owners were given compensation in the form of government stock and in the 1950s and 1960s this became the general pattern of finance, by stock issues. The final strand in the emergence of the public corporation as the legal instrument was the need to make it answerable to government. This had long been a bone of contention within the Labour Party which had opposed *ad hoc* boards like the Metropolitan Water Board and the Port of London Authority which were accountable to Parliament but not answerable to the relevant local government authorities. Indeed Morrison broke with Labour Party traditions in promoting the London Passenger Transport Board which was also *ad hoc* in this sense. All of which suggests a closer look at the role of both Labour and Conservative Parties is warranted and this forms the subject of the next chapter.

In summary, in the nineteenth century, government kept its distance from industry, preferring not to interfere with 'property'. The social and political forces which were already undermining that stance were enhanced in the inter-war years by the decline of the staple industries and the general loss of industrial leadership in both Germany and USA where large business organisations were coming to dominate the industrial scene. The reaction of British governments in the 1920s and 1930s was often hesitant and piecemeal. Price fixing and tariff protection were introduced to alleviate the worst affected sectors. The longer-term policy was to promote amalgamations of firms and rationalisation of industries to meet the new industrial competition. In transport, communications and fuel there were important scale economies to be realised but the government attempts to promote this by arm's length regulation came to be seen as ineffective and this explains some of the momentum towards public ownership in the 1940s. This line of argument is explored in several of the following chapters dealing with gas, railways, airlines and electricity. Other chapters address the puzzle of why some industries which appeared to have underlying structural weaknesses, like steel, cotton and motor vehicles were not nationalised. Water resource development moreover seemed to cry out for rationalisation but was untouched. Coal had all the properties of a classic competitive industry yet was the first major industry to be nationalised. Armaments and aircraft production remained in the private sector despite their strategic importance. There is, in other words, an overall mosaic to be explained and this is attempted in the last chapter.

REFERENCES

Alchian, A.A. (1965) 'Some economics of property rights', *Il Politico*, reprinted in A.A. Alchian *Economic Forces at Work* Indianopolis: Liberty Press, 1977.
Aldcroft, D.H. (1968), *British Railways in Transition*, London: Macmillan.
    (1986), *The British Economy: vol 1: The Years of Turmoil 1918–39*, Harvester.
Alford, B.W.E. (1988), *British Economic Performance 1945–75*, London: Macmillan.
Cadman Report (1938), 'Report of the Committee of Inquiry into Civil Aviation', Cmd. 5685, March.
Cairncross, A., (1985), *Years of Recovery: British Economic Policy 1945–51*, London: Methuen.
Chester, Sir N. (1979), *The Nationalisation of British Industry 1945–51*, HMSO.

Demsetz, H. (1983), 'The structure of ownership and the theory of the firm', *Journal of Law and Economics*, 11 (April): 375–90.

Dunkerley, J. and Hare, P.G. (1991), 'Nationalised industries', in N.F.R. Crafts and N.W.C. Woodward (eds.), *The British Economy Since 1945*, Oxford: Clarendon Press.

Edgerton, D.E.H. (1984), 'Technical innovation, industrial capacity and efficiency: public ownership and the British military aircraft industry 1935–48', *Business History*, 26(3): 247–79.

Fearon, P. (1974), 'The British airframe industry and the state 1918–35', *Economic History Review*, 26: 236–51.

Foreman-Peck, J. (1991), 'Industry and industrial organisation in the inter-war years: a survey of British experience', *University of Manchester Working Papers in Economic and Social History*, No. 5.

Foreman-Peck, J. and Millward, R. (1994), *Public and Private Ownership of British Industry 1820–1990*, Oxford University Press.

Hannah, L. (1976), *The Rise of the Corporate Economy*, London: Methuen.

(1979), *Electricity Before Nationalisation*, London: Macmillan.

Heim, C.E. (1983), 'Industrial organisation and regional development in inter-war Britain', *Journal of Economic History*, 43(4) (December): 931–52.

(1986), 'Inter-War responses to regional decline', in B. Elbaum and W. Lazonock (eds.), *The Decline of the British Economy*, Oxford: Clarendon Press.

Heyworth Report (19450, 'Report of the Committee of Inquiry into the Gas Industry 1945', Cmd. 6699.

Jevons, W.S. (1867), 'On the analogy between the Post Office, telegraphs and other systems of conveyance of the United Kingdom as regards government control', *Transactions of the Manchester Statistical Society*, pp. 91–104.

(1874), 'The railways and the state', in *Essays and Addresses: Owens College, Manchester*, London: Macmillan.

Kirby, M.W. (1973a), 'The control of competition in the coal mining industry in the thirties', *Economic History Review*, 26.

(1973b), 'Governmental intervention in industrial organisation: coal mining in the 1930s', *Business History*, 15.

(1974), 'The Lancashire cotton industry in the inter-war years: a study in organisational change', *Business History*, 16.

Lowe, R. (1978), 'The erosion of state intervention in Britain 1917–24', *Economic History Review*, 31.

McGowan Report (1936), 'Report of the Committee on Electricity Distribution', Ministry of Transport, May.

Ostergaard, G.N. (1954), 'Labour and the development of the public corporation', *Manchester School*, 22.

Parsons, W. (1988), *The Political Economy of British Regional Policy*, London: Routledge.

Reader, W.J. (1977), 'Imperial chemical industries and the state 1925–45', in B. Supple (ed.), *Essays in British Business History*, Oxford: Clarendon Press.

Samuel Commission (1935) 'Report of the Royal Commission on the Coal Industry', Cmd. 2600.

Savage, C.I. (1966), *An Economic History of Transport*, Hutchinson.

Supple, B. (1986), 'Ideology or pragmatism?: the nationalisation of coal 1916–46', in N. Mckendrick and R.B. Outhwaite (eds.), *Business Life and Public Policy: Essays in Honour of D.C. Coleman*, Cambridge University Press.

(1987), *The History of the Coal Industry: vol. 4: 1913–46: The Political Economy of Decline*, Oxford: Clarendon Press.

2   Labour, the Conservatives and nationalisation

John Singleton

Nationalisation was both a political and an economic issue. How, then, are we to disentangle the political from the economic variables accounting for the growth of the state sector in Britain? No two candidates for public ownership were exactly the same, and the political and economic cases put forward by the supporters and opponents of nationalisation differed from industry to industry. Clearly, all economic arguments for nationalisation had a political context and contained either an implicit or an explicit political message. If we accept McCloskey's view (1986) that economics is primarily a set of techniques for winning debates, we may never succeed in separating the economic from the political components of the nationalisation issue.

Recent research has stressed that nationalisation should not be treated in isolation from industrial policy in general. State intervention in business could take a number of forms, including the provision of technical assistance, the encouragement of industry-level planning, and the use of direct controls over the allocation of inputs. Nationalisation stood at one end of the continuum of options from which governments could select their policies for dealing with industrial problems (Mercer, Rollings and Tomlinson 1992). This interpretation is unobjectionable, although it does not alter the fact that nationalisation was a particularly radical form of industrial intervention. Moreover, the state in Britain was prepared to resort to nationalisation more readily than governments in some other countries, such as the United States and Canada (Grant 1989). Given that there was something very distinctive about the public ownership option, this chapter seeks to examine the politics of nationalisation in Britain from 1918 to 1950.

1   Nationalisation and the Labour Party 1918–39

Support for nationalisation in the Labour Party stemmed from a variety of economic and social concerns. Capitalism was both a moral evil and a source of economic inefficiency, in the opinion of early twentieth-century socialists (Dennis and Halsey 1988, Tawney 1922, Wright 1987). The economic historian and socialist activist, R.H. Tawney, argued that Labour's 'fundamental dogma is the dignity of man; its fundamental criticism of capitalism is, not merely that it impoverishes the mass of mankind . . . but that it makes riches a God, and treats common men as less than men' (Tawney 1964, p. 197). The abolition of the private ownership of industry, and its replacement by an economic system in which working men and women were in full control of their own destinies, was a precondition for the recovery of the human spirit from the horrors of industrialisation. Tawney's attack on capitalism was inspired by Christian socialist principles. An ethical approach to socialisation is also to be found in the statements of leading Labour politicians. Aneurin Bevan, the founder of the National Health Service, explained in his personal manifesto, *In Place of Fear*, that nationalisation would produce a gradual change in the attitudes of workers and managers towards each other, leading to full democratic participation in decision making, and 'that spiritual homogeneity that comes when the workman is united once more with the tools of his craft, a unity that was ruptured by the rise of economic classes' (Bevan 1976, p. 128). Other advocates of nationalisation, such as Sir Leo Chiozza Money, a First World War planner and convert from the Liberal Party, tended to stress more pragmatic considerations. Money had been impressed by the efficiency of state-owned munitions factories during the war and argued that this system should be extended to other industries in peacetime (Money 1920).

In 1918 a general commitment to the nationalisation of British industry was enshrined in Clause Four of the constitution of the Labour Party. The Labour Party was a diverse coalition of hundreds of trade unions and a handful of small socialist factions. At the end of the war Labour's leaders needed to devise a statement of economic principles which would unite and inspire the movement. Equally important, they needed to differentiate Labour's creed from those of the bolsheviks on the left and the Liberals on the right (Winter 1974, pp. 259–63). Clause Four was their solution, calling for 'the common ownership of the means of production, distribution, and exchange, and the best obtainable system of popular administration and control of each industry or service'. Its vagueness was deliberate, since it was designed to appeal to many shades of opinion. The unions accepted Clause Four at the 1918 Labour conference, although they were more interested in schemes for maintaining wartime controls over industry in order to stabilise incomes and prevent profiteering. An earlier draft simply called for the nationalisation of monopolies and essential raw materials, and McKibbin argues that the phrase 'means of production, distribution, and exchange' was inserted to appeal to middle-class activists (McKibbin 1974, p. 97).

Tomlinson, in minimalist vein, describes Clause Four as 'not an extended reflection on the nature of socialist policies but rather a variety of short-term, *ad hoc* points' (Tomlinson 1982, p. 3). For Gamble and Walkland, Labour's commitment to public ownership was merely one of the 'ideological totems which [have] concentrated debate into well-worn channels', thereby disguising the lack of real choice in British politics (Gamble and Walkland 1984, p. 177). Drucker is less dismissive and makes much of the distinction between the doctrine, or formal pro- gramme, and ethos, or culture and tradition, of a political party. Clause Four expressed the Labour Party's faith that a more egalitarian society was within reach. The fact that it did not specify a timetable of action or explain what was meant by 'popular administration and control' was irrelevant: 'Clause Four's continuance as the sole statement of principle in Labour's constitution holds Labour true to its past, true to what its originators wanted it to be: for labour and against capital' (Drucker 1979, p. 38).

The inter-war period was one of considerable disappointment for the Labour Party, which was unable to take full advantage of the decline of the Liberals and to establish itself as a serious challenger to the Conserva- tives. Labour was never strong enough to force through its programme for the socialisation of specific industries. Labour's 1918 policy statement *Labour and the New Social Order*, which was considerably more ambi- tious than the election manifesto of the same year, reaffirmed the Party's commitment to nationalise arms production, and promised the immediate nationalisation of railways, coal mines, and electricity, to be followed by land, canals, harbours, steamships, industrial life assurance, and the production and sale of alcohol. This list was the shape of things to come, and Miliband sorrowfully remarks that it confirmed the movement's lack of ambition and its pathetic belief in 'piecemeal collectivism, within a predominantly capitalist society, as the key to more welfare, higher efficiency, and greater social justice' (Miliband 1964, p. 62).

Labour's list of target industries fluctuated during the 1920s and 1930s. The mines, transport, and power were the most regular candidates for public ownership, but other industries cropped up from time to time, including cotton, the banks, and chemicals. Enthusiasm for nationali- sation increased during the early 1930s. Rising interest in economic planning, due to its apparent success in the Soviet Union, and the need to find an alternative to the market system which had failed to ensure full employment in Britain, enhanced the attractions of a policy of nationali- sation. Schemes for the public ownership of the banking sector were held to be of key importance (Pollard 1979). With the supply of credit in public hands, a Labour government would be able to divert resources towards those industries which it felt were essential to the national interest. Until

Table 2.1. *Nationalisation plans in Labour election manifestos 1918–51*

1918	1922	1923	1924	1929
Coal mines	Coal mines	Coal mines	Coal mines	Coal mines
Railways	Railways	Railways	Railways	
Electricity		Electricity	Canals	
Shipping				
Armaments				
Land				

1931	1935	1945	1950	1951
Coal mines	Coal mines	Coal mines	Sugar	'concerns
Transport	Transport	Transport	Cement	which fail
Iron and Steel	Iron and Steel	Iron and Steel	Water	the nation'
Land	Land	Land	Minerals	
Banks	Banks	Gas	Meat supply	
Power	Electricity	Electricity	Chemicals (?)	
	Cotton	Bank of England		
	Armaments			

Note: Other industries appeared as nationalisation candidates in interim policy documents without appearing in the election manifesto. It should be noted that the manifestos are not devoid of ambiguity.
Source: Craig 1970.

Keynesian demand management techniques had been properly thought out and disseminated, it seemed to most socialists that the only way to eliminate economic uncertainty and unemployment was to exert direct control over industry. For some this meant Soviet-style communism, but for the majority it meant nationalising the commanding heights of the economy – transport, banking, iron and steel, fuel and power – and using these sectors as levers through which to regulate the operations of other industries (Barry 1965, Durbin 1986). However, the split in Ramsay MacDonald's cabinet in 1931 rendered the Labour Party incapable of putting such radical notions into practice during the remainder of the decade.

The 1930s saw a painful struggle over the appropriate institutional form for the nationalised industries (cf. chapter 1). This was fought out between the advocates of the non-political public corporation, led by Herbert Morrison of the London County Council, and those, including Ernest Bevin of the Transport and General Workers Union, who wished to allow for some measure of worker participation in the management of state-owned industries. The 1918 Labour manifesto had promised democratic control of the nationalised industries, but this idea did not appeal to all sides within the Party. Morrison, in his influential *Socialisation and Transport*, argued that 'the majority of workmen are . . . more interested in the organisation, conditions, and life of their own workshop than in those finer balances of financial, and commercial policy which are discussed in the Board room' (Morrison 1933, pp. 224–5). This was a tactful way of saying that the workers should not try to rise above their station.

Morrison's public corporation model won the day, although the issue of worker control and participation returned to the surface from time to time. Morgan speculates that the preference of some Labour leaders for the public corporation was related to their upper-middle-class background, although Morrison himself could not be convicted on this score. Clement Attlee had been a pupil at Haileybury, a school with a strong imperial tradition, and Hugh Gaitskell was the son of an Indian civil servant. It was natural for them to imagine that the nationalised industries should be run along the same lines as British colonies – not by shop stewards or union officials – but by benign and incorruptible public servants (Morgan 1987, p. 294).

2   Nationalisation and the Conservative Party 1918–39

It was a Conservative government, under the archpragmatist, Stanley Baldwin, which took the lead in the extension of public enterprise, when it established a Central Electricity Board in 1926 in order to build a national electricity supply grid (Hannah 1977). Given the problems of the inter-war British economy, it was hard for the Tories to dismiss calls for public ownership as mere rabblerousing. In fact, many Conservatives had an ambivalent attitude towards the state. There was tension between their belief in the autonomy of the individual and their emphasis on the communal life of the British nation (Greenleaf 1973, Durham 1989).

Harris detects a rising groundswell of support for corporatist ideas in the inter-war Conservative Party. He argues that there were two strands of Tory corporatism. The pluralistic corporatists advocated state involvement in the promotion of cartels and schemes for industrial self-government, but were strongly opposed to nationalisation. The *etatiste* corporatists were more radical and were not prepared to rule out nationalisation as a last resort for industries which did not respond to other methods (Harris, N. 1972, pp. 48–61).

Prominent amongst the Tory *etatistes* were the young Harold Macmillan and his collaborators (Booth and Pack 1985, pp. 55–75). In their opening manifesto in 1927, *Industry and the State*, they urged both socialists and free marketeers to abandon their entrenched positions: 'the science of modern economics is neither simple nor clear-cut. Our knowledge of it is at the present time so limited that we have never been able to evolve any fundamental laws upon which to build a theory' (Boothby, Loder, Macmillan and Stanley 1927, p. 29). Only pragmatism could identify and solve the problems of British industry. Tory radicals believed that the economy was undergoing a process of evolution: the average size of firms was increasing, the pay and status of workers were improving, and power was passing from the capitalist class to a new and more responsible managerial class. Some industries, however, were not evolving as smoothly as others and they required special guidance from the government. Large firms which abused their monopolistic powers had to be disciplined, and old industries which had fallen on hard times might need help to rationalise their capacity and to introduce new technology. A range of treatments was available in the medicine cabinet, from plans for industrial self government to trust-busting legislation and the imposition of punitive taxes on rogue firms. Nationalisation was not a desirable option, since it led to an ebbing away of the competitive spirit, but exceptions were possible in the case of 'born' monopolies, such as the railways and public utilities, if other methods of control had been tried and found wanting (Boothby, Loder, Macmillan and Stanley 1927, p. 223).

Industry and the State met with a patronising response from the leaders of the Conservative Party (Macmillan 1966, p. 173). But a further attempt was made to bridge the chasm between socialism and capitalism in the mid 1930s, when Macmillan joined the Next Five Years Group, an alliance of independently minded thinkers drawn from industry, academia, and all the main political parties. This group identified excess capacity as the most urgent problem confronting British industry and advocated collective schemes for maintaining prices and scrapping excess capacity (Next Five Years Group 1935, Carpenter 1976, Marwick 1964, Ritschel 1991). Industrial self government was not the only solution advocated by the Next Five Years Group, and a handful of industries were recommended for nationalisation. Public ownership of the Bank of England would assist the government to channel more funds into industrial investment. The nationalisation of transport and the electricity industries would permit the better coordination of these services. Defence contractors had to be taken into the public sector to eliminate corruption and war mongering. Industrial assurance and the distribution of milk and coal could not be entrusted to private entrepreneurs who would exploit the poor. A public corporation along the lines of the BBC or the London Passenger Transport Board was deemed to be appropriate for these nationalised industries. As for their commercial policy, the group was rather vague: 'each concern must either pay its way fully . . . or must render a public service incontestably worth the net cost involved' (Next Five Years Group 1935, p. 92).

Macmillan issued a more personal statement, *The Middle Way*, in which he added further items to the shopping list, including coal, coastal shipping, the other public utilities, and the distribution networks for most dairy products, bread, potatoes and sugar. Coal was to be taken into state ownership because there seemed to be no other hope for it. Macmillan was concerned about the high levels of malnutrition in British cities. He thought that private wholesalers and shops were incapable of providing good food at a price which working-class mothers could afford. Under Macmillan's plan, bread and margarine would have been delivered to the housewife's door by an organisation resembling the Post Office. High technology National Bakeries would be built in order to secure economies of scale, although the production and distribution of scones and fancy cakes would remain in private hands (Macmillan 1938, pp. 227–37, 441–58). By the late 1930s there was little difference between the proposals of Labour and of the Macmillanite wing of the Conservative Party. In 1938 Macmillan went so far as to describe Labour's programme for the nationalisation of the Bank of England, coalmining, power, land and transport within five years as 'mild' compared with his own plans (Macmillan 1938, p. 117). The issue which continued to divide them was, of course, one of principle: should nationalisation be thought of as a stepping stone on the road to socialism, or was it simply a useful expedient.

The majority of Tories, while sympathetic to pleas for corporatist measures, remained deeply sceptical about the benefits of nationalisation. Public ownership, they argued, would encourage all sections of industry to opt for an easy life, in the knowledge that higher costs could be passed on to their customers, and that the taxpayers would cough up for any residual losses. Tory critics of state enterprise drew inspiration from such treatises as Lord Hugh Cecil's defence of the free market in 1912 and Hartley Withers's even more trenchant attack on socialism in 1920 (Cecil 1912, Withers 1920). At a more practical level, British voters were urged to reflect upon the failure of state-owned industries abroad. For instance, the state railways in Australia were reputed to be at the mercy of voracious union leaders and their lazy and overpaid members, while the government coal mines in Bulgaria were deemed to be hives of inefficiency. Hence Labour's plans to nationalise the British coal mines would lead to economic ruin and a state of 'virtual dictatorship by the miners' (Conservative Party 1928, p. 16).

Under a socialist government not even the pennies in a child's savings account would be safe. When Labour threatened to nationalise the commercial banks in the mid 1930s, Walter Runciman warned of the threat which reckless lending policies could pose to savers: 'If I were a large depositor, one of the first things I would ask [my bank] would be: "Are the principles of Sir Stafford Cripps [the radical Labour MP] carried on in this institution?" If they said "Yes", I would close my pockets and take them elsewhere – somewhere where it would be safer' (Conservative Party 1935). Hartley Withers argued that the socialists would stop at nothing once they were in possession of the banks. The Labour Party was full of 'cranks – teetotallers, vegetarians, non-smokers, and other earnest folk who think they know best what other people ought to eat and drink and wear', and there was a possibility that they would deny banking services to brewers and introduce prohibition by the back door (Withers 1934, p. 8).

Considering that the Tories were in government, in one form or another, for most of these years of high unemployment and declining public confidence in British industry, it is hardly surprising that the Party developed no clear strategy on nationalisation. Although no true Conservative welcomed the idea of nationalisation, some radicals came to regard the public ownership of some sectors as a contribution towards the solution of Britain's industrial problems.

3   The Second World War and the 1945 election

The Second World War led to a change in the balance of power between Labour and the Conservatives and greatly increased the state's control over economic life (Harrison 1988, Howlett 1993). The aircraft producer Short Brothers was taken into public ownership to combat inefficiency, and there was a rapid growth of munitions production in the state-owned Royal Ordnance Factories (Postan 1952, pp. 423–34). Labour ministers in the Coalition government were pledged not to introduce any divisive nationalisation bills, despite strong pressure from the left wing and the miners (Bullock 1967, pp. 168–70). Wartime economic controls familiarised the electorate with state intervention in the economy. They also showed that it was possible to plan British industry without changing its ownership (Addison 1975, p. 262).

At the 1944 Labour Party conference attention shifted to the nature of the post-war settlement (Schneer 1987). The nationalisation demands of the 1930s were resurrected and the left even succeeded in putting the public ownership of the steel industry into Labour's programme, although the right secured the exclusion of any reference to the democratic control of industry. According to Miliband, 'most people in the Labour movement believed that the nationalised industries [w]ould be examples of a new socialist spirit in industry, islands of socialist virtue in a sea of capitalist greed' (Miliband 1964, p. 288). This was wishful thinking, and Brooke suggests that the Party was never genuinely united behind the socialist policies of 1945. Growing acceptance of Keynesian policies, and pride in the achievements of the wartime planners, persuaded Labour intellectuals, such as Gaitskell, Jay and Durbin, that nationalisation was no longer the precondition for successful regulation of the economy. In other words, public ownership was now an optional extra rather than the cornerstone of socialist economic planning (Brooke 1989). A more cynical observer remarks that the 1945 election was the culmination of Labour's ambitions rather than a new socialist dawn. The Party's leaders were satisfied with 'collecting long-coveted trophies', such as the Bank of England and the mines, before they retired (Howard 1986, p. 18).

British Conservatives could not afford to assume that the war would be followed by a return to the political status quo. Industrial strategy was one area in which it was felt that a repackaging of Tory ideas would be advisable. The Macmillanites were encouraged by the outcome of the wartime Nuffield Industrial Conferences. At these meetings a group of prominent business leaders had confessed that they would not object to the public ownership of the transport and power utilities, on condition that these industries would be run efficiently and without political interference (Boothby 1943, pp. 88–110, 118, Middlemas 1986, p. 61).

Quintin Hogg urged Conservatives to cease fighting the battles of the past: 'in the modern extra political form of public control [he could discern] a Nationalisation which has lost its terrors' (Gamble 1974, p. 34). Oliver Lyttleton cautiously told Birmingham Conservatives in 1944 that the Party's belief in free enterprise 'does not mean that we are bound to oppose State or public ownership of anything at all times'. In particular, Lyttleton could see the benefits of the public ownership of 'certain common services' (Lyttleton 1944, p. 6). Given the public's increasing propensity to tolerate collectivism, tactical considerations determined that official Conservative Party thinking was tending towards fudge on the public ownership issue (O'Gorman 1986, pp. 48–9).

Labour's success in the 1945 general election had little to do with its advocacy of nationalisation. The voters were not afraid of nationalisation in 1944–5, as is shown by table 2.2, but it is probable that their approval was skin deep. On the eve of the general election only 6 per cent of voters said that nationalisation was the most talked about issue in the campaign. Housing (41 per cent) and full employment (15 per cent) were at the forefront of public debate (McCallum and Readman 1947, p. 150). Obviously, people cared most about the issues which directly affected their

Table 2.2. *Summary of Gallup polls on nationalisation March 1944–May 1945*

	Labour's nationalisation plans	
	Approve (%)	Disapprove (%)
Coal mines	60	16
Railways	54	26
Land	51	30
Bank of England	39	20

Source: Fielding 1992, table 1, p. 634.

lives and, compared with housing and full employment, nationalisation was of peripheral interest.

4   The Labour governments 1945–51

Labour successfully took into state ownership all of the industries mentioned in its 1945 manifesto (Morgan 1984, pp. 94–127, Pelling 1984, 75–96). Apart from steel and road transport, which aroused ferocious Conservative and business opposition, Labour's programme generated relatively little political heat. Although it is clear that the outright nationalisation of industries depended on Labour's electoral victory in 1945, even a Tory government would have had to restructure the energy and transport sectors. Ownership apart, the gap between the industrial policies of Attlee and Churchill may have been narrow.

Whilst it would be an exaggeration to say that the Tories were too shell-shocked to offer any resistance to Labour's first wave of nationalisations – they tabled 800 amendments to the gas bill – their attack lacked coherence, and the Conservative Party entered a further period of introspection (Jeffreys 1991, pp. 210–11). An Industrial Policy Committee, chaired by Rab Butler, was given the task of drawing up the *Industrial Charter* of 1947. The charter called for a new spirit of partnership between government, industry, and workers in the quest for competitiveness. It asserted that Labour was mistaken to equate planning with nationalisation and the control of industry from the centre. The government's role was to provide a framework for business success by regulating the macroeconomy, negotiating trade agreements, and stimulating research and development. Conservatives were opposed to nationalisation 'as a principle'. But what should be done with Labour's spoils? A reversion to private ownership was promised for certain sections of the road and air transport industries and the Liverpool cotton market, but this was to be the limit of privatisation. The charter explained that it would be too disruptive to switch major industries, such as the coal mines, into and out of public ownership every few years, and that in one or two cases, such as the Bank of England, nationalisation had done no real harm. Those industries which remained in the state sector would be made more efficient through managerial decentralisation, the curbing of ministerial powers of interference, and the strengthening of consumer councils. Butler later confessed that Churchill had told him not to commit the party to anything too specific whilst it was in opposition (Butler 1972, pp. 126–53, Harris, N. 1972, pp. 77–84, Hoffman 1964, pp. 133–71, Ramsden 1980, pp. 108–14). The *Industrial Charter* was an interim compromise between collectivists and free marketeers – it was the high-water mark of Tory *etatism* in the 1940s (Harris, N. 1972, p. 77).

Steel was the industry which caused the most bitter row in the House of Commons (Hodgson 1986). Even Labour's cabinet was divided over the nationalisation of steel. Hugh Dalton saw it as a test of whether the government was truly socialist: 'Practical socialism, I said, only really began with Coal and Iron and Steel, and there was a strong political argument for breaking the power of a most dangerous body of capitalists' (Pimlott 1985, p. 497). Aneurin Bevan saw steel nationalisation in terms of the redistribution of power from big business to the community. At a May Day rally at Blaenau Festiniog in 1947, Bevan accepted the Tories' argument that the steel industry was far more efficient than the mines, but added that this was no justification for leaving it in private hands: 'I am opposed to the Government taking over the cripples and leaving the good things to private ownership' (Foot 1973, p. 223). Herbert Morrison, supported by John Wilmot, organised resistance to the nationalisation of steel within the Party. They feared that the uncertainty caused by the threat of nationalisation would hamper the current production drive, and preferred to look for a compromise which would have left ownership unchanged (Donoughue and Jones 1973, p. 400). Nationalisation was not a fundamental socialist principle for Morrison, but a practical measure designed to improve the performance of carefully selected industries. Morrison later claimed to have spent much of his time 'battling for sanity' in the Party, and reflected upon the left's penchant for drawing up endless lists of industries which they thought were ripe for public ownership: 'the greatest danger of the [socialist] intellectual in politics is that he dwells too much in his own mind. He cannot dispel the feeling that if he is satisfied with a proposal then it is most unreasonable for others to remain unconvinced' (Morrison 1960, p. 287). Morrison clearly thought that Bevan was using the steel issue to play to the gallery. Attlee had no firm views about steel nationalisation, but he regarded it as his duty to implement the manifesto and eventually sided with Dalton, Cripps, and Bevan (Harris, K. 1982, pp. 342–4). Given a different balance of power in the cabinet, for example had Morrison replaced Attlee, it is probable that steel would never have been taken into the state sector.

For the Conservatives, the nationalisation of steel was totally unacceptable on both political and economic grounds. Nationalisation of a manufacturing industry was a far more serious matter than the taking into state ownership of a public utility. It struck at the very heart of British capitalism: 'This Bill no longer raises a technical question about the size of a blast furnace or the location of a melting shop . . . [or even] about a little more or a little less nationalisation. With this Bill a clear breaking point has been reached between social democracy and totalitarian Socialism' (Fraser 1949, p. 16). Tories argued that the steel industry was profitable and already had an adequate development plan, and that only political malice could explain the campaign for its nationalisation (Conservative Party 1948, Conservative Party 1949c). A state monopoly in steel, they believed, could hold the metal using industries up to ransom and would victimise firms unpopular with the Labour Party (Conservative Party 1949b, p. 16). Mr Attlee was likened to a 'medieval baron who commanded all the castles and strong points of his territory . . . [This tyrant] would have felt himself strong enough even if eighty per cent of the farmland had been held by peasants whose life and fortunes were at his whim and mercy' (Brogan 1949a, p. 10).

Did Labour run out of steam in the late 1940s? It had paid its debt to the miners, it had reorganised public transport and the power industries, and it had resolved to proceed with its controversial plans for steel. What else was there to do? Morrison believed that the time had come to consolidate Labour's gains and to concentrate on improving the efficiency of those industries which were safely in the bag. Cripps thought that further nationalisation schemes would alienate the business community whose cooperation was essential to the success of the export drive (Morgan 1987, pp. 286–90). Labour also had to keep an eye on the political mood in the United States, where nationalisation was viewed by the right as a threat to democracy. Senator James P. Kem of Missouri and Senator Homer Ferguson of Michigan opposed giving aid to Britain whilst Labour continued to nationalise private property. While there is no evidence to suggest that these protests affected US policy, they served as a reminder that socialist Britain was a welfare beneficiary of the midwestern taxpayer and had to watch its step (Hogan 1987, pp. 96–7, 190, 336, Pelling 1988, pp. 69, 73–4, 127).

But some in the Labour Party were not prepared to put up with a situation which left capitalists in command of 80 per cent of the economy. Bevan wanted to press on as quickly as possible. Although he recognised that the public wanted a mixed economy, he felt that the balance should be shifted in favour of the public sector, with private enterprise being reduced to a residual role (Foot 1973, pp. 258–63). Various industries were investigated, including wholesale distribution, chemicals, cotton spinning and merchanting, land, the discount houses, industrial and life assurance, shipbuilding, aircraft construction, aero engines, machine tools, and parts of the car industry (Pelling 1984, pp. 212–13, Morgan 1984, p. 125). In the 1949 policy statement *Labour Believes in Britain* plans were unveiled for the nationalisation of shipbuilding, industrial assurance, ICI, water supply, meat distribution, sugar, minerals, cement, and the bulk buying of commodities. To the distress of the left, the unions in these industries exhibited little enthusiasm for public ownership, being under the impression that their firms were neither bad employers nor demonstrably inefficient. Many Labour members thought that it was unwise to attack the industrial assurance companies, since they were well placed to conduct an anti-government propaganda campaign through their numerous collectors, and it was resolved to seek a compromise through the transfer of ownership of these firms to the policyholders. The ire of the largest sugar refiner Tate & Lyle was raised and Mr Cube, an outraged cartoon sugar lump, became famous as a saviour of free enterprise (Hugill 1978, pp. 145–73).

Labour's 1950 manifesto was suitably cautious, and argued for the nationalisation of sugar, cement, water supply, and meat distribution, and the mutualisation of industrial assurance, largely on the grounds that the consumer needed to be rescued from the clutches of private monopolies. Labour had good reason to be apologetic about these plans. According to Gallup, Labour had only modest approval ratings for these nationalisation plans: steel (32 per cent in favour), industrial assurance (31 per cent), cement (26 per cent), sugar (25 per cent), and meat distribution (20 per cent). At least half of those questioned were definitely opposed to these measures. Gallup also found that disillusionment with nationalisation had risen steadily over the lifetime of the 1945 government (Wybrow 1989, pp. 21–9).

Conservative opposition to nationalisation was rekindled by the steel controversy and received an additional fillip from the teething troubles of the new state-owned industries: 'The Socialists were never more wrong than when they believed that nationalisation would send the miners sprinting to the pit-head and keep them slogging all day long as merrily as the Seven Dwarfs' (Brogan 1949b, p. 22). Individual initiative was being strangled in the new public corporations, Lord Woolton told a radio audience in 1948, and it was no wonder that so many bright young people wanted to emigrate to the Dominions: 'The spirit of the race demands room for expansion and you don't get it in directed and nationalised industries' (Marquis 1948, p. 6).

Colonel Lancaster, the Conservative member for the Fylde, contributed a detailed critique of the National Coal Board. He accused the NCB of excessive bureaucracy and centralisation. Men without previous managerial experience had been appointed to senior regional posts. At the national level there was no provision for long-term strategic thinking. The NCB was a shambles and exhibited all the worst features of the civil service, including 'apoplexy at the brain and paralysis at the fingertips' (Lancaster 1948, p. 7). Even the treatment of miners had deteriorated under the NCB. The dispute at Grimethorpe showed that the state, with the connivance of union bosses, was prepared to threaten strikers with dismissal, black listing, and the denial of unemployment benefit (Utley 1949, p. 22, Hutchison 1949, pp. 19–23). The Conservatives' major policy document of 1949, *The right road for Britain*, gloated over Labour's mishaps. But, although the Tories promised to 'restore free enterprise where that is practicable', they did not want to disrupt the work of key industries at a time of national crisis. In other words, apart from the Liverpool cotton market, road transport, and steel, the public corporations would be allowed to soldier on (Conservative Party 1949a, pp. 26–9).

Morrison thought that Labour's 1950 nationalisation proposals were a collection of 'odds and ends' and Dalton described them as a 'dog's dinner' (Pelling 1984, p. 237, Dalton 1962, p. 375). Nationalisation, except in the case of iron and steel, had reached a dead end in 1950. Rogow and Shore reflected on the results. Between 1945 and 1951 Labour had taken certain industries into public ownership, but it had done nothing to alter the structure of power in British society. Nationalised industries were in practice run by the same old social elite. Dispossessed private shareholders had been paid compensation and were putting their money into other sectors. Did it really make much difference? (Rogow and Shore 1955, p. 171)

5   Explaining the politics of nationalisation

How are we to account for the progress of nationalisation in Britain between 1918 and 1950? Was the nationalisation of some industries inevitable, or did luck and electoral calculation have an important part to play in determining the course of events?

The economic analysis of politics supplies a framework which may be of help in explaining nationalisation. Olson argues that economic interest groups such as trade unions and business associations become increasingly entrenched and influential with the passage of time. These organisations use their bargaining power to manipulate the market and the political process for the benefit of their members, regardless of the costs to other citizens. For instance, a powerful business group may use its contacts in parliament to obtain higher import controls, winning profits for its members at the expense of the consumer. This behaviour is called rent seeking. Another example would be a trade union in a declining industry which campaigned for nationalisation in the hope that this would lead to greater job security and higher wages for workers. Perhaps the nationalised industry would have to increase its prices and draw upon government subsidies in order to maintain employment levels and pay good wages, thereby punishing consumers and taxpayers (Olson 1982, Mueller 1983, Tollison 1982).

While the rent-seeking model is useful, it does not provide a convincing general analysis of the movement for nationalisation in mid-twentieth-century Britain. Unions played an important part in discussions about nationalisation, but their influence was rarely decisive. Only in the case of the miners does the rent-seeking approach appear to hold any water. As table 2.3 shows, only the miners could muster a really powerful force of sponsored MPs, and this was only one of their sources of influence. Union demands for nationalisation of the mines had their origins in decades of poor wages, dangerous working conditions, and uncertain employment. Black Friday, the General Strike, and the miners' loyalty to the beleaguered Labour opposition after 1931, ensured that the miners had a unique hold over the Party. Bevin's biographer explains that 'nationalization of the mines . . . [was] the touchstone of British politics, an issue around which so much bitter feeling had accumulated that it had to be treated, not as an economic or technical, but as a political question' (Bullock 1967, p. 258).

No other industry generated the same intensity of political emotion as did the coal mines. No other union had a parliamentary representation as numerous as that of the miners. Since this did not stop other industries being taken into the state sector, it must be concluded that a strong union campaign was not a precondition for nationalisation. In some industries on Labour's list the unions had no clear policy. The leaders of the Iron and Steel Trades Confederation, for instance, were not transported with enthusiasm for public ownership (Pelling 1984, p. 111). Debates about the nationalisation of gas and electricity barely touched upon the interests of the unions, which in any case had no particular axe to grind. The rail unions supported public ownership and possessed the second largest

Table 2.3. *Union sponsored Members of Parliament 1918–50*

	1918	1922	1923	1924	1929	1931	1935	1945	1950
Miners	25	41	43	40	41	23	34	35	37
Railwaymen	1	3	4	4	9	0	4	13	12
Cotton	4	3	3	2	4	0	0	3	2
TOTAL	49	86	102	88	115	32	79	121	110

Note: Railwaymen includes both ASLEF and the NUR.
Source: Muller 1977, table III-1, pp. 62–3.

group of sponsored MPs, although their influence was nowhere near as great as that of the miners. Given that the railways were viewed as an essential public service, it is probable that Labour would have nationalised them regardless of the attitude of the unions – and the same could be said about the mines. Lancashire's cotton operatives, facing a hopeless struggle against overseas competition, had more to gain than most groups from nationalisation, yet their policy was marked by hesitancy and they failed to mount a persistent campaign for public ownership. If British trade unions were rent seekers in relation to nationalisation, it must be concluded that their rent seeking was neither very systematic nor very effective.

Another and more revealing strand of the economics of politics approach emphasises the process of putting together a manifesto and bidding for votes. In a democracy a party cannot implement its policies without gaining the support of the electorate. Since most voters occupy the middle ground, it would be inexpedient for a party to commit itself to extreme policies (Tullock 1976, Mueller 1989). During the Second World War the middle ground in British politics shifted to the left, due to the public's association of Conservative rule with mass unemployment, and their wish to see the expansion of state housing and welfare services. In 1945 Labour took advantage of this favourable climate of opinion and secured acceptance for policies which would have been deemed extreme before the war.

Parties have to appeal to two groups of customers: the electorate at large, and their own members and financial backers. If leaders want to retain the support of the various factions which make up a political party, they must formulate policies which are broadly acceptable. Robert Brady, an American visitor to Britain in the 1940s, claimed that the existence of so many factions in the Labour Party resulted in a 'highly unstable set of compromises' over policy (Brady 1950, p. 34). Consequently, it was necessary for the Party to stick to the lowest common denominator in setting forth its plans: better wages and conditions, full employment, public ownership of some essential services, and a welfare state. These policies would keep the Party quiet and also stood a good chance of winning the approval of the voters. Labour went beyond the lowest common denominator in its proposals for such industries as steel, sugar, and cement, and as a result ran into a storm of controversy.

6   Conclusion

The aim of this chapter has not been to suggest that economic arguments were of secondary importance in the debates about nationalisation. Its purpose has been to show that the political environment determined which economic policies were feasible and which were not. Whatever the economic justification for nationalising a given industry, the outcome depended on the balance of forces for and against this policy in the Labour Party, the House of Commons, and the nation at large.

Political factors, some of which were fortuitous, had a crucial impact on the course of nationalisation. Had there been no war in 1939, it is likely that the National government would have continued to muddle through with its economic strategy, and that Labour would have been denied a landslide in 1945. Had the left of the Labour Party been even stronger in 1944–5, it might have succeeded in inserting a far more radical set of proposals into the Labour manifesto, possibly at the expense of electoral defeat. Finally, it is not possible to separate the political and the economic justifications for nationalisation. Economic reason and political aspiration were two sides of the same coin and this was recognised by most interested parties at the time.

REFERENCES

Addison, P. (1975), *The Road to 1945: British Politics and the Second World War*, London: Jonathan Cape.
Barry, E.E. (1965), *Nationalisation in British Politics: the Historical Background*, London: Jonathan Cape.
Bevan, A. (1976), *In Place of Fear*, Wakefield: E.P.
Blank, S. (1973), *Industry and Government in Britain: the Federation of British Industries in Politics, 1945–65*, London: Saxon House.
Booth, A. and Pack, M. (1985), *Employment, Capital, and Economic Policy: Great Britain, 1918–1939*, Oxford: Basil Blackwell.
Boothby, R. (1943), *The New Economy*, London: Secker & Warburg.
Boothby, R., Loder, J. de. V., Macmillan, H. and Stanley, O. (1927), *Industry and the State: A Conservative View*, London: Macmillan.

Brady, R.A. (1950), *Crisis in Britain: Plans and Achievements of the Labour Government*, London: University of California Press.

Brogan, C. (1949a), 'Socialism conquers Labour', Conservative Party Archives on Microfilm, Pamphlet Collection, 1949/86, Harvester.

(1949b), 'They are always wrong', Conservative Party Archives on Microfilm, Pamphlet Collection, 1949/87, Harvester.

Brooke, S. (1989), 'Revisionists and fundamentalists: the Labour Party and economic policy during the Second World War', *Historical Journal*, 32: 157–75.

Bullock, A. (1967), *The Life and Times of Ernest Bevin*, vol. II, *Minister of Labour, 1940–1945*, London: Heinemann.

Butler, R.A. (1972), *The Art of the Possible: The Memoirs of Lord Butler*, London: Gambit.

Carpenter, L.P. (1976), 'Corporatism in Britain, 1930–45', *Journal of Contemporary History*, 11: 3–25.

Cecil, H. (1912), *Conservatism*, London: Home University Library.

Conservative Party (1928), 'World-wide failure of nationalisation: some official facts and figures', Conservative Party Archives on Microfilm, Pamphlet Collection, 1928/98, Harvester.

(1935), 'A policy of destruction: the socialist party and the banks', Conservative Party Archives on Microfilm, Pamphlet Collection, 1935/34, Harvester.

(1948), 'Inside steel', Conservative Party Archives on Microfilm, Pamphlet Collection, 1948/48, Harvester.

(1949a), 'Right road for Britain: the Conservative Party's statement of policy', Conservative Party Archives on Microfilm, Pamphlet Collection, 1949/23, Harvester.

(1949b), 'Steel: the lie and the truth', Conservative Party Archives on Microfilm, Pamphlet Collection, 1949/49, Harvester.

(1949c), 'Steel and you: can nationalization help?', Conservative Party Archives on Microfilm, Pamphlet Collection, 1949/76, Harvester.

Craig, F.W.S. (ed.) (1970), *British Election Manifestos, 1918–1966*, Chichester: Political Reference Publications.

Dalton, H. (1962), *High Tide and After: Memoirs, 1945–1960*, London: Muller.

Dennis, N. and Halsey, A.H. (1988), *English Ethical Socialism: Thomas More to R.H. Tawney*, Oxford: Clarendon Press.

Donoughue, B. and Jones, G.W. (1973), *Herbert Morrison: Portrait of a Politician*, London: Weidenfeld & Nicolson.

Drucker, P. (1979), *Doctrine and Ethos in the Labour Party*, London: Allen & Unwin.

Durbin, E. (1985), *New Jerusalems: The Labour Party and the Economics of Democratic Socialism*, London: Routledge & Kegan Paul.

Durham, M. (1989), 'The right: the Conservative Party and conservatism', in L. Tivey and A. Wright (eds.), *Party Ideology in Britain*, London: Routledge, pp. 49–73.

Fielding, S. (1992), 'What did the "people want?": the meaning of the 1945 general election', *Historical Journal*, 35: 623–40.

Foot, M. (1973), *Aneurin Bevan: A Biography*, vol. II, London: Davis-Poynter.

Fraser, H. (1949), 'What do YOU think . . . about the nationalisation of steel?',

Conservative Party Archives on Microfilm, Pamphlet Collection, 1949/51, Harvester.

Gamble, A. (1974), *The Conservative Nation*, London: Routledge & Kegan Paul.

Gamble, A.M. and Walkland, S.A. (1984), *The British Party System and Economic Policy, 1945–1983*, Oxford University Press.

Grant, W. (1989), *Government and Industry: A Comparative Analysis of the US, Canada, and the UK*, Aldershot: Edward Elgar.

Greenleaf, W.H. (1973), 'The character of modern British Conservatism', in R.N. Berks and B. Parekh (eds.), *Knowledge and Belief in Politics: The Problem of Ideology*, London: Allen & Unwin, pp. 177–212.

Hannah, L. (1977), 'A pioneer of public enterprise: the Central Electricity Board and the National Grid', in B. Supple (ed.), *Essays in British Business History*, Oxford: Clarendon Press, pp. 207–26.

Harris, K. (1982), *Attlee*, London: Weidenfeld & Nicolson.

Harris, N. (1972), *Competition and the Corporate Society: British Conservatives, the State and Industry, 1945–1964*, London: Methuen.

Harrison, M. (1988), 'Resource mobilization for World War II: the USA, UK, USSR, and Germany', *Economic History Review*, second ser., 41: 171–92.

Hodgson, G. (1986), 'The steel debates: the Tory recovery', in M. Sissons and P. French (eds.), *Age of Austerity*, Oxford University Press, pp. 283–304.

Hoffman, J.D. (1964), *The Conservative Party in Opposition, 1945–51*, London: MacGibbon and Kee.

Hogan, M.J. (1987), *The Marshall Plan: America, Britain, and the Reconstruction of Western Europe, 1947–1952*, Cambridge University Press.

Howard, A. (1986), '"We are the masters now"', in M. Sissons and P. French (eds.), *Age of Austerity, 1945–1951*, Oxford University Press, pp. 1–20.

Howlett, P. (1993), 'New light through old windows: a new perspective on the British economy in the Second World War', *Journal of Contemporary History*, 28: 361–79.

Hugill, A. (1978), *Sugar and All That: A History of Tate & Lyle*, London: Gentry.

Hutchison, J.R.H. (1949), *The Great Betrayal: The Impact of Nationalisation on the Worker and the Consumer, the Local Authorities and the Taxpayer since 1946*, London: Conservative Political Centre.

Jeffreys, K. (1991), *The Churchill coalition and wartime politics, 1940–1945*, Manchester: Manchester University Press.

Lancaster, C.G. (1948), 'What do YOU think ... about coal?', Conservative Party Archives on Microfilm, Pamphlet Collection, 1948/66, Harvester.

Lyttleton, O. (1944), 'Seven points of Conservative policy', Conservative Party Archives on Microfilm, Pamphlet Collection, 1944/24, Harvester.

McCallum, R.B. and Readman, A. (1947), *The British General Election of 1945*, Oxford University Press.

McCloskey, D.N. (1986), *The Rhetoric of Economics*, Brighton: Wheatsheaf.

McKibbin, R. (1974), *The Evolution of the Labour Party, 1910–1924*, Oxford University Press.

Macmillan, H. (1938), *The Middle Way: A Study in the Problem of Economic and Social Progress in a Free and Democratic Society*, London: Macmillan.

(1966), *Winds of Change, 1914–1939*, London: Macmillan.

Marquis, F.J. [Lord Woolton] (1948), 'The modern Conservative', Conservative Party Archives on Microfilm, Pamphlet Collection, 1948/19, Harvester.

Marwick, A. (1964), 'Middle opinion in the thirties: planning, progress, and "political agreement"', *English Historical Review*, 79: 285–98.

Mercer, H., Rollings, N. and Tomlinson, J. (eds.) (1992), *Labour Governments and Private Industry: The Experience of 1945–1951*, Edinburgh: Edinburgh University Press.

Middlemas, K. (1986), *Power, Competition and the State*, vol. I, *Britain in Search of Balance, 1940–61*, London: Macmillan.

Miliband, R. (1964), *Parliamentary Socialism: A Study in the Politics of Labour*, New York: Monthly Review Press.

Money, L.C. (1920), *The Triumph of Nationalization*, London: Cassell.

Morgan, K.O. (1984), *Labour in Power, 1945–1951*, Oxford University Press.

(1987), 'The rise and fall of public ownership in Britain', in J.M.W. Bean (ed.), *The Political Culture of Modern Britain: Studies in Memory of Stephen Koss*, London: Hamish Hamilton, pp. 277–98.

Morrison, H. (1933), *Socialisation and Transport*, London: Constable.

(1960), *An Autobiography by Lord Morrison of Lambeth*, London: Odhams.

Mueller, D.C. (ed.) (1983), *The Political Economy of Growth*, New Haven: Yale University Press.

(1989) *Public Choice II*, Cambridge University Press.

Muller, W.D. (1977), *The Kept Men? The First Century of Trade Union Representation in the British House of Commons, 1875–1975*, Hassocks: Harvester.

Next Five Years Group (1935), *Next Five Years: An Essay in Political Agreement*, London: Macmillan.

O'Gorman, F. (1986), *British Conservatism: Conservative Thought from Burke to Thatcher*, London: Longman.

Olson, M. (1982), *The Rise and Decline of Nations: Economic Growth, Stagflation and Social Rigidities*, New Haven: Yale University Press.

Pelling, H. (1984), *The Labour Governments, 1945–51*, London: Macmillan.

(1988), *Britain and the Marshall Plan*, London: Macmillan.

Pimlott, B. (1985), *Hugh Dalton*, London: Jonathan Cape.

Pollard, S. (1979), 'The nationalisation of the banks: the chequered history of a socialist proposal', in D.E. Martin and D. Rubinstein (eds.), *Ideology and the Labour Movement: Essays Presented to John Saville*, London: Croom Helm, pp. 167–90.

Postan, M.M. (1952), *British War Production*, London: HMSO.

Ramsden, J. (1980), *The Making of Conservative Party Policy: The Conservative Research Department since 1929*, London: Longman.

Ritschel, D. (1991), 'A corporatist economy in Britain? Capitalist planning for industrial self-government in the 1930s', *English Historical Review*, 106: 41–65.

Rogow, A.A. and Shore, P. (1955), *The Labour Government and British Industry, 1945–1951*, Oxford: Basil Blackwell.

Schneer, J. (1987), 'The Labour left and the General Election of 1945', in J.M.W. Bean (ed.), *The Political Culture of Modern Britain: Studies in Memory of Stephen Koss*, London: Hamish Hamilton, pp. 262–76.

Tawney, R.H. (1922), *The Acquisitive Society*, London: Bell.

(1964), *Equality*, London: Allen & Unwin.

Tollison, R.D. (1982), 'Rent seeking: a survey', *Kyklos*, 35: 575–602.

Tomlinson, J. (1982), *The Unequal Struggle? British Socialism and the Capitalist Enterprise*, London: Methuen.

(1993), 'Mr Attlee's supply-side socialism', *Economic History Review*, second ser., 46: 1–22.

Tullock, G. (1976), *The Vote Motive: an Essay in the Economics of Politics, with Applications to the British Economy*, London: Institute for Economic Affairs.

Utley, T.E. (1949), 'Essays in conservatism', Conservative Party Archives on Microfilm, Pamphlet Collection, 1949/26, Harvester.

Winter, J.M. (1974), *Socialism and the Challenge of War*, London: Routledge & Kegan Paul.

Withers, H. (1920), *The Case for Capitalism*, London: Eveleigh Nash.

(1934), 'Should the banks be nationalized?', Conservative Party Archives, Pamphlet Collection 1934/34, Harvester.

Wright, A. (1987), *R.H. Tawney*, Manchester: Manchester University Press.

Wybrow, R.J. (1989), *Britain Speaks Out, 1937–87: A Social History as seen through the Gallup Data*, London: Macmillan.

II

Case studies of industry organisation, performance and nationalisation

3   The coal industry: images and realities on the road to nationalisation

David Greasley

1   Introduction

On 1 January 1947 the assets of British coalmining were vested with the National Coal Board. The Board took control of an industry with over 1,200 pits and 0.7 million workers. Capital assets, including mineral rights, valued at £390 million thus came under the control of a single organisation (Ashworth 1986, p. 28). That there was little opposition to the transfer of these assets to a public corporation shows the minimal public esteem private ownership of the mines enjoyed by 1946 (Supple 1986, p. 228).[1] Yet less than a decade before the onset of the Second World War, a scheme by the Coal Mines Reorganisation Commission to concentrate production in six large undertakings, one in each of the major British coalfields, was ridiculed as economic nonsense, and throughout the 1930s more modest attempts at reorganisation foundered in the absence of wholehearted government support (Kirby 1977, p. 155). What was different by the time the Coal Industry Nationalisation Act received Royal Assent in 1946 was that the Second World War had both laid bare the frailties of British coalmining and transformed the labour market. By the end of the war the technology and organisation of the industry were adjudged inadequate, and private ownership deemed to have failed. Even *The Times'* (1945, p. 46) eulogy to British war production had to admit that coal was a problem. Equally important, both the miners' and the Labour Party's enthusiasm for nationalisation prior to the war had been tempered by an awareness that reorganisation might reduce employment (Political and Economic Planning 1936, p. 96). The acute difficulties in recruiting miners provided by 1945 a very different backcloth to the nationalisation debate.

    The proximate cause of the coal's nationalisation seems clear enough, the industry came under intense public scrutiny during the war and was found wanting. Nationalisation was more an adverse judgement on the private ownership of the mines, than a blueprint for industrial modernisation. The transfer of the industry's assets rested on the general and somewhat vague belief that a public corporation would make better use of them (Supple 1987, p. 627). Victory for the idea in 1946 that the public interest would be best served by rescinding the coal owners' private property rights had deep historical roots which came to fruition during the Second World War. Matching capacity with demand had long proved troublesome for coalmining. An industry allegedly suffering from chronic overcapacity during the 1930s failed to respond to modest increases in wartime coal demand. Only reduced exports along with new opencast production made possible a limited rise in domestic consumption and staved-off the ever-lurking threat of a wartime coal crisis (Court 1951, p. 107). Nevertheless the persistent threat of coal shortages emphasised that coal remained central to the economy, and kept the industry under critical and intense scrutiny from ministers, civil servants, and the public throughout the war years, fostering an irresistible momentum for change.

The public and political judgement on the coal industry's wartime performance could hardly have been more damning. The view that the industry failed, and that failure was unacceptable given coal's continued importance in the economy, was deep rooted and spread far beyond the miners and the Labour Party. Industry insiders, the engineers and managers on the Reid Committee, and civil servants at the Ministry of Fuel and Power, concurred that the technical efficiency of the coal industry was lamentable. The image of wartime failure cast a long back-ward shadow, fanning the disgruntlement with the industry's perform-ance which had arisen between the world wars. That coalmining had a bad war appeared to confirm that its organisation was inadequate, and that private ownership, both in conjunction with competitive markets in the 1920s, and the limited government interventions of the 1930s, had failed to produce an efficient industry. Coalmining's response to the state's sponsoring of cartels and encouragement of amalgamations under the provisions of the 1930 Coal Mines Act looked, on the basis of wartime performance, wholly inadequate. Since there was little expectation that the private owners would mend their ways public ownership seemed left as the only viable route to the modernisation of the British coal industry. This judgement was essentially pragmatic (Supple 1986, p. 248). Even *The Economist* (7 April 1945), commenting on the Reid Report (1945), agreed that if public ownership was proven necessary for efficient production opposition would melt away, and noted that the proof was near complete. After some prevarication both the Conservative Party and the owners' representatives accepted, without prejudice to their opposition to public ownership, that voluntary reorganisation would not suffice.[2]

Understanding coal's nationalisation as an institutional reaction to supply-side failure, rather than as a clearly articulated plan for the future, raises the central issue of explaining the industry's weaknesses so starkly exposed during the war years. The derelictions which might explain the demise of private ownership are legion, and surround the behaviour of the owners, the miners, and the government. Principally the allegations pinpoint the unwillingness of the owners to modernise the industry via amalgamation and mechanisation, the reluctance of miners to work under private ownership, and the validation given to inefficiency by government under the operation of the 1930 Coal Mines Act. To pre-empt, exploring the coal industry's alleged performance weaknesses does cast doubt on the view that private ownership was economically inefficient. Why private ownership was eventually deemed against the public interest may rest more on hazy beliefs that the industry should have done better than on persuasive and precisely articulated economic argument. Though the economic case against a privately owned coal industry may have been fragile, this did not weaken the force of the political argument. Indeed it appeared by the summer of 1945 that 'two and a half political parties favoured nationalisation' (Rogow 1955, p. 155). Labour's landslide victory in July 1945 presaged nationalisation not because of the miners' political clout, but from the near unanimous consensus that public owner-ship was the only avenue left for coal. Tacit acceptance by the industry's professionals, the engineers and managers on the Reid Committee, and civil servants at the Ministry of Fuel and Power, was buttressed by Labour's popular mandate for nationalisation. Certainly *The Economist*'s (18 August 1945) contention that there was only one controversial issue in the King's Speech following Labour's victory, the proposed nationali-sation of the coal industry, looks somewhat overstated given the breadth of public and professional support for the policy in the aftermath of the Second World War. This chapter examines the origins and veracity of the belief that nationalisation was the only road forward for British coal-mining by 1945.

2   Coalmining in the Second World War: the production problem

The nature of the coal problem during the Second World War was straightforward enough: deep-mined coal output fell in every year. In wartime circumstances output was the yardstick by which the industry was judged, and, quite rightly on this definition, found guilty. While other sectors of the economy, for example agriculture and the railways, appeared to respond well to wartime demands, coal was seemingly trapped treacle-like by a depressing pre-war legacy. Deep-mined coal output fell from 231 to 192 million tons between 1939 and 1944, the last full year of war. Though the threatened coal crisis never emerged, falling output occurred despite strong government efforts to reverse the decline. Lower export volumes helped avert crisis but were insufficient to maintain levels of household and industrial consumption, given the increased requirements of the railways and the electricity supply industry (Ministry of Fuel and Power 1945, p. 47). Thus the government took greater control of the coal industry in 1942, directed labour to the industry, and deployed scarce engineering capacity to make mining machinery in vain attempts to raise production. Government efforts, and almost continual exhortations for more effort from the miners, failed to reverse the output decline arising from a reduced workforce and lower labour productivity.

British coalmining remained a highly labour intensive business on the eve of nationalisation. As late as 1936 revenue per worker was only £213, well below levels in other staple industries. Hence the influence of the workforce on output was powerful, though of course the technical conditions of production helped to shape labour productivity. Before the war comparatively small output declines had been associated with big job losses, contributing to sour labour relations. Conversely wartime expansion required more workers from an economy moving rapidly towards full employment. However 84 thousand had left the pits by 1941 as miners, especially in the export fields found better paid work elsewhere. Thereafter direction of labour modestly increased employment in the pits, but the workforce was still around 7 per cent lower at the end of the war than it had been in 1938. By itself a reduced labour force cannot explain falling coal output during the Second World War. In the immediate post-war years official estimates put the elasticity of output with respect to labour at 0.75, which suggests the 7.3 per cent labour reduction in the period 1939–44 might have reduced output by 5.5 per cent, whereas the actual production fall was 16.7 per cent (Ministry of Fuel and Power 1951).[3] The remainder of the output fall resulted from the productivity problem. Unscrambling the complex cocktail which shaped miners' wartime productivity represents the first step to understanding the reservations surrounding the industry's longer-term performance which led to the post-war nationalisation of coalmining.

Much attention during the war focused on the behaviour of miners, especially their work effort and their absenteeism, as output per worker fell from 302 to 259 tons between 1939 and 1944. The suspicion among government and the public was that miners, believing the benefits would accrue to the owners, would not work wholeheartedly for the war effort (Court 1951, p. 309). Impetus was thus given to the idea that public ownership was essential for better industrial relations as the hostility of miners to the private owners appeared irrevocable. Yet it seems unlikely that falling labour productivity had much to do with a slackening of the miners' efforts. Absentee rates did rise, from 6.9 per cent to 13.6 per cent between 1939–44, but these rates are expressed as a proportion of shifts it was possible to work. Actual attendance at work changed little, since the average number of shifts worked per week was 5.08 in 1944 compared to 5.15 in 1939 and 4.96 in 1938 (Ministry of Fuel and Power 1944, p. 9).[4] Other dimensions of the miners' efforts are more difficult to measure though no doubt dilution of the workforce, 35 per cent of miners were over forty-five years old by 1945, and war weariness eventually took its toll. However the attendance of miners remained remarkably stable until victory was assured in 1945. The key to falling output to 1944 was not fewer shifts worked by miners, but falling output per man shift (OMS). Very little of the fall in OMS, down from 1.14 to 1 ton between 1938 and 1944, can be laid directly at the feet of coalminers.

The wartime output of coalminers was essentially shaped by pre-war industrial organisation. Harder work produced little extra output after 1939, since most fields outside the English midlands were already working close to the limits of their physical capacity. Curiously the capital stock of an industry allegedly plagued by excess capacity appears to have been heavily utilised by the onset of war. Substantial output expansion was not feasible without new mines or, at least, the major reconstruction of established pits, both of which were impractical during the war years. In the short term adding to the labour force might raise output a little, though at sharply declining marginal productivity. The disappointing wartime gains from concentrating production in higher than average productivity pits stemmed from barriers to capacity. Only high productivity pits in English midlands, notably in Nottinghamshire, had scope for expansion. The inability of these fields to sustain output gains beyond 1942 highlights that the production problem was national. Productivity between coalfields did exhibit remarkable disparity (see table 3.1) especially when adjusted for differences in shifts or hours. North Derbyshire and Nottinghamshire's OMS was 25 per cent above the British average in 1938, and 43 per cent above the level in south Wales, while output per labour hour in Yorkshire, Derbyshire, and Nottinghamshire was 44 per cent above the south Wales level. Output per labour year shows a more limited range. North Derbyshire and Nottinghamshire's output per labour year in 1938 was only 13 per cent above the national average, and 25 per cent greater than in south Wales. Even more strikingly output per labour year in Scotland was above levels in south Yorkshire and north Derbyshire, and only 2 per cent lower than in Nottinghamshire. Clearly labour utilisation varied widely, and the tendency was for lower productivity coalfields to work more regularly. By the peak of the 1930s trade cycle, pits in lower productivity regions were working at almost full capacity. Mines in Northumberland and Durham wound coal on average 5.31 days per week in 1937, while the figures for Scotland and south Wales were respectively, 5.57 and 5.52 days per week. In contrast higher productivity mines in south Yorkshire, north Derbyshire, and Nottinghamshire respectively wound coal on 4.71, 4.25, and 4.76 days per week in 1937, and the differences were greater in earlier years when the industry's capacity generally was less fully employed (Board of Trade 1938, p. 146).

On the eve of the Second World War the only mining regions with substantial excess capacity were the newer, higher productivity fields of the English midlands. Expressed somewhat crudely, high productivity Nottinghamshire pits were perhaps operating around 17 per cent below capacity (defined by a 5.5 day coal-winding week) in the best pre-war year. It was from here, and in adjacent counties, that increased wartime output might be expected. However without efficiency gains, the national increase in output would be confined by the comparative size of the Midlands coalfield. Here lies a major legacy of the industry's earlier performance, one influenced by the state's support for cartels, namely the limited regional restructuring of the industry between the world wars. By 1938 only 12.6 per cent of British coal came from high productivity pits in north Derbyshire and Nottinghamshire, a figure not much above the 11.2 per cent share in 1929. Regional restructuring did gather pace in the Second World War. Together north Derbyshire and Nottinghamshire became, for the first time, larger coal producers than the traditional areas of Durham, Scotland, or south Wales, accounting for 16.14 per cent of national output by 1944. Yet actual output in north Derbyshire and Nottinghamshire peaked in 1940 at only 4 million tons above 1938 levels, equivalent to less than 2 per cent of the annual pre-war national output, and after remaining static until 1942 fell for the remainder of the war. Seemingly high productivity pits in the midlands simply did not have the capacity to appreciably raise British coal output.

The output and productivity trends experienced by the Nottinghamshire and north Derbyshire fields (table 3.2), illuminate the constraints on raising British coal output during the Second World War. The sharp 14 per cent rise in output between 1938 and 1940, while employment remained static, suggests a rapid shift towards full capacity, though output was sustained over the next two years despite a small outflow of workers. It seems clear that the coalfield was working flat out in 1941 and 1942, the years of peak labour productivity, but did not have the capacity to offset declines elsewhere in British coal production. Falling north Derbyshire and Nottinghamshire output and productivity after 1942, chiefly indicate that the physical limits of the coalfield had been reached.

Table 3.1. *British coalmining productivity in 1938 (tons)*

	Output/labour year	OMS (tons)	Output/labour hour
Northumberland	295.8	1.14	0.143
Durham	274.3	1.07	0.135
South Yorkshire	310.7 ⎫	⎫	
West Yorkshire	270.6 ⎭	1.28 ⎪	
North Derbyshire	312.7 ⎫	⎬	0.173
Nottinghamshire	343.0 ⎭	1.44 ⎪	
South Derbyshire	268.1	⎭	
South Wales	261.8	1.01	0.120
Lancashire and Cheshire	245.1		0.126
Scotland	336.7	1.17	0.156
Great Britain	290.4	1.15	0.149

Sources: Ministry of Fuel and Power 1944, pp. 6–8 and Greasley 1990, p. 880.

Table 3.2. *Output and productivity in north Derbyshire and Nottinghamshire*

	Output (m. tons)	Labour (000s)	Output/Lab	OMS
1938	28.47	86.7	328.4	1.44
1939	30.64	87.0	352.2	
1940	32.52	86.5	375.7	
1941	32.45	84.9	382.2	
1942	32.46	85.2	381.0	
1943	30.95	84.4	366.7	
1944	29.69	85.2	348.5	1.40 estimated*

Note: *see note 2.
Source: Ministry of Fuel and Power 1944, pp. 50–5.

The modest fall in shift productivity between 1938 and 1944 offers scant support for the idea that miners lessened their efforts. Since new sinkings were not an option during the war, the only viable route to increased production was to raise efficiency throughout the British coalfields. Here again the pre-war legacy limited the potential gains, perhaps to an even greater extent than wartime planners realised. On the surface the scope for efficiency gains appeared immense. Not only were inter-coalfield productivity differences wide, but there was also considerable diversity within the coalfields. Thus bringing low productivity pits up to best standards, or concentrating output in more efficient mines, ostensibly offered a solution to the production problem. Neither route had much success, and the disappointment did much to inform the on-going debates on the value of public ownership. Industrial organisation, especially the fragmented character of the industry, appeared to be the major obstacle to raising output by greater efficiency. Since this judgement underpinned the economic case for nationalisation, the basis of the verdict warrants careful attention.

Fragmentation (see table 3.3) was a key characteristic of British coalmining. Over 1,600 pits were operating in 1944, around 230 less than in 1938. These ranged greatly in size, some pits employed less than ten men while others employed over 3,000. Productivity variation was remarkable, often OMS in the best pits was three times greater than in the laggards, suggesting reallocation of labour offered a route to greater production. That less than two thirds of pits had OMS within 20 per cent of the 20 cwts. industry average in 1944 perhaps best illustrates the extent of productivity dispersion. On a wider scale over 10 per cent of pits had OMS 50 per cent above or below the industry mean, with equal numbers of mines within each tail. Small wonder that civil servants in London pondering over these data should have scented the possibility of a free lunch (Supple 1987, p. 547). Yet the potential for making output gains via scale economies, either by combining adjacent mines or concentrating production in bigger pits, look minimal. Pits with OMS 25 per cent above the industry norm were evenly distributed by mine size, lending support to the owners' view that amalgamation was not a panacea for British coalmining. Smaller mines show greater productivity dispersion, but there was no simple link between scale and efficiency (Greasley 1993, p. 155). Labour might have been transferred to high productivity pits irrespective of their size, though again the potential for gains look minimal. Once the capacity constraints set by haulage and winding were reached, the value of additional workers in pits with high average productivity would not be great. Since most British coalfields were working close to capacity in the immediate pre-war years, labour transfers within traditional mining regions did not offer much scope for output gains. The position of the midlands was rather different since this high productivity region had an underemployed pre-war workforce. Once the slack was taken up by fuller use of the existing workforce, the scope for usefully deploying more men there was not great.

In practice concentration of labour could only raise production if conducted in conjunction with wider reorganisation or mechanisation to lift capacity constraints. This route was attempted, and scarce engineering resources were directed to mining machinery production during the war (Court 1951, p. 279). The percentage of output machine cut rose from

Table 3.3. *Mine size and productivity in 1944*

No. employed	OMS (cwts. % in each category)					No. Pits
	< 10	10 < 15	15 < 25	25 < 30	< 30	
< 100	10.5	14.7	58.0	8.8	8.0	726
100 < 250	3.4	17.6	66.9	10.1	2.0	148
250 < 500	2.3	20.1	66.2	8.1	3.2	222
500 < 1,000	0.90	19.3	66.0	11.1	2.6	306
1,000 < 2,000	=	8.2	71.0	13.9	5.7	194
> 2,000	=	2.6	84.2	13.1	=	38
all pits	5.4	15.5	63.6	10.0	5.4	1,634

Source: Ministry of Fuel and Power 1945, p. 12.

59–72 per cent, and that machine conveyed from 54–69 per cent in the period 1939–45. The productivity gains were modest. Effective machine mining required the integration of coal cutting, loading, hauling, and winding into an efficient continuous system. Establishing high throughputs was crucially dependent on mine layout since efficient underground haulage, the main bottleneck in mass production, needed the spatial concentration of workings. Pits in the older mining regions, with their legacy of previous mining and meandering networks of underground roads, were not readily amenable to modern methods of machine mining (Greasley 1990, p. 895). In the newer mining areas, Nottinghamshire especially, machine systems had been substantially introduced prior to the war. Elsewhere the piecemeal deployment of mechanical cutters and conveyors during the war could do little to raise productivity in the absence of thorough-going, and, in the short term, impractical, reorganisation of the mines.

A clear message emerges from pondering the limits to production and productivity in British coalmining during the Second World War. The barriers to expansion were set prior to the war, and these constraints were not so much in the minds of the owners and the miners as in the physical state of British coalmining. Remarkably, much of the industry outside the English midlands appears to have been working close to full capacity shortly before the onset of war, having successfully adjusted to a smaller market for coal during the 1930s. The adjustment was partially shaped by the cartelised coal market which meant the highest productivity pits were the least utilised, negating the incentives for modernisation and regional restructuring. Once modern pits in the English midlands were operating at full capacity, as they were by 1940, the realistic prospect of raising coal output in the short term disappeared. Indeed maintaining labour productivity in an extractive industry working at full capacity was impossible. Traditionally the British coal industry's response to excess demand was to draw labour, albeit at sharply diminishing productivity, into the pits by offering higher wages. Thus the coalmining workforce rose by almost a quarter million in the boom following the First World War. Twenty years later in a fully stretched economy finding a few thousand more workers proved immensely difficult. Yet, even had more labour been available, the physical barriers to increasing capacity would have largely precluded output gains. The legacy of the past inevitably condemned the coal industry to a bad war, while the war itself demonstrated the continuing importance of coal to the economy. The industry was deemed to have failed, and the price of failure was nationalisation.

3   The nineteenth-century origins of the production problem

The origins of the wartime production problem had deep roots which go back beyond the start of the twentieth century. The organisational form of British coalmining was shaped by nineteenth-century market forces. By 1913 2,662 coal mines were operating, each on average employing 408 men and producing 108 thousand tons of coal. By 1938 the main change was a down-sizing of production while the industry's organisation remained remarkably static (Supple 1987, p. 364). Output was down by 21 per cent on peak 1913 levels by 1938, but 1,870 pits survived, and on average employed 427 men and mined 121 thousand tons of coal each. The intervening increase in mine size defined respectively by employment and output of 4.7 per cent and 12.0 per cent provides ample testimony to the resilience of small mines. Looking at the industry's organisation from the viewpoint of the firm confirms the static picture over the quarter century to 1938. On average firms employed 756 workers and produced 199 thousand tons of coal in 1913, figures which respectively rose to 772 workers and 220 thousand tons by 1938. Firm structure was more concentrated than pit structure, but this was almost as much the case in 1913 as it was in 1938. The proportion of miners employed in larger undertakings with over 3,000 men rose only from 46 per cent in 1913 to 53 per cent by 1938, and most of the increase took place before 1924. This apparent unwillingness or inability of the private owners to concentrate production loomed large in the minds of the industry's critics, both between the world wars and during the wartime production problems. Since larger units seemingly, in the eyes of those outside the industry, yielded substantial benefits, the continuing fragmentation of the British industry appeared illogical, and was eventually unacceptable. The case for the public ownership of the mines was underpinned by the persistence of nineteenth-century patterns of industrial organisation. Since the industry's supply-side problems during the Second World War stemmed from pre-war rigidities, explaining the largely static organisational form of inter-war coalmining would appear central in the story of coal's road to nationalisation.

It does seem that British coalmining's nineteenth-century legacy was decisive in limiting organisational change and the modernisation of the industry between the world wars. Perhaps the most important element in the legacy was over 2,600 pits and a capacity to produce over 280 million tons of coal per year, though over one million men were needed to mine peak 1913 output. Indeed expansion of the industry in the quarter century before the First World War was increasingly dependent on the labour force whose growth exceeded that of output and the capital stock (Mitchell 1984, p. 43). Falling productivity, defined as output per man year, resulting from increases in the average age of pits and therefore longer below ground haulage, accentuated the demand for labour. Much of the industry's capacity in 1913 dated from developments started in the early 1870s boom, since the resulting excess capacity led to low coal prices and little new activity before the 1890s. Thereafter improved financial fortunes did encourage new investment in coal mines, but the average age of pits continued to rise. The upshot in the era of price inelastic demand for coal before 1914 was rising revenues, which allowed the industry to attract labour with comparatively favourable wages (Greasley 1985, p. 388). Yet adequate supplies of labour were forthcoming at rates which both allowed the industry to remain profitable and made machine cutting uneconomic in all but the thinnest seams (Greasley 1982, p. 251).

There seems little scope for an adverse judgement on the British coal industry's performance in the years before the First World War. In 1913 the industry was producing 25 per cent of world output and was responsible for over 50 per cent of world exports. The technology deployed naturally followed from conditions in the labour market, and the industry's capital stock was shaped by earlier ebbs and flows in the price of coal. Yet the legacy left by nineteenth-century market forces proved to be a profoundly problematical one, making unlikely a response to lower demand during the 1920s and 1930s that would be sufficient to stave-off public disquiet and lessen the clamour for nationalisation. Should this assertion be true, the roots of nationalisation lie in an era before most miners working in 1946 were born. The forces shaping the character of the nineteenth-century British coal industry were strengthened by the effects of the First World War. Output and exports fell over the war years, as did the labour force, but a doubling of coal prices resulting from deficient supplies served to heighten profitability (Redmayne 1923). Thereafter the post-war boom propelled the British coal industry to a peak of prosperity. In a financial sense 1920, not 1913, was the apotheosis of British coal-mining. Remarkably, 240 thousand miners were added to the workforce in the two years after 1918. Even more remarkably, the 24 per cent rise in the workforce increased coal output by less than 1 percent. Consequently output per man year waned to 189 tons, probably, barring years of major strikes, the lowest level achieved since the Napoleonic Wars. In the market conditions of 1920 the upshot was a sharp rise in coal prices to 65 per cent above 1918 levels, whereas prices generally rose 42 per cent. The effect was to raise the value of coal output to £396.9 million, which was greater than the real value of output in 1913, and amounted to over 7 percent of 1920 GDP. Seemingly the demand for coal was as price inelastic in 1920 as it had been at the start of the twentieth century (Greasley 1992, p. 142).

Falling productivity in 1920 was not uniquely experienced by coal-mining. Reductions in hours throughout the British economy served to depress annual output (Broadberry 1990, p. 271). Yet price inelastic demand for coal did make the industry's experience distinctive. The concomitant surge in prosperity attracted new miners in a fashion remi-niscent of the ninteenth century. The influx of workers was even stronger than that in 1900, and perhaps on a par with that in the early 1870s boom. Just as in the earlier peaks, additional labour offered the only feasible route to immediate output expansion in 1920. Shorter hours partly explain why the gains were so modest, but the physical capacity con-straints imposed by an aging capital stock were probably the more decisive. The barriers to increasing output, shown by falling labour productivity, were apparent in 1913, and limited investment during the First World War further weakened the supply side. For those in the industry the limits to supply had pleasant effects on both profits and wages, and prosperity did encourage new investment during the post-war boom. However the secular demand for coal was inexorably changing, and for the first time in over thirty years the terms of trade were about to shift decisively against the producers.

Nominal coal prices halved in the two years following the 1920 peak, while prices generally fell around 25 per cent, making the real price of coal less than in 1913. The resulting tension prompted speedy government decontrol of the industry, a three month coal strike, and defeat for the miners, their wages falling 43 per cent in 1921, broadly following the downward course of coal prices. In retrospect 1921 may appear to be a watershed in coalmining's fortunes demanding more effective response from the industry's private owners. Yet making this judgement at the time would have needed more foresight than perhaps could have been reasonably expected. The effects of the 1921 slump spread far beyond coalmining. Industrial output fell in Britain by 9 percent, and the downturn was felt throughout the world economy. Disentangling the longer-term prospects for coal in this depressed and confused environment was hardly straightforward. The owners had also won a striking industrial relations victory, bringing down production costs almost in line with coal prices to keep the industry generally profitable. The economy bounced back in 1922 and so did coalmining. Coal prices rose through 1924, against deflation elsewhere in the economy, and exports and output showed marked upward trends for the first time since 1913. Indeed exports hit record levels in 1923, and output in that year had only been exceeded in 1913. The favourable market, partly predicated on disruption elsewhere in the world, induced substantial investment, especially in 1923,[5] although activity was also reasonable in 1924–5, and renewed inflows of labour to levels in 1924 not much below those in the 1920 boom. A clear long-term decline in British coalmining can only be discerned from 1925.

The nature of Britain's national coal problem in the period 1925–38 was principally one of adjusting output to a lower level of demand. From the perspective of the owners the concern was to hang on to markets, and this meant, at least before the operation of the 1930 Coal Mines Act, cutting costs. It seems unlikely that lower coal prices, whether achieved by greater efficiency or a further attack on wages, would have much widened the market. In the domestic market consumption was largely static over the years 1913–38, irrespective of the price fluctuations. The chief problem for the industry was that a growing economy was not associated with greater coal demand as better fuel efficiency led to lower per capita consumption, down from 4.03 tons in 1913 to 3.69 tons by 1938 (Buxton 1978, p. 173). Coupled with static domestic consumption was the relentless, but surprisingly gradual, downward trend in coal exports after the record levels in 1923. By the mid 1930s exports were down by around 40 million tons from peak levels, as was British coal output, given stable domestic consumption. In part the export declines stemmed from slower growth of world coal demand, but Britain's share of world coal exports fell from 50 per cent to 30 per cent over the period 1913–38. Whether the decline need have been so precipitous remains an open question, though British coal exports remained generally above German levels throughout these years despite the oft-alleged technological superiority of the Ruhr (Supple 1987, p. 281). Barriers to trade, including substantial transport subsidies for continental European producers, make uncertain how much exports would have risen with better efficiency in British mines. The suspicion is that very little more coal would have been sold. Coalmining's export performance over the period 1913–38 does not compare unfavourably with British manufacturing, whose share of world trade was down from 30 per cent to around 20 per cent over the same period, suggesting there were deeper forces at work than those peculiar to coalmining. Secular decline was the inevitable operating backcloth for private ownership in the years 1924–38. Though the nature of the coal problem was precisely the reverse of that during the Second World War, the public response to the industry's performance was similarly adverse.

4   Private ownership and the image of failure

Stated boldly, the problem for British coalmining from 1924 to the onset of the Second World War was to shed around 40 million tons of capacity. Chiefly this was done by reducing employment by almost half a million, equal to over 35 per cent of the workforce. Since the output fall was only around 15 per cent, the contraction of the industry was accompanied by rising labour productivity. For the first time since the 1880s coal won per man year exhibited an upward trend, rising from the abysmal 184 tons in 1920 to 309 tons by 1937. Superficially at least these data do not portray an inflexible industry, poor management, and a reluctant workforce. Yet the public image of the industry between the world wars was very different, and best typified by Lord Birkenhead's biting comment, 'it would be possible to say without exaggeration that the miners' leaders were the stupidest men in England if we had not had frequent occasion to meet the owners' (Fine 1990, p. 19). The notion of inadequate response by British coalmining to difficult market circumstances gathered pace between the world wars, and was devastatingly reinforced by the publication of the Reid report in 1945. Deliberating against the background of wartime production problems, the mining engineers and managers on the Reid committee offered damning testimony to the technical and organisational frailties of British coalmining. Productivity achievements elsewhere, especially in Holland, the Ruhr, and Poland, seemingly showed what could have been done if the private owners in Britain had been more enterprising. Though the extent of international productivity differentials can be questioned, shift lengths varied widely and the data rest on uncertain sampling, there can be no doubt that the Reid enquiry offered an engineering blueprint for raising coalmining productivity (Greasley 1990, p. 899). Indeed there was no need to look overseas to demonstrate that better labour productivity was feasible, since productivity growth in Nottinghamshire had been on a par with best continental achievements. What was distinctive about the British industry was the deviation from best engineering practice and hence low average labour productivity.

Reid's engineering remedy for coalmining's woes, namely modernisation via more effective mechanisation, especially of underground haulage, also required the concentration of production and organisational change. Since private ownership had palpably failed to produce an organisational structure apposite to modernisation, the momentum for a change of ownership approached critical velocity following publication of the report in the dying months of the Second World War.

The views of the Reid Committee on coalmining's inadequacies represented an acceptance by industry insiders of opinion that had been gathering pace outside the industry throughout the interwar years. The proceedings and the reports of Royal Commissions had earlier exposed the derelictions of coalmining's private owners to the public gaze. Though the Sankey (1919) enquiry brought the issue of nationalisation to the forefront, the efficacy of the industry's production structure received only tangential attention. Rather the focus then was on distribution, the balance between wages and profits, and the alleged inequities stemming from private ownership. Thus the case for nationalisation was made, in the aftermath of the First World War, on moral, rather than on efficiency grounds. Had coalmining's post-war prosperity been less ephemeral, the deliberations of the Sankey enquiry may not have had lasting consequences. However the denting of public confidence in the private ownership of the mines during the proceedings that arose from the ridiculing of the owners at the hands of Tawney and the Webbs was never repaired. That first significant crack in the edifice of private ownership was soon to be widened by the judgement of the Samuel Commission (1925).

Most importantly the Samuel Commission provided a quantitative appraisal of the coal industry's technical efficiency, and these numbers powerfully shaped public sentiment towards private ownership. Though nationalisation was rejected, the idea that the public interest would be served by concentrating production in fewer, larger, and more efficient units received strong stimulus from the statistics gathered by Samuel, which appeared to show clear positive correlation between both the size of undertakings and mines with labour productivity. Representations from the owners, colliery managers, and engineers that the existence of scale economies beyond those already realised was illusory, and that larger enterprises might encounter managerial diseconomies were given short shrift. The owners already had a credibility problem, Samuel assumed their opposition to rationalisation stemmed from a fear that amalgamations would be the first step towards nationalisation. Yet in retrospect, and with the benefit of the Ministry of Fuel and Power's (1945) more detailed later assessments the benefits of larger scale appear dubious. Smaller pits were shown by the Ministry's data to have greater productivity dispersion, rather than a lower average. It may be that the limited sample of undertakings and pits, especially the paucity of data for smaller operations, on which Samuel's judgements were based, misrepresented the benefits of scale. However doubts about the veracity of the evidence mattered less than the verdict; the organisation of the industry under private ownership was found wanting.

The efficacious image of free market forces was also dented by Samuel's support for restrictive marketing associations. Initially the emphasis was on schemes relating to the export market, but the tacit approval for output restrictions and higher coal prices gained wider sympathy once the disruption, and perhaps the limited scope, of the alternative strategy to further attack wages costs became manifest in 1926. In a fiercely competitive coal market the owners were sympathetic to marketing schemes, but the tendency for private agreements to break down, along with the limited progress made towards rationalisation, led to more direct state action.[6] The Coal Mines Act of 1930, promoted by the minority Labour government to protect wages and employment in the industry, set the operating context of British coalmining until the onset of the Second World War. Another mile post on the road to nationalisation had been passed. By the very enactment of the legislation the market was deemed to have failed, and, just as importantly, the provisions of the act gave the owners yet another opportunity to convince civil servants, ministers, and the public at large that there was a chasm between their private and the social interest. Ostensibly the Coal Mines Act gave government the power to override private property rights and force amalgamations of colliery undertakings. The failure of the Coal Mines Reorganisation Commission to push through a single merger might be taken as eloquent testimony to the stubbornness, inflexibility, and political clout of the owners. Certainly officials at the Mines Department and the commissioners, especially their chairman Ernest Gowers, became convinced that reorganisation of the industry would not be achieved at the owners volition. On the other hand, the Reorganisation Commission palpably failed to convince industry insiders of the economic case for amalgamations (Kirby 1973, p. 281). Thus the early scheme of the commissioners to concentrate coal production in six large undertakings, one in each of the main coalfields, appeared to have no economic merit, and seriously damaged the Commission's reputation. More generally the deterioration of trade and rising unemployment after the legislation was passed reduced the incentive for government to pursue with vigour greater efficiency in coalmining. In particular the Labour Party's commitment to rationalisation was tempered by the growing awareness that displaced miners would have few employment prospects outside the industry (Political and Economic Planning 1936, p. 96). When conditions of excess demand returned to the labour and coal markets with the onset of war, recollections of the owners' obstinacy proved more enduring than those of the corresponding lack of the political will to force amalgamations.

To a large extent absence of sympathy for owners and the willingness of the state, by 1946, to revoke private property rights stemmed from the progressive undermining of public confidence in the coal industry. Thus the dents to the owner' reputations in the 1930s resulting from their hostility to amalgamation, which was felt to be in the public good, added to the unease fostered by the Royal Commissions in the 1920s. Curiously though the fatal blow to the image of private ownership of the mines came not from disquiet outside the industry, but from the colliery engineers and managers on the Technical Advisory Committee. The Reid report appeared to confirm what those outside the industry – ministers, civil servants, and the British public – already believed, that British coalmining was hopelessly, and under private ownership irrevocably, inefficient. It was an industrial dinosaur that had failed to shake-off the legacy of the nineteenth century. It should be recognised however that Reid's diagnosis of the industry's failings was different to that of Samuel. Specifically the mining engineers were able to show how better methods would raise labour productivity, rather than to simply infer from suspect data that larger units would be more efficient. It was the engineering solution, the efficient integration of coal cutting, loading, hauling, and winding, to the production problems exposed by the Second World War, that attracted almost unequivocal support. Even elements of the press sympathetic to the market economy and the owners, *The Economist* and *The Colliery Guardian*, saw merit in Reid's proposals (Supple 1986, p. 228). The organisational consequences of implementing the engineering blueprint were not spelt out by Reid, though the need for change was accepted. The force of Reid's recommendations lay not in their novelty, but that they gave authority and widespread publicity to what could, and indeed what was already being achieved in the industry's best pits. Reid himself worked in Fife, the highest productivity part of the Scottish coalfield, and more generally the recommended practices, including experiments with power loading, were already in effect in progressive English midland pits. The engineers were calling for the whole industry to be modelled on best practice, and received wide public support.

5   Private ownership and economic reality

Reid's moment was well chosen, an engineering solution to coal's problems was almost universally attractive in 1945. Coal was scarce, but labour was in short supply. The only realistic strategy for raising production appeared to lay through the emotionally appealing route of technical improvement, and the engineers had shown how this could be done. Whether the engineers offered an economic solution to the industry's problems appears much more questionable. Organising production on the lines defined by Reid did not necessarily need large pits, but did need modern ones. Age of pits was crucial to the provision of the efficient underground haulage which was central to the engineering solution. Meandering networks of roads and widely scattered workplaces, typical of much of the industry's capital stock, were not conducive to modern methods of machine mining. Ideally, to make the most of available technology, production should be planned for the sinking of the mine, rather than accumulated in piecemeal fashion over the decades. Hence Reid's (1945, p. 46) reference for retreating longwall systems, in which roads would be driven to the outer boundaries of the mine, and the coal taken when retreating back to the mineshaft on progressively shorter haulage lines. There can be no doubt that best engineering practice machine mining methods would have substantially raised labour productivity. On the other hand, Arthur Beacham's (1945, p. 209) doubts on the economic viability of Reid's blueprint appear well founded. As a vision for the distant future the engineers' plans had appeal. In the context of the immediate post-war years, and most especially as a judgement on the interwar performance of British coalmining, Reid's assessment seems remarkably illfounded.

Sir Roy Harrod's view that, 'economic efficiency does not consist in always introducing the most up to date equipment the engineer can think of, but rather in the correct adaptation of the amount of new capital sunk to the earning capacity of the old asset', needs little embellishment (Johnson 1973, p. 665). For new pits to be economically useful, their production costs, including capital, would have to match the current operating costs of existing mines. Less prosaically bygones are bygones, and labour productivity in new pits would need to be sufficiently high to offset the legacy of sunk capital in the old pits. Thus, as Salter (1960, p. 53) elegantly demonstrated, a range of unit labour requirements among firms in an industry does not necessarily indicate inefficiency. Old plant might be especially resilient if operating costs can be lowered by comparatively modest investment in new equipment, to deter major new entry into an industry. The economists' vision of efficiency differs sharply from that of the engineers on the Reid committee.

The economists' perspective seems central to understanding both the performance of the British coal industry between the world wars, and the forces which led to nationalisation. In 1944 only 6.2 per cent of British coal came from pits less than twenty years old (Ministry of Fuel and

Power 1945, p. 15). These new pits were chiefly located in the English midlands, and led there to labour productivity well above the national average as modern systems were introduced. The Samuel Commission noted in 1925 that nineteen new developments in south Yorkshire and the English midlands had commenced since the turn of the century, and with more projects planned or underway, looked forward to the increasing prominence of this field. Samuel's expectations were unrealised, and the share of the English midlands in British output made little further headway before the onset of the Second World War. The secular decline in the demand apparent from 1925 deterred the expansion of capacity, and the investment in new pits apparent in the early 1920s petered out. Once the prospect of a larger coal market disappeared, investment in new mines was only sensible if the operating costs of existing capital could be undercut. Even with modern machine mining methods, this appeared a dim and uncertain prospect. Modern mines had high capital costs, and established mines were able to bring running costs down somewhat with a more piecemeal introduction of machinery (Buxton 1970, p. 491). In the fiercely competitive coal market of the later 1920s, the upshot was rising productivity across the British coalfields, but the extent of these productivity gains were inevitably confined by the age of mines which deterred the shift to machine mining systems. Even in the tough competitive environment of the later 1920s, maximising labour productivity was not a sensible economic objective for the British coal industry, and the discipline imposed by the marketplace was soon to be diminished.

The thrust of public policy in the 1930s was largely inimical to the technical modernisation of British coalmining. At the time of Samuel's deliberations, lower costs from more efficient organisation might still be envisaged to raise coal demand, especially from overseas. By the 1930s the prospects for export growth, even with substantially lower costs, appeared hazy. Whether valid or not, Samuel's belief that larger units would lead to greater efficiency became largely irrelevant with the downturn of the world economy and the remorselessly rising unemployment in 'outer' Britain after 1929. Forcing amalgamations under the provisions of the 1930 Coal Mines Act to maximise labour productivity proved difficult for a number of reasons. Rescinding of private property rights jarred with ideas of natural justice, and the coal lobby remained powerful, but perhaps more importantly the notion of further reducing the colliery workforce in an era of mass, and increasingly long-term, unemployment lacked commonsense. In effect the reorganisation of British coalmining was to be held in abeyance for the duration of the depression, and the provisions of the 1930 Coal Mines Act relating to marketing schemes came to the forefront.

Again the direction of public policy, the support for cartels, can be traced back to the Samuel Commission, which noted the beneficial effects of the private schemes then operating. The competitive 1920s coal market limited success, especially in the export fields, of the attempts by the owners themselves to maintain coal prices. While the private schemes floundered under market pressure, the state sponsored cartel of the 1930s proved more enduring and restored an element of stability to the industry. By setting minimum prices and allocating output quotas on the basis of past production, the market pressure forcing efficiency and the exit of the least productive pits from the industry was lifted. The incentive for major new developments in British coalmining to replace less efficient mines may have been somewhat limited anyway in the depressed 1930s, but the cartel, by allocating quotas to established pits, all but ended the prospect of new mining developments. True, inefficient pits could sell their quotas, but the sinking of new mines in the hope that a quota might be purchased from an older colliery made little sense, even to British coal owners. By deterring new enterprise and regional restructuring the cartel did tend to raise unit labour requirements, and productivity stagnated in most British coalfields during the 1930s. Somewhat paradoxically these productivity weaknesses were to count heavily against private ownership when the market for coal was transformed during the Second World War.

In addition to deterring new developments in British coalmining, the cartel may also have served to lessen the efficiency of established mines. The spreading of production and employment across the industry did lead to lower capital and labour utilisation of more productive mines, especially those in the English midlands, thereby limiting the incentive for greater efficiency. Rising real coal prices, and a widening margin between costs of production and price, also offered a more comfortable market environment for the owners (Henley 1988, p. 276). By 1938 nominal coal prices were 30 per cent above 1929 levels, compared to generally static prices elsewhere. Given the weak demand for coal it seems clear that the cartel effectively restricted output and encouraged supply side ineffi-ciency. Only underutilised pits in the English midlands were able to sustain the productivity upturn of the 1920s, elsewhere labour produc-tivity was largely static (Greasley 1990, p. 883). The cartel helped preclude a greater output contribution from the midland's pits, thereby limiting overall productivity, though less efficient mines had incentives to reduce costs via mechanisation, since their margins would widen as the cartel held up prices. Even if the absence of market discipline did not completely destroy incentives, the scope for efficiency gains from machine mining was constrained by the age of pits. The absence of productivity growth during the 1930s outside the midlands perhaps provides the best testi-mony to the effects of the 1930s Coal Mines Act. The scope for productivity gains was limited unless more production could be concentrated in the high productivity midland's coalfield. To the extent the state sponsored coal cartel lessened the likelihood of the regional restructuring of British coalmining, the effects on productivity were detrimental. Indeed the coal cartel worked so effectively that not only did coal prices rise sharply, but local coal shortages appeared in the years immediately before the Second World War, as the limits of the physical capacity of the British coalmining were approached (Political and Economic Planning 1936, p. 134).

By most conventional criteria the British coal industry successfully performed in the first four decades of the twentieth century. The notion that private ownership was economically inefficient, and hence that nationalisation was just reward for the stubbornness and inadequacies of the owners, needs to be tempered. At the very least the economic case against private ownership remains unproven. For an industry often characterised as inflexible, and the private ownership thereof conventionally labelled myopic, the rapid downsizing of the coalmining workforce and the reductions in unit labour costs in the 1920s appears remarkable. Yet the organisational foundations of British coalmining were a product of the nineteenth century market for coal. This legacy made the matching of capacity and demand problematical, and shaped the industry's twentieth century performance. In the years to 1914 the chief characteristics of the market were price inelastic and secularly expanding demand, and a supply side that was labour intensive. The technical conditions of production made supply adjustments difficult. In the short run, in conditions of excess demand, the only option was to deploy more labour, typically at diminishing marginal productivity, which did little to dampen fluctuations in the price of coal. A longer term response required new sinkings, or at least the development of new seams, which took many years to come to fruition. The effect was for nineteenth-century coal prices to exhibit a cycle rather reminiscent of Kuznet's long swings, with prices peaking in 1873 and then falling as the new capacity came on stream. By 1900 demand was outrunning supply once more, coal prices were rising, and new investment was attracted by the industry. Coalmining's capital stock increased around 50 per cent in the period 1899–1913, almost matching the 55 per cent rise in the workforce (Mitchell 1984, p. 43). In the context of prevailing factor markets and feasible technology this final burst of pre-World activity presented a vigorous response to market demands. Quite sensibly coalmining remained a labour intensive industry, but one that had difficulty matching production to the vagaries of demand. These characteristics profoundly influenced subsequent events in the industry.

The experiences of coalmining during the First World War highlight the key production characteristics of the industry. Loss of labour to the armed forces inevitably led to supply difficulties. Moreover the limited new investment during the war made the industry even less able to cope with the sharp demand increases in the post-war boom. As in the nineteenth century the only short-run option was to increase the workforce, and, given the hours reduction of 1919, this had to be substantial. Since coal demand remained price inelastic, supply side constraints meant high profits. Whether these profits should have been used to more effectively modernise the industry remains a problematical issue (Alford 1986, p. 219). Investment did rise sharply in 1919 and 1920, but to the extent this added to capacity rather than replaced less efficient units, the subsequent price deflation was exacerbated. It was the legacy of the industry's pre-1914 capital stock, over 2,500 pits, that was the biggest obstacle to modernisation. The owners also won a decisive industrial relations battle during the 1921 deflation. Palpably wages were flexible in a downward direction, and that so many pits survived until 1929, despite government exchange rate policy, testifies to the industry's ability to bring costs down.

With hindsight, the modest extent of coalmining's contraction by 1929 appears remarkable. Output was only down 10 per cent, around 30 million tons, of the peak 1913 level, and was above the average production for the years 1903–12. Even more illuminating, in the light of the industry's poor productivity image, 1929 output was under 10 million tons less than in 1924 despite the shedding of 291 thousand jobs. Exports were averaging 60 million tons in the later 1920s, little different to pre-war averages, and presumably would have been greater without sterling's revaluation during 1924. Clearly the coal industry was under tremendous competitive pressure during the 1920s, and, given the labour intensity of production, the workforce bore the brunt of the attack on costs via lower wages and less work. Yet the industry was adjusting to a changed market place, and to characterise the industry, or private ownership, as inflexible appears unjustified. The form of the adjustment largely reflected the legacy of the industry's sunk capital and the labour intensity of production. In the tough competitive environment of the 1920s there was little wonder that the owners turned attention to stabilising prices as well as to reducing costs. Government sponsorship in 1930 to a coal cartel provided a very different operating context for private ownership.

The stability of British coalmining during the 1930s stands out against the backcloth of a collapsing world economy. Nominal coal prices held firm during the contraction of 1929–33, against deflation elsewhere, and were more than a third higher by 1938. Rising output after 1933 also helped to restore the industry to profitability, though production was some 30 million tons below 1929 levels in 1938. By contributing to coal price increases and allocating production quotas the cartel diminished the market discipline on private ownership, thus helping to ameliorate the pace of employment decline. The deterrent to new developments also helped to bring the industry's ability to supply coal back in line with demand. By implication the degree of excess capacity in British coalmining before the slump of 1929–33 appears to have been only around 30 million tons. Once this capacity was shed, as it largely was by 1936 by the non-replacement of worked-out capital, the industry was no better able to respond to short-run demand pressures that it had been in 1920. To an extent the cartel, by removing the incentive to replace old mines with new, more productive, capital, was responsible for supply-side inelasticity. Certainly labour productivity would have been greater had the market functioned more freely, and the industry would have needed less scarce manpower in the Second World War. What remains uncertain however is the extent a regional restructuring of British coalmining would have taken place, with production concentrated in modern higher productivity pits, had there been no cartel. The legacy of old capital would have still been there; it was not until 1936 that coal prices rose, and even then high productivity pits in the English midlands operated below capacity. The lead times for new developments perhaps suggest that wartime production would still have been a problem. Nevertheless private ownership can hardly be blamed for failing to respond to incentives that were not there. Given the context in which they operated the private owners generally made economically sensible use of the coal industry's assets. Thus the state's forcible acquisition of these assets still needs explanation.

6   The public image of private ownership

A simple idea lay at the heart of the decision to transfer the assets of the British coal industry to the public sector. Private ownership was deemed not to be in the public interest. Coalmining's historical record was judged inadequate, and, just as importantly, there seemed to be no prospects for future regeneration under private ownership. The origins of the public's perception that coalmining failed can be traced back to at least the turn of this century. Then the coal question focused on deficient supply and the tax on exports, as falling productivity raised coal prices in an era of price inelastic and expanding demand. Public concern was allayed by the Royal Commission on Coal Supplies (1903–5) investigations, but the battle for the eight hour day and the industry's industrial relations record served to keep the industry in the public mind during the years to 1914 (Jevons 1915, p. 520). Though the idea that coal was a troublesome industry was firmly planted in the Edwardian mind, the issue of ownership did not seriously surface until the First World War. That the industry could not meet the demands of war without direct state intervention served to further dent the public esteem of private ownership. Though control was financial and wartime circumstances exceptional, the rise in coal prices and profits gave weight to the view that the private interests of the owners and the public good might be widely divergent (Redmayne 1923).

It was against the smouldering background of wartime discontent that the proceedings of the Sankey Commission put the first serious crack in the edifice of private ownership. The Sankey enquiry was not a searching investigation of British coalmining's technical proficiency, rather the concern was with the equity of private ownership. The damage done to the reputation of the owners was immense. The privations in mining communities, contrasting sharply with image of the owners' wartime profiteering, seemingly offered some moral justification for the rescinding of private property rights. Though the force of the argument for nationalisation was not yet overwhelming – the miners themselves lost enthusiasm once their material aspirations had been met – the issue was indelibly on the political agenda (Supple 1986, p. 233). The attack on miners wages in 1921–2 coming so soon after the public exposure of the owners' avarice helped to keep the industry in the public arena. Soon the moral case for public ownership was powerfully reinforced by the Samuel Commission's diagnosis of coalmining's organisational failings.

The deliberations of the Samuel Commission resulted in a focused appraisal of the coal industry's supply-side weaknesses. The fragmentation of the industry, the proliferation of small undertakings and mines, was pinpointed as the major obstacle to raising efficiency and competing effectively with overseas producers. In retrospect the verdict of Samuel looks rather shaky. Almost to a man, the representatives of the owners, managers, and engineers denied the existence of scale economies in excess of those attained already, raising instead the spectre of managerial diseconomies. Samuel felt the owners' denial that benefits would accrue from larger scale rested on a fear that amalgamations would presage nationalisation, and preferred to rely on the findings of statistical investigations. These data appparently showed a clear correlation between size, both of pits and undertakings, and labour productivity, providing a simple agenda for public policy: the rationalisation of British coalmining. Whether or not Samuel's judgement was right on the value of scale mattered less than the momentum given to the idea that the industry was failing. Not only did the equity of private ownership appear questionable, and this view was soon reinforced during the General Strike, but serious doubts about the industry's productive efficiency now gained wide currency. The time for nationalisation had still not arrived, for the miners' wages and hours were the paramount issues, but the enactment of the 1930 Coal Mines Bill, with its provision for the compulsory amalgamations, served notice that the owners would only be given limited time to put their own house in order.

The passing of Labour's 1930 Coal Mines Act with Liberal support, shows how much government attitude to private ownership and competitive markets had changed since the end of the First World War. The act both legitimised marketing restrictions, and opened the possibility of rescinding private property rights. By 1938, the year royalties were nationalised, even the Conservative Party was willing to sanction the forcible acquisition of private assets. The downturn in trade after 1930 tempered governments' enthusiasm for amalgamations, and the one scheme submitted for judicial review by the Coal Mines Reorganisation Commission was turned down. The owners' view that many of the commission's proposals would have done little to raise efficiency may have been justified, but their implacable hostility to the commission did serve to cast the owners as inflexible. It appeared that the attitudes of the owners were now so entrenched that modernisation of the industry could never be achieved by their voluntary action. Even though public opinion, as exemplified by the Political and Economic Planning report of 1936, was willing to give the owners more time to arrange voluntary amalgamations, given the depressed labour market, the resignation that compulsion might eventually be necessary was plainly apparent.

In the shorter term the operation of part one of the Coal Mines Act, which provided for orderly marketing, was more significant. Rather surprisingly, while coal output fell by 25 per cent in the period 1929–33 and the industry shed 165 thousand jobs, nominal coal prices remained stable, while prices generally fell 8 per cent. Subsequently average coal prices rose 34 per cent by 1938. The cushion provided to the industry by the output restrictions and minimum prices allowed the margin between costs and price to rise. The cartel's effects on economic efficiency have already been noted, but restrictive marketing also shaped public perceptions of private ownership. Sheltering the industry from the chilly wind of the market might be publicly acceptable if the industry itself responded by reorganising production and improving efficiency. Increasingly the feeling, especially after the upturn in prices after 1936, was that the owners took the advantage of the cartel but failed to accept the social responsibilities. Again the depressed economy lessened the practical effects of these sentiments, but once rearmament began to stimulate revival in 'outer' Britain, and local coal shortages were felt in southern counties, public tolerance of coalmining's performance diminished. By the later 1930s the supply of and demand for coal were almost back to parity, and employment in the industry, along with prices, started to rise. Whether the cartel would have survived, or private ownership responded effectively to better market conditions will never be known, since the Second World War was to intervene. Inevitably the industry would have a bad war, given the absence of either substantial excess capacity or widespread modernisation. Adverse public sentiments towards the private ownership of the coal industry shaped by the industry's history, were soon confirmed by wartime production problems, and the time for nationalisation arrived.

Conclusion

A beguiling interplay between image and reality shaped coalmining's path to public ownership. Eventually nationalisation came not because of the veracity of the economic case against private ownership, but from a near universal belief that the industry had failed. Nationalisation in 1946 was essentially an adverse verdict on the performance of British coalmining over the previous half century. Ostensibly private ownership had so enfeebled the industry that by the Second World War even modest demand increases could not be accommodated. Therefore the public interest required the transfer of the industry's assets to the National Coal Board. Such judgement on the efficacy of private ownership has flimsy economic foundations. Both the capacity and efficiency of the British coal industry were moulded by market forces dating back at least to the turn of the twentieth century. The decisions of private ownership in the product and factor markets then prevailing were apposite, but profoundly influenced British coalmining in the years between the world wars. The legacy, the accumulated capital stock, could not simply be laid aside, and the organisation and technology of the industry was inevitably constrained by history. Responses by the private owners to secular demand decline, both in the competitive 1920s and cartelised 1930s markets, were in the prevailing circumstances typically economically efficient. That their decisions were eventually adjudged against the public interest, and their property rights rescinded, chiefly reflects the progressive undermining of the owners' reputations both during the world wars and the intervening years of turmoil. Victory for the idea that the assets of coalmining would be better used by a public corporation rested on the simple belief that the industry could be better organised. That the National Coal Board was only asked to operate in the public interest shows that nationalisation was more an expression of discontent with the past than a blueprint for the future.

NOTES

I would like to thank the editors and the participants of the conference on Industrial Organisation and the Road to Nationalisation at Manchester, April 1993, for helpful comment.

1 This paper and the associated NCB sponsored history provide the starting point for any discussion of coal's nationalisation.
2 Gwilym Lloyd George, Minister of Fuel and Power in the interim Conservative government, was forced to qualify his earlier support in Parliament for private ownership by accepting both the recommendations of the Reid Committee and that amalgamations might be compulsory. The third version of the Mining Association of Great Britain's chairman's, Robert Foot, plan for coal also conceded that reorganisation might be compulsory (*The Economist*, 2 and 16 June, 28 July).
3 The estimates are reported in an unpublished Ministry of Fuel and Power document dated February 1951, 'Investment in the coal mining industry'. Deposited in the PRO in file POWE 37/99.
4 The basis of calculating shifts worked, and hence OMS, changed when statutory returns became available in 1943. The 1944 data reported here are adjusted to conform with the earlier estimates.
5 New investment which was below one third of 1913 levels through the war years peaked in 1923 at a level similar to the average of 1906–13 (Feinstein 1972, p. T192, and Feinstein and Pollard 1988, p. 445).
6 Interestingly the British owners declined to participate in discussions to establish an international coal cartel at the World Economic Conference, 1933, given their dominant position in the trade (Political and Economic Planning 1936, p. 12).

REFERENCES

Alford, B.W.E. (1986), 'Lost opportunities: British businessmen during the First World War', in N. McKendrick and R.B. Outhwaite (eds.), *Business Life and Public Policy*, Cambridge University Press, pp. 205–27.
Ashworth, W. (1986), *The History of the British Coal Industry, vol. v: 1946–82, The Nationalised Industry*, Oxford: Clarendon Press.
Beacham, A. (1945), 'Efficiency and organisation of the British coal industry', *Economic Journal*, 95: 206–16.
Board of Trade (1938), *Annual Report of the Secretary for Mines*, London.
Broadberry, S.N. (1990), 'The emergence of mass unemployment: macroeconomic trends in Britain during the trans-World War 1 period', *Economic History Review*, 43: 271–82.
Buxton, N.K. (1970), 'Enterpreneurial efficiency in the British coal industry between the wars', *Economic History Review*, 23: 476–97.
  (1978), *The Economic Development of the British Coal Industry* London: Batsford.
Court, W.H.B. (1951), *Coal*, London: Longmans, Green and Company.
The Economist (1945), London.

Feinstein, C.H. (1972), *National Income, Expenditure and Output of the United Kingdom 1855–1965*, Cambridge University Press.

Feinstein, C.H. and Pollard, S. (1988), *Studies in Capital Formation in the United Kingdom 1750–1920*, Oxford: Clarendon Press.

Fine, B. (1990), *The Coal Question: Political Economy and Industrial Change from the Nineteenth Century to the Present Day*, London: Routledge.

Greasley, D. (1982), 'The diffusion of machine cutting in the British coal industry 1902–38', *Explorations in Economic History*, 19: 246–68.

(1985), 'Wage rates and work intensity in the South Wales coalfield, 1874–1914', *Economica*, 52: 383–9.

(1990), 'Fifty years of coalmining productivity: the record of the British coal industry before 1939', *Journal of Economic History*, 50: 877–902.

(1992), 'The market for South Wales coal 1874–1914', *The Journal of European Economic History*, 21: 135–52.

(1993), 'Economies of scale in British coalmining between the wars', *Economic History Review*, 46: 155–9.

Henly, A. (1988), 'Price formation and market structure: the case of the inter-war coal industry', *Oxford Bulletin of Economics and Statistics*, 50: 263–78.

Jevons, H.S. (1915), *The British Coal Trade*, London: Kegan Paul, Trench, and Trubner.

Johnson, W. (1972), 'Entrepreneurial efficiency in the British coal industry between the wars: a second comment', *Economic History Review*, 25: 665–8.

Kirby, M.W. (1973), 'The control of competition in the British coal-mining industry in the thirties', *Economic History Review*, 26: 273–83.

(1977), *The British Coalmining Industry, 1870–1946: A Political and Economic History*, London: Macmillan.

Ministry of Fuel and Power (1944, 1945), *Statistical Digests*, Cmd. 6639 1945 X, and Cmd. 6920 1945–6 XXI.

Mitchell, B.R. (1984), *Economic Development of the British Coal industry 1800–1914*, Cambridge University Press.

Political and Economic Planning (1936), *Report on the Coal Industry*, London.

Redmayne, R.A.S. (1923), *The British Coal-Mining Industry During the War*, Oxford.

Reid Report (1945), *Report of the Coalmining Technical Advisory Committee*, Cmd. 6610, 1944–5 IV.

Rogow, A.A. (1955), *The Labour Government and British Industry 1945–51*, Oxford: Basil Blackwell.

Royal Commission on Coal Supplies (1903–5), 1903 XVI, 1904 XXIII, 1905 XVI.

Salter, W.E.G. (1960), *Productivity and Technical Change*, Cambridge University Press.

Samuel Commission (1925), *Report of the Royal Commission on the Coal Industry*, Cmd. 2600, 1926 XIV.

Sankey Commission (1919), *Reports on the Royal Commission on the Coal Industry* Cmd. 84 et seq, 1919 XI, XII, XIII.

Supple, B. (1986), 'Ideology and necessity: the nationalisation of coalmining 1916–46', in N. McKendrick and R.B. Outhwaite, *Business Life and Public Policy*, Cambridge University Press.

(1987), *The History of the British Coal Industry, vol. IV, 1913–46: The Political Economy of Decline*, Oxford: Clarendon Press.

The Times (1945), 'British War Production', London.

4   The changing role of government in British civil air transport 1919–49

Peter J. Lyth

The establishment of the British air corporations as state-owned enterprises in 1946 was probably the least controversial element in the nationalisation programme of the post-war Labour government. The British Overseas Airways Corporation had already been taken into public ownership in 1939, and civil aviation in Britain, as in most other parts of the world, had a history of government control and subsidy stretching back to the earliest commercial flights. Unlike the obvious targets for Labour's nationalisation plans, such as the coal industry, air transport had no 'dues to pay' to a large and exploited labour force, nor did it in any sense occupy a position on the commanding heights of the British economy. Hitherto the preserve of the privileged, with passengers, pilots and engineers coming mainly from middle-class backgrounds, there was little immediate expectation that it would become a popular means of transport and no reason to see its development as especially important to the government's plans for the future. That Labour found it necessary to nationalise Britain's airlines instead of leaving them as amenable private monopolies, as envisaged in the previous government's White Paper, seems to have been prompted by a mixture of economic pragmatism and ideological consistency.

Civil aviation was barely a quarter of a century old in 1945. While older industries and natural monopolies had been targeted for nationalisation at various times since the adoption of Clause 4 in Labour's 1918 constitution, air transport had hardly figured in the Party's deliberations. Moreover at the end of Labour's term of office in 1951 its economic significance was still only a fraction of that represented by the other major state-owned industries.[1] However there were compelling reasons why civil air transport should have been of concern to Labour. The Second World War had shown the vital importance of air power, and Britain was committed both to the production of a new generation of airliners and to the operation of a wide range of international air services, 'showing the flag' as befitted its victor status. The airline industry had experienced a troubled history and policy towards it had fluctuated considerably; now was the time for a fresh approach.

What had those policies been? Why indeed did civil air transport need any government policy at all? Apart from the obvious safety considerations that required the state's involvement, there had been a number of economic and political reasons put forward to justify active government involvement, all of which were still common currency in 1945. Firstly, there was the geo-strategic requirement that a reserve of transport aircraft and operational routes be maintained for defence and for communications to the colonies. Secondly, there was the perceived advantage of providing a market for domestic aircraft manufacturers and encouragement to them to build the most advanced aircraft. Thirdly, there was a need to ensure air services to inaccessible points which were wholly unprofitable for airlines to operate under normal market conditions. Fourthly, there was the prestige factor, the rarely stated but generally understood desire that Britain demonstrate its commercial and technological prowess on foreign soil. Fifthly, there was the wish to ensure, by restricting the number of entrants to one or two *chosen instruments*, a high level of operational activity with the minimum amount of financial support.

Writing almost fifty years later, it is striking how few of these motives would be accepted as determining factors today. The defence and prestige principles vanished for all practical purposes with the Empire, while the idea that British airlines should be captive customers for the domestic aircraft makers died with that industry in the 1960s. The provision of 'social services' which were not offered by commercial airlines has a long tradition and stems from the fact that there was political capital to be made from establishing communications to isolated regions which were cut off from the surface transport network. Regular air services to the Hebrides, the Orkneys and the Shetlands, as well as to Belfast and the Isle of Man, were already in operation by 1935; ten years later it was an article of faith for Labour that they be maintained despite their hopeless economics.

Lastly, there is the vexed question of financial support, and the trade-off between entry restrictions and the granting of subsidy. Early British air transport policy appeared to have as its guiding philosophy the minimisation of charges on the public purse. Yet subsidy and air travel were virtually synonymous in the years between the wars, and there were no carriers operating anywhere in the world, including the United States, that did not receive direct or indirect subsidies on a regular basis. The challenge which faced all British governments from 1920 to 1945 was not so much to eliminate the subsidy, although there were figures in government who would have welcomed this step, but to create a system with the right combination of subsidy and regulation to fulfil the prevailing object- ives of civil aviation policy.[2] Since 1945, as major international flag- carriers like the British air corporations have shown that they can be self sufficient and make profits on a regular basis, the need for them to be protected with entry restrictions and monopoly privileges has faded away.

The nationalisation of air transport represented neither the achieve- ment of a political goal by Labour, nor the only choice remaining to government in 1945, but rather one further approach to the problem, given that the principles listed above were still determining factors in civil aviation policy. This chapter will be concerned with the road that was travelled to reach this solution.

1   The failure of early competition

The first regular international passenger air service was inaugurated in August 1919 by the British airline, Aircraft Transport & Travel [AT&T], between London and Paris. AT&T had been founded by George Holt Thomas, who had also set up the Aircraft Manufacturing Co. with Geoffrey de Havilland, and it was a typical feature of early commercial air travel that aircraft manufacturers and airline operators were often the same people. Handley Page and Junkers are other examples. AT&T's London–Paris service was an obvious route to begin with because it was the right distance for the aircraft of the time with their limited range, there was good traffic potential between the two European capitals, and it involved a sea crossing – a critical advantage of air travel over surface transport. The trip took about two and a half hours and cost around £15 for a single fare. Handley Page Transport began a Paris service about a week after AT&T and a third airline established by the shipowners Instone started Paris services in February 1920. In the summer Handley Page began flying to Amsterdam, sharing the route with the vigorous new Dutch airline KLM.

British civil aviation began therefore with open competition, but this state of affairs did not last long. Although in the summer months it looked promising, the traffic was far too thin to support so many firms and when two subsidised French airlines entered the market on the London–Paris route, losses mounted rapidly. Operating with rudimen- tary and uneconomic aircraft, the airlines' costs were so high that they would have had difficulty breaking even with load factors of 100 per cent; as it was they were lucky to take off with their planes half full. The DH.4s and DH.8s of AT&T 'lost money on every flight', irrespective of how many passengers or how much cargo was carried, and, beginning with

AT&T, the British firms folded one after the other, until for a while in 1921 there was not a single commercial airline in the country (Birkhead 1960, p. 138, Dyos and Aldcroft 1974, p. 403).

State subsidies for foreign rivals like KLM and the French operators were in evidence from the outset, but in Britain there had been little political support for the idea that the government should assume financial responsibility for the fledgling airlines (Higham 1960, pp. 39–42). If commercial air transport was to fly, said Winston Churchill, it 'must fly by itself'.[3] This oft-quoted remark has to be set in context. State involvement in British business was relatively unknown before the First World War and far less common than in the rest of Europe. The war had certainly brought a greater degree of intervention in the economy, but much of this was reversed after 1918 (Ashworth 1991, pp. 1–3). There was little knowledge of air transport's commercial dynamics, and no willingness to treat it differently from other industries. What changed this attitude seems to have been the humiliating prospect of air communications between Britain and the Continent being totally dependent on foreigners. Britain was the largest military air power in the world at the end of the First World War, and to have no part in the development of peacetime air transport was a situation which even the most complacent of governments could hardly contemplate. There seemed to be compelling defence and prestige reasons for helping British airlines face up to their subsidised competitors.

A scheme for the London–Paris service was quickly drawn up by the Cross-Channel Subsidies Committee chaired by Lord Londonderry under which British companies were guaranteed a 10 per cent profit on gross receipts from March 1921. This first air subsidy amounted to £85,671. Then from April 1922 a more complicated arrangement was introduced which covered three companies on the London–Paris service and one on London—Brussels. The subsidy was 25 per cent of gross earnings together with £3 per passenger carried. In so far as traffic did not increase significantly, the scheme failed, and from October 1922 competition between the British firms, previously considered essential, was rejected. A third 'revised scheme' was now implemented by which the four airlines were given separate routes with a subsidy according to the number of flights operated. This scheme, which cost the government a further £304,000 between October 1922 and March 1924, increased the share of traffic on British aircraft, but did nothing to make the airlines more financially viable, while the minimum performance stipulation provided no incentive to expand routes, acquire better aircraft, or generally enlarge their scale of operations (Higham 1960, pp. 43–75, Spurgeon 1956, p. 6).

On the other hand, the incentive to amalgamate was in any case weak at this stage, and the government's action in subsidising competing firms probably had little retarding effect. There were few scale economies to be gained as long as passenger traffic was so low and aircraft size so small.

The basic cause of the early airlines' losses was weak demand caused by high fares, poor regularity, and a doubtful safety record. Moreover while demand was lacking there was no stimulus to provide greater capacity, although an increase in aircraft size and the frequency of operations was the only way forward. Many people felt that until there was stronger demand for passenger travel the carriage of mail should form the basis of air transport development and this is what actually happened in the United States where the Post Office was the main source of subsidy in the 1920s (Birkhead 1960, p. 139). However in Europe, with shorter distances and a more developed surface network, the advantages of air mail were marginal. The central problem was the technical limitations of the aircraft which virtually eliminated all possibility of profitable operations. Even efficient operators could hardly cover a quarter of their costs at revenue rates which would attract passengers from the railways. As one of the industry's most experienced commentators has put it, the aircraft 'were so unsafe and unreliable and were so limited in their operations by unfavorable weather that they were incapable of competing with surface transport, except in a few special cases which were nothing like numerous enough to support the commercial growth of a new industry' (Brooks 1967, p. 164).

This was the situation when a government-appointed committee met in January 1923 under the chairmanship of Sir Herbert Hambling to look into the best way of subsidising British civil aviation and fostering its future growth. In its report the Committee drew the lesson that competition between British airlines would continue to cripple the industry until passenger demand increased. With the prevailing subsidy at double the revenue, the government was competing with itself and since the losses attributable to competition were passed on to the taxpayer, no increase in efficiency could result. The Committee recommended instead that the policy of subsidising a number of small companies be discontinued and a single large company with a 'privileged position as regards subsidies' created from the merger of the existing airlines, i.e., Handley Page, Instones, Daimler Hire, and a fourth unsubsidised carrier, British Marine Air Navigation. The benefit of competition under the present circumstances was 'illusory', argued the report. 'So far as efficiency of service is concerned, adequate incentive should be provided by the direct competition of foreign companies with large Government resources behind them' (Hambling Report 1923, para. 14).

Thus, after less than five years of commercial experience, competition between British airlines was at an end. The era of subsidy had already begun. Now monopoly privileges were to be added to civil aviation's operating environment. Henceforth a *chosen instrument* would have exclusive rights to financial assistance from the state; it was an important step towards public ownership.

2   Subsidised private monopoly

The *chosen instrument* was to be Imperial Airways. It was set up at the end of March 1924 with the former railway executive, Sir Eric Geddes, as chairman and George Woods Humphrey as General Manager. It had a total staff of 260, including nineteen pilots, and all the assets of the constituent airlines. Geddes had wide transport experience and had been Minister of Transport briefly in 1919. However, since he was also chairman of the Dunlop Rubber Company, he was never able to devote his full attention to running the airline. The government decided on a subsidy of £1 million to be paid in diminishing installments over ten years, at the end of which period it was hoped the company would be self supporting. In addition it was required to use only British-built aircraft (Higham 1960, pp. 76–83, Spurgeon 1956, p. 16).

A chronicler of the airline has described Imperial Airways' history as 'sixteen years of pioneering and development – sixteen years of glorious achievement' (Quin-Harkin 1954, p. 197). It was undoubtedly pioneering and pursued its goal of linking the far corners of the British Empire with missionary zeal. By contrast its interest in Europe declined and it would probably have preferred to abandon its services to the Continent altogether if the Air Ministry had allowed it to do so (Higham 1960, pp. 88–108, Pudney 1959, pp. 101–39). Attachment to the Empire remained a potent force in the 1920s, particularly it seems amongst aviators (Edgerton 1991, p. 21), and the adoption of Imperial Preference at the Ottawa Conference in 1932 strengthened an economic trend which civil air transport gladly followed. However Imperial Airways was also following the commercial dictates of the industry at the time. Air trials on the route between Cairo and Basra had shown that long-distance services to colonial outposts were likely to be considerably more profitable than flights to the Continent, on which the slow aircraft of the 1920s had to compete with express rail networks as well as the other European flag-carriers.

By the beginning of the 1930s two things about British civil aviation were already apparent (see table 4.1). Firstly it was going to take much longer than anticipated for airlines to 'fly on their own', and by 1929, with no sign of self sufficiency in sight, the government made a new ten year agreement with Imperial Airways (Higham 1960, pp. 81–2). Secondly there was a strong potential for conflict between the goal of financial self sufficiency and the requirement to operate British-built aircraft. In 1924 Imperial had agreed to complete a minimum yearly total of 800,000 miles, rising to one million miles after four years. But this provision did nothing to stimulate either the growth of passenger traffic or the development of faster, more modern aircraft, since the mileage could just as easily be done with small, slow aircraft as with large, fast ones. The airline was not only neglecting Europe but was flying antiquated aircraft. The stately Handley Page HP42 biplanes of which it took delivery after 1930 were barely faster than the Handley Page 0/400 bombers of fifteen years earlier. Of course they offered luxurious accommodation, but because Imperial's specifications had not required a cruising speed in excess of 100 mph, there was no incentive for the manufacturers to produce a more advanced aerodynamic design, such as were already being planned and built in the United States and Germany (Handley Page 1953, p. 110).

Another development of significance to the long-term future of civil aviation was the appearance between 1932 and 1935 of a whole rash of small domestic airlines. Lacking the prestige factor that had made the government so concerned about international services, these internal operators were allowed to fly in unfettered competition with one another, free to decide their frequencies, fares and equipment. They expanded rapidly in number, flying a great range of different routes from Cornwall to the north of Scotland, often exploiting the advantage of a short sea crossing, and frequently operating on the most precarious of financial foundations. The most important element in their midst was soon revealed to be the British railway companies (LNER, LMS, Great Western and Southern), which had spotted the threat to their long-distance passenger market posed by air travel. In March 1934 they established Railway Air Services (RAS), the first airline owned and directed by a competing form of transport. With considerable financial resources available to it, RAS set about establishing services on routes where the other airlines were striving to offer an alternative to the existing rail connections, their main object being to prevent outsiders developing air transport to the detriment of the railways' main transport operations (Aldcroft 1974, pp. 226–42).

Where RAS could not acquire competing airlines, they banned railway-accredited travel agents from taking bookings from independent airlines – an extraordinary practice which persisted until 1938, despite strong protests from aviation circles. However RAS's aim of consolidation amongst the many competing independent carriers, and its prescription of tight control for the domestic industry gained ground with legislators. In 1935 the Maybury Committee found little to fault in RAS operations, conclud-

Table 4.1. *Airline revenue, passengers and subsidies: Britain and Germany 1924–55*

| | Total British scheduled traffic | | Chosen instruments | | | | Deutsche Luft Hansa | |
| | Rev. pass. | Pass/ miles (000s) | Imperial Airways | | British Airways | | Rev. pass. | Subsidy (£000s) |
			Rev. pass.	Subsidy (£000s)	Rev. pass.	Subsidy (£000s)		
1924	10,321	2,482	10,321					245.0
1925	11,027	2,645	11,027	137.0			55,185[a]	
1926	16,621	3,746	16,621	137.0			84,594	
1927	19,005	4,296	19,005	152.6			102,681	
1928	27,303	6,477	27,303	235.1			111,115	988.5
1929	28,484	7,147	28,484	230.6			87,019	517.4
1930	24,027	6,003	24,027	364.6			76,894	732.7
1931	23,817	7,009	23,817	340.3			82,998	875.5
1932	48,200	16,007	45,844	467.5			86,578	740.5
1933	79,100	21,601	54,768	545.0			94,872	847.3
1934	135,100	29,162	54,875	543.7			130,758	1,010.8
1935	200,000	42,360	66,324	561.5		112.9	163,980	962.1
1936	236,300	41,144	60,374	426.6	15,508	11.6	232,061	1,038.3
1937	244,400	49,729	64,629	381.8	17,130	61.8	277,347	1,220.6
1938	222,200	56,348	51,287		22,562	110.6	254,716	1,148.1
1939	210,400	66,577	63,400					

Year			BOAC		BEA	
1940	71,400	53,429	27,200	na		
1941	88,200	73,337	30,900	na		
1942	111,800	107,335	48,100	na		
1943	135,600	128,693	63,400	na		
1944	175,600	189,572	99,500	na		
1945	259,600	322,769	142,600	na		
			BOAC/BSAA		**BEA**	
1946	423,500	362,841	149,500	8,964.0[b]	44,600	3,136.0
1947	586,500	441,140	109,300	6,560.0	462,900	3,400.0
1948	713,400	554,536	135,100	5,750.0	565,500	2,150.0
1949	917,200	613,383	148,900	6,350.0	709,200	1,535.0
			BOAC			
1950			200,500	6,000.0	939,600	1,000.0
1951			250,200	1,500.0	1,135,600	1,400.0
1952			290,600	nil	1,400,100	1,250.0
1953			305,000	nil	1,656,800	1,500.0
1954			291,136	nil	1,874,300	1,000.0
1055			385,800	nil	2,224,700	nil

Notes: [a] Luft Hansa was formed in 1926 from the two German airlines Deutsche Aero Lloyd AG and Junkers-Luftverkehr AG; 1925 figures are for the two companies combined.

[b] Includes grants made before the 1946 Civil Aviation Act.

Sources: Civil Aviation Statistical and Technical Review, 1937; Civil Aviation Report 1946–7, p. 48–9; Deutsche Luft Hansa AG, Jahresberichte 1926–38; Cadman Report 1938; BEA and BOAC Annual Reports, 1946–56; Higham 1959, p. 122.

ing that 'if air transport is to become fully self-supporting, it is a pre-requisite that cut-throat competition must be eliminated and that some measure of restriction must be applied to avoid indiscriminate multipli-cation of services' (Maybury 1937, para. 125). It is striking how much the sentiments of the Maybury Report repeat those of Hambling, a decade earlier, reinforcing the notion that 'wasteful competition' in civil aviation had to be avoided at all cost.

3   Subsidised competition

Imperial Airways and Railway Air Services were the means by which international and domestic air transport, using public and private subsi-dies, was consolidated in a regime of entry restrictions and monopoly. And the concepts of subsidy and monopoly are constant features of the landscape through which the road to nationalisation runs; the one offered hesitantly by governments, the other used to protect the investment. It would be wrong however to deduce that the government was entirely comfortable with a monopoly in international air transport and it was certainly aware of the shortcomings of Imperial Airways. Conveniently, after a series of mergers among non-subsidised airlines in late 1935, a challenger emerged in the form of British Airways Ltd.

The prospects for this private airline would have been doubtful in the absence of a subsidy, but an Interdepartmental Committee chaired by Sir Warren Fisher recommended that in view of Imperial's lacklustre per-formance in Europe, a subsidy should be given to the newcomer (see table 4.1). Prestige demanded that Britain put on a better show (Cadman 1938, Appendix B, 45). Thus the pre-1924 doctrine of subsidising more than one carrier was partly restored, with the important proviso that each airline operate in a designated sphere. In February 1936 Imperial Airways agreed to surrender its rights, unused since 1926, to territory north of a line between London and Berlin. British Airways began flying on the route London–Amsterdam–Hamburg–Copenhagen–Malmo,   as   well   as pioneering night mail flights to Sweden and Berlin, the latter hitherto a Deutsche Luft Hansa monopoly (Higham 1959, pp. 113–15).

In making British Airways a second *chosen instrument* the government concluded a subsidy agreement which required the airline to operate fast, i.e., 200 mph, services to compete with carriers like KLM and Swissair which were already using the new Douglas and Lockheed types. Since there was not a single British transport aircraft which possessed that kind of performance, British Airways was allowed to buy Lockheed Electras and some German Junkers JU.52.[4] The Electras immediately cut the time on the London–Paris service from Imperial's leisurely two hours to ninety minutes, thus restoring serious competition between British carriers on this premier route for the first time since the early 1920s (Higham 1959, p. 119).

Meanwhile the widespread parliamentary dissatisfaction with Imperial's performance had prompted the government to initiate a major committee inquiry into British civil aviation. The Cadman report which was published in 1938 saw a conflict between Imperial's private enterprise approach to the industry and the airline's wider obligations to the national interest. Its management was seen as too concerned with the balance sheet, and not enough with the development of competitive aircraft, smooth labour relations or the enhancement of British prestige abroad (Cadman 1938, paras. 43–6). It did not help matters that the airline, still a government subsidy recipient, had just declared a large dividend, much to the irritation of its flying staff. In Parliament it was attacked by Robert Perkins, a Conservative MP and founder of the British Airline Pilots Association, who accused it of unfairly dismissing pilots and cutting their salaries (Higham 1960, pp. 270–88, Cross 1982, p. 201). Labour relations at Imperial had been poor from the outset, indeed it had been hit by a pilots' strike on the very first day of operations in 1924. Its bad reputation with organised labour is clear from the opinion of a trade unionist and staunch supporter of the industry's nationalisation, writing in the early 1950s. 'The incorporation in the 1946 legislation of the provision that the state-owned air corporations should be model employers owed a lot to the trade unions' memory of Imperial's pre-war transgressions' (Jenkins 1953, p. 22).

In fairness to Imperial Airways and its managing director, Woods Humphery, it should be noted that the airline had performed its job reasonably well within the spirit of the 1924 legislation which, after all, had placed self sufficiency as a primary objective. 'Mr Woods Humphery was charged with making commercial aviation pay, and he came nearer to succeeding than anybody else in the world. The new executive chairman Sir John Reith (late of the BBC) is charged with making British aviation technically advanced, no matter whether it pays or not' (*The Observer*, 17 June 1938).

By concentrating on the less competitive Empire services, Imperial had actually come closer to financial autonomy than any of its major European competitors, i.e., Deutsche Luft Hansa, Air France and KLM (Cadman 1938, Appendix B, paras. 11–14). However the policy goals had changed in the fourteen years since Hambling, or at least there had been a shift in emphasis. Self sufficiency remained a cherished goal, but it was now an idealised one, like chastity. In the late 1930s aviation was at the cutting edge of international rivalry in Europe and the subsidies that drove it forward could no longer be dispensed sparingly. A glance at table 4.1 shows that the leading European airline, Deutsche Luft Hansa, was being subsidised at the rate of £8.9 per revenue passenger in 1928, £10.5 per passenger in 1931 and £5.9 per passenger in 1935. By comparison, the figures for Imperial Airways were £8.6, £14.3 and £8.5, which suggests that although the British airline's annual subsidy was averaging less than half the amount received by Luft Hansa, German taxpayers were getting better value for money. The Air Ministry map of European air routes for 1935 shows a Continent dominated by the black network of the German flag-carrier with only a few thin red lines stretching out from London. Of course state subsidies were not the only reason for Luft Hansa's successful expansion in Europe from the 1920s onwards. Unlike Britain, France, Holland and Belgium, it did not have the distraction of colonies and the accompanying urge to connect them to the motherland with tenuous air links. And the prohibition against the construction of any kind of military air force meant that Germany channelled all its resources and aeronautical expertise into civil transport (Joensson 1987, p. 47). However in an industry where consumer demand was still weak the whole-hearted financial support of the state undoubtedly made a difference.

Cadman's importance lies in the establishment of the principle that Britain also had to have a full network of air services between London and the principal capitals of Europe and that the nation's civil aviation effort would not succeed against foreign competition unless it was properly subsidised (Cadman 1938, paras. 34–5). Had the Report's recommendation to subsidise both Imperial and British Airways been fully implemented, it would have created a two-armed instrument for British civil aviation policy, closer to developments in the United States at the time, where four major trunk operators (American, United, Eastern, and TWA) had created the oligopoly that was to characterise American air transport for the next forty years. However in Europe where the market was very much smaller, governments had all opted for the single protected flag carrier to operate international services.

4   State-owned monopoly

The government may have been influenced by European practice at this juncture. In any event while it accepted Cadman's recommendation that the subsidy be increased, it decided to pay it to a single, publicly-owned air corporation formed by the merger of Imperial Airways and British Airways. As private companies, subsidised or not, they were bound to act in the interests of profit rather than 'real aeronautical progress', the new Secretary for Air, Sir Kingsley Wood, told Parliament in 1939; merging their operations would lead to a reduction in their administrative costs. As in 1924, the necessary competition would be provided by the foreign carriers.[5] In August 1939 the British Overseas Airways Corporation [BOAC] Bill received Royal assent, and on 1 April 1940, at the beginning of the new financial year, BOAC came into being.

Charles Mowat has called BOAC's creation a piece of 'Tory socialism' (Mowat 1968, p. 449). This probably exaggerates its significance. The interventionist idea had become acceptable even amongst Conservatives in the inter-war years and government support of one sort or another had become common for ailing industries like coal and cotton as much as for new ones like air transport. Public ownership had already spread to include the BBC, London Passenger Transport, and the Central Electricity Board (Gourvish 1991, pp. 114–16, Skuse and Jones-Owen 1983, pp. 25–6, Tivey 1973, pp. 23–5). The key was the emergence of the public corporation, a statutory body, controlled by government, but with separate finances and management, an institution with the lofty goal of maximising welfare instead of profit (Redwood and Hatch 1982, p. 5, Tivey 1973, pp. 33–5).

Unfortunately BOAC had no opportunity to put its peacetime charter as a public corporation into practice. When it began operations in April 1940, the skies were filled with the drone of combat aircraft, and it was immediately placed under the control of the Royal Air Force. Normal business procedures were suspended and BOAC's sole task was to ferry men and supplies along whatever international routes were still reasonably safe from enemy action. By the end of 1940 the only remaining European services from Britain were to Portugal and occasionally Sweden (Bray 1973, pp. 19–22).

The wartime coalition government pondered the shape of post-war civil aviation, but little was done before 1944. By then the war had stimulated revolutionary developments in aircraft design and manufacture, and it was obvious that air transport was going to be a great deal more important in the future. The problem for Britain was that the industry was likely to be dominated by the United States with its enormous fleet of modern transport aircraft. Consequently in the negotiations on the future shape of international air transport which took place at Chicago in November 1944, America sought the greatest freedom, Britain the greatest protection (Dierikx 1992, pp. 808–15, Dobson 1991, Joensson 1987, pp. 31–5).

The man who led the British delegation at the Chicago conference was Viscount Swinton, the Air Minister who had resigned at the time of the Cadman Report, now recalled from an African posting to assume the job as Britain's first Minister of Civil Aviation. As a senior Tory, Swinton had no ideological preference for nationalisation, but his championship of 'orderly development' at Chicago showed that he was hardly an enthusiast for free-market operations either, at least not in commercial air transport (Cross 1982, pp. 244–51). When he set about assembling his plan for British civil aviation in the winter of 1944–5 he was in search of a compromise between unrestricted private enterprise and state-owned monopoly. Having concluded that aviation was a transport business in which airmen were not experts, he decided to co-opt the skills and resources of those who were: the railways, the shipping lines, and the travel agencies.

Swinton's plan, as presented to the Cabinet in January 1945, envisaged British civil aviation in the hands of several organisations with mixed ownership. The major input for the plan seems to have come from two main sources: the wartime BOAC management and the railway companies. BOAC, under its chairman Lord Knollys, favoured an airline monopoly for international operations, with openings for private investors. Knollys argued that the participation of rail and shipping interests would serve to 'provide a means of giving a stake in the enterprise to those who may claim they are prejudiced by its activities'. This curious piece of reasoning, reminiscent of the RAS strategy in the 1930s, was dismissed by Sir George Cribbet at the Air Ministry as a 'desire to allow clamourous private interests to share in the swag at the expense of the taxpayer'.[6] But the railways maintained a similar line. Their *Railway Plan for Air Transport* outlined a scheme for a joint Continental and UK service, operated by a railway-led airline with the participation of the shipping companies, and confidently predicted that it would function without subsidy.[7]

The proposals of Lord Knollys and the railway companies, with their dubious prescriptions for private monopolies, could be safely disregarded were it not for the fact that they exercised a critical influence on the Swinton Plan, a substantial part of which was in turn adopted by Labour in its 1946 legislation.

When the Swinton Plan appeared as a White Paper in March 1945, the participation of surface interests had become central; they would be 'brought into a real and effective partnership with the organisations which will be responsible for transport by air' (British Air Transport 1945, para. 10). BOAC was to remain a state-owned enterprise but two new corporations, British European Airways (BEA) and British South American Airways (BSAA), would have mixed ownership, the majority private. Thus Sir Kingsley Wood's pre-war policy which had favoured a single corporation for all international services (BOAC) and domestic and charter operations being left to private independents, was changed (Corbett 1965, pp. 105–6). The dividing line was moved so that European services were separated from other international flights. The main share-holders in BEA, apart from BOAC with a minority stake, were to be the railways, the travel agencies and the short sea shipping lines, much as the *Railway Plan* had foreseen. The third carrier, BSAA, was to be respon-sible for services to South America, with majority ownership in the hands of four shipping companies, and with a smaller BOAC participation.

Why the Conservatives within the coalition had shifted to the view that a single instrument for international services would be unmanageable is unclear, since as we have seen this was the approach adopted by every other European nation, and there had been no opportunity to gain any meaningful commercial experience with BOAC in the war years. There were dissenters (chief amongst which was Lord Beaverbrook), but other-wise Swinton received broad Cabinet approval. This may be because it was seen by the coalition members as a non-political, all-embracing compromise, conceived along the faintly corporatist lines of Swinton's earlier effort at getting the British aircraft manufacturers organised for rearmament; his reputation as an expert on civil aviation was in any case restored by 1945.

Whatever its philosophical underpinning, the Swinton Plan aimed to fulfil a number of important criteria, which, because of their enduring influence on post-war policy, are worth recording. Firstly, to secure the provision of services in the public interest which were nonetheless inher-ently unprofitable, and to do so, not by direct subsidy, but by offering the airline monopoly rights on its profitable routes; asking it in other words to take 'the rough with the smooth' and to cross-subsidise.[8] Secondly to provide several chosen instruments flying in separate geographical regions. Although in a non-competitive relationship to each other, BOAC, BEA and BSAA were supposed to provide the benefits of differ-ent managerial styles, a questionable assumption bearing in mind the economics of the air transport business and the inherent differences between long- and short-haul operations. Thirdly to ensure that the airlines flew British aircraft, and fourthly that they did so without subsidy. The last criterion restored the pre-Cadman philosophy and is seen in the stipulation that the participating companies be chosen not just because of 'the positive contribution which they can make in skill and experience', but also because they were 'prepared to invest their own money without any Government guarantee' (British Air Transport 1945, para. 23).

The White Paper was debated in the House of Lords in March 1945. However its proposals lasted no longer than the government and by the end of the year Labour had produced its own draft legislation. Swinton's three corporations were mocked by Herbert Morrison in January 1946:

BEA was to 'square the railway interests', BSSA was for 'the shipping people, the Conservative believers in private enterprise', and BOAC? 'That is for the Socialists'.[9] It may seem today that the Swinton Plan was little more than a formula for appeasing as many existing transport interests as possible and that it took little account of the need to subsidise civil aviation until the introduction of modern aircraft and the growth in consumer demand allowed it to 'fly by itself'. In spite of Morrison's jest however much of it survived the change of government to reappear in Labour's nationalisation programme.

5   Labour's multiplicity of instruments

The new Labour Minister of Civil Aviation, Lord Winster, announced the government's plans for air transport to the House of Lords in November 1945 (British Air Services 1945). Until late October the Cabinet had seemed to be moving towards an option which was essentially Swinton with minor modifications: the shipping and rail interests in the new corporations would be reduced to minority holdings, but the mixed ownership plan remained. At this point, 'according to reports that are too circumstantial to be disbelieved', Labour back benchers threatened to organise a revolt in the Parliamentary party 'if capitalist interests were not wholly excluded' and the Cabinet opted for complete nationalisation (*The Economist*, 10 November 1945).

Although the 1946 Civil Aviation Act must obviously be seen within the context of Labour's general economic and political programme, its purpose was essentially pragmatic. In the main debate on the Bill, Labour stressed the need for subsidies and that nationalisation would enable these to be used effectively and without meddlesome supervision. The public corporation would actually give the airline's management a greater degree of independence than that enjoyed by the private company Imperial Airways. Curiously the Conservatives chose to criticise the monopolistic features of the proposals, rather than the ownership question, although the Swinton Plan had allowed for little else but mixed-ownership monopoly (Tivey 1973, p. 48).

Nationalisation was a new policy only in so far as the coalition government had made such elaborate plans for private interest participation. Seen in the longer term it appears as little more than a structural development, reversing 'the fusion policy of 1939/40 by splicing BOAC into three groups.' (Aldcroft 1986, pp. 225–6). Sir Stafford Cripps, who had held the post of Minister of Aircraft Production in the coalition government, had supported the case for having three separate corporations during the debate on the White Paper in March 1945. A 'multiplicity of instruments' would enable the testing of different techniques for civil air transport and the rigid uniformity of ideas that might come from a single monolithic structure would be avoided.[10] Distinct differences in the management and operating style of BOAC and BEA did in fact emerge before too long, although it is hard to see what the commercial advantages of this 'healthy rivalry' were, since they did not compete on the same routes.[11] Labour's policy in government followed the Cripps lead. 'Orderly, economic and efficient development of air transport' would take place, wasteful competition be avoided (an echo here of Hambling and Maybury), yet an effective spirit of enterprise be ensured by not placing 'matters of great national importance' in the hands of one single managerial group.[12]

Irrespective of whether there were any advantages to be gained with a 'multiplicity of instruments', the question arises as to whether the divisions between the instruments were in the right place. The separation of long-haul (BOAC) and short- to medium-haul operations (BEA) left the latter with a fundamental cost handicap. In addition BEA was burdened with the loss-making domestic services and would have to cross subsidise them from the outset. The divisions were of course inherited from the Swinton Plan, under which BEA would have had a wide range of owners, including the railways who could have been expected to develop domestic air services along RAS lines, but Labour was not obliged to adopt the Swinton structure any more than it had to accept its provisions for ownership (Lyth 1990, pp. 1–6). The question of uneconomic 'social services' and how they should be financed – direct subsidies or through the exploitation of the corporation's monopoly power – was to persist for the next twenty years.[13]

There were various proposals to unite the three air corporations into a single airline from as early as 1946, either to improve aircraft procurement or to enhance the marketing of British air transport.[14] These were all rejected, but following the crashes of BSAA's Tudor aircraft in 1948 the government did decide to reduce the number of 'instruments' from three to two and merge BSAA with BOAC. The fact that a single aircraft problem triggered BSAA's demise suggests that the airline was basically unviable and not that Labour was having doubts about its approach (Robson 1960, p. 111). However the corporations' monopoly was gradually loosened. In 1949 independent British carriers were allowed some scheduled services in 'association' with BEA, and in 1952 the new Conservative government went a little further and allowed applications for new services from independent airlines to be heard by the Air Transport Advisory Council – a first small gesture on the road back to competition.

6   Size and performance in airline operation

Airlines have always been helped by governments with taxpayers' money. Besides direct subsidies, they have received generous payment for carrying mail, the free provision of navigational and airport facilities, and substantial aid in the development and purchase of aircraft. Why nationalise therefore when you can subsidise?

The Labour government in 1945 was intent on taking all of Britain's surface transport services into public ownership, so apart from reasons of ideology there was legislative consistency in nationalising air transport. It was also aware that British airlines would need substantial support if they were to prosper in the post-war world, but could other methods of subsidy and control have achieved the goals laid out at the beginning of this chapter more effectively or at less cost? Pre-war experience and the Cadman Report suggested that privately owned carriers could not fulfil all the objectives of a national air transport policy because subsidising independent airlines from the Treasury always carried with it the potential for conflict-of-interest difficulties in commercial strategy, labour relations, aircraft procurement, and the all-important realm of prestige services. Assuming therefore that the new government accepted those earlier goals, then nationalisation was unquestionably the simplest and most effective solution for the post-war world. After all, it could point both to practice in other European countries and to the Conservative decision to create the state-owned BOAC in 1939 as indicative of the conventional wisdom on this point.

The early managers of the air corporations were certainly not opposed to nationalised undertakings. Many shared the opinion of Sir Peter Masefield, who was BEA's chief executive from 1949 to 1955, that in air transport the 'much debated issue of state or private ownership is quite immaterial' as long as the airlines were of an efficient size, were adequately capitalised, and the management was granted sufficient freedom to do the job properly. 'Only rabid and doctrinaire exponents of free enterprise or of nationalisation see only evil in the other' (Masefield 1955, p. 252).

What was an efficient size for an international flag-carrier, and what was the job it had to do? Nationalised industries aim at various targets, some of which can be loosely grouped under the heading 'public interest' and some of which have a strict commercial character (Preston 1975, pp. 70–1). With nationalised airlines, the 'public interest' can be summarised under three headings: the provision of 'social services' to isolated communities, the development of as wide an international network as possible, and the use of locally produced aircraft. The commercial goals are obviously to operate profitably, to operate efficiently, and (which may also be a 'public interest' goal) to operate without subsidy.

The problem for Britain's air corporations, to a greater degree than with other nationalised industries, was that 'public interest' and commercial goals were often in conflict with each other. Until the 1960s they were expected to fly British aircraft although these were rarely the most efficient or most likely to encourage profitable operations (Pryke 1981, p. 135). They were also expected, thanks to the negative experience with Imperial Airways, to be generous employers. In the case of BOAC, which got off to a difficult start and lost £7 million in its first year (1946/7), one early critic noted that 'the excessive leanness of Imperial Airways and British Airways (had been) replaced by an excessive fatness on the part of the Corporation' (Brancker 1949, p. 111). BOAC staff numbers were undoubtedly too high but that was a consequence of the airline's origins. During the war normal commercial procedures had not been followed and all expenses had been covered by the Treasury. It was an unfortunate regime under which to establish a new airline and the legacy of the war years left a lasting impression on BOAC's management culture. In April 1947 the corporation's Chairman listed a range of necessary economies, including a reduction in the number of establishments which were designed to employ the largest number of 'wartime subgrade staff'. However a year later a senior official at the Ministry of Civil Aviation found little improvement, with low output per capita, excessive manpower, and 'unjustifiably liberal standards of remuneration' throughout the airline.[15]

In fact, judged by labour productivity, both BOAC and BEA did markedly better than other nationalised industries in their first decade, with annual growth averaging 14 per cent between 1948 and 1958 (Gourvish 1991, p. 128). This is largely attributable to the rapid technological development of civil aviation, i.e., the introduction of larger and faster aircraft. In theory new capital investment leads directly to higher productivity and lower unit costs, although in air transport the productivity of an aircraft needs a matching rise in traffic flow before increased output can be achieved. In the event this was brought about by lower international airfares and a consequent expansion of the market for air travel in the 1950s (Wheatcroft 1964, pp. 14–15).

The most efficient size for an international airline depends on its objectives and its position within the industry. The case for monopoly relies to a large extent on proving that combining traffic and services in a single large carrier will yield economies that would not be available if the same work was performed by several airlines. Indeed this argument was employed at the time of BOAC's creation in 1939. In general however the airline industry, unlike aircraft manufacturing, is not subject to strong economies of scale, and firm size has not been an important variable in the production of air transport services since costs are determined by a combination of input prices, route structure, and aircraft utilisation (Straszheim 1969, p. 96). There is for example a strong tendency for operating costs-per-seat-mile to fall as aircraft size increases, so that an airline will try to use the largest aircraft possible for a given route distance (SCNI 1967, para. 306). But the use of larger aircraft does not require a larger airline or the reduction of competition. The repeated use of the phrase 'wasteful competition' by all parties to the debate on civil aviation in the years before 1946 was only a reflection of the underdeveloped state of the air transport market; with high fares, small aircraft and short ranges, there was rarely enough passengers for more than one airline per country.

The notable thing about Labour's 1946 decision is that it seems to have given less consideration to the implications of monopoly in air transport than in the surface industries. There was no provision for a central administrative body equivalent to British Railways for instance, nor was there an independent licensing authority such as the American Civil Aeronautics Board which could have challenged the monopoly power of the air corporations when necessary. Monopoly structures were accepted throughout the nationalisation programme in the belief that their adverse effects would be neutralised by the virtue of public ownership. This may have made sense with natural monopolies such as electricity generation whose profitability is largely a function of monopoly situation, but airlines are not in this category and their monopoly privileges are at the discretion of government (Aharoni 1986, p. 119). To grant the chosen instrument a monopoly of scheduled air services is a political decision, which, as we have already seen, had as its driving force the need to provide a substitute for greater dispensation of taxpayers' money.

It took another twenty years and an explosion in demand for passenger air travel in Europe and on the North Atlantic before competition between British airlines ('dual designation') was made officially respectable by the 1969 Edwards Report. It is significant that this Report – the most comprehensive investigation of British civil aviation since Cadman – gave BOAC and BEA an overall vote of confidence and, while recommending an end to their monopolies, saw no case for their denationalisation (Edwards 1969, paras. 495 [2]).

NOTES

1 I.e., the railways, coal, iron and steel, electricity and gas. The air corporations BOAC and BEA represented around 2 per cent of the turnover of state-owned

industries in 1951 (£2,234 million) and 1.1 per cent of the employment strength (2,314,900) (Gourvish 1991, p. 113).

2 I have drawn to some extent here on the illuminating discussion in Foldes 1961, pp. 160–1.

3 Hansard (1920), 5.Series, vol. 126, c.1622, 11.3.1920. Churchill was Secretary of State for War and Air until 1921.

4 For the weaknesses of the inter-war British aircraft industry see Fearon 1974, pp. 249–51 and 1985, pp. 31–2.

5 Hansard (1939), 5.Series, vol. 349, c.1831–1947, 10.7.1939.

6 'As a contribution from the chairman of a public corporation,' concluded Cribbet, 'I do not regard it as a high commendation of his qualifications for holding such an appointment' (Memorandum, 26.6.1944, PRO (1944), AIR 2/6937).

7 'Railway View of Post-War Operation of Internal and External Air Services', British Railway Companies Plans for Air Transport, June 1944. PRO (1944), AVIA 2/2462.

8 Swinton's Memorandum to the Cabinet, Lord President's Committee, LP[45]101, 10.5.1945, PRO (1945), AVIA 2/2760.

9 Hansard (1946), 5.Series, vol. 418, c.425, 24.1.1946.

10 Sir Stafford Cripps, Cabinet Papers, PRO (1946), CAB 129/CP(46)37.

11 The phrase is Ivor Thomas's. Brief for Minister, Socialisation of Industries Committee, 7.1.1946. PRO (1946), AVIA 55/38.

12 Winster, Minister of Civil Aviation, Cabinet Papers, 12.1.1946, PRO (1946), CAB 129/CP[46]37.

13 Domestic services were BEA's Achilles heel from the outset. They had a lower fare structure than Continental services, incurred heavier duty on fuel and used less economic aircraft. In Scotland in 1947 not a single route made a profit. Operating Results by Routes, April and July 1947, BEA Board Papers 12/14.

14 Civil Airways Corporations, Common Services Policy, 1946–1948, PRO (1948), BT 217/1506; Memorandum by Colonel Ducker, 1948, PRO (1948), BT 217/2127.

15 Ministry of Labour, BOAC Economy campaign, Ch.566, 9.4.1947, and 14.5.1948, PRO (1948), BT 217/2098.

BIBLIOGRAPHY

PRO (Public Record Office)

PRO (1944), AIR 2/6937, Memorandum, 26.6.1944.

PRO (1944), AVIA 2/2462, British Railways Companies' Plans for Air Transport, June.

PRO (1945), AVIA 2/2760, Lord President's Committee, LP(45) 101, 10.5.1945.

PRO (1946), CAB 129/CP(46)27, Cabinet Papers.

PRO (1946), AVIA 55/38, Brief for Minister, Socialisation of Industries Committee, 7.1.1946.

PRO (1948), BT 217/1506, Civil Airways Corporations, Common Services Policy, 1946–1948.

PRO (1948), BT 217/2127, Memorandum by Colonel Ducker.

PRO (1948), BT 217/2098, Ministry of Labour, BOAC Economy Campaign, Ch.566, 9.4.1947 and 14.5.1948.

Official publications
Cadman Report (1938), *Report of the Committee of Inquiry into Civil Aviation*, Cmd. 5685.
Edwards Report (1969), *British Air Transport in the Seventies*, Cmd. 4018.
Hambling Report (1923), *Report on Government Financial Assistance to Civil Air Transport Companies*, Cmd. 1811.
Maybury Report (1937), *Report of the Committee to Consider the Development of Civil Aviation in the UK*, Cmd. 5351.
Ministry of Civil Aviation (1945), *British Air Services*, Cmd. 6712.
Select Committee on Nationalised Industries (1967), *British European Airways*, HC 273.
Swinton Plan (1945), *British Air Transport*, Cmd. 6605.

Secondary References
Aharoni, Yair (1986), *The Evolution and Management of State Owned Enterprises*, Cambridge, Mass.: Ballinger.
Aldcroft, Derek H. (1974), 'The railways and air transport, 1933–9', in *Studies in British Transport History, 1870–1970*, Newton Abbot: David & Charles, pp. 226–42.
(1986), *The British Economy, vol. I Years of Turmoil 1920–1951*, Brighton: Harvester.
Ashworth, William (1991), *The State in Business 1945 to the mid-1980s*, London: Macmillan.
Birkhead, Eric (1960), 'The financial failure of British air transport companies 1919–1924', *Journal of Transport History*, 4(3): 133–45.
Brancker, J.W.S. (1949), 'The effect of nationalisation on air transport', *Journal of the Institute of Transport*, (May): 108–12.
Bray, Winston (1973), *The History of BOAC*, London: BOAC.
British European Airways (1947), Board Papers.
Brooks, P.W. (1967), 'The development of air transport', *Journal of Transport Economics and Policy*, 1(2): 163–72.
Corbett, D.C. (1965), *Politics and Airlines*, London: Allen and Unwin.
Cross, J.A. (1982), *Lord Swinton*, Oxford: Clarendon Press.
Dierikx, M.L.J. (1992), 'Shaping world aviation: Anglo-American civil aviation relations, 1944–1946', *Journal of Air Law and Commerce*, 57(4): 795–840.
Dobson, Alan P. (1991), *Peaceful Air Warfare: The United States, Britain and the Politics of International Aviation*, Oxford.
Dyos, H.J. and Aldcroft, Derek H. (1974), *British Transport. An Economic Survey from the Seventeenth Century to the Twentieth*, Penguin Books.
The Economist (1945), 'The bed of procrustes?' 10.11.1945.
Edgerton, David (1991), *England and the Aeroplane: An Essay on a Militant and Technological Nation*, Basingstoke: Macmillan.
Fearon, Peter (1974), 'The British airframe industry and the state 1918–1935', *Economic History Review*, 27(1): 249–51.

(1985), 'The growth of aviation in Britain', *Journal of Contemporary History*, 20(1): 31–2.

Foldes, Lucien (1961), 'Domestic air transport policy', *Economica*, (May): 156–75, (August): 270–85.

Gourvish, Terry (1991), 'The rise (and fall?) of state-owned enterprise', in Terry Gourvish and Alan O'Day (eds.), *Britain Since 1945*, Basingstoke: Macmillan, pp. 111–33.

Handley Page, Sir Frederick (1953), 'The influence of military aviation on civil air transport', *Journal of the Institute of Transport*, (May): 107–18.

Hansard (1920, 1939, 1940), House of Commons Debates.

Higham, Robin, D.S. (1959), 'British Airways Ltd, 1935–1940', *Journal of Transport History*, 4(2) (November): 112–21.

(1960), *Britain's Imperial Air Routes 1918 to 1939*, London.

Jenkins, Clive (1953), *British Airlines: A Study of Nationalised Civil Aviation*, Fabian Research Series, No. 158.

Joensson, Christer (1987), *International Aviation and the Politics of Regime Change*, London: Frances Pinter.

Lyth, Peter J. (1990), 'A multiplicity of instruments: the 1946 decision to create a separate British European airline and its effect on civil aircraft production', *Journal of Transport History*, 11(2) (September): 1–18.

Masefield, Peter G. (1955), 'British transport in the national economy and an appreciation of its major components', *Journal of Transport History*, (November): 244–61.

Mowat, Charles Loch (1968), *Britain between the Wars, 1918–1940*, London: Methuen.

The Observer (1938), 17.6.1938.

Peston, M.H. (1975), 'The nationalised industries', in R.M. Grant and G.K. Shaw (eds.), *Current Issues in Economic Policy*, Oxford: Philip Allan, pp. 61–79.

Pryke, Richard (1981), *The Nationalised Industries: Policies and Performance since 1968*, Oxford: Martin Robertson.

Pudney, John S. (1959), *The Seven Skies: A Study of BOAC and its Forerunners since 1919*, London: Putnam.

Quin-Harkin, A.J. (1954), 'Imperial Airways, 1924–1940', *Journal of Transport History*, 1(4) (November): 197–215.

Redwood, John and Hatch, John (1982), *Controlling Public Industries*, Oxford: Blackwell.

Robson, William A. (1960), *Nationalized Industry and Public Ownership*, London: Allen and Unwin.

Skuse, Allen and Jones-Owen, Robert (1983), *Government Intervention and Industrial Policy*, 3rd Edition, London: Heinemann.

Spurgeon R.W. (1956), 'Subsidy in air transport', *Journal of the Institute of Transport* (November): 5–18.

Straszheim, Mahlon, R. (1969), *The International Airline Industry*, Washington DC: Brookings.

Tivey, Leonard (1973), *Nationalization in British Industry*, Revised Edition, London: Allen and Unwin.

Wheatcroft, Stephen (1964), *Air Transport Policy*, London: Joseph.

5 The motor vehicle industry

Sue Bowden

1 Introduction

In October 1948, the Labour Party's Sub-Committee on Industries for Nationalisation agreed that the motor industry was unsuitable for nationalisation (Labour Party 1948a, no. 5, p. 2). How and why was this decision made?

As an important industry which occupied a key position in the economy, the motor vehicle industry appeared an obvious candidate for some form of public ownership or control. In 1948 one and a half million people were employed directly and indirectly in the manufacture, selling, maintenance and operation of vehicles, whilst the industry's annual turnover (estimated to be over £500 million) and the amount of raw material it consumed made it one of the five largest industries in the country (Labour Party 1948b, para. 219(1), p. 62). The health of the industry, moreover, had wider repercussions for industry in general, as its products provided transport equipment for industry and in particular for defence since the basic factories of the industry could be expanded at times of international crisis to provide road vehicles, armoured fighting vehicles and aircraft. The industry was also seen to contribute to economic progress and well being through the rapidity and safety with which goods and people could be transported from one place to another. It was with the wide-ranging and important position of the industry in the economy that a consultative report, which provides one of the most comprehensive and balanced surveys of the industry at mid century, was prepared for the Labour Party in May 1948 (Labour Party 1948b).

The starting point was to establish the basic objectives of the industry. The consultative document was clear that the industry had two overriding aims: to

provide motor transport at the lowest possible price, of the highest possible quality and performance and in the quantity required at the time it is required

and to

develop an export trade on a scale commensurate with the large share it takes of the nation's resources in manpower, raw materials, capital equipment and technical skill *and pull its weight with other industries in the struggle to redress the British payments deficit.* (my italics) (Labour Party 1948b, para. 220 (a) and (b), p. 62)

Of the two, the latter was to outweigh and supercede the former. Although discussion of the advantages and disadvantages of public intervention in the industry in the consultative document was largely based on how best to realise the two objectives, the eventual outcome was determined by the short-run need to contribute to export earnings rather than the long-term need to reorganise and rationalise the industry which would have caused disruption to exports.

The case for and against public ownership was based largely on the answers to two questions: Did the evidence suggest there was room for improvement and in what sense?; and, accepting the need for improvement: How might this best be realised?

2   Was there room for improvement?

Judged from its past record and position by 1948, the industry seemed a success whether measured on its own terms (tables 5.1 and 5.2) or relative to other UK manufacturing industries and its main European competitors.

Between 1920 and 1938, the annual percentage growth in output in vehicles was far in excess of any other industry and well above the average for all manufacturing industry,[1] whilst between 1937 and 1951 the industry was among the top performing industrial sectors in the economy.[2] From 1932 UK output had far exceeded that of France and of Germany,[3] whilst in 1949, when UK production had more than recovered its inter-war peak, UK motor car producers were achieving output volumes which were double those of France, nearly four times those of Germany and nearly eight times those of Italy (Society of Motor Manufacturers and Trades, Annual).

In 1949, the UK was the second highest car producing nation in the world and the pre-eminent European exporter, accounting for about 7 per cent of global output, whilst three years later, when commercial vehicle production accounted for just under 11 per cent of global output, the UK was the second largest producer in the world (Society of Motor Manufacturers and Traders, Annual).

In addition, strong domestic producers existed which, with varying degrees of success, had performed well relative to their major domestic competitors in the inter-war period and were showing signs of maintain-

Table 5.1. *Production of motor vehicles 1924–48 (000s)*

Date	Private cars and taxis	Index of production (1924 = 100)	Goods and passenger service vehicles	Index of production (1924 = 100)
1924	116.6	100	30.0	100
1938	342.4	294	105.2	351
1947	287.0	246	155.7	515
1948	334.8	287	173.3	578

Source: Political and Economic Planning (1950), *Motor Vehicles; A Report on the Industry*, table 2, p. 10.

Table 5.2. *Exports of motor vehicles 1924–48 (Value of complete new vehicles)*

Date	Private cars and taxis		Commercial vehicles		
	Number (000)	Value (£m)	Number (000)	Value (£m)	Total value (£m)
1924	11.0	2.9	1.7	0.8	6.5
1938	44.1	5.5	3.4	1.6	14.9
1948	194.7	55.6	36.6	16.0	115.5

Notes: Political and Economic Planning (1950), *Motor Vehicles; A Report on the Industry*, table 19, p. 79.
Source: The industry also exported chassis with engines for both private cars and commercial vehicles and parts and accessories. In 1948, the value of the former amounted to £20.6 million and of the latter to £16.3 million.

ing that record in the immediate post-war years. Motor vehicle production at this time was dominated by the 'Big Six' producers, Morris, Austin, Ford, Vauxhall, Singer and Rootes, of which Morris and Austin were the major producers. The major domestic producers moreover had shown an ability throughout the inter-war years to deal with and overcome periods of crisis.

Morris experienced two such periods of difficulty in the inter-war period. First in 1920 and 1921, when the combination of the post-war slump and the heavy costs of reorganisation at Cowley led to a doubling of the company's overdraft and extensive debts to suppliers.[4] This was overcome by an aggressive price-cutting strategy and standardised quantity production of models such as the Cowley and the Oxford, as a result of which Morris was not only to overcome the immediate problems of the post-war years but also boost his position as the pre-eminent UK producer.

The second period of difficulty came at the turn of the decade and the first few years of the 1930s as the company failed to react to the shift in demand to small horse power models and to the increased competition from Vauxhall and Ford. Recovery stemmed from the four pronged strategy of giving Lord full managerial control,[5] rationalising production, introducing conveyor belts and moving assembly lines and transforming into a limited company (Church and Miller 1977, p. 177).[6] In 1934 the recovery of Morris was further insured with the launch of the Morris Eight which was to become the major best seller of the decade.

Despite periods of difficulty, Morris had demonstrated a singular ability to react to and overcome problems. At no point between 1919 and 1938 did the company record an annual pre-tax loss; with the exception of 1933, the company maintained its position as the leading car producer in the country and, most crucially, was responsible for about a quarter of all UK car exports (table 5.3).

Austin also experienced financial difficulties in the post-war slump years but also reacted to and overcame these initial problems. In 1923 the Austin Seven was launched and by 1927 the modernisation programme at Longbridge was completed. For Austin the inter-war years were ones of steady growth with only a slight fall in post-tax profit in 1932. Despite competition from Vauxhall and Ford, and even in the face of the Morris recovery after 1934, Austin was more than able to hold its own (table 5.4).

Although the leading manufacturers, Austin and Morris, experienced periods of financial difficulty, both survived their respective crises and were profitable entities at the end of the 1930s. They had demonstrated an ability to grow; they dominated UK production and at the end of the inter-war years and in the immediate post-war years they were both financially viable. The Ministry of Supply was thus able to conclude that:

the industry has shown by its past performances that it is in itself vigorous and efficient, and has made effective response to the stimuli applied by its environment . . . if its future environment is such as to apply the appropriate stimuli, there is every reason to expect that it will respond to them vigorously and effectively. (Ministry of Supply 1947, para. 12, p. 10)

The question, of course, was whether the industry could have performed better and whether its present structure was appropriate to the changed conditions of the post-war period. The collapse of international trade in the inter-war years had effectively limited demand to domestic sales and manufacturers had to concentrate on the home market. In

Table 5.3. *The performance of Morris 1920–50*

Date	Total sales £000s	Pre-tax profit £000s	Car output	% UK car output	% UK car exports
1920	863	50	1,932	3.9	
1923	4,654	927	20,048	28.1	
1925	13,332	1,556	55,582	42.1	
1928	14,466	1,595	55,480	33.6	22.7
1932	12,182	971	50,337	29.4	14.1
1934	13,711	1,168	58,248	22.7	⎫
1935	17,124	1,442	96,512	31.0	⎪
1936	21,535	2,182			⎬ 28.8*
1937	19,170	1,784			⎪
1938	18,247	1,402			⎭
1947	31,060	2,856		20.9*	22.7
1948	30,097	1,407			22.9
1949	41,790	2,685			23.3
1950	61,154	7,229			17.6

Note: *Morris exports accounted for 28.8% of UK exports between 1934 and 1939 (Overy, table 7, p. 135).
Source: R.J. Overy (1976), *William Morris, Viscount Nuffield*, table 1, p. 128, table 2, p. 129, and table 7, p. 135; D.G. Rhys (1972), *The Motor Industry; An Economic Survey*, table 2.1, p. 19.

Table 5.4. *The performance of Austin 1922–38*

Year	Sales turnover £000s	Output	Pre-tax profit £000s	Car production at Longbridge as a % UK car production
1922	1,653		222	4
1928	8,790		861	25.7
1932	6,755	36,526	1,078	22.7
1935	11,331	77,171	1,469	23.6
1937	13,283	89,745	1,665	22.1
1938	10,430	64,053	1,283	19.2

Source: R.A. Church (1979), *Herbert Austin; The British Motor Car Industry to 1941*, table 6, p. 84; table 8, p. 114; table 14, p. 143.

addition, low average levels of income and the skewed distribution of income had restricted the market to the wealthier groups in society, namely the middle and upper classes who constituted 25 per cent of the population. In such circumstances, it was not rational for the domestic producers to invest in high throughput technology to produce high volume output (Bowden 1991, Bowden and Turner 1993a and b).

The post-war years altered the agenda. The balance of payments deficit in the UK and the global dollar shortage placed a high premium on large volumes of exports. Whilst it was generally believed that domestic demand would remain depressed in the short term, the prospect of an eventual recovery in the home market added to the incentive to produce large volumes of motor vehicles. The question as to whether there was room for improvement largely rested on the need to produce large output volumes and to realise economies of scale, the ultimate objective of which was to increase export volumes since 'the need for exports has become imperative' (Labour Party 1948b, para. 232, p. 63).

It was estimated in 1947 that to meet the government's export target, plus 160,000 cars for essential home requirements, the industry needed to produce cars at an annual rate of 475,000. This was subsequently revised to 500,000 cars and 170,000 commercial vehicles (Labour Party 1948b, para. 86, p. 27). In these terms, total output of cars in the UK (table 5.1) was too low; in 1948 the deficit was in the order of 165,200 cars and taxis. Commercial vehicles just exceeded the required target in 1948.

The document was correct to point out that mass production in the UK was hampered not only by the total output of the industry but also by market differentiation with no one producer achieving output volumes sufficient to reap economies of scale. In 1947 the minimum efficient scale of production for a firm was an overall output of between 100,000 and 150,000 units a year (Dunnett 1980, table 2.3, p. 22, Maxcy and Silberston 1959, pp. 77 and 79). In 1947 the largest firm's (Morris) production share was only 60,000 (Dunnett 1980, table 2.3, p. 22). The UK industry moreover was characterised by a higher degree of market differentiation than that experienced in other vehicle producing economies. In 1937, when the major UK producers (Morris, Ford, and Austin) held 61.4 per cent of UK production, Ford, Chrysler and General Motors produced 85 per cent of US output, whilst in Europe the three main producers in Germany and France accounted for 70 per cent and 74 per cent of output respectively (Political and Economic Planning 1950, pp. 26 and 111). In 1947, Austin and Nuffield together only held 39.3 per cent of the total production of cars in the UK (Maxcy and Silberston 1959, table 3, p. 117). Market differentiation thus presented a serious obstacle to large volume output and the realisation of economies of scale and, in this respect, threatened to place the UK at a competitive European disadvantage.

The consultative document was also correct in pointing out that the problem was compounded by the UK practice of product differentiation, with each firm producing a multiplicity of models. Before 1939, over thirty makes of car were being produced in the UK, with 136 basic models and 299 body variations. Such a strategy incurred heavy costs in the resetting of machinery and die changing (Political and Economic Planning 1950, pp. 129 and 131). It was estimated at the end of the 1940s, that the full advantages of volume production would only be secured when the annual output of a particular model (or two models in which similar engines and parts were used) was between 30,000 to 35,000 units a year. In these terms, just before the war, the only 'volume' models produced in the UK were the Austin Seven and Ten and the Morris Eight and Ten. The three best-selling models in the United States, by comparison, were achieving production volumes of between 350,000 and 600,000 each by 1939 (Rostas 1948, p. 63). By 1947 most manufacturers had trimmed down the number of models and engines they produced; in 1947 sixty-two basic models were being produced. Despite the obvious reduction in product differentiation it was still felt that the resources of the industry needed to be concentrated on an even smaller range of models if the full benefits of mass production were to be realised (Labour Party 1948b, para. 159, p. 48). In 1947, when nineteen American manufacturers produced over four million cars a year, with forty-two basic models, some of which had similar engines, twenty British manufacturers produced under 400,000 cars, with fifty-one basic models (Labour Party 1948b, para. 163, p. 49).

There was evidence then which suggested that the consultative document was correct in arguing that although the motor industry had been successful in the inter-war years, there was considerable room for improvement, most notably in terms of rationalisation of production and standardisation of product. The premium on such improvement was to intensify in the immediate post-war years, most notably in relation to the need to boost production for export purposes in order to alleviate the balance of payments problems. The question then was how might this be achieved?

3   The case for and against public ownership

The case for and against public ownership as presented in the consultative document largely rested on four issues: the structure of the industry, its financial record, the need to lower prices and the objection to monopolistic practices in the industry.

Much of the argument for and against public ownership hinged on the structure of the industry and the need to instigate rationalisation and standardisation. In this respect, although the consultative document was clear that rationalisation was needed and that nationalisation would force this through, the evidence indicated that the industry had taken steps over the years to deal with this problem itself. The structure of the industry had undergone considerable change in the inter-war years as the number of firms fell from one hundred and fourteen in 1914, to forty-one in 1929 and to thirty-three by 1938 (Overy 1976, p. 136), the decline in the number of firms in the 1920s being largely the result of the failure of these firms to survive the rigours of the economic environment and the intense price competition between manufacturers in the 1920s (Ministry of Supply 1947, para. 6, p. 8).

The objective of rationalisation was increased concentration of output in the hands of fewer producers who would be able to achieve scale economies. In the inter-war years increased concentration was largely the result of the exit process and the growing dominance of the 'Big Six'. Among the three dominant firms, only Morris combined with other motor vehicle companies. Wolseley was acquired in 1927, MG Car Company in 1930 and Riley (Coventry) Ltd in 1938 (Overy 1976, table 4, p. 131). The Wolseley acquisition was motivated by Morris's desire to effectively block any American challenge and to prevent Austin, his nearest rival, from becoming too strong, whilst the MG and Riley acquisitions have been described as motivated by reasons of sentiment and price (Overy 1976, pp. 27 and 92). In each case, as with the General Motors acquisition of Vauxhall in 1925, horizontal integration, such as it was, tended to be characterised by the acquisition of old established firms in financial difficulties; 'failure continued to be a prerequisite to horizontal combinations' (Maxcy 1958, p. 374).

Attempts at merger between successful companies had proved abortive. In 1924, when Austin was in the midst of financial difficulties, Dudley Docker of Vickers instigated merger proposals between Austin, Morris and Wolseley. The idea was blocked by Morris who resisted any attempt to diminish his personal control and independence and the negotiations went no further. In 1931/2 Austin approached Henry Ford with a view to discussing potential merger, but this proved equally short-lived as Henry Ford never responded.

It was argued that the process of rationalisation was further need to force the exit of the inefficient from the industry. Although it was claimed that public ownership would force this through, there were both positive and negative reasons against such action. Although the evidence on the decline in the number of firms suggests that the exit process had taken place during the competitive conditions of the inter-war years, the work of Foreman-Peck (1981) indicates that there were constraints on this process. Rover, for example, experienced serious financial difficulties in the inter-war years and in January 1932 there was a risk that the company would go into liquidation as a result of its inability to react to competition and reorganise for efficient production in the volume car market. In the event, the intervention of Lucas and Pressed Steel, two of the company's largest suppliers which had vested interests in the company not going into Receivership, and the banks, who wished to protect their short-term assets, aborted separate merger proposals with Standard, with Triumph and with Singer (Foreman-Peck 1981, pp. 191–207). Small producers with annual outputs of less than 35,000 units were incapable of reaping any economies, for a small firm was neither in the financial position nor had the required turnover to install costly machinery (Rostas 1948, p. 51).

For the consultative document, however, there was an even stronger argument against forcing through a major rationalisation project. The case against forcing through a drastic rationalisation scheme was the employment costs of instigating the closure of inefficient firms and plants and raising the spectre of creating large-scale unemployment in the industry:

The closing of even one of the factories would not be very popular with the several thousand employees – in Luton, Dagenham or Oxford they could not easily be absorbed in other local industries – even if they were told that it was necessary in the national interest and for the economical operation of the motor vehicle industry. (Labour Party 1948b, para. 224 (8), p. 65)

The second theme in the case for and against public ownership related to the issue of standardisation, both in relation to the number of models the industry produced and in the multiplicity of components supplied by the supplier industries. The consultative document claimed that before the war there had not been the 'slightest attempt to reduce the number of models and little attempt was made to standardise the fabricated materials or even raw materials used in their manufacture' (Labour Party 1948b, para. 225 (4), pp. 66–7). This was not strictly true; the industry had shown itself capable of reducing the number of basic models and engines it produced both before and after the war. Morris, for example, had cut the number of basic models from twenty-three in 1933 to seventeen in 1939 (Church and Miller 1977, table 9.1, p. 177). By 1946 most manufacturers had further trimmed down the number of models and engines and in 1947, the Society of Motor Manufacturers and Traders was able to claim that since 1939 the number of basic models had been reduced from 136 to sixty-two and that current rationalisation programmes were predicted to further reduce the number to forty-two. The Society also predicted that by 1949 body variations would have been reduced from 299 to forty (Ministry of Supply 1947, p. 3).

Where the consultative document was correct was in its criticism of the industry's failure to standardise after merger. When Riley was about to shut down, Morris took the company over and production was continued under the new management. The same happened when Rootes took over Sunbeam and Talbot and when Standard acquired Triumph. As a result of this policy:

innumerable opportunities of reducing the number and variety of models were lost, often because of purely sentimental attachment or the supposed goodwill attaching to a name. (Labour Party 1948b, para. 225 (4), p. 67)

The question was whether the industry's record on standardisation was sufficient if the industry was to realise economies of scale from large-scale production and to compete effectively for export markets. Many contemporaries believed that it was not.

We shall never get cars at prices low enough to popularise motoring at home and to compete in export markets without a degree of standardisation of design and manufacturing method which could not be achieved under private ownership. (Mikardo 1948, p. 14)

The above evidence suggests the fundamental truth of such views.

The third issue related to the financial position of the industry, both in terms of investment funding and risk. In terms of the former, it was argued that ample funds would be available for expansion, reequipment and modernisation and that new capital would be made available at rates of interest corresponding to those payable on government securities (Labour Party 1948b, para. 225 (9), p. 68). This, it was claimed, would have the added benefit of eliminating speculators 'whose only interest is to make the maximum profit they can' (ibid.). That the industry required a large investment programme – both to replace and update pre-war buildings and equipment and to raise capacity to produce large volume output cannot be disputed. At Singer 'there did not seem to be a single up-to-date machine tool in the place', very few of the specialist car firms 'were equipped with modern plant', whilst commercial vehicle firms such as 'Crossley and Maudsley worked with a good deal of semi-obsolete machinery' (Labour Party 1948b, para. 81, p. 25).[7] In 1943, of the forty-three motor vehicle companies surveyed by the Society of Motor Manufacturers and Traders, thirty-five had buildings which were over eleven years old, whilst ten had buildings which were over sixteen years old. Although many of the firms did have new buildings, they were not suited to mass production methods (Political and Economic Planning 1950, pp. 21–2). Investment was also needed to update machinery. The same survey revealed that twenty-four firms had machinery which was over eleven years old (ibid.). A conservative estimate of the cost of investment in building and fixed plant and equipment needed to raise output to the 470,000 vehicles required for export and essential home market requirements for 1948 amounted to £15 million (Labour Party 1948b, para. 90, p. 27).

The record however demonstrated the ability of the industry to finance its own investment programmes. The annual percentage growth rate of capital, at 3.1 per cent, in the vehicle industry had been among the highest in UK industry in the inter-war years (Matthews *et al.* 1982, table 8.7, p. 240), and, by 1935, investment in plant and machinery in the motor vehicle industry amounted to £12.4 million and constituted 77 per cent of investment in plant and machinery in the vehicle sector. The industry had invested heavily throughout the inter-war period and, relative to other sectors, had not experienced any investment shortfall. Among the major producers the inter-war years had seen large investment programmes with the gradual introduction of mechanised production techniques: notably moving assembly lines and machines which were used to produce individual items on a continuous basis (Labour Party 1948b, para. 82, p. 25). In 1923 a major investment programme in continuous flow production began at Longbridge as a result of which Longbridge became the first motor works in the country with a moving assembly line for chassis and car bodies (Church 1979, p. 100). Fixed assets at Austin had been valued at £2,076,408 in 1928; ten years later they amounted to £3,518,049 and during the 1930s average annual net investment in the company was in the order of £157,790 (Church 1979, table 13, p. 142). By 1938, Morris's total net assets at £11,464,000 were the highest among the major car-producing companies, additions to net assets between 1934 and 1938 being valued at £3,617,000 (Overy 1976, table 11, p. 56). The immediate post-war years also demonstrated the ability of the industry to finance investment programmes, most notably in the trend among the major motor vehicle producers to move to the automation of production. Austin and Standard, for example, began to install transfer machines in the late 1940s (Lewchuk 1987, p. 193, Maxcy and Silberston 1959, p. 59).

Whilst on one level, the ability of the industry to finance its own investment programme had been impressive, the concern was that it could have been higher and that the industry might not be able to finance a programme designed to raise capacity. The Labour Party may have disliked the industry's association with

company promoters whose only interest is to make the maximum profit they can, and all the other high priests of company share promotion whose only anxiety about a capital scheme is whether the public will swallow the carefully prepared bait without reading their prospectuses and which they are so careful to print in very small type. (Labour Party 1948b, para. 225 (9), p. 68) but a more serious constraint on the industry's ability to finance post-war investment programmes was government restrictions on imports from dollar countries and on investment in capital plant.[8] The chairman of Vauxhall had no doubts as to the ramifications of such policy:

Left to ourselves we should now be installing new plant machinery and equipment costing very large sums of money . . . We are not at present able to take all these steps. Indeed, we are very much restricted as a consequence of the Government's investment policy. (Labour Party 1948b, para. 83, p. 26)

If the United States industry is taken as the barometer of 'best practice', then the evidence did indicate that the UK manufacturers could have done better. Throughout the 1930s, Austin employed between £175 and £200 of fixed capital per employee, whilst at Fords in Detroit the amount of fixed capital per worker rose from $1,210 in 1908 to $3,194 in 1914, and $5,544 in 1921 (Lewchuk 1987, p. 146). The United States industry, however, was operating in a different league. In 1937, the US car industry was producing nearly four million cars a year (Maxcy and Silberston 1959, pp. 32 and 110) and between them Ford, Chrysler and General Motors accounted for 85 per cent of US output (Political and Economic Planning 1950, p. 111). Mass production techniques were viable in the US given the size of the market; market constraints in the UK were such as to negate the viability of investment in such methods (Bowden 1991).

There is evidence to suggest however that investment may have been sacrificed to the higher claims of dividends in the inter-war years. Between 1922 and 1939, Austin paid out nearly 70 per cent of its profits in ordinary and preferred dividends and in interest on long-term bonds (Church 1979, pp. 214–15). Between 1927 and 1951 Morris earned nearly £55 million in pre-tax profits, but retained only 26 per cent in the firm (Lewchuk 1987, p. 186, Overy 1976, p. 129). This policy has been explained by Lewchuk in terms of the fear that dissatisfied investors would replace existing managers by mounting takeover bids and of the decision not to switch to mass production technology and methods (Lewchuk 1987, p. 186).

The capital requirements and historical record of the industry thus did point to the need for heavy investment funding. But investment had taken place in the inter-war years and the absence of any large-scale trans-formation to Fordism was, in the event and in the short term, rational. Moreover, in the immediate post-war years, the industry had demonstrated its ability to react and to undergo a modernisation and auto-mation programme. In addition, the Labour Party, and this may have been the crucial deciding matter on the investment issue, was fearful of the risks involved in any financial commitment to investment funding in the industry. As the consultative document pointed out, the cost of introducing a new model could be anything from £500,000 to £1,500,000. If a mistake was made, the company either went out of business or made a fresh start. The losers were the shareholders who had to renounce dividends for a year or more. The risk of public ownership was the cost of such mistakes to the taxpayer (Labour Party 1948b, para. 244 (7), p. 65).

The final issue was that of pricing. There were two strands to the argument. The first related to the need for public ownership to eliminate 'all price rings, cartels, selling agreements, exclusive buying arrangements, monopolies and other forms of trustification (overt or hidden)' in order that the private motorist 'would pay a fair and reasonable price' (Labour Party 1948b, para. 225 (12), p. 68). The problem, however, applied not to the motor manufacturers but to component suppliers, notably the electrical components industry, and to the oil industry. To ensure a 'fair and reasonable' price involved public ownership (or some form of public control), not of the motor industry but of its principal suppliers (see below). The issue of fair price moreover was dependent on the realisation of standardisation and rationalisation, where the case for public ownership was by no means clear. Indeed, it was argued that if private industry could instigate its own rationalisation and standardisation programme it would compete effectively and one of the main reasons for private ownership was that the industry needed competition since

without this competitive element, design, performance and style would tend to stagnate and quality to be uniform (probably inferior). This is important so far as the home market is concerned. Competition is the life blood of the industry. It can be stimulated only under private ownership. No alternative system under which goods of great variety and types are made for resale to the public has shown results comparable with the results obtained under private ownership. (Labour Party 1948b, para. 224 (2), p. 64)

In the final analysis, three issues probably counted most against full public ownership. First, was the indisputed fact that under private ownership, the industry had grown to become one of the largest and most important industries in the country

in spite of the fact that it has never had a fair or a square deal so far as the taxation of its products is concerned. It has had to fight for its place in a very competitive market without getting a real chance to show what it could do. It has been like a boxer fighting with one hand tied behind his back. The amazing thing is that it is still in the ring and in reasonably good shape. It is very doubtful whether it could have given as good an account of itself if it had been under public ownership. (Labour Party 1948b, para. 224 (11), p. 66)

Such an argument, of course, presumed that the industry would continue to grow and prosper in the changed conditions of the post-war world and that it would effect its own rationalisation and standardisation schemes.

Second, the report viewed the American industry as the barometer of efficiency and low production costs and noted that the motor vehicle industry in that country was under private ownership and subject to hardly any control from the Administration – or at least certainly to much less control than the British industry (Labour Party 1948b, para. 224 (12), p. 66). The explicit assumption was that the 'superior' performance of the American industry followed from private ownership and the lack of control. As such, the consultative document ignored the very different market conditions in America, which allowed the realisation of economies of scale at large production volumes, and assumed that if the American industry were efficient, it was because it was left in private hands.

The third explanation however was undoubtedly the most critical and the one which, in the final analysis, explains why the industry was not taken into public ownership. Public ownership would have caused short-run disruption, would have acted as a major constraint on the industry's ability to attain maximum production and, as such, posed a serious danger to export earnings. Not only was the case of public ownership not proven, but also

the amount of rationalisation which would be called for, if the full benefits of public ownership were to be secured, would completely upset the tempo and smooth working of the industry at a time when maximum production is vital to the economic life of the nation. (Labour Party 1948b, para. 1, p. 95)

4   The case for partial public ownership

Private and public ownership did not exhaust the possibilities. Alternatives existed in the form of partial nationalisation and of government controls. In the case of partial nationalisation, three European blueprints existed – for the state, in the absence of a strong national producer to effectively create a national motor vehicle producer (Volkswagen in Germany); for the state to take over a company with a wartime history of collaboration with the occupying powers and with a history of poor labour relations (Renault in France), and close state cooperation with a private industrial giant (Fiat in Italy) (Bardou et al. 1982, p. 141, Jones 1981, pp. 36, 41, Political and Economic Planning 1950, p. 120). Of the three, only one was given serious consideration in the consultative document and only one pursued in subsequent years.

In the inter-war period both General Motors and Ford had a strong presence in the German motor industry. In 1929 General Motors took over Opel; nine years later the company was the largest car producing firm in Germany, holding 40 per cent of output. Ford, which opened a factory in Cologne in the 1920s, held equal second place with Daimler Benz at 10 per cent of car production (the remaining 40 per cent was shared among 'other' producers) (Jones and Prais 1978, table 3, p. 139). The decision to forge a new state controlled company was largely motivated by the fact that in the early 1930s the German car industry had demonstrated neither the willingness nor the capacity to produce the Nazi ideal of the low-cost car in high volumes for the masses. Neither Opel nor Ford actively promoted the development of the small car since the infrastructure and demand conditions in Germany were seen to be major constraints on the development of a mass market. Taxation was high, purchasing power was low, and efficient, alternative forms of transport existed in the low-price rail network (Tolliday 1991, p. 3).

From 1934 Hitler had urged the manufacture of a car for the masses and, in the face of the failure of the existing producers to produce such a vehicle, in 1937 called on Dr Porsche to design a small car for the masses and created Volkswagen in 1937 (Bardou *et al.* 1982, p. 141, Jones 1981, p. 41, Tolliday 1991, pp. 3–5). In 1937 Volkswagen was thus created and was 100 per cent owned by the state, although civilian production only began after the war. Initially, the framework and operating principles of the company were laid down by the government. Later Volkswagen was run on behalf of the nation by the industry trade association, Reichsverband der Deutschen Automobilindustrie (Tolliday 1991, p. 4).

The desire to create a small car for the mass market was not the only motivation behind the creation of Volkswagen. A key factor was the belief that the programme would stimulate employment and economic recovery (Tolliday 1991, p. 5). In addition, the company was seen to offer the Nazi regime 'a national champion able to symbolise German industrial power in the world' (Jones 1981, p. 41). The German model was thus motivated by the absence of strong national producers and by the desire of the government to forge mass markets for cars.

In the UK, however, strong domestic producers existed which, with varying degrees of success, had performed well relative to their major domestic competitors in the inter-war years and were giving every sign of maintaining that record in the immediate post-war years. In 1947, there was little to suggest that UK production would be dominated by Ford or Vauxhall since the domestic producers continued to hold the lion's share of the market (table 5.5).

The main criticisms of the Volkswagen strategy voiced by the Labour Party boiled down to the financial costs and risks. The possibility of launching a 'people's car' based on the Volkswagen model was given consideration. Such a project however

Table 5.5. *British motor vehicle production by firms, 1938 and 1947 (estimated percentages by numbers)*

	Cars and taxis		Commercial vehicles	
	1938	1947	1938	1947
The big six				
Nuffield	26.6	20.9	26.5	13.6
Ford	17.8	15.4	20.0	22.9
Austin	17.0	19.2	4.2	14.3
Vauxhall	10.1	11.2	24.6	20.3
Rootes	9.6	10.9	5.5	7.9
Standard	9.0	13.2		
Specialist car producers	9.9	9.2		
Heavy vehicle builders			10.0	11.4
Unspecified commercial vehicle production			8.2	5.3

Source: Political and Economic Planning, 1950, *Motor Vehicles; A Report on the Industry*, PEP Engineering Reports – II, January, table 14, p. 26.

could be launched only if the firms concerned merged completely their resources, and this they are not likely to do unless under compulsion, which means some form of nationalisation, the pros and cons of which have already been set out in some detail (Labour Party 1948b, para. 266, p. 88)

and even then it was claimed that three things were necessary for the launching of a 'people's car' such as the Volkswagen: (a) almost unlimited financial resources, (b) a design which was acceptable to the public – a cheap car in itself was not enough – and (c) a technically efficient car which could be produced in quantity at reasonable prices. The venture was not only likely to be extremely expensive but also high risk. Hitler, as the report noted, 'could do it because he was not troubled with making the venture a financial success, nor with questions from 600 masters (Parliament)', (Labour Party 1948b, para. 269, p. 88).

In terms of Renault, the Labour Party Research Department merely commented that 'the experiment has not been a failure although it may be too early yet to say that it has been a success' (Labour Party 1948b, para. 226 (4), p. 69). The model of cooperation with one firm, though never given serious consideration in the consultative document (or even mentioned in Mikardo's proposals) was ultimately realised in the government's heavy backing for Standard based on the premise of providing financial and other support to what appeared to be a progressive firm (Tiratsoo 1992, pp. 171–80). The partial control option discussed in the consultative document focused more on partial control of the Big Six, rather than on specific manufacturers. The idea of creating one large national producer, by forcing through an amalgamation of Nuffield, Austin, Rootes and Standard was never mentioned. This may have been because the focus of attention was on the rationalisation of production of the 'popular' end of the range (Labour Party 1948b, p. 69, Mikardo 1948, p. 14). The problem in this respect was that it inevitably raised the question of how to treat the multi-nationals.

The German model was partly motivated by the need to create a strong national producer in the face of the strong presence of the multi-national producers, Ford and General Motors. The presence of Ford and General Motors (Vauxhall) complicated the issue of public control of the motor vehicle industry in the UK in several respects.

In the inter-war and immediate post-war periods, the national producers dominated the motor vehicle industry in the UK. The history of Ford in particular was not robust in the inter-war period and did not constitute a major threat to the UK nationals. The 1920s was a troubled decade for the company – the principal difficulty being the unsuitability of their products for the British market since Ford cars were more suited to American rather than British roads, fuel prices and taxation conditions. Marketing problems were compounded by a period of managerial problems (Church and Miller 1977, p. 168). Despite evidence of falling output shares, Henry Ford refused to acknowledge that his product, which had been so successful in America, might not be suitable for the UK market. No substantial modifications to the Model T, which might have met UK demand conditions, were permitted and the plans for the new Dagenham factory were built on the assumption of producing an unchanged Model T. In 1927 the company launched the Model A which, with its smaller bore engine and horsepower of fifteen, was more appropriate to the UK market[9] (Church and Miller 1977, pp. 169–70). The Model A however still could not compete with the smaller cars then produced by Morris and Austin, which were not only cheaper to buy but also, and of particular importance in the UK market, significantly cheaper to run.

Although the dismal performance of the 1920s was to some extent turned round in the 1930s (largely due to the reappointment of Perry as Managing Director of the UK operations in 1928), Ford's record in that decade did not compare well to that of the UK nationals (table 5.6). It was not until September 1932 that a model suitable for the UK market (the model Y), which at a selling price of £120 directly competed with Morris and Austin, was in volume production. Ford's share of UK production fluctuated for the rest of the decade. The success of the Model Y was shortlived; in 1934 Morris introduced the Morris Eight which was to become the best-selling car in the UK before the Second World War. In the 1930s competition in the UK market was motivated by price quality rather than price competition (Bowden 1991, p. 263) and Ford was outsold by dearer competitors which 'offered more comfort, performance and sometimes even individuality' (Church and Miller 1977, p. 173).

Whilst Vauxhall replicated in many respects Ford's failure to dominate the car market, it constituted a major threat in the commercial vehicle market. In the early 1920s, Vauxhall had been a small-scale, ailing producer which concentrated on the manufacturer of high-grade vehicles with a weekly output of twenty-five to thirty vehicles in 1925 (Lewchuk 1987, p. 164). In December 1925 the company was taken over by General Motors for two and a half million dollars as the launchpad of Sloan's plan to expand General Motors production into Europe (Adeney 1988, p. 107, Church and Miller 1977, p. 171).[10] Although Vauxhall had already begun to move away from its exclusive reliance on quality cars, the American influence was to witness the development of production of small cars for the 'popular' market. In 1930 the Vauxhall Cadet was launched and by the end of 1934 the Luton plant was producing over 20,000 cars (Adeney 1988, p. 107) and by 1938 the company had been transformed from a minor to one of the Big Six producers. The company also became the country's largest producer of commercial vehicles by the end of the 1930s (table 5.5) and its pre-eminent position was reinforced in the immediate post-war years. In 1947 it held 21.2 per cent of the production of goods vehicles up to 5 tons capacity and 14.7 per cent of the production of goods vehicles over 5 tons and public service vehicles. Significantly, its nearest contender in 1947 was Ford which held just over 26 per cent of the production of goods vehicles up to 5 tons, but which did not produce public service vehicles and goods vehicles over 5 tons (Political and Economic Planning 1950, table 15, p. 34).

The presence of the multinationals created additional problems in the debate for partial public ownership. The discussion of partial ownership by the Labour Party's consultative document focused on the possibility of nationalisation of the 'Big Six' vehicle producers. Partial public ownership which only covered the UK producers (Morris, Austin, Rootes and Standard) was never mentioned. The argument of the consultative document was based on the premise that partial public control of the mass producers was more desirable than full public control of both the mass and the specialist producers and the heavy vehicle builders. The implicit argument appears to have been that partial control was only viable if it

Table 5.6. *Ford and Vauxhall's share of total 'Big Six' car production 1929–38*

Date	Vauxhall	Ford
1929	1.1	5.7
1930	5.9	7.0
1931	6.4	3.5
1932	5.6	7.5
1933	7.1	18.9
1934	8.7	15.5
1935	8.6	17.4
1936	6.4	22.1
1937	8.1	22.3
1938	11.3	19.0

Source: G. Maxcy and A. Silberston (1959), *The Motor Industry*, table 2, p. 107.

included *all* the mass producers. It was argued, for example, that the Big Six were 'the only manufacturers of vehicles who really matter as they account for 90 per cent of the production of cars and at least 70 per cent of the production of commercial vehicles' (Labour Party, 1948b, para. 226 (2), p. 69). Ford and Vauxhall between them held 26.6 per cent of car and taxi and 43.2 per cent of commercial vehicle production in 1947 (table 5.5). The notion that one large-scale UK producer might have been formed, which would have competed against the multinationals, is perhaps the most noticeable omission from the consultative document.

It was argued that public ownership of the Big Six would achieve the advantages of nationalisation, namely rationalisation, standardisation, enhanced output, etc., whilst retaining the essential competition in the industry by forcing privately owned companies to improve techniques and general efficiency in order to survive (Labour Party 1948b, para. 226 (3), p. 65). Partial control of the Big Six manufacturers however would attract the same problems as full public ownership, not least of which was the short-run disruption to production and its consequent costs for export earnings such a programme would have involved.

In addition, partial control of the Big Six would have involved a state takeover of two major US multi-nationals which, by the end of the 1930s, had established manufacturing bases and relatively strong market positions. Both Ford and General Motors had vested interests in the continuation of their UK subsidiaries: in the inter-war period as part of the policy of extending exports whilst overcoming tariff barriers[11] and post-war, as part of the drive to secure firm holds within national markets. The Labour

Party's consultative document never directly addressed this issue but merely noted that if Ford and Vauxhall were taken under public control 'they would not be able to call on the technical resources and advice which their controlling organisations in the United States now give them' (Labour Party 1948b, para. 224 (12), p. 66). The possibility of the state taking over these US subsidiaries was in the circumstances non-existent. Nor was it at all likely at this time that the UK government would have been willing to offend US interests by broaching the subject. The Report thus concluded that 'the advantages of partial nationalisation, such as a scheme to bring the "Big Six" vehicle manufacturers under public owner- ship do not outweigh the disadvantages' (Labour Party 1948b, para. 4, p. 95). The disadvantages were not explicitly stated.

There were three main divisions of the manufacturing industry: car and commercial vehicle manufacturers; manufacturers of components, parts and accessories; and the motor vehicle retail and repairing trade. The notion that the retail trade might be taken into public ownership was quickly dismissed by the consultative report (Labour Party 1948b, para. 224 (7), p. 65). The question of the heavy vehicle manufacturers and the components industry proved somewhat more complicated since pro- duction was not divided between manufacturers of commercial vehicles and manufacturers of motor cars. In both the inter-war and the immedi- ate post-war years, the major producers held the largest shares of both car and commercial vehicle output (table 5.5). The alternative, recommended by the Labour Party's consultative document, was to take into public ownership one or two of the heavy commercial vehicle manufacturers (Labour Party 1948b, para. 4, p. 95). Why then was this recommendation not implemented?

The Transport Act of 1947 transferred to state ownership the responsi- bility for the transport of both peoples and goods (Dunkerley and Hare 1991, p. 388). The aim was to provide the central planning required if an integrated, coordinated, and efficient transport service for both goods and people were to be available and, particularly in the case of the railways, to provide the large sums necessary to rectify decades of under- investment and to modernise the transport network. The Act of 1947 directed its attention to transport *services* and the public transportation of peoples and goods. The nationalisation of transport thus raised the important issue of the split between the manufacture of commercial vehicles, be they heavy goods vehicles or buses and coaches, and the provision of services from such vehicles. As it was, the state was to provide the flow of services whilst private industry provided the capital goods. This would seem to have created a conflict of interests. If the state were to assume responsibility for the provision of the services then it might have made sense for government to take over the manufacture of the goods.

The conflict emerged in the drafting and passing of the 1947 Transport Act. Drafts of the initial Bill contained Clauses which stipulated that the Transport Commission would be empowered to construct and maintain all equipment other than the construction of chassis of road vehicles for the use of the National Transport Commission. Later amendments included the stipulation that the Commission would not be involved in the construction of the chassis of road vehicles other than for the purpose of experiment or research (Chester 1975, pp. 201, 203). This would appear to have been a clear statement of the government's intention not to engage in manufacturing activities which would impair the motor vehicle industry. Subsequent Clauses, however, did empower the Commission to manufacture what vehicles it required for its own activities and to carry on any activities which were carried on by an acquired undertaking. Such Clauses immediately came to the notice of the Society of Motor Manufacturers and Traders (SMMT), which was quick to realise the implications and tabled a series of amendments to be put down in the House of Lords.

The Ministry of Transport, and Morrison in particular, appears to have been eager to mollify the anxieties of the motor vehicle industry. A series of limitations which would 'clarify' the issue and overcome the objections of the SMMT were prepared. The limitations included preventing the Commission under inherited powers from manufacturing for sale and placing a complete embargo on manufacturing by the Commission of the chassis of motor vehicles and of motor vehicles or parts of motor vehicles. It was hoped that the SMMT would be satisfied with the first such limitation – that the Commission would not manufacture for sale as a result of its inherited powers.

The SMMT, backed by the Federation of British Industries, were not however won over and throughout June and early July of 1946 meetings were held between the Ministry and representatives of the SMMT. In the event, the SMMT were to announce on 7 July that 'the latest draft amendments represented a complete settlement of the points raised by the manufacturers with regard to both chassis and bodies of road vehicles' (Chester 1975, pp. 208–9).

The motor vehicle industry had thus satisfied itself that its interests were not jeopardised by the provisions of the Transport Act. In the Report stages of the Act, a lengthy amendment was introduced by the government and agreed which placed strict upper limits on the power of the Commission to manufacture chassis and bodies as well as major components and to maintain and repair road vehicles. The Commission was also subject to stringent limitations on the purchase of road vehicles for the purpose of sale.

In the event the demarcation between the production of goods and the provision of services was maintained. The limits on the power of the Commission to manufacture the commercial vehicles it owned and operated were such as to ensure the continuation of a strong independent private commercial vehicle sector. Once the Transport Act threatened the interests of the vehicle lobby, the government was quick to retreat and to pacify their concerns. Whilst the motor manufacturers could deliver the goods, meet export targets and thus contribute to the balance of payments, their bargaining position was assured.

Another variation of partial nationalisation strongly recommended by the Labour Party's consultative document was to bring under public ownership such companies in the industry which might be considered monopolies or to set up publicly owned or government sponsored companies to compete with concerns which had a monopoly in their particular field. The main target of this recommendation was the monopoly position of the Lucas group as principal supplier of electrical components, such as electric batteries, lamps, dynamos, starters, windscreen wipers, and direction indicators (Labour Party 1948b, para. 6, p. 4, para. 14, p. 5, paras. 40, 44, and 45, p. 15 and para. 226 (8), p. 70). Control of the Lucas company raised however the possibility of ICI's involvement since the chairman of Lucas was a director of ICI (Labour Party 1948b, para. 14, p. 5).

Plans to deal with components suppliers again would have involved the multi-nationals since American interests were also represented in this sector with two of the main producers of sparking plugs, Champion and A.C. Delco, being subsidiaries of American companies, whilst the major body-building section, Briggs, was directly controlled by its parent company in the US before 1953 when it was taken over by Ford (Silberston 1958, p. 11). At a time when no UK manufacturer was as highly integrated as the major manufacturers in the United States, the relationship between assemblers of vehicles and their key supplier industries presented another dimension to the multi-faceted structure of the industry and created a further complication to any nationalisation plans.

5 Why not stay as we are?

In the final analysis, the consultative document recommended that the Party could achieve its aims of integrating the motor vehicle industry into the planned economy whilst not disturbing the industry's all important contribution to export earnings, by opting for controlling the industry. As the Report noted, industries had been controlled during the war mainly through the allocation of manpower and raw materials by the government. Control during the war moreover had demonstrated that the government could, in the final analysis, win the argument and force manufacturers to do as required. This was most noticeably shown in the case of the disagreement between Morris and the aircraft designers at the shadow factory at Castle Bromwich in 1940. Morris argued for standardised parts in order to achieve a rapid flow of production. The cost of his plans was twofold: the delay whilst the arrangements were put into place and the resultant inflexibility of a standardised product. The air force, on the other hand, needed both immediate supplies of aircraft and the flexibility to improve models as the occasion arose. Whilst Morris was trying to implement his ideas, he was countered by the plane designers, who produced a string of modifications as they learnt the lessons of combat and tried to implement improvements (Adeney 1993, p. 153). Morris took his quarrel to both Beaverbrook and Churchill but ultimately lost to the 'higher' claims of flexibility and modification to the aircraft of the Royal Air Force (Adeney 1993, p. 154). There is a strange irony here in that Morris's plans were based on standardised products from long, rapid production runs, which in the end were negated by the modifications required by the aircraft designers (Adeney 1993, p. 154).

Moreover, controls notably over the allocation of raw materials, had continued in force after the war. This gave government scope for control without jeopardising the export trade. The motor industry needed steel, fuel and other raw materials in order to produce vehicles. The allocation of these basic inputs to the industry was made dependent on the industry exporting a very high percentage of its products. Controls could and ultimately were used to integrate the industry into the planned economy and to deal with the short-run overriding necessity of gaining export earnings. If the industry did not meet its export targets, then its share of raw materials would be reduced for 'in so far as these post-war controls have diverted sales from the home market to the export market they have been successful' (Labour Party 1948b, para. 230, p. 70). In 1946 the industry was required to export 50 per cent of production; a year later this was raised to 75 per cent (Dunnett 1980, p. 32). The government could also easily exercise further controls since control of new building operations and the purchase of new equipment for factories from the main source of supply, the hard currency areas, made it easy for the government to limit or assist the expansion of the individual units of the industry (Labour Party 1948b, paras. 228 and 229, p. 70).

What then was to happen when the supply of raw materials was no longer limited? The Report's answer to this was to point out that the balance of payments problem would continue for many years and that 'there is no prospect of that gap being closed without a very big contribution from exports. In other words, the export drive will have to continue indefinitely although its tempo and direction may change' (Labour Party 1948b, para. 231, p. 71).

The motor vehicle industry was to play a major role in achieving that objective.

The Report went to some length in outlining the advantages of control as opposed to full or partial ownership of the industry. Four main areas were identified. Firstly, it was argued that controlling the industry via export quotas would ultimately force through rationalisation as the inefficient would be squeezed out of the market once they failed to reach export targets. Second, it was argued that manufacturers would be compelled to reduce the number and variety of models if export targets were sufficiently high and the penalty for failure to attain them sufficiently onerous. As such, standardisation would be achieved without having to take the industry into full or partial control. It was further argued that in the bid to attain export earnings, the industry would have to be competitive and, as such, the benefits of private ownership and competition would be retained. Finally, control overcame the difficulties of defining the boundaries of the industry (Labour Party 1948b, para. 232 (2)–(7), p. 71). It is not difficult to see why this solution appeared so attractive at this time – it offered the promise of overcoming the key problems of rationalisation and standardisation whilst maintaining the 'competitive spirit' and avoiding the short-run disruption of full or partial ownership and the consequent costs to export earnings.

How was such control to be effected? The consultative document recommended a controlling body empowered to allocate production between home and export markets. It also recommended that such a body should 'deal with' such issues as the number and type of models produced, the standardisation of fabricated parts and raw materials, the position of specialist car manufacturers, distribution arrangement, price-fixing arrangements, research, and training. What was meant by 'deal with' was not stated (Labour Party 1948b, para. 235 (2–8), p. 72). The possibility that control might best be achieved through government export quotas was ceded in the Report's acknowledgement that

the difficulty of finding people in the industry itself who have the necessary qualifications and who would be willing to co-operate in an effort to carry on the industry as to get the best possible results from the workers, plant and materials available need hardly be stressed (Labour Party 1948b, para. 236, p. 72).

6   Conclusion

The motor vehicle industry was not taken into full public ownership or subjected to some form of partial public ownership after the war. Not only was the case for nationalisation not proven, but also the costs of any rationalisation programme would have raised the spectre of unemployment and completely upset the tempo and smooth working of the industry at a time when maximum production was vital to the economic life of the nation. The balance of payments problem and the contribution of the motor vehicle industry to export earnings also explain why it was felt that control via the allocation of raw materials was the best way to control the industry.

So long as they performed their allotted tasks of producing vehicles or other motor goods and of exporting their quota, manufacturers would be free to go about their job in their own way. (Labour Party 1948b, para. 232, p. 71).

This, in the final analysis, was what the government required of the industry and this is the solution that was finally applied. So long as the industry met its export quotas, then it would be free to go its own way – under private ownership.

NOTES

Thanks to Nick Crafts, James Foreman-Peck, Neil Rollings, Steve Tolliday, Paul Turner and the editors of this volume. The usual disclaimer applies. This research was funded as part of a larger project on the post-war motor vehicle industry by the Nuffield Foundation under grant SOC/100/(50).
  1 The average for all manufacturing industry was just under 3 per cent; that for vehicles was just under 7 per cent (Aldcroft (1983), table 13, 43).
  2 Its annual growth rate was 3.6 per cent per annum (Matthews, Feinstein, Odling-Smee (1982), table 8.7, p. 240).
  3 Just before the War, UK production, at 341,000 motor cars, had been well in excess of that of France (199,800), Germany (276,600) and Italy (59,000).
  4 In September 1920 the overdraft had doubled to £84,315 and a debt to suppliers of around £50,000 had been run up (Adeney 1988, p. 97).
  5 Leonard Lord, previously production and lay out organiser at Wolseley, was brought in by Morris in 1933 to effect the complete reorganisation of the Cowley factory and to introduce new models. His stay at Cowley was limited to three years. After a row with Morris (said to be based on a disagreement over Lord's salary) he left – initially to look after the Nuffield Trust for the Special Areas – but later in 1937 to take over at Longbridge where he was responsible for the Austin Eight which competed head on with the Morris Eight.
  6 Between 1933 and 1934, the layout and equipment at Cowley were reconstructed and the proliferation of models which had characterised the Morris

production line (most notably in 1933, when nine basic models and twenty-six styles were offered), was reduced. By 1937, the number of basic models had been reduced to five, with ten styles (Overy 1976, table 6, p. 134).

7 The comments on Singer were subsequently deleted from the report.

8 This related to imports of American machine tools.

9 The usual horsepower for regular American models was 24 (Church and Miller 1977, p. 170).

10 As with Ford, the move was also a reaction to the imposition of tariffs against imported cars.

11 The nominal rate of protection for vehicles was 33.3 per cent; the effective rate was 53.5 per cent (Capie 1983, table 81, p. 118; table 3.1, p. 43).

REFERENCES

Adeney, Martin (1988), *The Motor Makers; The Turbulent History of Britain's Car Industry*, London: Collins.

(1993), *Nuffield: A Biography*, London: Robert Hale.

Aldcroft, D.H. (1983), *The British Economy Between the Wars*, Oxford: Phillip Allan.

Bardou, Jean-Pierre, Chanaron, Jean-Jacques, Fridenson, Patrick and Laux, James M. (1982), *The Automobile Revolution; The Impact of an Industry*, Chapel Hill: University of North Carolina Press.

Bowden, S.M. (1991), 'Demand and supply constraints in the inter-war UK car industry; did the manufacturers get it right?', *Business History*, 33(2): 241–67.

Bowden, S.M. and Turner, P.M. (1993a), 'Some cross section evidence on the determinants of the diffusion of car ownership in the interwar UK economy', *Business History*, 35(1) (January): 55–69.

(1993b), 'The UK market and the market for consumer durables, *Journal of Economic History*, 53(2) (June): 244–58.

Capie, F. (1983), *Depression and Protectionism: Britain between the Wars*, London: George Allen & Unwin.

Census of Production, Fifth Census (1935), Summary Tables.

Chester, Norman (1975), *The Nationalisation of British Industry 1945–1951*, London: HMSO.

Church, R.A. (1979), *Herbert Austin; The British Motor Car Industry to 1941*, London: Europa.

Church, Roy and Miller, Michael (1977), 'The British motor industry, 1922–1939', in Barry Supple (ed.), *Essays in British Business History*, Oxford: Clarendon Press, pp. 163–86.

Dunkerley, J. and Hare, P. (1991), 'Nationalized industries', in N.F.R. Crafts and Nicholas Woodward (eds.), *The British Economy since 1945*, Oxford: Clarendon Press, ch. 12, pp. 381–416.

Dunnett, Peter J.S. (1980), *The Decline of the British Motor Industry; The Effects of Government Policy, 1945–1979*, London: Croom Helm.

Foreman-Peck, J. (1981), 'Exit, voice and loyalty as responses to decline: the Rover company in the inter-war years', *Business History*, 23(2) (July): 191–207.

Hare, P. (1984), 'The nationalised industries', in P.G. Hare and M.W. Kirby (eds.), *An Introduction to British Economic Policy*, Brighton, ch. 11, pp. 151–64.

Jones, D.T. (1981), 'Maturity and crisis in the European car industry; structural change and public policy', Sussex: Sussex European Research Centre, University of Sussex.

Jones, D.T. and Prais, S. (1978), Plant size and productivity in the motor industry: some international comparisons', *Oxford Bulletin of Economics and Statistics*, 40(2): 131–51.

Labour Party (1948a), Sub-Committee on Industries for Nationalisation, Minutes (2) 13 October, Labour Party Archive, National Museum of Labour History, Manchester.

Labour Party, Research Department (1948b), 'Report on the British motor industry; possibilities of future development with special reference to the advantages and disadvantages of public ownership', May, Labour Party Archive, National Museum of Labour History, Manchester.

Lewchuk, Wayne (1987), *American Technology and the British Vehicle Industry*, Cambridge University Press.

Matthews, R.C.O., Feinstein, C.H. and Odling-Smee, J.C. (1982), *British Economic Growth, 1856–1973*, Oxford University Press.

Maxcy, G. (1958), 'The Motor Industry', in P.L. Cook and R. Cohen (eds.), *The Effect of Mergers*, London: Allen and Unwin.

Maxcy, G. and Silberston, A. (1959), *The Motor Industry*, London: Allen and Unwin.

Mikardo, Ian (1948), *The Second Five Years; A Labour Programme for 1950*, Fabian Publications, April, Research Series No. 124.

Miller, M. and Church, R.A. (1979), 'Motor Manufacturing', in Neil K. Buxton and Derek H. Aldcroft (eds.), *British Industry Between the Wars; Instability and Industrial Development, 1919–1939*, London: Scolar Press, pp. 179–215.

Ministry of Supply (1947), National Advisory Council for the Motor Manufacturing Industry, Report on Proceedings.

Overy, R.J. (1976), *William Morris, Viscount Nuffield*, London: Europa.

Political and Economic Planning (1950), *Motor Vehicles; A Report on the Industry*.

Rhys, D.G. (1972), *The Motor Industry; An Economic Survey*, London: Butterworths.

(1980), Motor Vehicles in P.S. Johnson (ed.), *The Structure of British Industry*, London: Granada, pp. 179–206.

Rostas, L. (1948), *Comparative Productivity in British and American Industry*, Cambridge University Press.

Silberston, Aubrey (1958), 'The Motor Industry', in Duncan Burn (ed.), *The Structure of British Industry; A Symposium*, vol. II, Cambridge, ch. X, pp. 1–44. Cambridge University Press.

Society of Motor Manufacturers and Traders, *The Motor Industry of Great Britain*, Annual.

Thoms, David and Donnelly, Tom (1985), *The Motor Car Industry in Coventry since the 1890s*, Beckenham, Kent: Croom Helm.

Tiratsoo, Nick (1992), 'The motor car industry', in Helen Mercer, Neil Rollings and Jim Tomlinson (eds.), *Labour Governments and Private Industry; The*

Experience of 1945–1951, Edinburgh: Edinburgh University Press, ch. 9, pp. 162–85.

Tolliday, Steven (1991), 'Rethinking the German miracle; Volkswagen in prosperity and crisis 1939–92', Harvard University, Business History Seminar; Competition and Industrial Structure, November.

(1993), 'Transferring Fordism: the first phase of the overseas diffusion and adaptation of Ford methods, 1911–1939', mimeo, University of Leeds.

6 The railway companies and the nationalisation issue 1920–50

Gerald Crompton

1 The post-war settlement

The idea of railway nationalisation was no novelty in 1914, and had made some modest headway on the basis of support from trade unions and from railway customers in the small business sector. But it was the First World War which brought the issue to the fore, and indeed made it hard to evade. This was partly because of the success of wartime arrangements, when the railways were operated 'as one complete unit in the best interests of the state' (Boscawen 1931, p. 21) and an increased volume of traffic was handled by a smaller labour force. A further consideration was that many of the smaller companies would have been unviable at post-war levels of cost. As in other areas of policy, wartime experience automatically posed the question of whether the gains of state intervention ought to be secured for the future, even if this involved permanent reorganisation. For a short time at the end of the war 'a political consensus existed for the implementation of a centrally adminstered transport scheme' (Grieves 1992, p. 24).

In 1919 a bill was introduced to set up a new ministry which would control virtually all forms of transport, and even gave the government authority to assume direct ownership by issuing Orders in Council. This reached the statute book by August, but without its more radical clauses. By 1920 the political climate had changed, and a white paper in June set out the essentials of the new policy. This retained private ownership, with compulsory amalgamation into four territorial groups. These were to be launched as regulated oligopolies, heavily constrained in both their pricing and wage fixing, and carrying strong obligations to act as 'public' utilities. Despite the newly rationalised structure, this legislation was based on pre-war thinking, and gave expression to anti-monopoly assumptions 'at precisely the moment when the monopoly began to disappear' (Railway Companies Association 1937, p. 7). These assumptions were reflected in the railways' status as common carriers, forbidden to exercise price discrimination, and in the attempt to define 'standard revenue'. This norm, eventually fixed at £51.4 million, was based on 1913 earnings. Four fifths of any excess profits were to be devoted to the reduction of prices. But the standard was to prove unattainable.

The 1921 act was no doubt a 'pale shadow of larger aspirations' (Grieves 1992, p. 39). It must have been disappointing both to pre-war advocates of nationalisation and to the first Minister of Transport, Sir Eric Geddes. This former railway manager, described by a former colleague as having 'a passionate devotion to efficiency',[1] took a broad view of the significance of railways for national economic development. He also had a strong grasp of the potential for cooperation with the electricity industry. Others were dissatisfied with the post-war settlement for quite different reasons. The Railway Gazette denounced government policy as 'nationalising the railways without paying for them'.[2] The companies themselves were worried both by the financial implications and by the extent of ministerial powers. Even within the industry, however, there was some disposition to accept the government's claim that the legislation 'merely carried to its logical conclusion the practice of railways in the past, the object being operating economy and administrative efficiency' (Boscawen 1931, p. 24).

The reorganisation clearly created major opportunities for economies as each of the groups proceeded towards integration. Geddes himself, not surprisingly for one who set out the three key words of 'order, economy and enterprise' as the objectives of the Railways Act (Kidd 1929, p. 112), had initially made some of the most optimistic predictions. He suggested that savings of £25 million a year might be achieved within six or seven years. A much shrewder assessment came from one of the new general managers, Wedgwood, who recognised that amalgamation-derived economies 'cannot by any ingenuity be isolated; the only savings that really count must be spread out over many years'.[3]

It was less clearly appreciated that before financial advantages could be secured, there were major organisational problems to be overcome first. A common phrase of the time, 'the fruits of amalgamation', may have encouraged the misconception that easy pickings were available. In fact the mergers necessitated a managerial exercise unprecedented in scale. It could not possibly have been accomplished without friction. Four years after grouping, the Chairman of the LNER (London and North Eastern Railway) recalled that 'we had to start with seven traditions, seven loyalties, and with more than one language'.[4] In the late thirties Gilbert Szlumper of the SR (Southern Railway) had written that the old companies had 'long-standing and valuable traditions, many of which were lost in the fusions, and during the transition period there was a noticeable falling away of the esprit de corps which had previously existed'. He also recognised that there had been a 'period of stagnation', when senior staff were 'engaged mainly upon the problems of reorganisation'. In consequence the railways had been 'unable to throw the whole of their energy into the traffic battle',[5] and lost ground to road transport. This interpretation helps to explain what is often alleged to have been a belated response to the emergence of road competition and perhaps also the loss of the pre-war impetus towards electrification.

Between 1923 and 1929 the railways made slow progress towards the target of standard revenue – an increase of about 4 per cent in net receipts from railway operations alone. The form in which this gain was realised is significant. Receipts fell by approximately £13 million, but expenditure declined more quickly by about £14.5 million. The most serious losses were in passenger traffic, where receipts dropped by 13 per cent. This reflected increased competition from buses and private cars. On the freight side of the business, diversion of traffic to the roads was a less serious problem, but here the railways were adversely affected by the poor performance of their major customers, the staple export industries.[6] It was calculated in 1931 that if railway gross receipts had increased in line with the output of the whole economy, they would have been more than £40 million higher (about £228 million instead of £183 million). The railways had not taken their full share of the economic growth of the twenties. Their position had additionally deteriorated in the sense that reserves had been depleted, and investment income reduced. Over £15 million, equal to more than a quarter of the post-war government compensation award, was taken from reserves simply to maintain dividends in the strike-hit year of 1926[7] (Fox 1932).

Although the reduction in expenditure in the first six years after grouping had kept only narrowly ahead of falling receipts, the achievement was not insubstantial. It had been conventionally calculated that well over half (sometimes two thirds) of railway expenditure was 'fixed', or not likely to vary in proportion to fluctuations in the volume of traffic. In the past it would have been regarded as very difficult to improve net revenue in a situation of declining demand. This reinforces the presumption that part of these economies were attributable to amalgamation. In the years after 1923 the context of gradually dwindling revenue and gently falling prices probably encouraged railway management to concentrate primarily on simple cost reduction, rather than on more rapid standardisation measures requiring large-scale reequipment. Indeed it seems to have been accepted at an early stage in the life of the new groups that standardisation would not be achievable until large quantities of the existing and highly variegated capital stock (e.g., locomotives) had finally reached the end of their physical viability. Kidd's book, published in 1929, concluded that, for this reason, 'many of the larger economies have been postponed until 1940–1950' (Kidd 1929, p. 132). The famous criterion used by the Railways Rates Tribunal, 'efficient and economical working' contained a potential paradox: certainly the second adjective came to be honoured more than the first. The circumstantial pressure to adopt a relatively short-term or a defensive outlook was never lifted. What had been thought of as unfavourable conditions in the twenties got worse, not better. After 1929 came first severe depression and then a recovery accompanied by rising costs, intensified freight competition from the roads, and growing capital shortage. The seriousness of this latter problem could not easily have been envisaged at the end of the twenties, when the railways could invest around ten million pounds in bus companies, and still face criticism for maintaining free reserves of at least £45 million.[8] But in many respects, and especially the assumption that financial prudence dictated cost cutting rather than aggressive spending in order to expand revenue, railway management was set in the 1920s in a groove from which it was hard to escape.

A combination of the requirement to compensate employees made redundant by the grouping, and the 1919 reduction of working hours meant that the labour force declined only slowly until the mid twenties.[9] Another financial handicap was the normative obligation to maintain virtually the entire existing network of routes and stations. Only occasionally was the principle explicitly discussed, as when the President of the LMSR (London Midland and Scottish Railway) in 1928 referred to two lines serving the same area, commenting that 'where the stronger line absorbs the weaker generally both must remain open'. Others found examples such as the town where five out of seven goods depots now belonged to one company, but all five were still open in 1929 because of pressure from local traders (Kidd 1929, p. 132). Railway route mileage did not peak until the late twenties. Rationalisation and closure of underused facilities was pursued more actively in the thirties. But pressure to act as a public utility was unremitting, and the railways remained dependent on public and parliamentary sympathy in the hope of legislation to ease the disadvantages from which they suffered in relation to road transport.

2   The re-emergence of the nationalisation issue

For advocates of railway nationalisation, progress towards their goal must have seemed as slow during the twenties as the improvement in railway finances appeared to stockholders. It was true that four regulated groups had replaced a hundred separate companies, that pre-war strategies of stimulating competition had been discredited, and that the position of the trade unions was securely entrenched. But the settlement embodied in the Railways Act had an air of authority, if not of finality, about it. On the other hand, the case for both unification and standardisation was better understood. The Balfour Committee, concerned primarily with the needs of industry, reflected in its report that 'the question naturally arises' whether the public interest would be better served by the consolidation of the railway system under some form of National Board or Trust (Balfour, 1929, pp. 76–8). But an issue like nationalisation was an obvious one to pass over to the Royal Commission on Transport, which had been appointed before Balfour reported.

Reporting a couple of years before the slump had rearranged the economic landscape, the Commission members still thought it premature to pass judgement on the 1921 act. They were also anxious to steer clear of political controversy as far as possible, and noted that 'the very word "nationalisation" has become . . . a party badge'. However, in a significant distinction, only one particular type of nationalisation was deemed impossible to discuss 'without raising political differences of a party character'. This was 'the ownership and operation of one or all the means of transport by a Government Department under a political chief' (Boscawen 1931, p. 172). Balfour had also expressed distaste for this form of state ownership. But the Boscawen Commission outlined in implicitly favourable terms a scheme for a Public Transport Trust 'entirely divorced from political action'. It would be non-profit making but would operate on commercial lines. Such a framework was said to be compatible with current ministerial thinking on the reorganisation of London transport, and, in any case, to be the system which had usually been employed 'when anything of the kind has been attempted in this country in recent years'. A Trust on these lines was described as one of four possible forms which unification might take. No doubt was felt, however, that coordination of transport as a whole was highly desirable. In fact complete coordination, amounting to a 'controlled monopoly' of all transport services, was defined as an ideal – 'a state of affairs whereby every passenger travelled, and every ounce of goods was consigned, by the most economical route and form of transport' (Boscawen 1931, p. 170). The extreme difficulty of realising the ideal was clearly and sensibly recognised. Indeed the warning given against any attempt to enforce coordination by compulsory methods heavily underlined the elusiveness of the goal.

A minority addendum, or 'additional recommendations' was supplied by three members added to the Commission by the Labour government, who had also signed the main report.[10] They presented their conclusion, the nationalisation of a large proportion of Britain's transport facilities, as a logical extension of the remarks about unification and coordination in the main report. Their central arguments advocated public ownership as a rational development of the existing transport system. What they wanted was a National Transport Trust which would arrange coordination 'in the interest of national industry and trade', and would operate 'for service rather than profit', though it was envisaged that it would pay 'a reasonable rate of interest on capital'. It was pointed out that independent railway companies were likely to continue to fare badly in competition with the roads. A speech by a senior railway official, predicted serious consequences if nothing were done to halt this trend. These included withdrawal of unprofitable services, higher charges on remaining rail traffic, and the danger that 'large physical developments would suffer'. Directors were blamed for the fact that 'a considerable proportion' of railway capital was now 'dead', and did not represent assets with real earning power. On the other hand, railway professionals, right up to general manager level, were conspicuously praised ('there is perhaps no better type in the country of the organiser trained by experience'). Under nationalisation all board members and senior managers would be there 'because of their special fitness and capacity and should not be connected with any other business'. Despite the huge scale of the organisation envisaged, the challenge was anticipated with some confidence ('this is the age of big businesses').[11] All the essential elements of what later came to be known as Morrisonian nationalisation were thus present in the minority document of 1930, both the analysis of the defects of competition, and the purpose and forms of the institutions which would be needed to achieve coordination.

The Boscawen report confirmed a shift in the terms of debate which was already under way. The positive evaluation of unification and coordination, and the benign attitude towards ownership through a public corporation, could only strengthen the case for nationalisation. It may be that the Commission had been favourably influenced by some of the trade union witnesses, at least in their disavowal of nationalisation as a party issue, and insistence that there should be 'a definite national point of view' on transport questions. The same witness also made scathing comments on the progress towards standardisation, both internally and nationally, of the four groups. One charged that the LMSR 'have hardly yet decided what colour their engines shall be painted', and another complained that 'it [i.e., standardisation] could be done by the Companies, but, as they are Companies, of course it is not done'. Less attention was paid to these points.[12]

3   The redefinition of the issue

After 1930 nationalisation of railways alone was slightly downgraded as an issue because it clearly offered a less comprehensive solution than in the past. In itself it could not necessarily end ruinous competition, or bring about an acceptable reorganisation of all transport. As the Final Report noted, 'co-ordination of a certain character is comparatively easy, i.e. co-ordination of the traffic of a particular form of transport' (Boscawen 1931, p. 170). This point, although glib in its understatement of both the problems and the potential of the unification of a single mode, was often repeated. The Next Five Years Group (1935), for example, judged that 'so far as the railways are concerned, socialization would present few difficulties and few advantages', before proceeding to argue that in order to ensure that the nation's transport facilities were used to the full, 'a community of financial interest between road and rail was essential', and that this would require 'some degree of national control, if not ownership'.[13] But widening the scope of nationalisation proposals brought greater obstacles into view as well as expanded opportunities. Apart from road transport interests, resistance was more likely from anyone who doubted the ability of ministers and transport managers to devise some effective and even-handed coordination. It became a common argument that if railway nationalisation had occurred in the past, then the presumptive interest of the state in protecting its own assets might have led to the stifling of road competition. This was in fact the position taken up by a Conservative spokesman opposing the Transport Bill in 1946. He claimed 'the basic factor was always the same – that the position of the railway should be maintained not by improving the service, but by cutting the throat of its principal competitors'. If a nationalised railway were left 'open to the virile competition of a free road haulage industry', it would soon be 'showing the most colossal losses'.[14]

Such attempts to invoke fear of railway inertia and market power sought to tap a long tradition of hostility. The Royal Commission of 1928–30 had reflected that 'it cannot be denied that in the days of their monopoly the railways had in some way insufficiently studied the needs of the public, and that their policy had become unduly conservative'. The companies were accused of having forgotten 'the truth of the doctrine that facilities create traffic' (Boscawen 1931, p. 37). The Commission had taken a more positive line on current problems, recommending success-fully that pooling of traffic and revenue should now be permitted. After this and other recent legislative gains (the granting of road powers in 1928 and the remission of passenger duty in 1929), plus the introduction of a measure of regulation for road transport in 1930 and 1933, it could be argued that the railways were, to some compensating degree, the beneficiaries of government intervention, rather than merely the objects. By the 1930s it was apparent that an earlier stage of public regulation, one concerned basically with the protection of traders and consumers against local monopolies, had given way to a new phase in which the purpose was control in the interests of efficiency, via the complex reconciliation of a number of conflicting interests (Compton and Bott 1940, p. 108).

Hence, as *The Economist* explained in 1939, 'co-ordination is a blessed word'. Its meanings were multiple. It might refer to the ideal sketched out by the Royal Commission in 1930 – a means to ensure that 'traffic always moves by the route and on the systems which involve the smallest social cost'. Or it might mean an arrangement based on deals negotiated by competitors 'with the object not so much of maximising their joint efficiency as of stabilising their present positions'.[15] This implied that alternative and potentially competitive services would continue to exist, but, as long as agreements remained effective, would cease to undercut each other. Coordination in the first, and more blessed sense, was the aim of transport nationalisation, which was the only plausible method of turning the ideal into reality. Coordination in the second sense was more likely to be the outcome of a voluntary road–rail agreement. This had the merit of being attainable in principle without compulsion, but was wide open to traditional objections to cartelisation and restrictions on price competition.

By 1938 the railway companies, having suffered renewed financial setbacks after a lengthy period of recovery, launched a 'Square Deal' campaign for the removal of most of their remaining legislative constraints, especially those affecting classification and pricing of goods. War prevented the implementation of this scheme – a fact which emphasises the tardiness with which inter-war governments modified their view of railways as a sheltered sector and moved towards an appreciation of the extent of their handicaps *vis-à-vis* road competition (Crompton 1985). The 'Square Deal' was commended to the public as a contribution to the goal of coordination, the distinctive feature of the railway position being the belief that greater equality among the different modes of transport was a prerequisite. A series of articles in the journal *Modern Transport* in 1938, written from a railway standpoint, summed up the nationalisation issue as whether a self-sustaining, adequate and properly coordinated transport system could be best achieved under public ownership or 'under a combination of private enterprise and uniform state regulation'.[16] Herbert Morrison's reasoning was similar, when he said in the debate on the Transport Bill in 1946 that the real choice lay between 'private quasi-monopolies', with state-regulated coordination, and 'an integrated national transport system'.[17]

The Royal Commission had stated bluntly one fundamental reason why the aims of coordination and harmonisation were of vital importance: despite the impact of newer forms of transport, railway services were still 'indispensable'. Furthermore, 'an immense proportion' of capital had been invested in them, and 'the Nation cannot afford to place this capital on the scrap heap or even to render it partially unremunerative' (Boscawen 1931, p. 45). Failure by privately owned companies to earn satisfactory returns was thus accepted as a matter of public concern, and as a potential threat to the viability of the transport system. The implication of this analysis was that substantial long-term deterioration in net revenue, coupled with the inability to negotiate a satisfactory agreement with road interests, was bound to produce pressure for state-imposed coordination.

Between 1929 and 1932 all the railway groups were hit hard by the general decline in economic activity. Gross receipts fell heavily within a range from 15.9 per cent (SR) to 23.6 per cent (LNER). The only compensating factor was that every company succeeded in reducing expenses significantly. The decline varied between 12.4 per cent (SR) and 17.9 per cent (LNER). Cost reductions on this scale were greeted by *The Economist* as 'distinctly creditable to their managements'.[18] They were clearly assisted by continuing gains from amalgamation. Nevertheless by 1932 £260 million of railway capital was going without dividend. Only the GWR paid anything at all to ordinary shareholders, and only by drawing on reserves. At the other extreme the LNER made full interest and dividend payments only on debentures and guaranteed stocks (about 48 per cent of its total capital).[19]

The years 1933 to 1937 brought an important measure of recovery. However, only the SR showed higher net revenue at the peak in 1937 than in 1929 (and still fell short of standard revenue). The other three suffered falls of between 12 per cent and 22 per cent from the 1929 level. All companies had a lower return on capital in 1937 than in 1929, with the SR registering the smallest decline. These returns, calculated on railway operations alone, varied from 3.3 per cent to 4.15 per cent. Three of the four groups were carrying more passengers in 1937 than in 1929, and on average for longer journeys. These gains reflected both the acceleration of services, and also the cheaper 'penny-a-mile' fares which had been progressively introduced, experimentally in 1933, and on a regular basis from 1934. They also indicated the ability of railways to withstand competition from buses on all except short journeys. As one analysis put it, passenger traffic will show 'an elasticity of demand, responding to lower charges and careful publicity'. But freight was a far more intractable problem. The volume of goods handled by the railways fell 9.1 per cent between 1929 and 1937. The lighter and more profitable categories of merchandise declined by more than the average. The railways plainly failed to share in the general economic recovery of the 1930s, and were losing business to road haulage. This was apparent from the figures for 'recovery' goods of a type suitable for rail transport. The year 1936 was a record year for building, but fewer bricks travelled by rail than in 1929.[20]

Despite general recovery, important economic trends were clearly unfavourable to the railways. Several heavy industries, whose products inevitably went by rail, were still experiencing sluggish demand. Overseas trade, which often required long hauls by rail to and from ports, declined proportionately as the economy expanded. Some industries located or relocated themselves on the basis of proximity to markets, and many retailers began to order their supplies in smaller quantities and at shorter intervals. This both raised handling costs, and made the use of road transport more probable. During the recovery the railways were subject to rising costs, especially of raw materials, and in some years increased traffic required a slight rise in the number of employees. Yet it proved difficult to recoup higher costs, and the 5 per cent increase in charges in 1937, which was unfortunate in its timing, was partly negated by falling trade. In 1938 a renewed and serious downturn in receipts, following the general trend of the economy, reduced the return on railway capital to approximately the same level as in 1932. This was a financial performance which inevitably put the future independence of the railways in some jeopardy.

4   Electrification

For many critics of the inter-war railway companies one of the most appropriate criteria of their financial soundness, managerial resourcefulness and commitment to modernisation is their record on electrification. This deserves examination in some detail. Electric traction had been employed in Britain since 1890, and more than 100 route miles had been converted by 1914. Interest in the possibilities of large-scale electrification was to quicken after the war on the basis of well-justified expectations that current would be available at lower prices and without the need for railways to provide their own power stations. Progress was disappointingly slow, however, except on the SR, as the Minister admitted to Parliament in 1925.[21]

The Royal Commission of 1928–30 was favourable to electrification, especially for suburban traffic. However, it deferred to the judgement of the Weir Committee, whose report in 1931 was the most systematic survey to date of the case for comprehensive electrification. But by the time of publication, few could have expected its proposals to be taken up promptly, in such an unfavourable economic climate. The authors believed that the investment required – £260 million net by the railways, and about £80 million by the Central Electricity Board and others – was such that 'the magnitude of this would be unique in the history of world enterprise'. They also acknowledged that the estimated return on this expenditure, net of interest charges, would be unattractive 'from a business point of view'. The margin of around 2 per cent would be 'too narrow for the risks involved'. In fact the consistent caution of the Weir procedures, and the unfavourable impact of assuming that all non-suburban lines would be converted, and within a twenty-year period, meant that the conclusions could serve only as a lower-bound estimate of the benefits of electrification. The overall gross return was calculated at 6.7 per cent. An additional investment of £45 million for intensified electric working of suburban routes was expected to yield around 13 per cent within the context of a general scheme. Given the lower interest rates prevailing within a short time after publication of the report, both these figures could have been interpreted as encouraging.[22]

Further examination of the assumptions behind the Weir calculation reinforces this impression. The Committee had made no allowance for any increase in demand, and the benefits anticipated were based entirely on economies in handling existing traffic. Such an ultra-prudent approach may have been suggested by the fact that railway turnover was actually falling whilst the committee was at work. But this declining trend had been reversed by 1933, and electrification schemes invariably did succeed in increasing traffic, as the SR had demonstrated, and as indeed Weir noted. The Railway Gazette pointed out four years later that with a national electrified system, or even simply with greater demand for current and higher load factor, 'it should be possible to reduce the cost of current below the unit figure assumed' by Weir.[23] Other strikingly conservative assumptions embedded in the report were that the total number of tractors (i.e., locomotive units) would be reduced by only 30 per cent, and that no acceleration would occur in express services. It was naturally conceded that many advantages of electrification were difficult to quantify. These included greater cleanliness, improved punctuality, acceleration of local, suburban and stopping services, and reduction of shunting and signalling movements. There were also important external benefits. The electrical manufacturing industry obviously stood to gain from a steady flow of work. This would be on such a scale that, given standardisation and a common technical policy, it was envisaged that orders might be fulfilled at prices 10 per cent to 15 per cent lower than those used in the committee's estimates. Continuous employment would be created for about 60,000 over twenty years. Virtually all expenditure, except for purchases of copper, would ultimately be translated into wages in Britain. Offsets against these positive effects would include reduced demand for labour in the locomotive grades, and a decline of almost ten million tons a year in coal consumption, with a consequential impact on employment.[24]

One reason for making calculations based on the conversion of the entire railway network was the alleged impracticability of eliminating the 'appreciable mileage of light traffic lines where electrification would not be justified'. Of course what was impracticable in a cost–benefit exercise would have been quite simple in practice. Much of this mileage would have been more appropriate for closure than conversion to electric traction. The effect of including obviously unsuitable routes was to understate the probable returns from a realistically defined electrification programme. Another possible justification for the comprehensive approach was the disappointing and inconclusive results of a couple of regional studies which the committee had commissioned from Merz and McLellan. One focused on a section of the LNER, and although this included substantial low density areas of Lincolnshire, indicated a respectable return of 7.22 per cent. But the LMSR study, although it covered a smaller area with denser traffic, showed a discouraging yield of 2.5 per cent. The crucial difference seemed to be that the latter exercise assumed that surrounding lines were still steam-operated, that much dual-working was unavoidable, and the number of locomotives would fall by the minute figure of 2½ per cent. It is hard to say how seriously these Merz and McLellan projections were taken by the companies. But it may have been unfortunate that the more tempting prospects were held out to the group with the least ability to raise capital, whilst the weaker inducement was extended to the rather better-resourced LMSR.[25] A more convincing example of a limited scheme was submitted by a correspondent to *The Economist*, K. Johnston. He proposed an initial electrification of 750 double track miles, consisting of a trunk route from London to Scotland, with connections to half a dozen cities in the north and midlands. *The Economist* approved this economical plan, noting its similarity in principle with rationalisation in industry: it offered selective modernisation and concentration of activity on areas judged likely to produce the maximum return.[26]

In actuality the Weir report did not stimulate electrification, of either the overall or the piecemeal variety. The SR did pursue a vigorous policy of conversion, but here it was simply continuing on its chosen path, having already made its mind up about the merits of the question. The company inherited eighty-three electrified route miles from three of its constituents. By the end of the decade the SR had converted nearly 300 route miles, representing 17 per cent of its track mileage, and handling more than a third of its passenger train miles. As Weir noted, the SR accounted for well over half of the British total of 487 electrified miles (excluding tube lines, but including over fifty miles of Metropolitan and District). A major extension to Brighton and Worthing (described by Weir as 'almost a main line scheme, but electrified for suburban traffic reasons') was already under way at the time. What followed was essentially a rolling programme, which was scarcely interrupted even in the worst years of depression. This included services, especially the Portsmouth direct route, with its scanty local traffic, which were unambiguously 'main line'. From 1936 electric mileage overtook steam on passenger services, and by 1939 was over 60 per cent of the total. The SR then possessed one of the largest electrified systems in the world, with well over 600 route miles, and nearly 2,000 track miles. These developments would have been taken further but for the war, and indeed the SR produced a post-war plan by which all principal routes east of a line from Reading to Portsmouth would have been converted to electric traction, with branch lines operated by diesel (White 1982, chapter IX, Cox 1937).

It was obvious that the SR had committed itself definitively to electrification, and that in this respect it stood alone among the big four in Britain. By 1939 the amount of track electrified was just over 5 per cent for the whole country, but only around 1 per cent for the area north of the Thames (Johnston 1949, p. 328). The introduction of international comparisons fails to establish a clear picture of British backwardness in this respect, although it would undoubtedly succeed in doing so but for the contribution of the SR. Several European countries, including Germany, had electrified a smaller proportion of their track. Most of the national railway systems which had been electrified to a significantly higher degree than the British were characterised by a combination of the problem of mountainous terrain and the advantage of abundant hydro-electric power (as in Switzerland and Scandinavia). Relative scarcity of indigenous coal was also a factor. These circumstances had allowed the Weir Committee to state that 'the causes for most foreign electrification schemes do not apply in Britain'.[27] Although perhaps literally accurate here, they did have to concede that absence of water power was not a critical handicap, as electricity could be generated as cheaply by other methods. Furthermore differences in geographical conditions could not altogether explain the more rapid adoption of railway electrification during the thirties in France, Holland and Italy (Johnston 1949, pp. 158, 328–31).

The main questions arising from British experience are the enthusiasm and the success with which electrification was taken up by the SR, and the contrasting coolness or inactivity of the other groups. One fundamental difference was the unusually low dependence of the SR on freight, and its possession of one of the densest suburban passenger networks in the world. The fortunes of the company were linked to traffic of a type for which the potential of electrification had been most apparent from the outset. It served one of the most prosperous parts of Britain, and was largely unaffected by the gloom cast by the prolonged inter-war depression of the heavy industries, which had a major negative impact on the two northern groups. Furthermore two of the SR's predecessor companies had already made out the case for electric traction, albeit on a small scale. They had both discovered that whereas a policy of lower costs (i.e., fewer trains) was no answer to falling receipts, regular electric services were capable of reversing a declining trend in passenger traffic. This was the lesson the SR took to heart, relying on the 'sparks effect'. The cheaper running costs of electric traction were exploited so as to provide a more frequent and reliable service, which attracted more passengers. Thus a greatly increased train mileage could be run with no rise in expenditure. Gross running costs would remain roughly the same, and the yield on the investment consisted basically of the increased receipts. One estimate, in round figures, suggests that the company 'saved' (increased revenue by) about £2 million a year in consequence of a total capital outlay of about £19 million. What is certain is that electrification on the SR brought increased traffic wherever it was implemented, and that the benefits were not confined, as in Weir's premise, to merely economising on the cost of existing services (White 1982, pp. 180–1, Johnston 1949, p. 175).

The attitude of the other groups remained unenthusiastic despite periodic assertions that the question was under consideration, and that minds were open. Stamp claimed in a published interview soon after his arrival at the LMSR that electrification 'of various parts of the line' was currently 'under review' and that the outcome would depend on 'whether it is an economic possibility'. But he was decisive enough to predict that 'it would be a long time before the electrification of long-distance main line traffic could be justified'.[28] Wedgwood, the LNER's general manager and a member of the Central Electricity Board, sat on the Weir committee himself, but seems to have acted as a drag on the enthusiasm of the chairman. He insisted on a watering-down of the first, more positive, draft of the report (Hannah 1979, pp. 164–5). The chairman of the GWR made the inference from Weir that the project was commercially unjustifiable, 'a highly speculative venture', on which his company had no intention of embarking. He stressed, though, that the matter had been investigated, in relation to 'particular sections of our line' 'on more than one occasion during recent years'.[29] It is indeed known that the GWR twice (at least) considered electrification schemes, though the second instance was in the late thirties.

The first idea was for the electrification of coal traffic in south Wales and was not implemented. The second, and better-known case, related to the main line west of Taunton and other selected West Country routes. The consulting engineers concluded that an investment of about £4 million would yield derisory returns of less than 1 per cent. Unsurprisingly this project was also scrapped. In retrospect, the area was a curious choice. Assumptions were made which virtually nullified the normal advantages of electrification. These were, *inter alia*, the exclusion of acceleration, the employment of as many electric locomotives as their previous steam equivalents, and the need to cater for high traffic peaks, especially on summer weekends.[30] There is a suspicion that the GWR may not have been completely desolated by the negative verdict of the study. One historian has suggested that the covert purpose of the whole exercise was to warn colliery owners that the company was growing dissatisfied with the rising price of coal and was willing to contemplate alternative sources of energy (Semmens 1986, pp. 81–7).

Another extreme contrast with the SR was the LNER, which made negligible progress in improving its North London suburban services. These attracted frequent criticism, and appeared to be suitable cases for electrification. Between 1923 and 1925, and again between 1929 and 1931 the company worked on schemes for the suburban lines out of King's Cross. Both foundered, through a mixture of worry over capital costs, the difficulties of building a connection with existing tube lines, and the threat of new, competing tube routes. It was the announcement of the Piccadilly's extension to Cockfosters which laid the LNER's plans to rest in 1931. Electrification of the former Great Eastern suburban lines out of Liverpool Street seems to have been regarded as an intractable problem because of the need for expensive track-widening near the terminal. It was only after responsibility for these matters had passed to the LTJC (London Transport Joint Committee) in 1933 that a start was eventually made on the Liverpool Street–Shenfield route. No other LNER lines in the London area were selected, and the LTJC generally gave priority to tube extensions (Butterfield 1986, pp. 37–40).

One recent study has concluded that by the mid 1920s the LNER 'was looking for government assistance to undertake projects it certainly wished to proceed with'. More basically, 'there was very little in the way of innovation on the LNER for the simple reason that the company could not afford it unless the rewards were significant and certain'. Wedgwood's statement to a minister in 1929 that 'expectation of a 10 per cent return was demanded before new works were regarded as justifiable' certainly helps to explain his role in the shaping of the Weir report (Butterfield 1986, pp. 37–40). This factor was also the main explanation of the LNER's minuscule electrification achievements – essentially a share with the LMSR in the Manchester–Altrincham route and a beginning of the Manchester–Sheffield–Wath scheme.

5   Financial weakness and its implications

The LNER was the weakest of the big four, but a similar necessity for great caution over investment expenditure weighed heavily on the other companies too. This fundamental constraint overshadowed lesser and more specific issues in the debates over electrification. There was of course a number of perfectly rational objections which could usually be mobilised against any proposal. Some required abnormally expensive conversion, especially if connections with adjacent lines were sought, some would have meant continuation of steam operation within the electrified area, thereby postponing the full benefit, some would have relied speculatively on a large increase in traffic to justify the initial cost. There was probably a genuine tendency to underestimate the advantages on routine main-line operations, and to think of electrification as applicable essentially to areas with dense suburban traffic or difficult terrain. This may explain some of the surprising choices of location for pilot studies. A general worry was that large-scale change of fuel would further damage the coal industry, which was of course a major customer of the railways, as well as a supplier. An alleged technical conservatism, rooted in the belief that steam locomotive design and practice had not nearly reached its limits, was another factor which may have checked electrification. Stamp once made a suggestive distinction when he pointed out that in locomotive construction, as in signalling, 'improvement has come from within' under the impetus of changing operating requirements, but in matters of electric traction, 'the drive in discovery has come from general electrical research outside' (Williamson 1933, p. 169). Yet it seems doubtful whether any of these sources of inertia or conservatism would have been significant barriers in a warmer financial climate. Some were probably not so much real motives for inaction as public rationalisations and excuses for not doing what was privately judged technically desirable but financially impossible. With a typical reflex a railway director MP fell back on some familiar defences when the railways were criticised in parliament in 1939. Sir Richard Glyn emphasised that Weir's 7 per cent profit figure was no more than 'a speculative estimate', that electrification had 'a detrimental effect on the coal industry', and that during the thirties 'abnormal' improvements had been made in the steam locomotive.[31]

This reply, though serviceable as a series of debating points, was less compelling than the attack which prompted it. Herbert Morrison, for whom this was a favourite target, had deplored the railways' record on electrification. With the exception of the SR, which was commended for 'pluck' and 'enterprise', he suggested that 'business men with courage and initiative' were rare on the railways. When their leaders had responded to the Weir report by asking Morrison (then Minister of Transport) for financial assistance, he had countered by enquiring 'when they were going to get into a decent business enterprise frame of mind, instead of a public assistance frame of mind'. He had thrown in a pointed reference to persons 'not genuinely seeking work' adding that he 'would like to apply a proper test to capitalists who do not genuinely seek enterprise'.[32] In similar vein in the debate on the Transport Bill in 1946, Morrison argued that the railways' failure to electrify without state assistance was evidence of 'degeneration into a poor law frame of mind' and amounted to 'a confession that they could not adequately do the job'. Nationalisation, he then claimed, 'would enable cheap capital to be made available as soon . . . as it becomes practicable and expedient'. In the 1939 debate, from a position of much less political strength, he had made the essential connection. If railway leaders claimed they were capable of running their undertakings, then they should electrify: if not then he would 'draw a Socialist deduction from that answer'.[33]

Morrison's account of the reception of the Weir report in the summer of 1931 omitted one particular. Having already been informed by Weir himself of the likely railway response, he had tried unsuccessfully to persuade the cabinet to offer assistance. It was true that he had then met the company chairmen to urge them to electrify on their own initiative. Their refusal to discuss the matter further without state guarantees thus reduced the report to 'no more than a scrap of paper in the Minister's waste basket' (Hannah 1979, p. 165).

Even in 1939 Morrison's criticisms were felt to be sufficiently damaging to merit a considered response. Lord Stamp gave the 1940 LMSR annual meeting an overview of relations with government over the previous two decades. Whilst the railways had asked for the removal of unfair handicaps, he denied that 'we have ever asked for charity'. On the contrary, railway shareholders had been 'called upon to give the public assistance only too often'. In November 1922 it had been agreed at the request of the Prime Minister to carry out major development works to assist national trade and employment. In 1929 railway lobbying helped to obtain abolition of passenger duty, but 'on terms which were designed to aid the government's unemployment relief policy'. In the same year, the railways began employment-creating works 'out of our own resources', on which the state paid part of the interest costs for periods of up to fifteen years. But this help related only to projects 'which would not otherwise have been undertaken at that time'. The railways also had their rating liabilities reduced, but kept nothing themselves, being 'merely used as the channel for passing the derating allowances on to certain heavy industries'. Finally the Railway Finance Corporation Loan raised capital 'at rather lower rates than railway credit alone would have made possible', through government guarantee. But again, only schemes 'outside or beyond the regular railway programme' were eligible for benefit – those unlikely to be 'so profitable as to justify the expenditure of ordinary railway funds'. Seen in this perspective, according to Stamp, 'the "public-assistance-minded" idea fades into the air on examination'.[34]

This counter-attack no doubt served its immediate purpose. But Stamp could hardly refute Morrison's central charge: that the railways, or most of them, were unable or unwilling to embark on large-scale electrification and modernisation programmes, and that only additional state assistance could have changed this position. Stamp acknowledged the reality of government-railway cooperation, including elements of subsidy. His aim was to emphasise the marginality of subsidy, and to present the relationship as one in which the railway shareowner was helping the public, rather than vice versa. The danger, from Stamp's viewpoint, was that people other than Morrison might deduce that the railways were incapable of performing adequately on the basis of their own resources. If injections of public capital were seen as essential to stimulate either railway revenue or the economy, then private ownership and independence could soon be undermined. One indication of the spread of critical attitudes was the comment by the Next Five Years group that whilst electrification had been judged to be not worth while for the railways as private companies, a different conclusion might have been justified, if 'judged by the wider calculus appropriate to the community as a whole'.[35]

On other occasions Stamp himself had spoken in different terms about relations with government. In 1935 before an audience of stockholders, he denied that the government had brought pressure to bear on the railways over the recent works programmes, or that the companies had any intention of 'acting as philanthropists, mainly for electoral purposes'. On the contrary, Stamp insisted, the LMSR had accepted a Treasury guarantee on a loan of £30 million, because the conditions had been 'much more favourable than the railways could obtain on their own credit, unaided, at the present time'. A clinching consideration had been that money might not remain 'as cheap as it was today indefinitely', and that the government's offer might not stay open for ever. After emphasising the company's efforts to minimise the costs of investment, Stamp set out the rationale behind the capital expenditure which did take place. So far from crowding out dividend payments, it was designed to protect and enhance future dividends. The reason was that all capital schemes were designed either to prevent revenue from falling, or to 'improve, increase or consolidate' it. Alternatively their purpose was to enable existing revenue to be maintained on the basis of lower expenditure. Any capital proposal was always accompanied by a statement of the effect on net revenue, and railway officials had become 'expert at making extremely fine estimates'. A full basic rate of interest on the capital in question was always included in working costs.[36]

Stamp's ultra-cautious approach no doubt ensured that, individually, the new capital projects selected by his and other companies were adequately profitable. But as was apparent to critics, 'the immediate fact is that these satisfactory innovations have only served to check the fall in earnings. If they are ever to go to the length of raising them, a very large new investment will be required'.[37] Major electrification schemes would have come into this category. In fact, by normal standards railway investment did not seem to be negligible. *The Economist* had referred on a previous occasion to the substantial increase in capital investment between 1929 and 1937. It estimated this at £26.3 million on railway assets alone, and around £40 million in total.[38] When a railway spokesman presented a financial survey to the Railway Rates Tribunal in 1939 (covering the eleven-year period since the new standard charges became operative in 1928), he claimed that total expenditure on works was £260 million – equivalent to 22 per cent of capital employed.[39] In some of their general publicity material, the companies boasted of 'staggering' levels of spending on 'new works and reconstructions', citing in one case a figure of £450 million between 1923 and 1939.[40]

However the distinctive accounting practices followed by the railways make all such figures difficult to compare with those for firms in other sectors. Critics argued that a reasonably conservative industrial company would normally charge to revenue the cost of keeping equipment up-to-date and competitive, even if the replacement of assets involved some element of betterment. On the railways any betterment was supposed to be charged to capital, not revenue. The effect of this procedure was to produce flattering figures for revenue, but to require more frequent injections of fresh capital – in fact an almost continuous stream of fresh capital if there was to be any improvement in the average standard of railway equipment. These unusual accounting methods would not have caused any problem if healthy profits had allowed substantial allocations to reserves, in order to cover investment needs, without compromising dividend payments. But this condition could not be fulfilled in the thirties. Net revenue, even though inflated in the accounts, was modest, and usually consumed by dividends, which were still insufficient to satisfy ordinary shareholders, or to sustain the price of the stock. The result, inevitably, was that railway companies were unable to raise new capital, except by issuing further fixed interest securities, which created additional prior charges, and made the capital structure even more top heavy. Another consequence was that companies resorted to sources other than the capital market to fund the projects deemed essential. Capital was obtained from sales of land, liquidation of non-railway investments, such as government securities, and from liquid surpluses in superannuation funds. Between 1929 and 1938 the net deterioration in the interest situation on superannuation funds was £2.78 million. Overall, each of the four groups continued to spend more capital than they were raising. The debit on capital account widened by £35.1 million from £47.7 million in 1929 to £82.5 million in 1938.[41]

The underlying financial problems explain why, despite occasional boasting about their activity, railways boards were anxious to limit capital expenditure, and to operate on essentially defensive assumptions. They also explain why from time to time the accusation was made that the railways were 'overcapitalised' and that capital ought to be written down. This was a point of extreme sensitivity in railways circles. Stamp himself was at least twice stung by unacceptable comments in *The Accountant* and *The Economist* into writing letters of protest.[42] There was particular resentment of any suggestion that railway capital was 'watered'. In truth virtually all capital had actually been subscribed. However the original costs of land purchase, construction and parliamentary approval had been grossly inflated, so that even before 1914 a burden of unremunerative capital was being carried. The process of grouping in 1921–3 did involve a minor degree of writing down, not surprisingly given that some of the smaller companies could not have survived independently. By the late thirties the four groups were making less than three fifths of standard revenue, much of the capital was receiving nothing, and a further substantial fraction enjoyed less than its full return. The conclusion was irresistible that earning power had declined permanently, and that a fair part of the existing capital was not matched by earning assets. A standard argument from the railway camp was that much of the accumulated capital stood at pre-war prices, and the true value, and of course the replacement cost, of the railway system comfortably exceeded the nominal capitalisation. But the issue of replacement cost was increasingly 'academic'.[43] The main practical point of advocating writing-down of capital was that if profit could be increased by further capital expenditure, then it would be easier to attract subscribers to a new issue. The prospects for such an operation would of course be best in a period of rising net revenue, such as occurred between 1933 and 1937, and again during 1939. *The Accountant* helpfully cited some precedents for writing-down from both the railway and other sectors.[44]

The viewpoint from the railway board room was quite different. The nominal capitalisation was in a sense the quantitative expression of the railway's historical contribution to the economy. To companies struggling to defend their autonomy, self-preservation instincts no doubt suggested the necessity of insisting that the figures represented full value for money. If revenue was currently inadequate, as was freely conceded, this was attributable to a combination of the economic difficulties experienced by the whole country since the last war, and to the unfair disadvantages which railways faced in competing with road haulage. The collapse of earning power was not accepted as permanent. It was an important theme of the Square Deal campaign that Britain's railways constituted one of the few independent and self-supporting systems in the world, and intended to retain that status (Railways Companies Association 1939).

6   Organisation

Financial weakness certainly did not prevent, and may well have stimulated, organisational innovation. This is best exemplified by the largest of the four groups, the LMSR. They faced the biggest problems of integration and had most to gain from finding solutions. After three years of slow consolidation a radical break with tradition occurred with the appointment of a chief executive from outside the industry, Sir Josiah Stamp. From 1927 an American-style management hierarchy was adopted. There was no longer a general manager, but a small executive committee responsible to the board. This was headed by a President, with three Vice Presidents, who collectively were responsible for all general policy questions. Each Vice President acted as General Manager for a number of specific departments, the heads of which reported to him, and through him to the board. This system made the LMSR the most effectively centralised of the groups, and rationalisation, already under way, proceeded at an impressive pace once the new organisation was in place. Concentration of purchasing policy facilitated dramatic reductions in the number of different items stocked (Williamson 1933, pp. 181–2, LMSR 1946, p. 11). The new methods in fact extended considerably further than simple rationalisation. From 1931 a form of budgetary control was introduced which set fixed limits of expenditure for various units against an estimated given income. The aim was to push financial responsibility as far down the managerial line as possible. The LMSR was also innovative in marketing and research. In the thirties surveys were carried out of market potential in the thirty-five districts of the Company's territory, and a scientific research department was set up which employed sixty science graduates.

Some of the most important changes were made in the group's various locomotive and carriage works. A new system of cost and statistical records was adopted early in the Stamp regime, along with a progressive repair system by which a locomotive moved along a line through the erecting shop at Crewe. The average time spent in the shops was soon reduced from sixty to twelve days (Larkin and Larkin 1988, pp. 106–7, LMSR 1946, p. 6). More rapid progress was made in the thirties towards reducing the number and variety of the group's locomotives. By 1945 there were 8,049 steam and forty diesel locomotives in 133 classes (in 1923 10,316 in about 400 classes). However, 4,438 out of the 1945 total fell into the seventeen classes then deemed to be the company's standard types. Even so almost half (48.6 per cent) of the locomotive stock, 33.3 per cent of the passenger coaches and 31.5 per cent of the freight wagons were still of pre-grouping vintage (LMSR 1946, p. 6).

Improvements in many sections of the company were naturally reflected in the operating department. An internal study covering the years 1927–37 showed gains in efficiency by every criterion. These ranged from the relatively modest (2.0 per cent increase in freight train speed, 1.44 per cent reduction in coal consumption per engine mile) through the very respectable (7.27 per cent increase in wagon miles per engine hour, 4.78 per cent reduction in freight shunting per 100 train miles) to the spectacular (15.66 per cent reduction in coaching shunting per 100 train miles, 20.05 per cent increase in engine miles per locomotive in use, and 30 per cent for the whole locomotive stock).[45] Most of these indicators had appeared even more impressive a few years earlier because by 1937 greater priority was being given to speed and frequency of service than to operating economy. The reality of acceleration was beyond question, and affected local and freight trains as well as the spectacular long-distance passenger expresses. It reflected competitive pressures and was expressed through more powerful locomotives, automatically braked rolling stock, and modernised marshalling yards (Fisher 1938). The thirties also saw a consolidation of standards of reliability and punctuality. The LMSR was already claiming by 1933 that 70 per cent of freight consignments were delivered the day after despatch, and 94 per cent by the second day (LMSR 1946, p. 14). By 1938 Stamp announced 91 per cent punctuality for passenger trains.[46]

Of course not all the groups were as proficient organisationally. Not all faced such fundamental problems. One easily explained paradox is that the most managerially conservative of the four, the GWR (Great Western Railway), was the most financially successful. This was partly because its territory was on balance more prosperous than that of the two northern groups, and also because the GWR, as the largest of the pre-grouping companies, had merely had to absorb a number of far smaller organisations after 1921, and thus experienced far less disruption than the others. The least successful of the big four was the LNER. It was dependent on the freight flows generated by a number of hard-hit heavy industries. Several large or medium-sized pre-grouping companies required painful integration. Nevertheless the LNER did show some distinctive and creative managerial responses. It relied on a divisional structure, with three major centres apart from head office, and with directors being expected to draw on local knowledge and contacts by involving themselves in divisional affairs. The LNER also developed the most effective traffic apprenticeship scheme for the training of future senior managers. Recruited partly internally, and partly from the universities, this institution was sometimes thought to explain the high proportion of ex-LNER personnel in senior positions in British Railways (Hughes 1992, p. 173, Bonavia 1980, p. 71).

7   The refocusing of the issue

Although nationalisation never appeared imminent until after the 1945 election, it has been plausibly suggested that it 'was never far below the surface of political debate' (Gourvish 1986, p. 15) in the inter-war years, and more especially in the 1930s. A cluster of new developments at the beginning of the decade brought the issue back into focus. These were the Boscawen and Weir reports, the London Passenger Transport Board (LPTB), renewed pressure from labour following the 1931 pay cuts, and underlying all these factors, the crisis of profitability. Most of these considerations were mobilised in a slightly alarmist article in *The Accountant* in mid 1931, which anticipated early nationalisation on unfavourable terms. It drew attention to the very low market price of railway stock, the dependence of the Weir recommendations on state subsidy, and the fact that the government's plans for London transport 'may be used as an argument for the nationalisation of the main lines'.[47] All these were points of real substance, especially coming from a source basically unsympathetic to nationalisation. And they omitted growing labour discontent. The 1931 decision by the National Wages Board to reduce wages provoked both a pro-nationalisation addendum to the decision by the trade union representatives on the Board, and a deputation to the Prime Minister. When the LPTB finally materialised in 1933, it was generally regarded as a success by both supporters and opponents of nationalisation. The aim of coordination of passenger transport in the capital commanded widespread support, and the method, in the words of one Conservative MP, was 'forced upon us not by theoreticians but by facts' (Macmillan 1933, p. 28). It was the first occasion on which shareowners in private concerns had been compulsorily dispossessed, and compensated with securities in some kind of public corporation. The climate of opinion was further affected by a public statement at the end of 1937 by the LNER chairman, William Whitelaw. He said that provided the terms were fair, he did not think railway stockholders would resist nationalisation. He believed that 'the control of the railway industry by the State has reached a point at which accuracy can barely designate it as a private undertaking'.[48] One reaction was the suggestion from a source friendly to the railway interest that £856 million would be an appropriate, if hypothetical, price for the state to pay. This figure was pitched high, but more remarkable than the precise calculation was the fact of public debate about compensation terms, initiated by the railway camp, in the absence of any immediate threat of nationalisation.[49]

One basic limitation from which the inter-war railways could not escape was their division into four groups. Consolidation around four poles was a slow and painful process, but still left them well short of unity, even within their own sector, let alone the whole transport system. Each of the four standardised to a large extent on a company, not a national basis. On one flank they were open to all the normal criticisms attracted by oligopolies and cartels, and on the other invited the thought that if one hundred-plus companies would go into four, then why should four not be made into one. The four did stick together, often through the medium of the Railway Companies Association, and were sometimes said to move at the pace of the slowest. One literal application of that point was the agreement to avoid competition on train speed, which held good until the early thirties. Problems were caused in various respects by insufficiency of either competition or coordination. Butterfield's study of the LNER's passenger policy found examples where every proposal to economise by reducing services met objections based on competitive considerations. When pooling with the LMSR was finally instituted, very little was done to exploit it, except for minor savings on a few local services. Coordination of timetables between companies was another area in which progress was minimal (Butterfield 1986, pp. 27–32). A final failure of coordination was the inability of the companies to develop the proposals of the Gore–Browne report of October 1942, which was probably their last attempt at a positive approach to issues of post-war organisation.

There had been agreement on the basic principles of private ownership, the need to combine road and rail interests, and the value of a central board and executive. But this intiative foundered on the insistence of the companies on keeping their separate identities after the war (Gourvish 1986, pp. 22–3).

Within the formidable constraints of their situation, the railway companies achieved a good deal between the grouping and nationalisation, including a respectable standard of efficiency in routine operations. The main deficiencies were those of omission, and related usually to shortage of capital for purposes of investment and modernisation, plus their inability, unaided, to bring about unification and coordination of transport. Derogatory comments by critics of the industry and advocates of nationalisation were not usually directed against the general quality of railway management and services, but were concentrated instead on the poor physical condition, or obsolescence of railway equipment, along with the failure to electrify. Morrison's own typical line of criticism was exemplified by his remarks that much of the railway system was 'really not very creditable before the war', that much of the rolling stock was 'pretty bad', that there was 'much sheer obsolescence', that many of the stations were 'the most dreary things imaginable'. Electrification, in contrast, would have produced 'cleaner and brighter railways'. Dalton saw things the same way when he referred to 'a very poor bag of physical assets'.[50]

Labour and trade union spokesmen usually expressed confidence in railway staff and management, and in their willingness to cooperate with each other.[51] It was assumed that the professional abilities of railway employees, up to a senior level, could be abstracted from the context of private ownership. Directors and shareholders, on the other hand, were associated with financial and stock exchange considerations, and were seen as representative of particular interests, both their own and those of other companies. Their role was one which distorted and divided the transport system, rather than helping to make it work efficiently. Under a nationalised regime, in contrast, railways would be run by a semi-autonomous public corporation, with board members appointed on the basis of ability and experience, with no concern other than the public good. Under independent and disinterested management, such a concern would be 'absolutely free to go for sheer efficiency right from the beginning'.[52]

Before the end of the thirties Morrison and his co-thinkers had made out a strong case for nationalisation as 'good business for the nation' (Labour Party 1932). They had done so through a coherent analysis of the shortcomings of the inter-war transport system. It was one which became more persuasive as the 1921 settlement was slowly drained of credibility. Gradual revision of the regulatory regime, though favourable to the railways, always lagged behind events, and left the companies unable to contrive an independent financial salvation. In the context of a general decline in belief in the efficiency of competition, the long-term advocates of nationalisation were gradually joined by many others in preference for this solution rather than a continuation of non-intervention and hope for an effective voluntary road–rail agreement. The economic effects of war and the result of the 1945 election completed the change in the balance of the argument.

NOTES

1 Sir Ralph Wedgwood, in *The Times*, 25 June 1937.
2 *Railway Gazette*, 10 December 1920 and 14 January 1921.
3 *The Economist*, 16 September, 1922.
4 *The Times*, 10 January 1927.
5 *Modern Transport*, 3 December 1938.
6 *Westminster Bank Review*, no. 211, September 1931, pp. 5–7.
7 Ibid., p. 7.
8 *The Accountant*, 31 January 1931.
9 *The Accountant*, 8 April 1933. The labour force peaked at 735,000 in 1921, was still over 700,000 in 1925, but under 600,000 by early 1932.
10 Royal Commission on Transport, Final Report. Additional Recommendations, Cmd 3751 by R. Donald, F. Galton and W. Leach (Boscawen 1931).
11 Ibid., pp. 223–9.
12 Royal Commission on Transport, *Minutes of Evidence*, Evidence of C.T. Cramp, 16 January 1929, and J. Bromley, 17 January 1929 (Boscawen 1931).
13 Next Five Years Group (1935), p. 93.
14 Speech by P. Thorneycroft, Parliamentary Debates, House of Commons, vol. 431, 18 December 1946, cols. 2029–2030.
15 *The Economist*, 27 May 1939.
16 Nationalisation of Transport, no. 8, *Modern Transport*, 9 April 1938.
17 Hansard (1946), Speech by H. Morrison. Parliamentary Debates, House of Commons, vol. 431, 18 December 1946, col. 2076.
18 *The Economist*, 27 February 1937.
19 *The Accountant*, 8 April 1933.
20 *The Economist*, 19 March 1938 and 4 March 1939.
21 Hansard (1925), Speech by Col. Ashley, Parliamentary Debates, House of Commons, vol. 184, 21 May 1925, col. 722.
22 *Railway Gazette*, 1 May 1931, pp. 669–74.
23 *Railway Gazette*, Electrical Supplement, 5 April 1935.
24 Ibid., p. 673.
25 *Railway Gazette*, 1 May 1931, p. 671. Ibid., 15 May 1931.
26 *The Economist*, 18 April 1936.
27 *Railway Gazette*, 1 May 1931, p. 669.
28 *Railway Gazette*, 18 November 1927.
29 *Railway Gazette*, 26 February 1932.
30 Ibid., 19 May 1939.

142   *Gerald Crompton*

31 Hansard (1939), Speech by Sir R. Glyn, Parliamentary Debates, House of Commons, vol. 349, 5 July 1939, col. 1374.
32 Hansard (1946), Speech by H. Morrison. Ibid., col. 1372.
33 Hansard (1946), Speech by H. Morrison. Ibid., vol. 431, 18 December 1946, col. 2078.
34 *Railway Gazette*, 22 March 1940.
35 Next Five Years Group (1935), p. 50.
36 *Modern Transport*, 30 November 1935.
37 *The Economist*, 4 March 1939.
38 Ibid., 5 March 1938.
39 *Railway Gazette*, 16 June 1939.
40 British Railways Press Office, Great Western Railways *et al.* (1946), p. 4.
41 *The Economist*, 4 March 1939.
42 Ibid., 26 March 1938. *The Accountant*, 12 December 1932.
43 *The Accountant*, 13 May 1939.
44 Ibid., 7 March 1931, 9 January 1937.
45 Operating the LMSR, *Railway Gazette*, 27 May 1938.
46 *Railway Gazette*, 3 March 1939.
47 *The Accountant*, 13 June 1931.
48 *Modern Transport*, 1 January 1938. *Railway Gazette*, 31 December 1937.
49 *Modern Transport*, 2 April 1938. The figure was based on twenty years' purchase of the average net revenue for 1923, 1929 and 1937.
50 Hansard (1946), Speeches by H. Dalton and H. Morrison. Parliamentary Debates, House of Commons, vol. 431, 17 December 1946, col. 1809, and 18 December 1946, col. 2072 and 2078.
51 Speech by W. Sparks, ibid., 18 December 1946, col. 2046.
52 Speech by H. Morrison, ibid., 18 December 1946, col. 2079.

REFERENCES

The Accountant (1931–9).
Balfour (1929), *Final Report*, Committee on Trade and Industry, Cmd 3282.
Bonavia, M.R. (1980), *The Four Great Railways*, Newton Abbot: David and Charles.
Boscawen (1931), Royal Commission on Transport. *Final Report, with Additional Recommendations*, Cmd 3751.
British Railways Press Office (1944), *British Railways in Peace and War*, London.
Butterfield, P. (1986), 'Grouping pooling and competition', *Journal of Transport History*, 7: 2.
Compton, M. and Bott, E.H. (1940), *British Industry*, London: Drummond.
Cox, E.C. (1937), 'The progress of the Southern Railway electrification', *Journal of the Institute of Transport*, 18 (January).
Crompton, G.W. (1985), '"Efficient and economical working"?: the performance of the railway companies 1923–33', *Business History*, 27: 2.
The Economist (1922 and 1936–9).
Fisher, S.H. (1939), 'Acceleration of Railway Services', *Journal of the Institute of Transport*, 20 : February.

Fox, W. (1932), *Ten Years of Railway Finance*, London: Labour Party Research Department.

Gourvish, T.R. (1986), *British Railways 1948–73*, Cambridge University Press.

Great Western Railway, London Midland and Scottish Railway, London North Eastern Railway, Southern Railway (1946), *British Railways and the Future*, London.

Hannah, L.J. (1979), *Electricity Before Nationalisation*, London: Macmillan.

Hansard (1925, 1939, 1946), Parliamentary Debates, House of Commons.

Hughes, G. (1992), 'The Board of Directors of the LNER', *Journal of Transport History*, 13: 2.

Johnston, K. (1949), *British Railways and Economic Recovery*, London: Clerke and Cockeran.

Kidd, H.C. (1929), *A New Era for British Railways*, London: Benn.

Labour Party (1932), 'The national planning of transport', London.

Larkin, E.J. and Larkin, J.G. (1988), *The Railway Workshops of Britain*, London: Macmillan.

London Midland and Scottish Railway (1946), *London Midland and Scottish Railway, A Record of Large Scale Organisation and Management 1923–46*, London.

Macmillan, H. (1933), *Reconstruction*, London: Macmillan.

Modern Transport (1935, 1938).

Next Five Years Group (1935), *The Next Five Years: An Essay in Political Agreement*, London: Macmillan.

Railways Companies Association (1937), 'The railway crisis', London.

    (1939), 'Clear the lines!', London.

Railway Gazette (1920–40).

Semmens, P. (1986), *History of the Great Western Railway, vol. II*, London: Allen and Unwin.

The Times (1927, 1937).

Westminster Bank Review (1931).

White, H.P. (1982), *A Regional History of the Railways of Great Britain, Vol. II, Southern England*, Newton Abbot: David and Charles.

Williamson, J.W. (1933), *A British Railway Behind the Scenes*, London: Benn.

7 The motives for gas nationalisation: practicality or ideology?

John F. Wilson

When the gas industry came into public ownership in May 1949, this terminated over ten years of debate about the most effective form of organisation for a utility which had evolved as an essentially localised service. The atomistic nature of gas supply and its ownership structure, intensive competition from electricity, socialist doctrine, the need for an integrated national fuel policy, and a feeling that the wartime planning techniques ought to be retained once victory had been achieved were all factors of significance in this debate. In analysing why the industry was nationalised we need to assess what role they played in affecting the final decisions. Essentially, we shall be trying to distinguish between the orthodox view that nationalisation was driven by ideological forces, as opposed to questions of industrial organisation as emphasised by Millward (chapter 1 above, also 1991), by tracing the main events in a story which reveals a variety of influences determining the final outcome.

In identifying the main reasons why gas supply was nationalised, it is important to discuss Millward's (1991, p. 19) interpretation of the reasons for the late 1940s move towards public ownership of network industries. Millward is less concerned with ideological influences, stressing instead inter-war attempts at state-assisted rationalisation, the ineffectiveness of arms-length government regulation of utilities, and the need for post-war reconstruction, revealing what he claims to be 'a political consensus for the reorganisation of the undertakings in the network industries into large business units'. More recently, Millward and Singleton (1992, pp. 2, 12 and 29) have also claimed that 'the broad support for public ownership came from the desire to improve industrial organisation', pointing to the groundswell of 'informed opinion' which advocated 'larger business units in gas supply, electricity retail distribution and coal . . . on a regional or subnational scale'. They are willing to concede that 'it is not possible to prise apart the political and economic justifications for nationalisation', but their primary emphasis is on the desire to improve the performance of these industries by forming public corporations charged with the task of concentrating production and distribution. Morgan (1984, p. 96) also links the ideological with the functional, emphasising how in the 1940s the socialist belief in public ownership was associated with central planning and improved economic performance. On the other hand, Cairncross (1985, p. 494) feels that nationalisation was 'a response to strongly-held political and moral convictions', albeit in the context of 'an economic philosophy favouring large, nationwide units of control', indicating the central importance of ideological factors in this move towards public ownership (Clegg 1952, p. 426).

These introductory points serve to focus attention on the key issues influencing the mid-twentieth-century debate about nationalisation. Kelf-Cohen (1958, p. 110) was prepared to state that by 1948 'the gas industry was even anxious to be nationalised', but this view ignores both the historical reluctance of many undertakings to envisage large-scale integration and the circumstances which dictated the industry's response to the political threat, indicating the need for a more detailed analysis of the event. Government papers, technical journals, independent surveys and internal industry reviews provide much of the material for this assessment, giving a balanced insight into the greatest political challenge affecting gas supply since the emergence of municipal trading in the mid nineteenth century.

1   Background history

When the gas industry emerged in the early nineteenth century, it was characterised by a highly localised nature, with undertakings outside London having been formed to supply a particular town and its immediate environs (Wilson 1991, pp. 1–56, PEP 1939, pp. 41–55). One must also note that until the 1880s gas was used almost exclusively for lighting purposes, but with the advent of electric lighting around that time diversification into heating, cooking and even industrial markets was being attempted with some success. As table 7.1 indicates, both sales and the number of consumers expanded significantly in the period 1882–1912, in spite of the competition from electricity. On the other hand, sales per consumer had fallen by over 15 per cent, but this simply reflected the success of the introduction of prepayment meters after 1880 which allowed more working-class houses to take gas, while a new incandescent mantle provided a much cheaper and better quality of lighting for the domestic user. One should also note that the substantial rise in number of undertakings recorded in table 7.1 largely arose because many un-authorised ventures were securing statutory status in that period, the vast majority of communities having established a public gas supply prior to 1880. In effect, the average size of undertakings, measured in sales and

Table 7.1. *The British gas industry 1882–1937*

	No. of statutory undertakings	Gas sales (m. therms)	No. of consumers	Capital invested (£m.)	Sales per consumer (therms)
1882	500	333	1,972,000	50.8	169.0
1912	826	995	6,876,000	137.0	144.6
1921	797	1,177	7,599,000	153.1	154.8
1930	767	1,383	9,344,000	194.6	148.7
1937	706	1,494	11,010,000	225.8	134.6

Sources: PEP (1939) and Heyworth Report (1945).

capital, was rising at unprecedented rates in the thirty years prior to the First World War, emphasising how at this time the industry was able to deal effectively with the challenge posed by its new rival.

It was in the inter-war years that the competition from electricity in the lighting, cooking and heating markets really started to affect the gas industry. Gas sales continued to grow between 1921 and 1937, as table 7.1 indicates, but the rate of growth was much slower than in the earlier era, while between 1929 and 1934 they actually fell (Chantler 1938, p. 19). In contrast, total electricity sales had expanded nearly six-fold between 1920 and 1939, from 3,707 gigawatt-hours to 22,234 gigawatt-hours, a trend accelerated by the construction of a national grid under the auspices of the state-created Central Electricity Board after 1926 (Hannah 1979, pp. 427–9). One must also emphasise how gas sales per consumer (see table 7.1) continued their long downward trend, because the industry developed a growing dependence on domestic prepayment consumers who were hiring increasingly efficient domestic gas appliances, while the incandescent mantle only required one-eighth the amount of gas used by its predecessors (PEP 1939, p. 81). In fact, by 1937 lighting accounted for only 7 per cent of the total gas load, even though approximately 70 per cent of total sales was used in the home. This indicates how important cooking and heating had become to the industry by the inter-war years, and in recognition of the changing nature of the business the 1920 Gas Regulation Act allowed undertakings to charge according to the heat capacity of gas (the therm), rather than its luminosity value (measured in cubic feet). The industrial market was also certainly beginning to expand at this time, but in 1939 it still only took between 10 and 20 per cent of gas sales, and most attention was still being paid to serving the domestic consumer (PEP 1939, p. 49).[1]

The sluggish growth of gas sales, the fall in consumption per customer, and the ascendancy of electricity in lighting and industrial markets were naturally worrying trends, but the internal response only highlighted some of the more fundamental obstacles to mounting a successful counterattack. On the one hand, vigorous publicity campaigns were introduced by the larger undertakings in an attempt to expand and diversify sales, and the British Commercial Gas Association (founded in 1912) continued and intensified its efforts at persuading housewives in particular of the advantages of gas cooking and heating. At the same time, the latter revealed only the need to coordinate many other aspects of the industry – tariffs, appliances and costs – if national campaigns were to have any impact (PEP 1939, pp. 148–9). The market potential in the considerable comparative advantage gas possessed over electricity in the field of heating could only be effectively exploited when sales teams were provided with the resources to contact potential and actual consumers,[2] but it was clear by the 1930s that many undertakings did not possess the kind of expertise required in this situation. Furthermore, there seemed little likelihood that the necessary degree of coordination would ever emerge as a result of the industry's own efforts.

2   The economics of gas supply

The gas industry up to 1949, because of its localised nature, had always been characterised by a pyramidical structure, with a small minority of substantial undertakings and a plethora of relatively tiny operations. This is borne out by the information supplied in table 7.2, where we see one company (the Gas Light & Coke Co, of London) at the peak, a further 179 undertakings selling over one million therms per annum, and 1,070 authorised and non-statutory businesses forming an extended base. In fact, 86 per cent of sales came from 180 suppliers, highlighting the potential case for wholesale changes in structure if the industry was to improve its competitiveness by rationalising production and enhancing its marketing skills. At the same time, gas managers were increasingly concerned at the decline in returns on capital employed in the gas industry during the 1930s, with companies earning just 5.2 per cent on average in 1937, compared to 5.8 per cent in 1930, and municipal undertakings experiencing a fall from 6 per cent to 4.6 per cent over those years (BoT 1937, part II, p. 3). There is no evidence in the Board of Trade returns of a mass write down of capital employed in the industry in order to maintain dividends, but with profits falling and competition intensifying the very future of the industry was being questioned very seriously.

In view of these problems, it might seem surprising that the gas industry was not moving towards the kind of grid structure employed in electricity

Table 7.2. *The size distribution of gas undertakings in 1937*

Annual sales (m. therms)	No.	Sales	% of total sales
Authorised			
250 +	1	253.8	16.3
100–249.9	—	—	—
10–99.9	23	602.5	38.8
1–9.9	156	475.5	30.6
Under 1	526	163.2	10.2
Unauthorised			
Under 1	544	56.0	3.6
Total	1,250	1,551.0	—

Source: PEP (1939), p. 29.

supply after 1926. One of the obvious pitfalls to avoid when discussing a possible rationalisation of gas supply, however, is likening these two industries. While electricity suppliers could exploit substantial economies of scale by generating from a small number of large stations and transmitting at high voltages across a nationally integrated grid distribution system, gas suppliers were not in such an advantageous position. The key criterion to consider was the position of each gasworks in relation to both its coal supplies and market, bearing in mind the relative costs of delivering fuel, as opposed to the price of supplying gas from a large works to a neighbouring community. Coal-gas was produced at such a low pressure that distribution costs could be prohibitively expensive when considering integrating systems, reducing the benefits to be gained from producing in centralised works. A further factor to consider was accessibility to a market for the coke produced in town-gas manufacture, because by the inter-war years most undertakings relied on the income generated from this by-product (and many others) to such an extent that its loss could result in a significant increase in the price of gas. Indeed, measured simply in terms of production and distribution costs, a small isolated works could be just as efficient as its much larger counterparts, confounding any suggestions that gas supply ought to imitate the grid system established for the electricity supply industry in 1926 (Pryke 1971, p. 366, Wormsley 1954, pp. 16–31). On the other hand, a strong case could be made for regionalising gas supply by concentrating production and distribution in areas where inefficient undertakings could be linked into larger, well-managed businesses with the resources to exploit any available economies of scale.

There was, indeed, a growing number of expert commentators who were advocating a 'regional' solution to the industry's situation, and some were willing to provide estimates of minimum efficient size for supply undertakings. A PEP study (1939, p. 119) identified the notional figure of one million therms as 'large enough for economic production' (including a full range of by-products), and by this measure table 7.2 indicates that 1,070 undertakings could be defined as uneconomic. By the mid 1940s, the influential Heyworth committee (1945, paras. 87–8) was arguing that, after carbonisation techniques in large works had been improved by the application of the latest improvements, and the use of high-pressure distribution had been diffused more extensively, the minimum efficient size could be raised to 1.25 million therms per annum. Heyworth was particularly concerned that many of the smaller works operated with a technical efficiency of just 65 per cent, compared to the weighted average of 75 per cent for the whole industry, arguing persuasively that in densely populated regions considerable scope existed for interconnections and plant closures.

The PEP and Heyworth reports had consequently identified considerable possibilities for rationalisation of gas supply, a point further substantiated by Wormsley's analysis (1954, p. 31) of gas supply economics. His figures revealed that net production costs would fall from 19.0 pennies per therm in undertakings with an output of up to 50,000 therms per annum to 8.66 pennies per therm where output exceeded one million therms. Further increases in scale only provided marginal cost reductions,[3] but as 680 of the 998 undertakings in 1950 produced less than one million therms per annum it is evident that opportunities existed for some improvements in this area. Wormsley (1954, p. 31) also pointed to the inability of these smaller undertakings to introduce the most efficient methods of gas manufacture, namely, vertical retorts and mechanical stoking, because 'the indivisibilities inherent in all these techniques only permitted their installation when the heavy capital cost could be spread over a large output'. Of course, bearing in mind the isolated location of some small supply operations, high transmission costs could still have prevented the interconnection of all 680 networks with a larger neighbour, but because most of these smaller undertakings were within thirty miles of a plant producing over one million therms annually Wormsley was confident that the use of high-pressure transmission techniques would lead to the development of highly efficient regional grids.[4]

It is clear, then, that, while a national grid was not an economically viable proposition, most authorities agreed that the atomistic structure so typical of gas supply up to the 1930s should be substantially overhauled along regional lines. This innovation would not only lead to some economies of scale in the production and distribution of gas and its by-products, it would provide even more substantial gains in the areas of finance and bulk purchasing, while in marketing and personnel recruitment significant deficiences could also be eradicated. The personnel issue was, in fact, seen as one of fundamental importance to the future of gas supply, Heyworth (1945, para. 238) giving as one of the main considerations determining his advocacy of larger groupings the hope that: 'The units should be able to attract personnel at least the equal in imagination, initiative, judgement and energy of those of other fuel industries.' Many of the smaller undertakings were especially poorly staffed in crucial areas like technical development, marketing and sales, with 'Jacks-of-all-trades' running many different aspects of the business for which they were palpably ill-equipped (PEP 1939, p. 153). The medium-sized and larger undertakings were much better served by the steady supply of articled engineers who had passed through the Institution of Gas Engineers' accreditation system, but it could be fairly claimed that this created a bias towards the technical side of the industry, leading to some neglect of the commercial areas like marketing and sales. An additional issue of concern was the propensity of municipal gas undertakings to pay much lower salaries than those available in private industry, leading to the recruitment of poorly qualified staff in what were some of the largest gas supply businesses (Heyworth 1945, para. 74). These defects in the overall quality of both technical and commercial staff had to change if gas supply was to compete more effectively with its rivals, providing a challenge to the whole culture of an industry which had been slow to develop the required degree of cooperation in these, and many other, areas.

3   The regional solution

The earliest proposal for a regional solution to the problems outlined in the last sections had actually come from an economist, P. Chantler (1938, pp. 134–6), who in the debates of the following decade played a decisive role in fashioning the rationalisation proposals eventually pursued at the national level. Apart from his own book, Chantler was also largely responsible for drafting the PEP report (1939, pp. 173–6) which advocated the creation of a small number of area gas supply authorities as the most effective means of achieving the necessary degree of coordination in engineering, sales and personnel policies. Both reports also stressed the need for a central authority to supervise the coordination process, but, as PEP concluded, rigid centralisation was to be avoided in order not to stifle local initiative and prevent management from losing touch with conditions within individual communities. On the other hand, a central body would be capable of standardising gas pressures across the country, reducing the need for domestic appliance manufacturers to modify their products according to local circumstances.[5] Bulk purchasing of coal and domestic appliances, easier access to capital, and the coordination of commercial and technical policies would also be possible in this revised structure, providing considerable economies of scale which had only ever been available to the very large undertakings.

Of course, as table 7.1 reveals, during the inter-war period the number of statutory undertakings had fallen, from 797 in 1921 to 706 in 1937, while in the 1930s forty non-statutory suppliers were absorbed (Wormsley 1954, p. 4). One of the reasons for this trend was the formation of joint boards among municipal gas ventures, but the last of these occurred in 1922. Of far greater significance was, firstly, the concentration of gas production in London, accounting for thirty-four absorptions between 1920 and 1938 (Heyworth 1945, para. 19), and, secondly, the emergence of holding companies after the 1932 Gas Undertakings Act had allowed the acquisition of financial interests in other undertakings without parliamentary approval. The 1933 report of the Gas Legislation Committee, instituted by the Board of Trade, was especially supportive of the holding company movement, because it could offer to smaller operations the possibilities of easier access to capital, a central technical and commercial service, and the bulk purchase of coal and appliances on more favourable terms (Heyworth 1945, para. 20). On the other hand, there were limitations to their impact at that time as a result of a variety of economic and legal factors largely beyond the control of individual holding companies.

To contemporaries, holding companies seemed to presage many of the developments later advocated by those in favour of regional concentration, with *Gas World* (1 May 1937, p. 423) using the headline 'Aspiration and Achievement' to report the activities of one of the largest, the United Kingdom Gas Corporation. By 1945, fourteen holding companies had acquired 310 separate operations, resulting in the closure of fifty-three gas works and the laying of interconnecting mains between 126 towns (Wormsley 1954, p. 11). The leading businesses like the United Kingdom Gas Corporation and the South Eastern Gas Corporation had also established central management services which provided extensive technical, commercial and financial support to their subsidiaries, linking as many of the operations as possible and developing a cohesive strategy for future progress.[6] Unfortunately, however, this kind of integration was not pursued as extensively in all holding companies, largely because acquisition policies were pursued in a haphazard fashion even in the well-managed organisations, with little attention paid to geographical or economic factors. For example, six of the holding companies had subsidiaries in more than three of the areas later established as administrative regions at nationalisation (Pryke 1971, p. 365). It is fair to note, though, that a lack of cooperation from neighbouring undertakings often limited the degree of holding company integration, resulting in a general failure to exploit the potential benefits of this movement. On the other hand, a distinct lack of planning also contributed to this development, and once again another opportunity to improve performance through greater coordination appears to have been missed.

Another fruitful means by which integration could have proceeded in the inter-war years was the purchase by small undertakings of a bulk supply of gas, particularly where cheap coke-oven gas could be secured from colliery or steel companies. A Select Committee set up in 1930 to investigate the feasibility of building a coke-oven gas grid had rejected the idea of a national system, but it did recommend that the Sheffield Gas Co. should be granted powers to move along these lines (Chantler 1938, pp. 39–43). This idea was also seized upon by the United Kingdom Gas Corporation in 1939, when they formed the West Yorkshire Gas Distribution Co., an unique venture whose function was to purchase and supply coke-oven gas along a grid to West Riding towns (Heyworth 1945, paras. 22 and 72). This system proved to be a technical and commercial success, but relatively few gas undertakings were willing to follow the example. In fact, by 1945 in total fifty-three undertakings purchased 241 million therms of coke-oven gas, accounting for just 12 per cent of total gas sales, and one can only conclude that the full potential in this relationship between coke producers and gas suppliers had yet to be exploited. PEP (1947, pp. 193–9) regarded such statistics as further evidence of failure, and in demanding a central body to negotiate agreements which would provide easier access to a cheap source of gas and would overcome the main obstacles to greater integration, it was underlining how, from the late 1930s, the movement for change was beginning to gather momentum.

4   Obstacles to integration

Undoubtedly, one of the main reasons why up to the 1940s gas supply had not moved towards a more rational structure was the intransigence of local authority gas committees. Municipalisation of gas supply had not been as extensive as in other utilities, but as table 7.3 reveals 274 local authorities accounted for almost 39 per cent of sales from statutory undertakings by 1945, while in Scotland and many English counties north of Birmingham the proportion would have been considerably higher (Wilson 1991, p. 56). The 1920 Gas Regulation Act had allowed neighbouring municipal bodies to merge their supply and distribution systems, but by 1945 only five of these joint boards had been formed, the last one being in 1922, while only seven local authority undertakings featured in the 112 gas industry mergers between 1921 and 1935 (Wormsley 1954, p. 9). As Heyworth (1945, para. 74) noted: 'Local patriotism often makes it difficult for municipal undertakings to co-operate with surrounding undertakings in framing joint schemes . . .', an example being the refusal of Glasgow Corporation to participate in a central Scotland coke-oven grid because it would have meant the scrapping of its plant (PEP 1939, p. 124). The key problems with this insular attitude were that, firstly, no rule existed which declared a natural relationship between town boundaries and the economically appropriate gas supply area, while, secondly, most of the larger towns also ran their own electricity undertakings, inhibiting any experiments with gas prices as a means of generating more sales (Heyworth 1945, para. 74).

The intransigence of local authorities had only served to reinforce the impression gained by outside commentators that the gas industry was incapable of reorganising itself (PEP 1939, p. 127). Of course, one must not heap all the blame on to municipal ventures, because as Wormsley (1954, p. 9) noted the vast majority of small private companies were just as loath to merge their systems and lose the comfortable earnings to be made from retaining control and ownership. Nevertheless, the arguments of commentators like Chantler and PEP, that regional groupings and a central authority ought to be established, were given additional strength when such conservatism was demonstrated by so many undertakings. The national industry organisations like the National Gas Council (founded in 1916) had never been intended as vehicles for rationalisation policies, although the British Gas Federation had been formed in 1934 to provide a forum for elaborating a consensus view on general matters of gas industry policy (Williams 1981, p. 74). These bodies purported to represent a membership accounting for up to 90 per cent of gas sales, but at no time was it ever envisaged that they would have powers to compel any undertaking, large or small, private or municipal, to follow preconceived strategies. Indeed, PEP (1939, p. 160) remarked on the British Gas Federation's lack of influence in the 1930s, and only when in 1945 the British Gas Council appeared as the industry's response to the threat of nationalisation did senior gas men wake up to the need for a body with powers to negotiate for real change. By then, however, as we shall see, the industry was faced with a *fait accompli*, and its traditional belief in self government was about to be shattered.

An indication of the lack of success achieved by the British Gas Federation and its counterparts was the failure to persuade a sceptical

Table 7.3. *The ownership structure of statutory gas undertakings 1910–45*

	1910		1945	
	No.	Sales (M. cu. ft)	No.	Sales (M. cu. ft)
Private	511	115,342	406	225,792
Municipal	298	67,492	274	144,186
Total	809	182,834	680	369,978

Sources: PEP (1939) and Heyworth (1945).

government of the need to up-date a panoply of anachronistic statutory controls which had first been introduced when gas enjoyed a monopoly of the lighting market (Chantler 1938, pp. 96–132). These regulations had naturally been framed in the interests of consumers, but with the intensifying competition from electricity and oil it was obvious to many by the inter-war years that market forces would provide much greater security against exploitation than any artificial limits on prices and dividends (PEP 1939, p. 172). Furthermore, the controls were regarded as an obstacle to the elaboration of more ambitious commercial policies, because of the way in which up to 1920 prices and dividends were linked through the sliding scale first introduced in 1875. The 1920 Gas Regulation Act allowed the introduction of a more flexible pricing code, but even in 1945 only thirty-one statutory companies had adopted this system, while 374 retained the older methods of calculating prices and dividends,[7] indicating a further need for standardisation.

As early as 1928, the National Fuel and Power Committee of the Board of Trade had advocated a greater degree of freedom from such restrictions, but apart from easing the regulations on raising capital little was achieved in the following decade (Chantler 1938, pp. 96–132). During the war, of course, additional regulations were introduced on prices, investment strategy, and mergers, leading Heyworth (1945, para. 132) to conclude that 'a solution must be found which will permit the abolition rather than the perpetuation of these controls'. In this sense, Millward (1991, p. 19) is right to stress the inadequacy of arms-length government regulation as one of the main reasons influencing the move to public ownership, and the Chantler–PEP suggestion of a National Gas Authority with supervisory powers over such matters was regarded by many in the industry as a viable alternative in this highly competitive phase for the industry.

5   The Second World War

It was perhaps unfortunate that the reports by Chantler and PEP proposing radical structural change within the gas industry should have been
published just as the country embarked on a Second World War. Such
were the gas industry's difficulties over that six-year period that management was obliged to concentrate on more immediate issues like the
availability of coal, labour and equipment, and simply keeping the works
at full capacity. In fact, between 1938 and 1945 sales grew by 19 per cent,
from 1,530 to 1,821 million therms, compared to a 27 per cent increase in
sales between 1920 and 1938 (PEP 1947, pp. 170–2). This was achieved
largely as a result of new demands from both industry and domestic
consumers using gas as a substitute for scarce solid fuel. By-products like
benzole and tar were also required in greater quantities, putting considerable strain on an industry badly affected by the combined effect of
extensive bomb damage and severe shortages of labour and equipment.
At the same time, exacerbating these difficulties, the industry was faced
with the rising cost of coal, while the Board of Trade carefully controlled
gas price increases, especially after 1941 (PEP 1947, p. 173). This prevented the accumulation of sufficient reserves for new investment programmes, and as there had been an acute wartime shortage of plant, much
of the industry by 1945 was in a run-down state. This problem had
long-term origins; Wormsley (1954, p. 23) estimated that in 1946 almost
53 per cent of the industry's plant had been laid down prior to 1930. But
the war had certainly prompted the need for a much improved
replacement programme. As PEP (1947, p. 169) noted, 'reserve and
usually old manufacturing plant had been put into permanent commission; plant due for renewal was kept in almost continual service; and new
plant (not always the most suitable, but what could be most rapidly
erected) had to be installed'.

The dilapidated state of much gas-making equipment by 1945 was, of
course, well known to government ministries, because during the war
close contact with such vital industries was maintained by the relevant
authorities. Initially, the Board of Trade was responsible for gas affairs,
but in 1941 a Directorate of Gas Supply was set up to supervise the
industry's war effort, while in 1942 this function was taken over by a
newly established Ministry of Fuel and Power with specific responsibility
for coordinating activity throughout this sector (PEP 1947, pp. 298–9).
This latest development fitted in well with the growing contemporary
interest in the need for a sound national fuel policy, particularly in view of
the economic and industrial relations problems experienced in coalmining
since the 1920s. A National Fuel and Power Committee had appeared as

early as 1928, under the auspices of the Board of Trade, but the two reports it produced failed to arouse much industry support for greater integration (Heyworth 1945, para. 50). Both Chantler (1938, p. 136) and PEP (1939, p. 116) had voiced their proposals for rationalisation of gas production and distribution in the context of a national fuel policy, but it was only in response to wartime conditions that political and industrial attitudes started moving in the same direction on this matter.

There is little doubt that in the early years of the war senior figures in the gas industry were beginning to recognise a need for the kind of changes recommended by Chantler and PEP. The managing director of the United Kingdom Gas Corporation, after talks with the director-general of gas supply at the Board of Trade (E.W. Smith), reported to his board in December 1941 that the company's subsidiaries would have to be integrated more effectively 'if they were to take part in the general reorganisation of the gas industry, which will almost certainly take place after the war' (UKGCBM, 16 December 1941). A report by E.V. Evans (1941) for the National Gas Council in 1941 also echoed these sentiments by proposing the full implementation of the structural changes suggested by Chantler and PEP, and two years later the Post-War Planning Committee of the British Gas Federation (1943) published its scheme for the concentration of production in seven principal areas. The latter proved especially influential, because during 1943 the British Gas Federation endorsed the plans and proposed the formation of a Central Council with statutory powers to compel integration, providing a model on which future progress could be based (PEP 1947, p. 301).

The factors stimulating this conversion to the need for closer integration within the gas industry were no doubt related to the interaction with government ministries increasingly anxious to formulate a cohesive national fuel policy. That such a policy did not take shape at this time need not concern us here, but the gas industry was anxious not to be ignored in the planning stage, and consequently attempts were made to persuade the authorites that wholesale changes were being envisaged. The Ministry of Fuel and Power, however, remained sceptical about the sincerity of these moves, and consequently appointed in June 1944 what came to be known as the Heyworth Committee 'to review the structure and organisation of the Gas Industry, to advise what changes have now become necessary in order to develop and cheapen gas supplies to all types of consumers, and to make recommendations'. It was this committee which was to precipitate a dramatic transformation in the structure and ownership of gas supply, noting that the industry recognised its 'existing structure is restrictive of further progress', yet had only tackled the much-needed organisational changes 'with varying degrees of energy and success' (Heyworth 1945, para. 228).

6   The Heyworth Report and nationalisation

The Heyworth Report, published in December 1945, was momentous because it not only brought to a head all discussion of the plans to reorganise gas supply, it placed the focus of the debate on ownership by coming out in favour of outright nationalisation. This reveals another reason why the industry had been moving in favour of structural change since the late 1930s, because it had been known since at least 1937 that the Labour Party intended to bring such utilities into public ownership when a majority could be secured in the House of Commons (Morgan 1984, p. 95). PEP (1939, p. 159) had also claimed that nationalisation would find general support 'if it can be suggested that the structure of the gas industry is unsuited to modern needs and that its outlook is unprogressive', striking a note of fear in the wartime deliberations of gas industry planning committees.

There is no doubt that up to 1945, with the exception of a few municipal undertakings,[8] the gas industry was stridently opposed to nationalisation. Even the Association of Municipal Corporations and the Association of Smaller Municipal Gas Corporations were in faovur of retaining the prevailing ownership arrangements (PEP 1947, p. 302), albeit with much more use of the joint board structure to provide for integration and rationalisation, while all the evidence Heyworth received from the private sector was unambiguously against public ownership. The main industry bodies were equally dismissive of the benefits arising from nationalisation, members of the British Gas Council declaring by 461 votes to seventy-eight against the principle. Notwithstanding this firm position, the same organisation also voted 423 to ninety in favour of cooperating with the Ministry of Fuel and Power should the industry be taken into public ownership (*Gas World*, 31 August 1946, p. 215). The reasons given for this apparently swift change of mind were those expressed by British Gas Council (BGC) Chairman, A.E. Sylvester, who had earlier stated that the industry should not take part in political controversy (*Gas World*, 15 December 1945, p. 586). More realistically, though, members were much more concerned about influencing Ministry decisions on such issues as compensation, organisation and management, leading them to mandate the organisation to negotiate favourable terms. At the same time, the BGC delegates were left in no doubt as to the Labour government's position on the matter, Emmanuel Shinwell, the Minister of Fuel and Power, stating firmly at their first meeting that the act of nationalisation 'was not open to discussion'.[9]

The election of a Labour government committed to the principle of nationalisation had consequently precipitated a sharp change in the debate about possible changes in the organisation of gas supply. In several senses, the Heyworth Report had actually been a victory for those advocating the need for a rationalisation of gas supply, because he recommended the division of the country into ten regions and the establishment of regional boards with responsibility for managing all the undertakings within their areas (Heyworth 1945, para. 248). These were the common denominators linking schemes proposed by Chantler, PEP and the British Gas Federation, although Heyworth failed to include a national authority in his plan,[10] giving instead the Ministry of Fuel and Power much greater powers of intervention than the industry would have liked. The BGC was able to persuade the Ministry of the need for a central coordinating body, and it is no coincidence that the first chairman and vice-chairman of the nationalised body also held those positions in that organisation.[11] On the other hand, of course, most of the industry would have preferred private, rather than public, ownership, but on this issue the government was not going to change its mind.

In the period leading up to vesting day on 1 May 1949, much of the BGC's efforts were devoted to ensuring that both adequate compensation was provided to former owners, and a national body was built into the constitution of a future organisation. To facilitate these negotiations, in July 1947 the British Commercial Gas Association and the National Gas Council were liquidated and all their affairs taken over by the British Gas Council, while two months later plans were submitted to the Ministry outlining the need for a central body and thirteen area boards (*Gas World*, 5 July 1947, p. 7). In fact, twelve area boards were to be formed in 1949, after the Ministry had investigated the matter further,[12] but the industry's plans were to prevail over those of Heyworth on the subject of a central body, confirming the efficacy of the cooperation policy pursued from the outset. The government was to face strident opposition to its Bill in parliament, largely because by 1948 the Conservatives were beginning to rebuild some of the confidence lost after their shattering election defeat of 1945 (Kelf-Cohen 1973, p. 56). There is no evidence, however, that the industry encouraged this rearguard action, although *Gas World* (14 May 1948, p. 773) featured a photograph of the six Tory MPs who fought against nationalisation at a record-breaking sitting at committee stage under the headline: 'They Battled to the Last!'.

While gas industry managers in general were mostly against nationalisation, it is perhaps important to note that the trade unions representing most manual and clerical workers were mainly in favour of the move (Nabb 1986, p. 523). By the 1940s, after a series of union mergers, manual workers were represented by either the General & Municipal Workers' Union or the Transport & General Workers' Union, while the municipal clerical staff had been recruited into the National Association of Local

Government Officers,[13] and these organisations supported Labour policy on the need for public ownership. In fact, there had been relatively few industrial relations problems to handicap the industry's performance (Heyworth 1945, para. 156), partly because of the many co-partnership schemes which the larger gas companies had introduced since the 1890s. A National Joint Industrial Council had also been formed in 1919, and under the effective chairmanship of Sir David Milne-Watson this had become an effective negotiating medium between management and workers. Kelf-Cohen (1973, p. 164) has actually claimed that 'workers in the gas and electricity industries . . . showed no enthusiasm for expelling the capitalist' in the 1940s, but he ignores both the degree of municipal ownership in the industry, and the lack of any active lobbying by the unions in favour of private ownership. Indeed, many leading trade unionists accepted positions on the Area Boards created by the 1948 Gas Act, indicating a fair degree of support for nationalisation which was not always forthcoming from this sector in other industries, for example steel.

7   Ideology or practicality?

The compliant approach adopted by the industry and its official representatives could be used as evidence to support Millward's (1991, p. 19) argument that by the mid 1940s 'an opportunity for public intervention' had appeared which allowed the Labour government to nationalise the network utilities and coalmining. As we noted earlier, Millward feels that 'a political consensus' in support of this policy existed at that time, a consensus which was based on the pre-war interventionist approach towards the old staple industries, the inadequacy of government regulations on prices, dividends and quality of service, and a perceived need for planned reconstruction. Morgan (1984, p. 109) has also noted how, in explaining why 'the champions of private enterprise had only limited zest for the fight', one must remember the widespread enthusiasm for establishing 'the new era of planning, rationalisation, and integration that Labour seemed to embody'. Indeed, planning was a key feature of the post-war consensus, and when one combines this with the ideological commitment to nationalisation expressed in Labour Party strategy there seemed to be little room to manoeuvre for the network utilities.

Kelf-Cohen (1958, p. 114) has argued that nationalisation occurred 'at a most convenient time for the [gas] industry', particularly in view of the dilapidated state of much gas-making and storage plant, the bulk of which he described as 'scrap'. We have already seen how in 1945 the industry was faced with an enormous investment bill as a result of both the attentions of the Luftwaffe and an inability to replace worn-out plant worked to full capacity at a time of acute shortages in this area. There is no reliable estimate of the investment needs of gas supply in 1945, but it is interesting to note that in the eleven years following nationalisation £401.5 million (at current prices) was spent augmenting the net value of fixed assets (Kelf-Cohen 1973, p. 58), while Heyworth (1945, para. 270) put the value of the industry in 1945 at £272.25 million. Clearly, undertakings would have been faced with the urgent need to raise substantial quantities of capital, and in the mid 1940s such sums might not have been forthcoming. In the first place, their major rival, electricity, had already been nationalised, along with coalmining, and bearing in mind the government's avowed aim to fashion an integrated national fuel policy it would have been extremely difficult to persuade investors that the gas industry could have survived as an independent entity. Indeed, it would have been foolhardy had the gas industry resisted government policy, and the fact that nationalisation occurred after coal and electricity supply indicates how far down in the order of priorities it had fallen by that time. Falling under the state's wing provided the guarantee that gas supply would have access to the capital required in participating in the development of any new energy strategy, securing the industry's future more reliably than under the old system.

Of course, when one considers the Labour government's wholehearted commitment to nationalisation, it is important to stress that the British Gas Council was powerless to prevent this change in ownership. Moreover, the run-down state of the industry, the earlier nationalisation of coal and electricity supply, and an increasingly weak market position convinced senior gas men that compliance was the only rational strategy to pursue in the collectivist atmosphere of the 1940s. On the other hand, it is interesting to hypothesise about what Heyworth would have recommended had he been reporting to anything other than a Labour government which had already expressed its wish to acquire utilities as part of its commitment to plan the economy 'from the ground up'. Heyworth, after all, would have been persuaded of the need to restructure gas supply after listening to the evidence produced by most of his witnesses, but in between his appointment and the publication of the report a newly elected government had stated its intention to nationalise the industry, and this could have been the decisive factor in fashioning his final recommendations. He could just as well have proposed a scheme with no element of public ownership, having listened to the ideas of the British Gas Federation, but this would have been rejected by Labour as only a half-way house in its move towards nationalised industries run by large public corporations.

By the 1940s, there was undoubtedly a widespread belief in the need for both the regionalisation of gas supply and the formulation of more effective regulations governing the industry, sentiments reinforced by the industry's inertia and failure to envisage wholesale internal change. At the same time, much greater political interest was being shown in the need to coordinate activity in the fuel sector, and with a Labour government committed to the introduction of planning and the nationalisation of network utilities as essential ingredients of its economic and industrial policies there seemed little prospect of gas supply remaining in private or municipal hands. This sense of inevitability about the move towards public ownership is borne out by Cairncross (1985, p. 494), and in many respects one might argue was fostered by the industry's reluctance to reorganise itself. As Heyworth (1945, para. 233) noted of gas supply: 'No voluntary process is likely to be sufficiently speedy to satisfy present and future requirements.' In effect, he felt that state compulsion was the only way an industry with widely varying levels of operating and managerial efficiency could be brought up to the necessary standards of performance which would be demanded if the integration of fuel policy was to succeed, and in the ideological climate of 1945 this would inevitably mean nationalisation.

As far as gas supply is concerned, then, Millward (1991, p. 19) is correct in identifying 'a political consensus for the reorganisation of the under-takings in the network industries into large business units', but one must not forget the role played by socialist ideology in fashioning the actual solution. The alternative to nationalisation would have been government-initiated compulsory mergers of undertakings, with area boards and a national authority given responsibility for imposing the necessary policies on a reluctant industry. In 1945, however, little faith in such schemes was expressed by the Ministry of Fuel and Power, leaving no room for compromise once Emmanuel Shinwell was placed in charge after the Labour landslide election victory of 1945. There were problems with the arms-length government regulations, the industry had failed to rationalise itself, a mounting investment bill faced most undertakings after the war, and many recognised the need to compete more effectively with electricity, but the chosen instrument for reform owed most to the Labour government's belief in the political and moral correctness of public ownership, and it was this ideological position which swung the debate.

NOTES

This article forms the first stage in a project generously sponsored by British Gas North Western which aims to chart the origins, history and legacy of the North Western Gas Board. I am indebted to Professor R. Millward and Dr John Singleton (and those who attended the conference) for stimulating my thoughts on the issue of nationalisation, and, along with Terry Mitchell of British Gas North Western, for commenting on earlier drafts of this article.

1 The figures are vague because PEP made no attempt to break down the official returns on gas sales.

2 The Fuel Research Board had noted in 1919 that gas was 'the cheapest known means of distributing potential heat energy in a convenient form' (Quoted in PEP (1939), p. 95).

3 According to Wormsley (1954, p. 31) for outputs in excess of ten million therms per annum the net production cost was 7.58 pennies per therm.

4 Wormsley (1954, p. 163) actually identifies fifty separate regional grids which would have lead to the closure of 511 small works.

5 PEP (1939, p. 130) demonstrated the wide variations in the calorific value of gas produced in Britain: the average undertaking operated at between 475 and 500 British Thermal Units per cubic foot, but the spectrum ranged from 375 to 600. The problem here is that domestic appliance manufacturers would have to modify products according to local circumstances, increasing their price.

6 The South Eastern Gas Corporation had been formed by the Gas Light & Coke Co., while the United Kingdom Gas Corporation had financial links with two major banks, Hambros and Erlangers, indicating the depth of the resources on which they could call.

7 The 1920 Act allowed the introduction of 'basic prices', whereby companies were able to prevent an automatic reduction in dividends when gas prices rose as a result of factors beyond their control. According to Stemp & Wills (1949, p. 6), basic price companies accounted for 50 per cent of gas sales from statutory undertakings, while those on the sliding scale or maximum price scheme were responsible for the other half.

8 Glasgow Corporation, for example, gave evidence in favour of nationalisation. *Gas World*, 23 September 1944, p. 302.

9 'Memorandum on meeting between the Minister of Fuel and Power and representatives of the British Gas Council on the 18th December, 1945.' Howard Greenfield Archive.

10 Morgan (1984, p. 109) incorrectly claims that he did recommend the creation of a national gas authority.

11 These men were, respectively, A.E. Sylvester and H.C. Smith. *Gas World*, 17 April 1948, p. 583.

12 British Parliamentary Papers, 'Gas Supply Areas', Cmnd 7313, 1947–8.

13 None of the clerical and managerial staff in the private companies had been unionised by the 1940s.

REFERENCES

BoT (1937), *Board of Trade Returns on Gas Supply*, parts I and II.

British Gas Federation (1943), *Report on a Survey of the Gas Industry in Great Britain*.

British Parliamentary Papers (1947–8).

Cairncross, A. (1985), *Years of Recovery. British Economic Policy, 1945–51*, Methuen.

Chantler, P. (1938), *The British Gas Industry: an economic study*, Manchester University Press.

Clegg, H.A. (1952), 'Nationalized Industry', in G.D.N. Worswick and P.H. Ady (eds.), *The British Economy, 1945–1950*, Oxford University Press.

Evans, E.V. (1941), *The Place of the Gas Industry in Post-War Reconstruction and Development*, British Gas Federation.

Gas World, 1937–1949.

Hannah, L. (1979), *Electricity before Nationalisation*, Methuen.

Heyworth Report (1945), *The Gas Industry. Report of the Committee of Enquiry*, Cmd. 6699.

UKGCBM, United Kingdom Gas Corporation Board Minutes, deposited in the Howard Greenfield Archive, British Gas North Western, Partington.

Kelf-Cohen, R. (1958), *Nationalisation in Britain. The End of a Dogma*, London: Macmillan.

(1973), *British Nationalisation, 1945–1973*, London: Macmillan.

Millward, R. (1991), 'The causes of the 1940s nationalisations in Britain: a survey', Working Papers in Economic and Social History, University of Manchester, no. 10.

Millward, R. and Singleton, J. (1992), 'The political economy of nationalisation in Britain, c. 1920–1950', mimeo.

Morgan, K.O. (1984), *Labour in Power 1945–1951*, Oxford University Press.

Nabb, H. (1986), 'A history of the gas industry in the South West of England before 1949', unpublished Ph.D., Bath.

PEP (Political and Economic Planning) (1939), *Report on the Gas Industry in Great Britain*.

(1947), *The British Fuel and Power Industries*.

Pryke, R. (1971), *Public Enterprise in Practice*, MacGibbon & Kee.

Stemp, L.F. and Wills, R.A. (1949), *The Gas Act, 1948*, Butterworth.

Williams, T.I. (1981), *A History of the British Gas Industry*, Oxford University Press.

Wilson, J.F. (1988), *Ferranti and the British Electrical Industry, 1864–1930*, Manchester University Press.

(1991), *Lighting the Town: a study of management in the North West gas industry, 1805–1880*, Paul Chapman.

Wormsley, B.H. (1954), 'Some technological and economic problems of the gas industry', unpublished Ph.D., London.

8 Public ownership and the British arms industry 1920–50

David Edgerton

1 Introduction

Although, in certain contexts, the Royal Ordnance Factories, the Royal Dockyards and the Shadow Factories, are well known to historians, they do not occupy the place they should in the history of public ownership. Neither do they exhaust the story of public ownership in arms production. The total, cumulative, state investment in armaments capacity between 1936 and 1945 was around £1 billion. About £2.6 billion was paid out in compensation for the major nationalisations of the late 1940s. Nevertheless, even historians familiar with the history of war production do not take armament factories (or research and development (R&D) facilities) into account in the history of public ownership. William Ashworth – the official historian of wartime armament contracts[1] – argued in his recent study of nationalised industries that 'the Second World War saw little change in the extension of state ownership to business undertakings' (Ashworth 1991, p. 17); the nationalisation of Short Brothers and the creation of the North of Scotland Hydro-Electric Board 'were tiny modifications in the relations of the public and private sectors' (Ashworth 1991, p. 18). The reasons for this misunderstanding become clearer when we note that Ashworth, like most historians, argues that from the inter-war years 'when large new additions were made to public ownership of industry the form of institution used was always some sort of public corporation.' (Ashworth 1991, p. 60). Although he recognises that other forms of public ownership existed – local authority and central government operation, and state-controlled limited companies – he ignores their subsequent development. Public ownership becomes equated with the *transfer* to the central state, in the form of the public corporation, of privately owned, or local authority owned enterprises, in other words with *nationalisation*.

If, instead of adopting this implicit definition, we ask explicitly about the quantity of industrial capacity owned by the state, we get a significantly different picture, not only about the scale and timing of public ownership, but also its incidence and form. During the late 1930s and early 1940s the state built up armaments capacity to which it retained ownership, but did not manage, on a huge scale. Furthermore, it created and ran a huge network of Royal Ordnance Factories, operated by 'industrial civil servants'. In addition, it acquired a number of private companies, notably Short Bros. and Power Jets; the Ministry of Supply took over nine other firms (Ashworth 1953, p. 222). None of these initiatives proved to be temporary wartime measures: all continued into peacetime. Indeed, after the war the state launched major new industrial operations within a civil service structure, notably the atomic bomb programme. The arms sector deserves a significant place in the historiography of public ownership of the 1930s and 1940s, even if it has a minor, though interesting place in the history of nationalisation.[2]

This chapter, by highlighting an important but neglected part of the history of public ownership, will also bring to the fore some neglected aspects of public ownership in general. There is a useful analogy to be made between the armed services and the nationalised industries, both as monopolies, and as monopsonies.[3] The armed services and the nationalised industries were purchasers of some of the most complex and large-scale capital equipment: aircraft, generating sets, boilers, nuclear reactors, locomotives, and so on. The machines, structures and processes used by nationalised industries were central to their performance, but this aspect of their histories has rarely been discussed by their historians. What role the nationalised industries and armed services should play in the design, development and manufacture of the equipment they needed was to prove a complex and controversial question. In armaments the role of the state in design and production was very significant, but so was it in many other industries.

In an earlier paper on public ownership and the aircraft industry I placed my argument in a context of changing relations of demand and supply for aircraft, and economies of scale, especially in aircraft design (Edgerton 1984). The whole issue of economies of scale is central to the debate about nationalisation, as this volume shows. In this chapter I want to highlight a very important source of market failure in armament procurement and design, that arising from uncertainty. The standard argument is that the prime source of market failure in wartime, and hence the rationale for the creation of state-controlled war economies, arises from the fact that war economies are siege economies. To this is added the argument that in war there is a clear, nationally agreed goal: victory. But in wartime, and indeed in peacetime, warfare is subject to great risk and uncertainty. In such circumstances the state must step in to undertake investment in war production, and hence has to make decisions about what investments to make (Devons 1950, p. 4). This in itself leads to planning. Secondly, there is great uncertainty about the military value, at any particular time, of any given quantity of weapons of a particular type: a military value reflected in a price would result in wildly varying prices which a market system could not cope with (Devons 1950, pp. 10–121). These strategic and tactical uncertainties are compounded by technological uncertainties about the operational performance of weapons in development. I will show that uncertainty about demand for armaments forced the state to supply vast quantities of capital for armaments production, and that high levels of uncertainty in aircraft design were a good reason for eschewing possible economies of scale.

Two other neglected aspects of the story of nationalisation are brought out clearly by considering armaments. The conventional history of nationalisation is a subset of the history of the Labour Party and the trade unions. In the case of armaments, neither played a particularly important role; the peace movement and, above all, the state itself, were more important in shaping the extent and the character of public ownership. Looking at armaments also forces one to notice that different government ministries pursued different policies for public ownership. Indeed, it is striking how little reference the literature on nationalisation makes to the nationalising departments of state, as opposed to the industries themselves, and their trade unions: it is rarely even commented on that there were many nationalising ministries: Fuel and Power, Transport, Supply, Board of Trade, Treasury, and Civil Aviation. To this list we need to add the Admiralty, War Office, Air Ministry, and the Ministry of Aircraft Production.

2   The armaments industry

The general trend in armament production, in both peace and war, was upwards. Warlike production was greater in the Second than in the First World War; it was greater in 1930 than in 1904, greater in 1938 than in 1913, and greater in 1949 than in 1934. The Second World War, much more than the First, led to a great ratcheting up of peacetime procurement expenditures, which would then be increased again by rearmament in the early 1950s. The major arms firms of the late 1940s were larger than those of the 1930s, themselves larger than those of the Edwardian years. It is also important to note the size of the British military-industrial complex in comparative perspective. Before the First World War, the British naval-industrial complex could, and did, outbuild any other naval power. But even in the 1920s and early 1930s Britain was probably the largest producer of armaments in the world, and certainly the largest exporter. In the 1940s and 1950s Britain came third behind the USA and the USSR (Edgerton 1991a).

However, the total level of production of armaments, unlike that of civil products, was subject to extremely violent swings. In 1907 the Royal Dockyards and the Ordnance Factories, together with the two largest private armourers, Vickers and Armstrong-Whitworth, employed over 88,000 workers. At the end of the First World War, Woolwich alone almost as many, Armstrong-Whitworth employed 78,000, Beardmore 42,000 and Vickers 107,000 (Warren 1989, pp. 192, 195). In the 1920s and early 1930s defence expenditure was around the £100 million mark; at the outbreak of war it was about £600 million, and it peaked in the war at around £5,000 million, falling to about £800 million in the late 1940s. In terms of aircraft production there was a forty-fold expansion between 1935 and 1943; and a ten-fold contraction immediately after the war. There were also violent changes in the composition of demand. Changing state policies, and changing strategic priorities had huge industrial impacts. Before 1939 Britain's peacetime army was small, and it was generally expected that Britain would also have small wartime armies. In fact, in both 1914 and 1939 decisions were taken to create huge armies which required huge increases in output of artillery, small arms, and so on. Before the First World War aviation took an insignificant proportion of procurement expenditures, but, in the inter-war years, the new Air Ministry ran the Navy a close second; the Army was very much the 'cinderella service'. By 1950 'electronics' formed an important part of a much greater and more balanced arms industry.[4] This massive variability in demand was the context for an enduring state concern with reserve production capacity for armaments, which came to be called 'war potential': the state sought to ensure that swings in the level of capacity were not as violent as those in production. But wartime peaks of production were so high that it was inconceivable that anything but a small margin of unused capacity could be kept. Rearmament programmes invariably meant restrictions on civil production and the creation of new armament capacity. Given the variability in demand, and the uncertainty about the variability, the state had to step in to maintain capacity, and to create it on a very large scale. Private companies could not be expected to bear the risk of finding themselves with large quantities of excess capacity.

In the early 1930s procurement for the Navy was still at the centre of the military-industrial system. The naval-industrial complex had been created in the Edwardian years, and expanded massively in the First World War to supply the Navy, and especially Britain's new mass armies. This complex is not easily described, given its distribution across industrial sectors and the highly diversified nature of the dominant firms.

Table 8.1. *Expenditure on armaments and warlike stores 1923–33*

Year	Royal Navy	Total New ships	RAF	Army
1923/4	11.8	5.0	4.9	2.6
1924/5	13.0	6.0	6.9	2.6
1925/6	14.1	5.4	7.6	2.2
1926/7	16.0	8.3	7.4	1.8
1927/8	16.3	9.0	7.6	1.8
1928/9	15.0	8.5	7.1	2.0
1929/30	14.7	7.7	7.9	2.2
1930/1	10.7	5.0	8.9	1.5
1931/2	10.3	4.8	8.7	1.8
1932/3	10.7	6.0	7.8	1.6

Source: Postan 1952, table 1, p. 2.

Perhaps the easiest way of grasping it is to focus on it in geographically.[5] In Sheffield one had plants making armour plate and heavy forgings operated by such firms as Vickers, John Brown, Cammell Laird, Firth and Hadfield. On the Tyne there were above all the works and shipyards of Armstrong-Whitworth (Elswick, Scotswood, Walker Yard), as well as the steel works and shipyard of Palmers. On the Clyde the great armament, armour plate and shipyard of Beardmores was complemented by the shipyards of John Brown, Fairfield and Scotts. At Barrow in Furness there was one firm only, Vickers, which had a shipyard and massive gun and gunmounting works. On the Mersey, Cammell Laird had an important shipyard. In the South of England were the great government works: the shipbuilding yards attached to the Royal Dockyards at Devonport, Portsmouth and Chatham, the huge government factories at Woolwich, and the smaller works at Waltham Abbey and Enfield. In Kent Vickers had two important plants (Erith, Dartford).

The greatest Edwardian and wartime armourers – Vickers, Armstrong-Whitworth, John Brown, Cammell Laird and Beardmore were among the very largest manufacturing employers (Shaw 1983, Jeremy 1991). To varying extents, and in different ways, they were highly vertically integrated, diversified, multi-plant enterprises.[6] All made armour plate; all built warships; all built marine engines; all built heavy guns and large mountings and aircraft (John Brown, Cammell Laird, together with Fairfield, did this through Coventry Ordnance Works); Vickers, Armstrong-Whitworth, Hadfield and Beardmore built motor cars. These companies came out of the First World War extremely powerful and rich, and determined to diversify into new areas: the electrical industry (through Metropolitan-Vickers and English Electric) was just one route. However, the crisis in shipbuilding and heavy engineering in the late 1920s and early 1930s saw a wave of rationalisations within the naval-industrial complex, which led to disinvestment in ancillary activities. The extent of vertical integration was much reduced, and firms rationalised their activities horizontally. Thus Vickers-Armstrong was formed to take over the steel, arms, engineering and shipbuilding work of Vickers and Armstrong-Whitworth (Barrow, Sheffield, Erith, Dartford, Elswick, Openshaw, Walker Yard) while some plants, notably Scotswood, which Armstrong-Whitworth retained, were taken out of arms production. John Brown, Fairfield and Cammell Laird ceased to maintain Coventry Ordnance as a gun and mounting maker (it became part of English Electric). The Vickers-Armstrong steel and armour plate plants at Sheffield and Openshaw were merged with those of Cammell Laird (Sheffield) to form the English Steel Corporation (Burn 1961, pp. 438–9, Carr and Taplin 1962, pp. 439–50). On the shipbuilding side National Shipbuilders' Securities closed down the Beardmore and the Palmer yards.[7] At the same time, the arms firms divested their interests outside armaments: Vickers sold Metropolitan-Vickers; John Brown and others sold English Electric; Armstrong-Whitworth sold its aircraft and car companies; Vickers sold Wolseley cars; Beardmore and English Electric left the aircraft industry. However, as a holding company, Vickers emerged as easily the most important armament firm, operating right across armaments: it had two significant aircraft companies (Vickers Aviation and Supermarine), and controlling shareholdings in English Steel Corporation, the largest maker of armour plate and gun forgings, and Vickers-Armstrong, the largest warshipbuilder, maker of guns and mountings, machine guns, tanks, and so on. By the early 1930s Vickers dominated armaments as never before, indeed it was very largely an armament company. In 1935 Vickers was the third largest manufacturing employer, after Unilever and ICI (Jeremy 1991). Nevertheless John Brown, Fairfield, Scotts, Cammell Laird, Beardmore and Hadfield were still important members of the naval-industrial complex.

In the twenties and early 1930s the number of plants producing any given product was much lower than before the First World War, and there was generally surplus capacity. Only Vickers of the private yards supplied submarines, only Hadfield and Firth provided armour piercing shell. Vickers-Armstrong was the only supplier of heavy naval gun mountings. However, through the fixing of contract prices the Admiralty ensured that capacity was maintained. A good example is armour plate. At the end of the First World War armour plate capacity stood at 60,000 tons per annum; the Admiralty subsidised English Steel, Beardmore and Firth-Brown to keep at least 18,000 tons of capacity; well ahead of current requirements in the 1920s and early 1930s (Gordon 1988, pp. 82–5). Nevertheless, in the 1920s and 1930s there was substantial warship-building. In the 1920s three great battleship/battlecruisers were launched, and four large warships were converted to aircraft carriers. The inter-war years as a whole saw the building of more than thirty large cruisers of just under 10,000 tons displacement; very crudely the equivalent of seven very large battleships. In 1939 and 1940 five battleships and four aircraft carriers were launched, which gives an indication of warshipyard capacity of the pre-rearmament years, since no new yards were built.[8] As we shall see the investment in warshipbuilding capacity in rearmament and war was trivial by comparison to capacity for the Air Force and Army.

The second major chunk of the arms industry of the early 1930s was the aircraft industry. Much more so than the naval-industrial complex this industry was utterly dependent on warlike orders, at home and abroad: some 75 per cent of work was warlike. To a significant extent the aircraft industry was developed within the naval-industrial complex, but by the early 1930s most of the aircraft firms were independent of the traditional armourers. By 1924 the industry had been stabilised by the Air Ministry, which retained around fifteen airframe units and four engine units. In the late 1920s Air Ministry procurement grew significantly, and by 1930 it had nearly reached naval levels (see table 8.1). The rise of the air force is more to blame for low naval procurement than a reluctance of inter-war governments to spend on armaments. The individual units of the aircraft industry were smaller than the firms in the naval-industrial complex, but an important process of financial concentration was underway. In 1935 the merger of two multi-firm groups led to the creation of Hawker-Siddeley, a group which included Hawker, Avro, Gloster, Armstrong-Whitworth, and Armstrong-Siddeley. Hawker-Siddeley and Vickers-Armstrong were easily the two largest private arms makers of the Second World War (Edgerton 1991b).

3   Socialising the 'merchants of death'

The early 1930s, even before the rise of Hitler, were years not only of economic depression but of war. The most dramatic such war was the Japanese invasion of Manchuria in 1931. Furthermore, as some pointed out, the expenditure on armaments in the world was high by historical standards: the war to end war had left a world better armed than the world of the late nineteenth century. This prompted many to seek an explanation in the existence of private manufacturers of arms, and in the private arms trade. Calls for the control of the arms industry and the arms trade ranged into the centre-ground of British politics. A good example is the Next Five Years group:

We urge the Government to agree to the fullest measure of international control and supervision of this traffic, including annual inspection on the spot by an international commission and publicity for all orders for armaments received by armament makers; and steps should be taken, with regard to the manufacture of casualty-producing weapons by private enterprise, to ensure that this shall no longer be a source of private enrichment.

Either the state should take over the manufacture of all casualty-producing weapons, or else a public authority should be constituted which would be responsible for the assembly and completion of all such arms not completed in Government factories.

A special responsibility rests upon Great Britain in this matter, for this country is the largest exporter of armaments in the world. . . . The traffic in armaments is now a source of private enrichment to British firms to the extent of some millions of pounds a year; but the injury to the world's peace and confidence which results from this traffic under present conditions is of far greater importance to the public interest than the maintenance of the present system (Next Five Years 1935, p. 292).

The Labour Party in its 1934 programme, *For Socialism and Peace*, called for the abolition of the private manufacture of armaments, but the 1935 manifesto was more circumspect:

Labour will propose to other nations the complete abolition of all national air forces, the effective international control of civil aviation and the creation of an international air police; large reductions by international agreement in naval and military forces; and the abolition of the private manufacture of, and trade in, arms (quoted Craig 1975).

Arthur Henderson, in an official statement of Labour's foreign policy, said that Labour would propose to the League of Nations a plan which would include 'the nationalization and drastic international control of the manufacture of and trade in arms' (Henderson 1935, p. 45). This was not, then, a unilateral commitment to nationalise the British armament industry. But it was pressure from Labour, together with a groundswell of public opinion, which led the National government to establish a Royal Commission to look into the private manufacture of armaments. This commission sat from late 1935 into early 1936, taking evidence in public even from the Cabinet Secretary. The Royal Commission had been invited to look at a possible means of ensuring disarmament, but ended up examining nationalisation as a means of promoting rearmament. The general conclusion of the commission was that the arms industry should remain in private hands, but that state control should be increased (Scott 1962, Sampson 1977, Davenport-Hines 1979).

In the early 1930s the emphasis of radical critics had been on the dangers and immorality of private companies making a profit out of war, as 'merchants of death' and members of a 'secret international' (for example, Brockway 1933). With rearmament in the late 1930s emphasis on much of the left switched to criticism of inefficiencies in armament production, and of the very high profits the armourers, and the aircraft firms in particular, were getting (Cockburn 1985, pp. 247–55). Within the Labour Party too there was a shift from nationalisation as a means of reducing the production of armaments, to public ownership for greater efficiency. In 1937 the Labour Party's Defence Sub-Committee considered a paper which looked into various forms a publicly owned arms ministry might take: state-owned companies, government manufacture, and a public board.[9] The 1939 party document, *Labour and the Armed Forces* proposed that:

The Minister of Supply would be responsible for the existing state armament factories and under a Labour Government he would be under instructions to expand these factories or to set up new factories whenever possible, when an increase in industrial capacity was called for (Labour Party 1939).

After 1939, and especially 1941, the British armourers were no longer 'merchants of death' or profiteers. On the contrary, the pre-war arms industry was seen as the victim of governments of 'guilty men' unwilling to build armaments in sufficient quantities. Far from being inefficient, the armourers had created new scientific weapons in full collaboration with labour. It was not an industry which needed the strong medicine of nationalisation to bring it up to scratch. Furthermore, there was no powerful, much less a unified, claim from the trade unions for the nationalisation of a highly complex network of firms and plants. The 1945 Labour manifesto contained no reference to the nationalisation of the arms industry, even though wartime Labour ministers argued that a larger part of the aircraft industry should come under state control.[10] But from the left of the party there were reminders of the positions of the thirties. At the Labour Party Conference of 1945 there was a resolution demanding that arms production should become a government monopoly. It drew the following response from Philip Noel Baker – the great campaigner for disarmament and student of the private arms industry – for the National Executive: 'Our Party has always stood for the abolition of the private trade and manufacture of arms. We stand for it today. We are pledged to the hilt, and our pledges will be carried through.' The resolution was referred to the National Executive, to be buried (Labour Party 1945, pp. 149–50). The issue did not arise at the 1946 conference. At the 1945 TUC the AScW and the AEU spoke in favour of maintaining shadow factories and ROFs in public ownership (TUC 1945, pp. 358, 360). The question was referred to the General Council, who discussed the matter with Cripps to no great effect (TUC 1946, Report of the General Council). Thereafter, despite some pressure for nationalisation of the arms industry from the AEU, the TUC took no action.

In 1948 the Labour Party considered the nationalisation of the air-craft industry.[11] The aircraft industry, argued the research department of the party, was an arms industry for which there was a 'moral and political' case for nationalisation supplemented by the fact that the state was the principal purchaser of aircraft and did a great deal of research. Further-more, the aircraft firms could not be considered 'capitalist' in that they were guaranteed against loss by the state. Nationalisation, it was argued, would allow better planning and coordination of resources. The case against, also put by the research department, was that technical progress required a measure of freedom from control; there was no widespread demand for nationalisation from the trade unions; and that the state as monopoly purchaser had all the powers required to control the indus-try.[12] John Freeman, the Parliamentary Secretary to the Ministry of Supply, argued that in peacetime waste of resources was unavoidable if 'war potential' was to be maintained, but most important of all 'any undue centralisation on nationalisation would undoubtedly impoverish the main tide of technical thought'; he had little doubt that 'the keen and healthy competition which at present exists between design teams is essential to success'. He concluded that: 'There is no reason arising out of the purely physical difficulties of pursuing research and development, and maintaining or expanding productive potential, which requires the Government to take any new powers of control over the industry.' Such difficulties that had arisen in the post-war years were 'either inevitable or arise from a weakness in policy or administration on the part of the government and do not arise from an inherent lack of power' (quoted Edgerton 1984, pp. 269–70). In other words, the whole issue was regarded as an administrative one in which questions of ownership of property were irrelevant. But in fact they were far from irrelevant. The issue of public ownership arose in the arms industry after 1935 in many complex, but far from abstract, ways. Interestingly, Labour ministers, MPs and sympathisers, had little or no understanding of the actual involvement of the state in arms manufacture. There was, however, one, incidental, indeed accidental, nationalisation of armaments under the Labour government, that of English Steel. This was not an ordinary steel company – it was the main armament steel producer. It was later bought back by Vickers and Cammell Laird, at a profit (Scott 1962, chapter 29).

4   Public ownership and competition in research, development and design

The armed services were expert users of highly specialised equipment. Historically, they had designed much, perhaps most, of it themselves. The late nineteenth century saw a greatly expanded role for the private sector in the design of armaments, and thereafter there was a shifting balance between the public and private sectors. One particularly interesting case was the Army Aircraft Factory, renamed the Royal Aircraft Factory in 1912. This was not really a factory, since its production was minimal, but was one of the most important design centres for British aircraft. Largely because of opposition from the aircraft trade, it ceased to design aircraft or engines in the First World War, and continued in existence as the Royal Aircraft Establishment (RAE), concerned with testing, research and experiment (Edgerton 1991b). But the new Air Ministry, created in 1918, did make an important and expensive venture into design: the design and building of the R101 airship at what was called the Royal Airship Works at Cardington. This project was started under the 1923–4 Labour government and completed under the 1929–31 government: the Air Minister responsible, Lord Thompson, died in the crash of the R101 on its maiden flight. Even in this case, the Air Ministry had ordered a second airship, to a different design, from a subsidiary of Vickers (Masefield 1982). The Air Ministry was deeply committed to private design, and to competition between many private designers.

By contrast, the War Office, and the Admiralty were major designers of arms. The Admiralty, through its Corps of Naval Constructors, designed all warships; but it did not design their engines, their guns, or their gun mountings. It relied a great deal on the private trade. The War Office designed small arms, artillery, gunmountings and tanks. It also designed some naval guns and gunmountings for the Admiralty. Its only significant competitor was Vickers-Armstrong: sometimes they competed in design; at other times one or other was called to design; for some products one or other had a virtual monopoly (Postan, Hay and Scott 1964, pp. 464–5). For example, the War Office left tank design largely to Vickers-Armstrong after about 1930. In the late 1930s other private firms – Nuffield Mechanizations, the LMS railway, Vauxhall, Harland and Wolff, Leyland, Birmingham Railway Carriage, and the Vulcan Foundry – were brought in, with disastrous results (Scott and Hughes 1955, p. 282). Only in the last months of the war did the Ministry of Supply start designing tanks, and these tanks were put into production, for the first time, in an Ordnance Factory (Postan *et al.* 1964, p. 352). But the role of the inter-war research and design departments at Woolwich should not be underestimated. They designed the 14″, 8″ and 4.5″ naval guns, the 4.5″ army gun, the 4.5″ AA gun, an important tank gun, the 25 pounder field gun, and the important new explosive RDX (Scott and Hughes 1955, p. 273). As J.D. Scott, historian of war production and design, and later of Vickers put it:

> Before and during the First World War both Vickers and Armstrongs had been at least abreast of the government agencies in the design and development of all the armaments in which there was any competition in design, and had considered themselves in many respects to be well ahead. In the period between the wars they had remained competitors, and Vickers were still admittedly ahead, or rather alone, in a number of important fields, including tanks and mountings. . . .

However, after 1945 there was the risk that Vickers might become 'merely an armament jobbing shop, manufacturing to other people's designs' (Scott 1962, p. 302). This somewhat overstates the case, given Vickers' huge interest in aviation, but it broadly captures the shift away from private firms, especially ones like Vickers, to the state, in design capacity.

In the 1930s and 1940s the argument was made a number of times that the Air Ministry/Ministry of Aircraft Production should engage in design as did the War Office/Ministry of Supply and the Admiralty. Indeed, one of the most important arguments for and against the nationalisation of the aircraft industry concerned potential economies of scale in design. Ronald McKinnon Wood, a socialist aeronautical engineer who had worked at the RAE Farnborough between 1914 and 1934, argued that there were too many private design units: they were too small to be efficient, there was duplication of effort, and lack of diffusion of expertise. Nationalisation could help overcome these difficulties (Royal Commission 1936a, p. 150). The Royal Commission on the private manufacture of arms recommended the development of an Air Ministry design centre (Royal Commission 1936b, para. 130). But the Air Ministry was insistent on competitive, private design. As Lord Weir, industrial adviser to the Air Minister, put it:

> I know of many industries where I would consider [full state] control necessary and valuable, but in Air, which is still developing its scientific possibilities, and which demands engagement of the imagination and enterprise of the individual, I am frankly rather scared at the possible dangers of centralised direction (Quoted in Reader 1968, p. 287).

The government argued that 'in an industry of which the principal characteristic at present, and probably for a considerable time to come is rapid development and improvement sometimes of an almost revolutionary character . . . the strongest possible competition in design – inspired by the best brains working under conditions most favourable to and provocative of invention and progress – is essential to the maintenance of the highest levels of efficiency'. (Royal Commission 1936c, p. 493). That meant private enterprise. In late 1938 the Air Member for Development and Production, Sir Wilfrid Freeman, and Sir Henry Tizard, chairman of the Aeronautical Research Council, were in favour of an element of state design.[13] Furthermore, during 1943 the MAP Reconstruction Committee proposed the establishment of a government factory for design and construction. Indeed, the very first meeting of the War Cabinet reconstruction committee discussed the issue.[14] These efforts came to nothing in the field of airframes.

In aero-engines the story was rather different. Although the Air Ministry was highly dependent on the four major aero-engine companies for engine research and development, in the case of jet engines the aero-engine firms played no part in their initial development. Instead the key figures were an employee of the RAE, A.E. Griffiths, who developed the axial-flow turbine, and above all, an RAF officer, Frank Whittle. Frank Whittle's firm Power Jets had been formed in 1936 with private funds, and designed Britain's first jet engines under contract to the Air Ministry. The production of engines, however, had been turned over to private firms, notably Rover, Rolls-Royce and de Havilland, some of which also started designing engines of their own. Whittle, then a socialist, urged that the whole jet engine industry should be nationalised. In a letter to the Minister of Aircraft Production, Stafford Cripps, in April 1943 he noted that:

The case for nationalisation seems to me to be overwhelmingly strong, so much so that the public would be entitled to raise a vigorous outcry through Parliament if a few private firms were allowed to grasp for the benefit of their shareholders that which should properly be the property of the state (Quoted in Whittle 1953, p. 263).

Cripps, however, nationalised only Whittle's firm, and merged MAP's own gas turbine research establishment into it. Power Jets became a limited company owned by the state, which Cripps intended should continue to design jet engines and to manufacture them on a small scale. However, the private firms objected strongly and MAP would not authorise Power Jets to design and manufacture new engines. The election of the Labour government gave hope to Whittle that this decision would be reversed but, in early 1946, the government decided to convert Power Jets into the National Gas Turbine Establishment, a civil service organisation devoted exclusively to research, like the RAE. As Whittle himself put it, it was a 'striking paradox' that a 'Government company was virtually smothered to death while a Labour Government was in office' (Whittle 1953, p. 302). Whittle, and his team, resigned, never to design an aero-engine again.

In other very new areas the state was also very much in the lead. Radar was developed in the 1930s in state laboratories, not industrial ones. During the war MAP created a huge research and design organisation, the Telecommunications Research Establishment. This was the source of most of the new radar equipment. Universities and industry also played a role, but the industrial role, carried out mostly in the laboratories of GEC, BTH, Metro-Vick, EMI and STC, was largely one of 'development for production' (Postan, Hay and Scott 1964, p. 429). But perhaps the most striking case was nuclear weapons. The independent British programme, started in 1945, was entrusted not to the private sector (ICI was considered), but rather to the post-war Ministry of Supply, which built up an unparalleled scientific, technological and industrial organisation, the size of a large firm. The British bomb was built within the civil service, but a hived-off nationalised industry called Atomic Energy Authority would be created by the Conservative government in 1955 (Gowing 1964, 1974).

There were in fact two shifts taking place. The shift from the private to the public sector, and a shift from many to fewer designing institutions. Both shifts were connected to the growing scale of design and development activity for any given weapon system. Already before the war, aero-engine design was much more concentrated than airframe design, reflecting the much greater costs of designing engines. But in the 1930s and 1940s design costs were pushed up spectacularly, so much so that in some areas, notably nuclear weapons, only one programme was possible, at least in Britain.[15] In the case of aircraft and aero-engines, however, there does not appear to have been a reduction in the number of design units until the 1950s. There were certainly virtues in duplicating design activity given the uncertainty in aircraft design. It was perhaps just as well that firms like Armstrong-Whitworth, Fairey and Gloster, all very successful in the 1920s, did not come to monopolise aircraft production in the 1930s and 1940s, at least if one is to judge from their later records. Equally, it was fortunate that a small flying boat maker like Supermarine did not go out of business, or a firm like Avro, which made trainers. The Air Ministry and Ministry of Aircraft Production found it necessary to put three heavy bombers into production during the war: the Stirling, Halifax and Lancaster. After the war the Ministry of Supply ordered three nuclear bombers into production in the 1950s: the Valiant, Victor and Vulcan. This suggests, at least in part, that duplication was still necessary, and possible, into the 1950s (see Devons 1958).

5   Public ownership and the production of armaments

If the story of state involvement in design and development is complex, so too is the role of the state in the production of armaments. Again, there were significant differences between the policies of the three service ministries.

In the inter-war period the Air Ministry relied entirely on private production, while the Admiralty built about one third of its new tonnage in the Dockyards: in 1932, for example, the Dockyards had work on hand and allocated of a tonnage equal to 70 per cent of Admiralty work in the private yards (Hornby 1958, p. 67). The 1920s saw attempts to commercialise the Dockyards, but these were firmly resisted (Ward 1988, p. 85). The Admiralty also had a cordite factory and a torpedo factory (Scott and Hughes 1955, p. 7). The War Office had major plant at Woolwich, employing about 7,000, and smaller plants at Enfield and Waltham Abbey, which each employed hundreds (Hornby 1958, p. 83).

When, in the mid thirties, the decision was taken to embark on a massive rearmament programme, decisions also had to be taken as to where to expand, and how to finance expansion of capacity. It was to be rearmament overwhelmingly in the air and at sea. Although there was plenty of shipyard capacity, new plant had to be built for guns, gunmountings and armour plate; and for aircraft production new plant would be needed right across the board. In addition new capacity for making propellant, explosive, bombs and ammunition would be needed. One point that was clear to the planners was that the private sector could not be expected to finance more than a small proportion of the new capacity required. Rearmament was expected to involve only a temporary expansion of production so firms would be left with excess capacity if they invested to meet this demand. They were not to know that arms production would expand rapidly for nearly ten years. The question was then how the state would finance, and organise the operation of, the new armament capacity. One important principle laid down in 1936 was that the state would retain ownership of plant it financed.[16] While this rule was to hold generally, Vickers-Armstrong was able to obtain complete ownership of new gun-mounting pits which were 60 per cent financed by the Admiralty (Gordon 1988, pp. 147, 191–2). In 1937, however, the Admiralty and War Office bought and reequipped the Scotswood plant from Armstrong-Whitworth, at a cost of £2 million, and then leased it to Vickers-Armstrong (Gordon 1988, 206–9).

The issue of who would operate government-owned plant is best illustrated by looking at the different policies of the War Office/Ministry of Supply and the Air Ministry/Ministry of Aircraft Production. The War Office/Ministry of Supply both ran new factories itself (the Royal Ordnance Factories), gave new factories to private firms to run on an 'agency' basis, and financed new capacity at contractor's works. Its largest agent was Imperial Chemical Industries; indeed, in the late 1930s ICI was building agency factories worth only slightly less than the current ROF programme (Hornby 1958, 157–8). More than forty new Royal

Ordnance Factories were built or were acquired from the late 1930s, to make arms, explosives and propellants, and ammunition. Many of these factories were conceived of as larger replacements for Woolwich, which was deemed too old and too vulnerable to air attack. Chorley, in Lancashire, was the site of the first major new Ordnance Factory. It was built between 1936 and 1938, and in its wartime peak it employed 27,000 workers filling shells, bombs and ammunition. Some older factories were purchased for state operation. A former National Factory in Nottingham was bought from Cammell Laird in 1936; the famous Nasmyth works at Patricroft were bought in 1940; and another former National Factory at Birtley was bought from Armstrong Whitworth; Beardmore's closed Dalmuir plant was also purchased in the 1930s (it was later operated as an agency factory). By contrast the Air Ministry/MAP continued its policy of not running any industrial capacity itself. All its new capacity was run by private firms. In the late 1930s motor car companies were the main managers of new aero-engine and airframe plants (the Shadow factories). By 1938, however, there was a switch to investing in plant to be operated by aircraft firms themselves. The Air Ministry/MAP invested more in 'extensions' to the work of private contractors, than in the better-known Shadow factories, and the War Office/Ministry of Supply, invested more in 'agency' factories and in extensions than it did in Royal Ordnance Factories. The American term 'government-owned, contractor-operated', or 'GOCO' best captures the dominant form of state finance of war production capacity.

There were some calls for Air Ministry operation of aircraft factories, for example by J.T.C. Moore Brabazon MP in 1938 (he was wholly against state design).[17] Within the air ministry in late 1938, consideration was given to the development of state-run factories for aircraft production. The politicians, however, were against the idea.[18] In 1943 the MAP Reconstruction Committee proposed the establishment of a government factory.[19] Certainly in 1944 the SBAC became concerned at the possibility of nationalisation, and planned to lobby non-Labour MPs.

One reason for this nervousness was that MAP had nationalised the old and famous firm of Short Brothers in 1943, for refusing to toe the MAP line and for being inefficient (Edgerton 1984, Howlett this volume).[20] Another was that state-owned factories were more efficient than private ones. The reason for this was that production runs were longer in Shadow and agency factories because parent plants bore the brunt of modification and change; there was a two-tier industry.[21]

By the end of the war the cumulative total of state investment was over £1,000 million. Nearly £400 million went on aircraft production, and over £500 million was spent by the War Office/Ministry of Supply; the

Table 8.2. *Government actual expenditure on fixed capital for war production 1 April 1936–31 March 1945 (£m.)*

	Total	Admiralty	Air Ministry MAP	War Office MoS
Capital Assistance Schemes and Agency Schemes	767,300	43,100	384,600	339,600
Government Operation	262,100	45,500	—	216,600
Total	1,029,400	88,600	384,600	556,200

Source: Ashworth 1953, p. 252.

Admiralty invested less than 10 per cent of the total (see table 8.2). Unfortunately we do not have figures for private investment or for the value of privately owned capital. Ashworth was able to obtain a figure of £8 million provided by the aircraft industry itself before 1939 for investment covered by the Capital Clause scheme, and £25 million put in by private firms in contributory schemes (Ashworth 1953, p. 227). It was estimated after the war that in 1944 the aircraft industry used some £60 million of privately owned capital, while the total value of assets used was at least £200 million.[22] It seems probable that the vast bulk of new capacity for war production was supplied by the state. Of course, older privately supplied capacity was also used for war production. Postan estimated that 25 per cent of munitions workers were employed in state-owned plant, but this underestimates the position since he appears to include in the private sector workers who worked in state-owned extensions to arms-makers' firms (Postan 1952, p. 434). On the basis of figures supplied by Hornby we can make a crude estimate of war production employment using state-provided capital. This suggests that something like one-half of all employment was on state-owned plant (see tables 8.3 and 8.4).

One consequence of the high level of state provided capital, in aircraft at least, was that firms made high profits in relation to capital employed, since it appears that state-owned plant was used gratis.[23] The structure of ownership, and of operation, appears to have had a direct effect on the nature of labour relations in the arms factories. The Royal Ordnance Factories, and especially ROF Nottingham (a gun factory), saw much activity by Trotskyist militants, who controlled the ROF Shop Stewards' Committee. One indication of their success was the very late setting up of Joint Production Committees in many ROFs: these were very strongly supported by the Communist Party but denounced as collaborationist by

Table 8.3. *Distribution of government financed fixed capital for war production, cumulative 1 April 1936–31 March 1944. (Percentages)*

	Capital Assistance Schemes			Government operation
	Govt-owned	Contributory	Agency	
MAP*	54.5	1.5	34.1	—
MoS	34.0	2.6	24.5	38.9
Adm†	37.9	3.3	5.5	53.3

Notes: * as at 31 December 1944.
† adds to 90.1% due to other expenditure.
Source: Ashworth 1953, tables E, G, J, pp. 249–62.

Table 8.4. *Employment in government-owned factories and plant June 1943 (thousands)*

Type	Employment Ministry		Total			Government as % of total
ROF	268	MoS/Adm	865	MoS/Adm	2,250 MoS/Adm	38%
Dockyards	37					
Agency						
MoS/Adm	210	MAP	776	MAP	1,400 MAP	55%
MAP	300					
Capital Assistance						
MoS/Adm	350					
MAP	476					
Total	1,641		1,641		3,650	44%

Source: Hornby 1958, p. 383 for employment in ROF, Dockyards, and Agency schemes. Employment figures for Capital assistance plant estimated by author assuming constant capital/labour ratio and using figures for distribution of capital in table 8.3. Other figures are estimates taken from Hornby.

Trotskyists (Bornstein and Richardson 1986, pp. 59–63, Croucher 1982, 173–8). In the shadow factories there was an awareness by workers that these were government-owned factories, and in 1945 there was a campaign to keep these shadow factories operating, under the government, or at least producing for the government (Croucher 1982, 326–40).

Such campaigns had very little effect. The coalition had decided to sell government factories, but not to the highest bidder. Instead they would be leased for ten years taking into account locational and other grounds, with an option to buy (Hargreaves and Gowing 1952, pp. 622–3). The Labour government certainly sold a great deal of capacity. Between 1946/7 and 1949/50 the Ministry of Supply realised £61 million through sales of capital assets (Comptroller and Auditor General 1950). Between 1945 and 1950 half of the Ordnance Factories were closed or transferred to other uses. From 1947 plant was sold to aircraft firms; most appear to have bought some. English Electric bought much, though not all, the government plant it operated – at Preston, and the plant operated by its subsidiary Napier in Liverpool, as well as a tank factory in Stafford (Jones and Marriot 1970, p. 177). At the end of the war the government had surplus machine tools worth £100 million (Hancock and Gowing 1949, p. 552). Machine tools were also sold separately on a large scale: by late 1946 some 50,000 were sold, for around £12 million.[24]

Nevertheless state-owned capacity for armament production was retained in the arms industry. Ely Devons tried to estimate its importance in the aircraft industry in the late 1950s, and he is worth quoting at length:

On the present system of government accounting it is quite impossible to get any idea from published figures of the extent to which the industry is now using government-owned buildings and plant; and it has not been possible to get sufficient information from individual firms to form a general picture for the industry as a whole. But figures for one or two firms are sufficient to indicate that government-owned facilities are still of very substantial importance. In some firms at least, including one or two of the major ones in the industry, government-financed capital facilities are equal to those privately financed, and in some cases are actually substantially greater (Devons 1958, p. 80)

Even in 1965, 20 per cent of employment in the main aircraft firms was in seventeen plants owned by the Ministry of Aviation (Plowden 1965, table IV).

6   The structure of the arms industry in 1950

The private sector of the armaments industry created in the late 1930s and during the war was larger than that of 1914–18. The great armament firms of the First World War, in their new guises, produced more of the traditional weapons in the Second World War. According to one official historian, Vickers-Armstrong, Beardmore, ICI and BSA produced more in the Second World War than their predecessor companies had done in the First World War (Hornby 1958, pp. 150–2).[25] There is no doubt that state-provided plant was instrumental here. But these firms, and many others, developed whole new branches of arms production, notably aircraft. The aircraft firms approached the employment levels of the greatest armourers of the First World War, reaching well over 50,000 for such firms as Vickers, Hawker-Siddeley and Bristol. As well as massive expansion, rearmament and war brought a renewed tendency towards diversification. One example was that warshipbuilders acquired aircraft companies. Thus the Vickers aviation companies were put under Vickers-Armstrong; Swan Hunter took over Airspeed; John Brown and BTH took over Westland. William Denny and Harland and Wolff formed joint companies with Blackburn and Short: Blackburn Denny and Short and Harland. Metropolitan-Vickers and English Electric became major subcontractors for airframes in the late 1930s, and each went into aero-engines. Metro-Vick briefly designed jet engines; English Electric took over Napier. During the war English Electric produced 2,700 tanks, 3,150 bombers, and 4,500 large aero-engines (Jones and Marriot 1970, p. 144). After the war English Electric became a major designer and manufacturer of jet aircraft, and through its purchase of Marconi in 1946 a key defence electronics firm.

The post-war arms industry was much larger than that which existed in 1935. The aircraft industry employed five times the number it did in 1935; the Royal Ordnance Factories employed some three times more workers (Edgerton 1992, pp. 98–9). Nine out of the top fifty employers in 1955 were major defence contractors, each employing between 21,000 and 75,000 workers (Jeremy 1991). The role of the state in research, development and design was much greater too. The defence departments employed some 5,500 scientists and engineers on R&D in 1947, compared with 10,000 in industry, many of whom were also working on armaments (Edgerton, 1992, p. 104). We may illustrate some other changes by looking at the north-west of England. Before the Second and First World Wars, the only significant centres of arms production were Barrow (Vickers), Birkenhead (Cammell-Laird) and Openshaw (Armstrong). In 1950 the picture was very different: in addition to the above there were three important Ordnance Factories (Chorley, Patricroft and Blackburn) and state-run nuclear facilities at Risley, Drigg and Sellafield. There were also many aircraft factories: a number of Hawker-Siddeley (Avro) aircraft plants around Manchester; Fairey in Stockport; English Electric in Preston and (as Napier) in Speke, as well as de Havilland in Chester.

Conclusion

The lack of attention to arms production in the historiography of public ownership is an instance of a wider phenomenon: the failure of historians to take account of the warlike aspects of the state, even in wartime, and even when they had major consequences for the civil economy (Edgerton 1991a, 1991b, 1992). The wartime, and post-war, military industrial complex was not brought into being merely by the state demanding armaments. Most of the capital – on the scale of a large national utility, and employing perhaps one and a half million workers – was provided by the state. 'War socialism' was not a matter of business, labour and government coming together; it was rather a matter of the state taking over one of the key prerogatives of private enterprise: the finance of, and decisions about, investment (as well as decisions over production). The market failed, as it was bound to, to give the nation the capital base for arms production in either rearmament and war. Much of this capacity was operated by private industry, and much found its way into private industry after the war. Indeed, the Labour government privatised a very great deal of industrial capacity. But much remained in the public sector. The postwar years saw the maintenance and expansion of huge public sector organisations for research, development, design and production of armaments, largely under the Ministry of Supply, that dwarfed even the largest armament firms. One index of this is the fact that many of the firms privatised in the 1980s, or which are candidates for privatisation, had never been nationalised in the first place: Amersham International, BNFL (British Nuclear Fuels Limited), the UKAEA (United Kingdom Atomic Energy Authority), and Royal Ordnance. Furthermore, the 1980s saw the privatisation of the management of the Royal Dockyards and the AWRE (Atomic Weapon Research Establishment), Aldermaston. These measures, together with the denationalisation of aircraft manufacture (British Aerospace and Rolls-Royce) and the principal remaining war-shipbuilders (Yarrow, VSEL (Vickers Shipbuilding and Engineering Limited, Barrow), Cammell-Laird, Swan Hunter), meant that for the first time in history nearly all armaments production was in the hands of the private sector.

NOTES

1 See Ashworth 1953. None of the official histories of war production give an adequate account of public ownership (Edgerton 1984).
2 The arms sector has the predominant place in the history of the nationalisations of the 1970s: Rolls-Royce, Ferranti, BAC, Hawker-Siddeley, Scottish Aviation and the shipbuilders, were all defence contractors.
3 It is worth noting too that the post-war Ministry of Supply acted as a supply ministry not only to the armed forces, but also to government as a whole, and to a number of nationalised industries (Edgerton 1992).
4 See Hornby 1958, p. 28 for a comparison of production of various weapons in Britain in the two world wars.
5 The best sources for the inter-war arms industry are Hornby 1958, Davenport-Hines 1979, 1984, Gordon 1988.
6 To some extent, however, the extent of vertical integration even in the inter-

war years was more apparent than real. The reason for this was that the Admiralty (and later the Air Force) typically did not place orders for complete warships or aircraft. In the case of warships they placed separate orders for hull, armour, machinery, guns and mountings; similarly the Air Force ordered engines and airframes separately. The final assembly might take place in a private yard or aircraft factory, but the yard or factory would have a significant proportion of the components as 'Admiralty supply' or 'embodiment loan' items. For export orders, however, private contractors were indeed 'prime contractors', and it may well have been for this reason that vertical integration developed.

7 The latter was part of the background to the Jarrow Marches, see Wilkinson 1939.

8 In the 1930s many of the older battleships and battlecruisers were rebuilt in the Royal Dockyards: the 'complete modernisation' of *Warspite* cost £2,362,000: *Queen Elizabeth*, *Valiant*, and *Renown* were 'rebuilt on generally similar lines' (Brown 1983, p. 146).

9 Labour Party Defence Sub-Committee, 'Preliminary memorandum on public ownership and control of the arms industry', December 1937 (Labour Party Archives).

10 Minutes of War Cabinet Reconstruction Committee, 20/12/43. PRO (1943), CAB 87/5. This was the very first meeting of the Committee.

11 Civil aviation had become a state monopoly in 1946. The major airline, BOAC, had been nationalised in 1940. The Labour government additionally created BEA and BSAA.

12 Labour Party (1948a), 'The aircraft industry 1948'. See also Labour Party (1948b), Sub-Committee on Industries for Nationalisation, Minutes, 8/11/48, 8/12/48.

13 PRO (1939), AVIA 10/306. Note of meeting 25 January 1939.

14 War Cabinet Reconstruction Committee 20 December 1943, PRO (1943), CAB 87/5.

15 In the USA, after the war, a second warhead design centre was established; the USSR created a second 'Installation' in the 1950s.

16 For the contractual arrangements, see Ashworth 1953, pp. 142–56, 197–228.

17 Hansard (1938), House of Commons Debates, vol. 341. Cols. 1161–62, 17 November 1938.

18 PRO AVIA 10/306. Note of meeting 25 January 1939.

19 War Cabinet Reconstruction Committee R(43) 1st, 20 December 1943, PRO (1943) CAB 87/5.

20 In 1943 the Admiralty nearly 'took over' Harland and Wolff, the huge Belfast warship-builder (Moss and Hume 1986, p. 342).

21 As is made clear in a recent unpublished paper by Sebastian Ritchie.

22 PRO (undated, probably 1946), AVIA 65/1731, 'Financial Development of the Main SBAC firms from the beginning of the Rearmament period'.

23 Ibid. Furthermore aircraft firms distributed a higher proportion of wartime profits in dividends than comparable non-aircraft engineering firms. Ashworth gives figures of 20–30% return on private capital employed in aircraft during the war (Ashworth 1953, *Contracts and Finance*, p. 91).

24 *British Industries*, vol. 31, no. 9 (1946), p. 231. In an interesting editorial of

6 October 1946 *The Economist* noted that the machine tools would be sold off cheap, and saw this as a once and for all opportunity to reequip British industry with the latest machine tools. It is worth noting that 50,000 machine tools was very roughly the same as the British annual production of machine tools.

25 Three important new arms firms were created in the late 1930s: Nuffield Mechanisations (tanks); British Manufacture and Research (20mm cannon) and New Crown Forgings (shell forgings) (Hornby 1958, p. 152).

REFERENCES

Ashworth, William (1953), *Contracts and Finance*, London: HMSO.
      (1991), *The State in Business: 1945 to the mid 1980s*, London: Macmillan.
Barry, E. Eldon (1965), *Nationalisation in British Politics*, London.
Bornstein, Sam and Richardson, Al (1986), *War and the International: A History of the Trotskyist Movement in Britain 1937–1949*, London: Socialist Platform.
British Industries (1946).
Brockway, Fenner (1933), *The Bloody Traffic*, London: Gollancz.
Brown, D.K. (1983), *A Century of Naval Construction: The History of the Royal Corps of Naval Constructors*, London: Conway Maritime Press.
Burn, Duncan (1961), *The Economic History of Steelmaking, 1867–1939*, Cambridge University Press.
Carr, J.C. and Taplin, W. (1962), *History of the British Steel Industry*, Oxford: Blackwell.
Cockburn, Patricia (1985), *The Years of The Week*, London: Comedia. First published 1968.
Comptroller and Auditor General (1950), *Report of the Comptroller and Auditor General, Civil Appropriations Account (Class IX) 1949/50*, p. vii, pp. 1950/51, vol. XXV.
Craig, F.W.S. (1975), *British General Election Manifestos 1900–1974*, London: Macmillan.
Croucher, R. (1982), *Engineers at War, 1939–1945*, London: Merlin.
Davenport-Hines, R.P.T. (1979), 'The British Armaments Industry during Disarmament', University of Cambridge Ph.D. thesis.
      (1984) *Dudley Docker: The Life and Times of a Trade Warrior*, Cambridge University Press.
Devons, Ely (1950), *Planning in Practice*, Cambridge University Press.
      (1958), 'The Aircraft Industry', in Duncan Burn (ed.), *The Structure of British Industry: A Symposium*, vol. II, Cambridge University Press.
Edgerton, D.E.H. (1984), 'Technical innovation, industrial capacity and efficiency: public ownership and the British military aircraft industry, 1935–1948', *Business History*, 26: 247–97.
      (1991a), 'Liberal Militarism and the British State', *New Left Review*, 185 (Jan–Feb); pp. 138–69.
      (1991b), *England and the Aeroplane: an essay on a militant and technological nation*, London: Macmillan.
      (1992), 'Whatever happened to the British warfare state: the Ministry of Supply, 1945–1951', in Helen Mercer *et al.* (eds.), *Labour Government and Private Industry: the experience of 1945–1951*, Edinburgh: Edinburgh University Press, pp. 91–116.

Gordon, G. (1988), *British Seapower and Procurement: A reappraisal of rearmament*, London: Macmillan.

Gowing, Margaret (1964), *Britain and Atomic Energy, 1939–1945*, London: Macmillan.

(1974), *Independence and Deterrents: Britain and Atomic Energy 1945–1952, vol. I: Policy Making, vol. II, Policy Execution*, London: Macmillan.

Hancock, M. and Gowing, M.M. (1949), *British War Economy*, London: HMSO.

Hansard (1938), Parliamentary Debates, House of Commons.

Hargreaves, E.L. and Gowing, M.M. (1952), *Civil Industry and Trade*, London: HMSO.

Henderson, Arthur (1935), *Labour's Way to Peace*, London: Methuen.

Hornby, W. (1958), *Factories and Plant*, London: HMSO.

Jeremy, David (1991), 'The hundred largest employers in the United Kingdom, in manufacturing and non-manufacturing industries in 1907, 1935 and 1955', *Business History*, 33: 93–111.

Johnman, Lewis (1986), 'The Large Manufacturing Companies of 1935', *Business History*, 28: 226–45.

Jones, R. and Marriott, O. (1970), *Anatomy of a Merger*, London: Cape.

Labour Party (1945), *Report of the 44th Annual Conference, 1945*, London: Labour Party.

(1937), 'Preliminary memorandum on public ownership and control of the arms industry', Labour Party Defence Sub-committee, Labour Party Archives, December.

(1939), *Labour and the Armed Forces*, London.

(1948a), 'The Aircraft Industry 1948', Labour Party Archives, RD182.

(1948b), Minutes, 8 November and 8 December 1948, Sub-Committee on Industries for Nationalisation, Labour Party Archives, RD182.

Masefield, Sir Peter (1982), *To Ride the Storm: the story of airship R101*, London: Kimber.

Moss, M. and Hume, J.R. (1986), *Shipbuilders to the World: 125 Years of Harland and Wolff, Belfast, 1861–1986*, Belfast: Blackstaff Press.

Next Five Years (1935), *The Next Five Years: An Essay in Political Agreement*, London: Macmillan.

Plowden Report (1965), Table IV. Cmnd 2583, 1965.

Postan, M.M. (1952), *British War Production*, London: HMSO.

Postan, M.M., Hay, D. and Scott, J.D. (1964), *Design and Development of Weapons*, London: HMSO.

PRO (Public Record Office) (1939), AVIA 10/306, Notes of Meeting, 25 January.

(1943), CAB.87/5, Minutes of the War Cabinet Reconstruction Committee, R(43), 1st Meeting, 20/12/1943.

(undated, probably 1946), AVIA 65/1731, 'Financial development of the main SBAC firms from the beginning of the rearmament period'.

Reader, W.J. (1968), *Architect of Air Power*, London: Collins.

Royal Commission (1936a), *Minutes of Evidence taken before the Royal Commission of the Private Manufacture of and Trading in Arms, 1935–1936*, London: HMSO.

(1936b), *Report of Royal Commission of the Private Manufacture of and Trading in Arms, 1935–1936* Cmd. 5292, PP 1935/36, vol. vii.

(1936c), *Statement Relating to the Report of the Royal Commission on the*

Private Manufacture of and Trading in Arms, 1935–1936, Cmd. 5451, PP. 1936/37, vol. xxi.

Sampson, Anthony (1977), *The Arms Bazaar*, London: Hodder and Stoughton.

Scott, J.D. and Hughes, R. (1955), *The Administration of War Production*, London: HMSO.

(1962), *Vickers: a history*, London: Weidenfeld and Nicolson.

Shaw, C. (1983), 'The large manufacturing employers of 1907', *Business History*, 25.

TUC, 1945. *TUC Report (1945)*, London: TUC.

TUC Report (1946), London: TUC.

Tweedale, G. (1987), 'Business and investment strategies in the interwar British steel industry: A case study of Hadfield Ltd and Bean Cars', *Business History*, 29: 47–72.

Ward, Stephen (1988), *The Geography of Interwar Britain: the state and uneven development*, London: Routledge.

Warren, Kenneth (1989), *Armstrongs of Elswick: Growth in Engineering and Armaments to the Merger with Vickers*, London: Macmillan.

Whittle, Sir Frank (1953), *Jet: The Story of a Pioneer*, London: Muller.

Wilkinson, Ellen (1939), *The Town that was Murdered*, London: Gollancz.

Winston, Philip (1982), 'The British Government and Defence Production, 1943–1950', Cambridge University Ph.D. thesis.

9 The water industry 1900–51: a failure of public policy?

John A. Hassan

1 The economic and management problems of water resource development

The management and use of water are governed by the water cycle. This is initiated for present purposes when rain water replenishes upland gathering grounds and concludes when estuaries or other outlets release water to the sea. The water industry performs three different sets of functions within the water cycle. It supplies consumers with water. Secondly after use, effluent is returned to the cycle having been more or less purified at treatment works. Thirdly there are river conservancy tasks, touching upon the control, conservation and release of water, flood control and land drainage. All these functions interact. Sewage disposal may pollute sources used for domestic consumption; abstraction of water from a river may effect its capacity to dilute and carry effluent, and influences the interests of many other users, such as industry, canals and fisheries. Physical interdependencies have important implications for the management of water resources. From the time of Edwin Chadwick it has been argued that all these functions should be carried out by integrated river-basin based undertakings. These would be able to achieve an efficient and coordinated use of water resources and resolve the numerous human conflicts which arise in that connection.

Throughout the first half of the twentieth century, however, the water industry remained fragmented both across and within the three sectors. Water supply and sewage works were too small and numerous from the point of view of technical efficiency. Table 9.1 traces trends in the number of water supply undertakings. Even allowing for definitional discrepancies it shows that while ownership was not as widely dispersed in 1956 as in 1914, it was still very widely dispersed indeed. The period 1914 to 1945 was one of muted change in industrial organisation.

The ownership structure did not change greatly if at all, the private water companies being responsible for some 25 per cent of supplies throughout the period. Project development was also limited, especially

Table 9.1. *Estimate of numbers of undertakings in the water supply industry 1904–70*[1]

	Local authorities	Water boards and joint committees	Water companies	Other	Total
1904	870	0	221	—	—
1914	786	34	200	1,055[2]	2,100
1934	790	48	173	c 1,000[2]	c 2,011
1944	—	—	—	—	1,196
1956	883	42	90	15	1,055
1970	64	101	33	—	198

Notes:
[1] Survey numbers are not comparable as each estimate was carried out on a different basis.
[2] Includes very small private and/or non-statutory, companies.
Sources: The Municipal Year Book, 1910, p. 456; *Return of Water Undertakings*, PP 1914, LXXXIX, p. xxi; *Joint Committee on Water Resources and Supplies*, vol. II, minutes of evidence, PP 1934–5 (121), p. 1; Department of the Environment, *The future management of water in England and Wales: A Report by the Central Advisory Committee*, London: HMSO, 1971, p. 9.

compared to the pre-1914 and post-1950 periods. Water engineers looking back from the vantage point of 1945 were in no doubt that the great era of progress in their industry was 1870–1900, rather than the recent past. As the President of the Institution of Waterworks Engineers claimed (Taylor 1946, p. 27):

it is fair to say that between 1870 and 1896 there was an enormous development in works of water supply and the number of schemes designed and constructed during that period . . . was prodigious, and many of them are to their credit operating successfully today.

In the 1920s and 1930s the history of source development was characterised by consolidation and postponements. Did consumers of water services suffer as a result of this inertia? Attention given to the plight of the rural population and to the effects of drought conditions did highlight certain supply deficiencies. In general, however, the growth of demand of approximately 1.5 per cent per annum per head in the country as a whole over the first half of the century and less than 1 per cent in the urban population in the 1920s and 1930s, never put more than fleeting pressure on undertakers in satisfying market needs.

Developments for the other two sets of functions performed in the water industry are less easy to summarise. Sewerage and sewage treatment were the statutory responsibilities of the local authorities. Throughout the period up to 1900 local authorities carried out these operations, acting independently of one another, not only within the same river basin but also often with several separate sewerage works situated along the same stretch of river. Summing-up a great deal of evidence pertaining to sanitation it can be concluded that although there was no collapse of underground networks between the wars (this happened later), the physical infrastructure was rather neglected. By 1965 an estimated 60 per cent of all sewage works failed to meet Royal Commission standards laid down at the beginning of the century (Smith 1972, p. 178). The management of sewage and sewage treatment remained disorganised throughout the period.

A wide range of operations were undertaken by land drainage and river conservancy bodies. This sector has a long and complex history going back to the drainage of Romney Marsh in the reign of Henry II. By 1927 a heterogeneous collection of 361 drainage authorities, controlling some 2.9 million acres in England and Wales, had come into existence, exercising a great variety of powers and functions, without any uniformity of method. The Land Drainage Act of 1930 led to some rationalisation of river management. By 1943 fifty-three statutory Catchment Areas and 377 Drainage Boards had been established. This still represented a situation very remote from the ideal of integrated river management. The Boards, for example, had little or no power to control pollution, abstractions, or the activities of sewage treatment works.

These (ignored) physical interdependencies led to experts and official inquiries repeatedly calling for industrial reorganisation. Physical linkages, moreover, translated into economic ones and buttressed arguments for the creation of multi-functional large-scale units. Focusing upon water supply, the water industry is the classic natural monopoly, the duplication of distribution networks in a competitive situation being inefficient. Scale economies and falling long-run average costs were present. Under conditions prevailing in the late nineteenth century municipal enterprise appears to have performed better in satisfying public and private needs than private companies (see Hassan 1985 and Millward 1989 for fuller discussion). Externalities were also associated with the water industry, a wide variety of benefits including public health and fire-fighting advantages being generated by efficient distribution systems, but inadequate waste removal creates serious pollution. The social values and costs associated with water use present a strong case for public regulation. Others may prefer alternative solutions, but from a socialist point of view in the 1940s the case for nationalising the water industry was overwhelming. The fact that municipal ownership prevailed evades the point: the atomistic disorganisation of the industry was a bar to its efficient management. What was required were the advantages of large-scale operations under state control. As Ian Mikardo claimed, rationalisation would 'eliminate the very wide variations which exist in efficiency of operation between varying water undertakings throughout the country'. Smaller enterprises did not have the resources to produce a good service. There were all these guns 'shooting at the same target from big howitzers down to little popguns' producing a very differentiated output (see *Hansard*, 30 January 1948, pp. 1409–15).

Indeed nationalisation of the water industry had become official Labour Party policy in 1934, being adopted at the annual conference and set out in a 1935 document 'Water supply a national problem and its solution' (referred to in 'Water supply as a public service', PRO (1948), HLG/SO/2274). This was confirmed with the adoption at the 1943 annual conference of 'Labour's post-war water policy'. This document deplored the lack of 'national planning or control of our water resources' and advocated a National Water Commission and national plan to rectify these faults. It will be shown below, however, that Labour's interest in and commitment to this policy was weak. The industry was omitted from the nationalisation programme.

A prominent feature of the history of the water industry over the period under study was the caution displayed by Parliament when faced with opportunities to pass measures which would promote industrial modernisation. This legislative timidity reached its culmination with the Labour government's record between 1945 and 1951. Apart from a technical enactment in 1948 and notwithstanding measures on pollution control and land drainage, this radical nationalising administration failed to legislate at all on water supply reorganisation in England and Wales.

Given almost eighty years of reform proposals and given rather strong grounds for intervention as described above, this history of hesitation and non-action over the whole period and especially by the Labour government, is rather surprising. One purpose of this paper is to explore reasons for this negative outcome. In order to pursue these aims, in section 2 themes relating to policy issues and legislative proposals over the first half of the century will be explored. Later sections focus on explanations of the disappointing history of reform. Emphasis is placed upon the impact of interest politics, and the particular political situation of the late 1940s, including the government's prioritisation of its objectives.

2   Legislative and policy issues 1900–45

The foundations of the modern water industry were laid in the nineteenth century. Although there were some antecedents it was only from this period that water supplies and sewage disposal were formally organised in many communities. In the post-1850 years of rapid development organisational and legislative solutions were evolved, which may have served current requirements well enough, but which subsequently had the effect of locking the industry into a fragmented structure and which made reform more difficult to achieve.

The water supply industry grew up in a piecemeal fashion. Water undertakings were governed by legislation dating from 1847 and 1863. This provided a code of practice touching upon the obligation to supply, financial provisions and technical aspects. Statutory requirements to supply and increasing demand obliged expanding boroughs like those in Manchester, Glasgow and Birmingham to carry out evermore distant source developments. Public water supplies were developed by towns, for example, acquiring land and therefore water rights to aquifers, rivers and lakes. Under the law the undertakers had the power to impound or abstract water from a river only if all riparian owners agreed. In practice the exercise of this power was negligible because unanimous agreement by owners was rarely obtainable. Local authorities and companies had therefore to obtain additional local Acts of Parliament to develop new sources. A great disunity of practice emerged 'not infrequently the results of "Parliamentary bargains" between the water undertakings and their opponents rather than any settled course of policy' (*National Water Policy*, p. 14). Each proposal came to Parliament, furthermore, hydrologically devoid of any regional perspective. An unregulated, uncoordinated and wasteful system of provision resulted, the outcome of a competitive scramble by undertakers to obtain the right to develop sources. Sources claimed were not used to their full capacity. Smaller localities might be without supplies. The legislative process also enabled special interests to plead their case, notably the 'formidable interest' (Smith 1972, pp. 25–6) of millowners. They secured grossly generous allocations of compensation supplies, equivalent to from one-third to two-thirds of the yields of the impounding schemes authorised by waterworks legislation.

Friction over the distribution of supplies also arose over access to underground aquifers, an important source in London and the west Midlands. Water undertakers had no power to prevent landowners from draining off supplies, undermining the former's ability to execute their statutory obligation to supply customers. But landowners and other local interests were aggrieved by the abstractions of water undertakers which had some damaging effects, such as a lowering of the water table. This prompted the preparation of the Water Supplies Protection Bill in 1910, devised to 'restrict the power of authorised water undertakings' in various ways. The measure did not proceed, but the episode highlighted various defects in the framework governing water-resource development in the early twentieth century.

A Joint Select Committee examining the Bill made recommendations for industrial reorganisation, which echoed and anticipated the conclusions of earlier and later inquiries. After the First World War, for example, a Water Power Resources Committee was convened to advise on schemes which would promote employment and stimulate industry. To be effective it was found that the Committee's brief should be extended to cover the management of water resources as a whole. In the Committee's view the 'allocation of water has become too serious a matter to be left solely to a succession of Parliamentary committees which are constituted from time to time to deal with a particular Bill and have no continuity of existence' (*Second Interim Report* 1920, p. 5). It made a number of fairly interventionist recommendations, including the setting up of a Water Commission charged with the general control of water allocation, responsible directly to the Ministry of Health.

The post-war climate favourable to reform proved fleeting, however, and was followed by a rush for economism and decontrol. The Ministry of Health had taken over responsibility for public health and water supply matters from the old Local Government Board in 1919. In the 1920s the main avenues used for developing water policies were an Advisory Committee on Water formed in 1922, and Regional Advisory Water Committees. The latter were at the core of the government's policy towards water reorganisation in the inter-war years, but were really the means by which it could do nothing. The regional committees were supposed to coordinate the efforts of undertakers in developing joint schemes and to provide investigations of local needs and resources, out of which somehow a 'national policy' would emerge (Greenwood, *Hansard*, 22 July 1929, p. 939, 25 July 1929, p. 1485). The committees, however, were weak bodies, without any powers, covering only a fraction of the country by 1939, and undoubtedly they had a minimal impact upon the development of the water industry.

Drought in 1933 and 1934 along with other factors stimulated debate over the need for a National Water Policy. There was even belief that national control was 'inevitable and necessary' (Gourley 1935, p. 19). In anticipation of governmental action, interest groups such as the Institution of Water Engineers, sought to organise themselves better so as to influence water industry reform. As Sheail (1983, pp. 390–1) had described, the Minister of Health, Sir Edward Hilton-Young endeavoured to take advantage of heightened public interest in water supplies and was instrumental in the preparation of proposals. These, aiming to resolve the knot of organisational deficiencies besetting the industry, were set out in a draft White Paper: the Ministry would be empowered to regulate the acquisition of water rights, create joint boards, revise areas of supply and distribution, adjust compensation supplies and appoint regional advisory committees.

Between 1934 and 1939 the history of water reform is characterised by agonising legislative progress, political decisions being deferred by referring policy questions to additional bodies, and finally by failure. The two areas of discussion were the need to modernise and consolidate the waterworks code, which was regarded as a necessary preliminary to a modernisation of the industry's structure; this would be achieved by instituting greater ministerial powers along the lines of the Ministry of Health's 1934 proposals. Over these five years a Joint Select Committee deliberated, a new Central Advisory Committee (the Milne Committee) was formed and published two important reports, Parliamentary Bills were prepared, the water industry held conferences, and a great deal of presentation of special arguments by interested parties took place. All the time the Ministry of Health tried to nudge the process of reform along.

In 1939 a Bill was introduced with a view to simplifying and standardising waterworks legislation. It was anticipated that a measure to promote the comprehensive reform and reorganisation of water supplies would follow *after* this proposal had become law. Although the measure had received exhaustive examination by a Joint Committee of both Houses of Parliament and had passed the requisite stages in the House of Lords, the government decided, once the Second World War broke out, that it could not devote sufficient attention to the Bill and it was therefore withdrawn. There was no question of wider industrial reform measures materialising after the withdrawal of this Bill. Thus far from revolutionary attempts to take steps to modernise the water industry were thwarted.

In this chapter it is argued that there was a failure of public policy in relation to the water industry, in the sense of government failing to formulate and pursue to a successful outcome legislative proposals for the modernisation of the water industry and that this failure extended into the 1940s. This may appear harsh, as perhaps on three occasions between 1914 and 1951 the 'tide of events' intervened to abort the reform process including the initiative of 1934–5. That reform should be so long drawn out, leading to events interrupting the process, is revealing. It illustrates the difficulties of achieving reform where the strength of government commitment on the one hand is balanced against the influence of sundry interests anxious to modify or halt legislative proposals on the other.

Notwithstanding the set-back of 1939 the climate of opinion shifted during the course of the war, opening the way to the possibility of more significant reforms being achieved. Policy discussions first focused on land drainage. Lord Milne writing to the members of the Central Advisory Water Committee in November 1942 believed the moment was opportune to press government on the need for 'comprehensive river authorities'. Milne regretted that the Committee's work had to be suspended by the outbreak of war, its secretary having been called off for war service 'elsewhere'. The reason why Milne, and others engaged in land drainage management, perceived an opportunity for promoting proposals at that time was the initiation already of 'many planning activities . . . for dealing with local and national affairs after the war' (PRO (1942), HLG/ 50/1882, Milne to Central Advisory Committee members, November 1942). The Committee's subsequent report was extremely critical of the existing fragmented and incomplete approach to river management in England and Wales. Following earlier inquiries, the arguments for river-basin based river authorities were made again, with responsibilities for pollution prevention, land drainage and river conservation, along with most of the powers and duties of existing catchment, fisheries and navigation authorities to be transferred to them (Central Advisory Water Committee, *Third Report*, 1942–3).

In fact the Committee did not urge a radical restructuring of water management, so as to achieve an integrated approach to all the three main aspects of water use. The Committee preferred instead a separation between the power of the new river authorities it was advocating, and those of existing water supply undertakers. A failure of vision hampered the reform process throughout the 1940s. The Ministry of Health had already devoted much time and attention to drafting reform proposals and its aspirations appeared to have been limited to a sectoral approach.

3   The 1945 Water Act

In May 1943 the War Cabinet's Reconstruction Committee under the chairmanship of the Lord President received a memorandum from the Ministry of Health. This sought authorisation essentially to reintroduce initiatives which had been torpedoed by the outbreak of war. The Cabinet Reconstruction Problems Committee was asked to examine and report back on the question of water policy. Its recommendations followed closely on the Milne Committee reports of 1938–9 and 1942–3. This involved, firstly, devolving powers to the Ministry of Health for the scheduling of underground supplies, reassessing compensation supplies, and creating new undertakings by Order; and secondly creating new River Boards. As the Committee noted, these proposals involved a devolution of powers to the Minister of Health which had been firmly rejected in 1935. Since then, however, the situation had changed (PRO (1943), CAB/117/18, Lord President's Committee, Committee on Water Supply, Report, 30 July 1943, see also Sheail 1983, p. 394):

Indeed there is now a general readiness, both in Parliament and outside, to contemplate constitutional changes that would have been strongly opposed before the war. It is highly probable, therefore, that Parliament would be disposed to a substantial measure of devolution if it were represented – as we are convinced it might be – as essential to rapid progress in water supply.

Certainly by the following year there was a reasonably widely held assumption that legislative action, leading to organisational reform and a more involved role by central government in the water industry, was imminent and desirable. There was a fair degree of sympathy and support in some circles for what the Minister of Health was trying to achieve. The Ministry of Health's Permanent Secretary, Sir John Maude, was written to in a Cabinet Memorandum with respect to his minister's legislative proposals: 'Larger issues of policy arise on your proposed Bill to secure the better planning and use of water resources. We certainly wish you the best of luck in this enterprise' (PRO (1944), HLG/50/1876, memo to Maude, 5 February 1944).

The Cabinet, however, was against the more socialistic proposals favoured by some of its members, fearing 'fierce opposition' would be provoked if an attempt was made to replace the existing '1,100 odd undertakings' with a less devolved system of control. The decision to take a more cautious approach was significant: it led to the passing of the 1945 Water Act, arguably an inadequate measure, which would complicate the Labour government's position on water industry reform over the following years.

As Sheail (1983, pp. 394–5) has shown in his admirable treatment of these events, the Minister of Health successfully obtained government backing to set out legislative proposals, based on earlier Milne Committee reports in a government White Paper. Willink introduced the proposed Bill in the House of Commons in a positive manner. Some MPs reacted by welcoming the Bill. Others were much more critical. To one 'this "hugger-mugger" of a thousand concerns messing about with the water supply is altogether too bad . . . We want one competent national authority to deal with the problem . . . in a masterly fashion, and not in a local, tin-pot, parish-pump attitude of mind'. Adapting this analogy Mander (*Hansard*, 3 May, p. 1360) stated: 'We started with the parish-pump; now we have got beyond that but still have 1,000 authorities'.

While some politicians were very disappointed with the White Paper, the water supply industry was quite receptive to it. This was undoubtedly because a minimalist reform was being promoted which would not offend many of the interested parties in the industry. There was an extensive exchange of views between the Ministry of Health and a wide range of bodies – professional and local authority associations, water undertakers, water users and others. Most organisations, especially in the water supply sector, were broadly in favour of the principles behind the reform. They made a variety of detailed technical or representational submissions specific to their own interests. The British Waterworks Association, for example, was generally sympathetic to the measure. Reflecting the tenor of much water industry politics, however, it observed that 'the over-whelming majority of persons' on the Central Advisory Committee (which was to be retained), 'represent interests which are avowedly seeking to extract concessions from the water industry. The water supply industry therefore views with considerable alarm the perpetuation of the present structure of the Committee', and appealed for an adjustment (PRO (1944), HLG/50/1884, British Waterworks Association, 'Memo-randum', November 1944). A central principle of the government's atti-tude towards the reform was that the web of existing interests should be taken into account. Despite this, the Act is often seen as a turning-point. Porter (1978, p. 24) noted it greatly increased the involvement of central government with water supply problems and the supervision of water undertakers and, she said, marked the beginning of a national water policy. For Smith (1972, p. 29) the measure was the 'first real attempt at water resource legislation in this country'. Contemporary expectations were also often positive (*MYB*, 1945, p. 289).

The Act followed the 1944 White Paper closely. It gave the Minister of Health the statutory duty of promoting source developments and the conservation of resources; his 'planning policy' was to be assisted by advice and information supplied by a system of central and regional Advisory Committees, the former now being elevated to statutory status; the Minister had the power, subject to Parliamentary procedures, to create joint water boards, vary limits of supply and arrange for bulk distributions.

This apparently highly significant legislative breakthrough, however, did nothing to restructure water management. As noted above decisions had been made to keep separate the reform of water supply on one hand, and river management on the other. The White Paper of 1944 specifically (p. 22) recommended that in future regional River Boards should 'have no responsibility for water supply as such, nor would they have any power to veto the abstraction of water from the river by a water undertaker'. Nevertheless the River Boards Act of 1948 did represent an important step forward. New comprehensive River Boards were established, but they still possessed very limited powers indeed over source developments and the possibility of conflict with water supply undertakers remained high.

An argument being developed in this chapter is that legislation passed between 1945 and 1948 failed to provide an effective framework for the efficient management and utilisation of water resources in England and Wales. River management has been touched upon. Sanitation was not affected by 1940s legislation and remained chaotically disorganised. The most acute question, however, revolves around the 1945 Act: did it deliver the long-awaited reorganisation of the water supply sector?

As indicated Ministerial responsibilities for the promotion of an efficient provision of water supplies, as well as for the 'direction of a national policy relating to water', were stipulated in the Act. It did not, however, create effective machinery for the discharge of these duties. Like the River Boards the Minister had no direct power to develop waterworks or storage reservoirs for conservation purposes (Smith 1972, p. 31).

The main failure of the Act, however, lay in the provisions for promoting rationalisation. In principle it did now give the Minister of Health compulsory powers to achieve regroupings. Certainly in the late 1940s and early 1950s there was a flurry of administrative activity, inspectors' surveys into regional provisions were carried out, recommendations were submitted and Ministerial Orders were made. Unfortunately they made little impact on the overall picture. Significant reorganisation did not happen. There were 1,196 water supply undertakers in England and Wales in 1944, still 1,055 in 1956.

The reasons for this failure include the inadequacy of ministerial powers specified in the Act, and local resistance. Parochial mentalities and a desire to maintain autonomy led to few enterprises being prepared to 'admit that conditions would be improved if they joined with others', in the words of a Ministry of Health official (PRO (1948), HLG/50/2274, 'Water: Some Notes on Public Ownership', 24 August 1948). Bevan the Health Minister acknowledged he was empowered to form joint boards by compulsion. Because of safeguards written into the Act, however, procedures under it were expensive and involved. In each case lengthy preliminary inquiries with local authorities were necessary, followed, if there were objections, by a public inquiry into the draft Order and consideration by a Joint Select Committee of both Houses if objections were pursued. Parliamentary agents, counsel and expert witnesses had to be retained and appear before the Select Committee. As Bevan complained, each opposed Order could well be the equivalent of an opposed private Bill with all the expenses that incurred (PRO (1950), CAB/124/234 (Bevan), 'Nationalisation of public water supply', 10 March 1950). As his official conceded: 'It is very doubtful whether more than a thousand undertakings can be reviewed on this basis' (ibid.).

Even in the early 1970s an inquiry discovered organisational defects in the water industry strikingly similar to those prevailing at the beginning of the century: operating units were too small technically, conflicts arose over source developments between river and water supply authorities, and a variety of obstacles stood in the way of the planning and development of major regional and large-scale schemes (Central Advisory Committee 1971, pp. 33–9).

4   The role of interest groups

Labour's (non-interventionist) record on the water industry in the nationalisation period may be set within the longer-term story of policy prevarications and developmental inertia. Sheail's study (1983) emphasises Parliamentary and governmental reluctance to tamper with the rights of property-owners and water users. This was certainly one ingredient in a complex interaction of factors. This chapter will bring responsibility back more to the water supply sector itself by examining the role of interest group politics and governmental priorities in the late 1940s.

There are a number of themes and sectors which could be explored to develop arguments relating to the role of interest politics in the water industry. This discussion will be limited to the municipal water authorities and the professional associations. By the 1920s the local authorities occupied an entrenched position. This was the outcome of the role played by local government in acquiring responsibility for the development of sources during the second half of the nineteenth century; it was also the result of the close connection between water supply and other local government functions or interests, such as public health, fire-fighting, street cleansing and more indirectly the maintenance of urban property values and low industrial costs. As previously indicated, the industry expanded as a matter of many individual initiatives, without any regional dimension. Municipal authorities developed a jealously protective attitude towards their waterworks enterprises. By the early twentieth century they were demanding freedom of control from government supervision. The Municipal Corporations Association submitted the argument in 1912, in relation to a proposed ministerial Order: 'In order that the water authorities may discharge their responsibilities effectively, it is essential that they should have a free hand in the management of their undertakings . . . and that they should not be interfered with by another body constituted for an entirely different purpose' (*Second Interim Report* 1920, p. 21).

The desire to assert their own autonomy, furthermore, led to conflict both among water authorities, and between supply authorities and other sectors. The competitive scramble for upland sources in the nineteenth century led to smaller and rural communities losing out. There were also serious conflicts over access to, and use of underground sources, especially between London County Council and Hertfordshire (Sheail 1982, pp. 398–9). The fragmented structure of water management also led to conflict between water supply undertakings and river conservancy interests. Land drainage and conservancy boards had aims pertaining to the conservation, flow and redistribution of resources within river basins, which frequently collided with water authorities' intentions to impound the upper reaches of streams.

The large municipal water authorities, however, came to represent a powerful lobby. There are few examples of their proposals for large-scale projects being obstructed by Parliament. Their attitude is reflected in the statement of Sir A.M. Samuel before the Joint Committee on Water Resources (1935–6, p. 41) which acknowledged that an impression had been created 'that the claims of the water authorities are either *pari passu* or competitive with the claims of riparian owners, catchment boards, the Federation of British Industry . . .', but, he affirmed 'the claims and demands of the water authorities are absolutely paramount'. The municipal authorities, furthermore, both demanded (and obtained) their right to be consulted in the process leading up to the revision of water legislation (*Report by the Joint Committee*, 1938–9, p. 41).

In relation to the imminent reform of the industry, submissions by the Municipal Corporations Association on the 1944 White Paper reveal, however, defensive and cautious thinking. The corporations were generally fearful of possible transfer of powers from local to central government and a diminished role for municipalities in the water industry. While broadly favourable towards the White Paper, a number of provisos were made. The Association believed that representation of the municipal undertakings on the Central Advisory Water Committee was 'most inadequate', and in relation to increased Ministerial powers 'viewed some of the matters with grave anxiety' (*MYB* 1946, p. 288).

The Labour Party in government was aware of the susceptibilities of the large municipal undertakings and perhaps conscious of the relative importance of Labour councils within the Labour movement. When the Cabinet got round to considering water nationalisation and reform, there was anxiety not to alienate the local authorities. This concern influenced the form in which proposals were drawn up. Morrison pointed out that it would be unwise to present the large local authorities 'with a scheme prepared in advance. We have to remember that large cities, for example,

Manchester, Sheffield . . . have become responsible for vast schemes and successful systems of supply' (PRO (1950), CAB/124/234, Memorandum by Lord Privy Seal, 'A National Water Supply Scheme', 11 May 1950). The Cabinet was warned that the proposals for nationalisation which were being drawn up would involve a substantial encroachment upon local government, which would be 'much resented . . . The experience of the Northern Area Passenger transport scheme is a pointer to the extent of opposition which may be aroused' (PRO (1951), CAB/124/234, JAR Pimlott, 'Water', 14 February 1951).

Initially Bevan, then Dalton, took a strong line on water nationalisation in 1950, and preferred a model which would have concentrated power considerably at the centre. Ultimately, in deference to resistance from the local authority associations and misgivings in Cabinet, work was started on a Bill which envisaged a much more devolved system of management than originally planned, and which retained major local authority involvements (PRO (1951), HLG/68/104, Memorandum by the Minister of Local Government and Planning, July 1951).

The municipal water authorities were a civic lobby. Another overlapping but distinct area of interest was that which was represented by a professional or industrial lobby. Behind the public and private water undertakings were the professional associations representing owners, directors, managers and engineers. They emerged in the late nineteenth and early twentieth centuries and came to exercise a crucial influence upon government policy in the 1930s and 1940s. The most professionally orientated of the three main bodies was the Association of Waterworks Engineers (AWE) with 874 members in 1945. The membership of the British Waterworks Association (BWA) consisted of 167 Local Authorities and seventy-six water companies in the mid-1930s. Thirdly, fifty-eight companies also belonged to the Water Companies Association. In the period immediately after the First World War, in the context of the financial and supply difficulties faced by water undertakings, and also the publication by the Water Power Resources Committee of its proposals for industrial reorganisation, the President of the AWE advocated a coordinated approach 'with the British Waterworks Association and other kindred bodies for the purpose of enlightening Parliament and the public' as to the position of the water industry (Dixon 1920, p. 15). This initiative was seized upon by the BWA, and the two organisations did collaborate closely in presenting their arguments before government and the Water Power Resources Committee. These two bodies, opposed to the establishment of further 'bureaucracies' concerned with the industry, did recognise the need for the creation of an extra-Parliamentary body to supply government with information and advice, which would be representative of all water interests. But they maintained 'such a body already exists in the British Waterworks Association acting jointly with its technical brother institution, the Institution of Waterworks Engineers'. They concluded that these two bodies should 'bring their joint influence to bear', to present their arguments before government ('Memorandum on the Final Report' (1922), p. 244).

Perhaps a little surprisingly this self-interested argument was accepted by government, and the newly established Minister of Health appointed the Advisory Committee on Water in 1922, comprising nominations from the three professional associations. This was a very small body, with only six members in 1929 and thirteen in 1935. There were many criticisms from water users that it was a very sectional body, and in 1937 the separate Central Advisory Committee on Water was created, representative of a much wider range of interests. Also known as the Milne Committee, it was a very influential source of advice to government between 1937 and 1945, but recommended nothing that seriously threatened municipal, corporate or professional water-supply interests.

The position of the professional lobby on water industry reform was conservative. The BWA submitted at its 1922 conference that 'any system of national control over the allocation of water resources . . . must adequately provide for supreme control to be vested in Parliament alone' ('Water supply matters' (1922), p. 493). A joint opinion of the BWA and AWE reaffirmed this position: 'The State exercises its authority through Parliament, it follows consequently, that no final control whatever can be vested in any department of the Government, the final decision . . . must remain with Parliament' ('Memorandum on the Final Report' (1922), p. 241). This was an argument for the preservation of the nineteenth-century practice, whereby individual undertakers developed sources and works on an uncoordinated, one-scheme-at-a-time, basis.

The professional associations exerted themselves energetically in the mid-1930s to influence the reform process proactively. There was even some threatening talk of water nationalisation in the air. The AWE instructed its members to restrict their allegiance only to that body, and resign membership of any other organisation, in the belief that this would strengthen its ability to influence policy making. Professional mobilisation reached its climax in the holding of a Triple Conference of the three associations in 1934–5. A variety of conservative motions were passed. The government's weak system of regional advisory committees was supported. The Triple Conference also urged that 'Water Undertakers should remain autonomous, except the existing measure of control . . . Any outside interference with the local management of water undertakings . . . would be disastrous' ('Report of the Joint Conference' (1935), pp. 4–5).

This philosophy influenced the thinking behind the 1945 Water Act.

The second principle of the 1944 White Paper (arising out of the Milne Committee's earlier proposals) was that responsibility for water supplies should rest with democratic bodies – at the centre with the Minister and Parliament, at the circumference with the local authorities – but that unnecessary organisational change should be avoided (Ministry of Health (1943–4), p. 3).

Fragmentation in the water sector's industrial structure may be contrasted with a reasonable degree of *political* coordination of the industry's interests through pressure groups. As the industry perceived its interests to be served largely through a defence of the status quo, insofar as lobbying was successful the net impact was to sustain industrial disorganisation.

The way in which the water industry developed in the nineteenth century appeared to encourage the proliferation of discrete interests and bodies. By the 1920s the structure crystallised. Vested positions had been built up. Many organisations in principle were in favour of reforms and rationalisation, but on terms which did not threaten their own autonomy and rights of representation. Voluntary mergers foundered on the fragmented structure of the industry, but the industry's difficulty in influencing government policy because of its disorganised structure was partially overcome through more cohesive political organisation.

5   Contrasts with electricity and gas

If an impression is created that government was more susceptible to pressure groups in the water field than was the case for other industries there are a number of reasons why this may have been the case. Firstly, there was a counterpart to the fragmented structure of the industry in the fragmentation of the responsibilities of government departments in this area. Departmental involvements were divided up between the Ministry of Health, the Board of Trade, the Ministry of Agriculture and Fisheries and the Department of Scientific and Industrial Research, and even within these Departments there were internal divisions and conflicts. This created a fertile field for lobbying. Moreover, the separate departments frankly viewed themselves as patrons of sectional interests. Sheail's (1983, pp. 390–2) examination of the Minister of Health's promotion of new proposals in 1934 demonstrates the conflicting positions taken up in Cabinet and the acrimonious discussion which arose and which undermined the chances of agreement being reached on reform. Yet it was also striking subsequently, perhaps partly because of this experience, the extent to which a successor at the Ministry was unwilling to antagonise the numerous interests in the water services field, when formulating proposals which reached fruition in the 1945 Water Act. Willink present-ing the Bill in the Commons stated that 'many sectional interests', refer-ring to 1,000 water supply undertakers, and canal, industrial and agri-cultural interests, must be given a chance to put their case. He added that there must be 'ample protection for those concerned' (*Hansard*, 3 May 1944, p. 1342).

A second issue is that the 'defence of property rights' could be expected to attract a positive response in some government quarters in this period. But the nature of the interests involved in the case of resistance to water reform should be understood. Industry was a significant owner of riparian rights and deployed leading representatives from the FBI and large enterprises such as ICI to present its point of view (for example before the Joint Committee on Water Resources and Supply of 1935–6). Under the existing situation, which reform threatened to disturb, industry's use of the water resource was especially privileged in a number of respects: industrial property, besides generous compensation supplies, enjoyed uncontrolled access to underground sources, for example, and virtually uncontrolled use of rivers as sewers to remove polluting effluent. Cabinet reluctance to agree to measures which infringed property rights might give the impression that landed wealth was involved, but equally manu-facturing interests were at stake.

In the 1940s attention moves to the municipal water lobby and the impression that the Labour government was more susceptible to it than was the case with electricity or gas. This stemmed from a number of factors. Firstly, the local authority stake in water was older, bigger and more complex (given public health and other municipal responsibilities) than was the case with electricity and gas. Secondly, there was nothing analogous in water to the maturing of franchises which brought the issue of electricity distribution to the fore in the 1940s. Finally, the Labour government had a great interest in the pursuit of a national fuel policy, with which the nationalisation of the two power utilities was associated. There was nothing comparable to this in the case of water.

Beyond these specific explanations for the apparent strong impact of lobbying in the water industry in this period, there is a more general question relating to the role of scientific and technical knowledge in the environmental field. The disciplines involved, such as bacteriology and water analysis, were still quite young, and there appears to have been a dearth of specialist expertise, certainly among the relevant leading civil servants and politicians. This left the latter at a disadvantage insofar as lobbies were able to manipulate specialist knowledge, for example through the use of expert witnesses at inquiries (Sheail 1982, p. 406, Luckin 1986, chapters 2 and 3). At another level it is noticeable that the

Ministry of Health depended heavily upon Advisory Committees in its development of policy between the 1920s and 1940s, which reflects a lack of internal expertise. The Advisory Committees were not much more than representative organs of various water interests, and were certainly not as independent of the industry, as was the Heyworth Report which advocated state compulsion for the gas industry in 1945 or the Jowitt Report which advised on electricity.

Given the readiness of ears in Cabinet to listen to pleas from pressure groups, given the rigour of lobbying, given that support for reform was always conditional on sectional interests not being harmed, and given the neutralising effects of interdepartmental rivalries, it is hardly surprising that water industry reform proceeded at a snail's pace between 1910 and 1945.

6   Labour's nationalisation policy in the 1940s

Through the 1940s and down to 1948 it cannot be pretended that the labour movement at large was especially agitated by the problems of the water industry. It was included in the nationalisation shopping list adopted at the 1943 conference, but interest at grass-roots level appears to have been thin. *One* isolated communication, political in character, was received by the Ministry of Health when it was canvassing opinion on the 1944 White Paper. The Northampton Trades Council urged the government 'in their deliberations on post-war reconstruction to adopt the principle of nationalisation and wide expansion of our water supplies' (PRO (1944), HLG/50/1884, G.H. Lovell to Ministry of Health, 21 April 1944). In 1946 a motion from the Pitsea, Vange and District Ratepayers Association stung the local council to press the government to nationalise all water undertakings and to communicate their advice to the Prime Minister and Minister of Health (PRO (1948), HLG/50/2274, Pitsea, Vange and District Health Committee, letter, 6 June 1946). Otherwise Labour adopted a generally silent position on the issue of the country's water supplies.

Further, up to early 1948 the government's more-or-less official view was that the 1945 Water Act was working satisfactorily. John Edwards, Parliamentary Secretary to the Minister of Health said in the House of Commons that the Act was 'working very well, on the whole'. The Minister had already made ninety Orders, and other schemes were being developed. 'The House will agree that these are fruitful results after two years' experience of the working of the Act' (*Hansard*, 30 January 1948, p. 1394). In some quarters expectations had been high that the new administration would transform the way water supply matters were handled. In August 1945 an MP in the Commons said: 'I should like the new Minister of Health to be here, because a great dynamo of energy is going to affect the Department and it will concern not only housing and a supply of vitamins, but a policy of supplying water'. The speaker seemed to believe that water nationalisation had already been achieved (*Hansard*, 17 August 1945, p. 232).

In 1948 the misinformed silence on the water industry was broken and the subject of its reform and nationalisation came to the fore in the Labour Party and government. There were a number of reasons for this. First, the promotion of a procedural measure to revise parts of the 1945 Water Act reopened the issue of industrial organisation. Second, some members of the government, especially Bevan, were beginning to come to the conclusion that the 1945 reform had not been a success. And third, there appears to have been a genuine motivation to continue the process of socialisation.

A Water Bill was introduced to iron out certain defects in the 1945 Act, with a view to facilitating the formation of new undertakings and joint boards. It was a relatively minor measure but it did give the occasion to those impatient with the government's hitherto neglect of water reform to vent their spleen. Ian Mikardo in the Parliamentary debate presented an acute argument in favour of the advantages of rationalisation in the water industry. Mikardo did not criticise the government's handling of the water industry as such. Others were more critical and were looking for something more dramatic from government than the technical measure being proposed. 'The Bill is a disappointment . . . it means the maintenance of the *status quo* based upon evolution that comes from legislation passed 100 years ago', Ellis Smith perceptively observed (*Hansard*, 30 January 1948, pp. 1405–8) continuing: 'expediency, expediency, expediency . . . The Bill is a product of a Victorian mind . . . is not worthy of Labour . . . We should have adopted in accordance with Labour's policy, a national water policy . . . This Bill perpetuates the multiplicity [of undertakings]'.

Pressure for more decisive action was, therefore, building up by 1948. Later that year was an exchange of correspondence and confidential reports among individuals in the Labour Party, including Bevan himself, and officials in the Ministry of Health, on the subject of water nationalisation. By October 1948 a decision to adopt the policy of nationalisation had been made by the Cabinet's Industries for Nationalisation Sub-Committee (PRO (1948), HLG/50/2274, Young to Bevan, 13 November 1948). This followed a cogent case being made for the policy circulated in a confidential paper which concluded (ibid., 'Water Supply a Public Service', September 1948):

To sum up, the main proposals of this paper are for the nationalisation of the water industry under a National Water Commission, with regional boards on the analogy of the nationalisation of gas and electricity but with further dispersal from the regions to the local authorities where they have already proven they can do the work.

Over the next two-and-a-half years the government continued to develop its water nationalisation policy. In July 1951 Dalton sought Cabinet approval for a proposal to prepare a Bill for the nationalisation of the industry. Among the interesting aspects of the episode is that the commitment to undertake a further significant nationalisation measure was more positive at this stage than some accounts suggest (Gregg 1967, p. 79). On the other hand, as previously indicated the events underline the power of the municipal lobby at that time. The Minister met local authority associations in March 1951. Afterwards he presented a considerably watered-down version of plans previously energetically advocated by himself and Bevan. It was envisaged that local authorities would retain a strong role in 50–60 new Joint Boards (PRO (1948), HLG/50/2274 and 68/104, sundry documents).

Ultimately this proposed reform of the water industry, like a number before it, was swept away by events. Mounting difficulties associated with the Korean War, inflation, petrol-rationing and budgetary problems led Attlee to call a further General Election, which brought the Conservative Party to power with a majority of seventeen seats on 25 October 1951. If Labour had survived it is almost certain that the water industry would have been nationalised. Rather than dwell upon this conjecture, however, the remainder of the discussion will focus on why it was left too late, that is why water was not included in the first wave of nationalisation measures, given the strong arguments which existed for its inclusion.

There are a number of reasons why water was excluded from the first nationalisation programme. Firstly, there was the almost historical accident that the Water Act had been passed just prior to Labour assuming power which nullified, to some extent, the need for a fresh reorganisation proposal to be prepared. As one MP said at the time of the 1948 revision of the Act: 'I fully recognise, as we all must do, that there are practical difficulties in introducing a large-scale measure at the moment. The Water Act, 1945, is not so very old and was indeed a great improvement on the state of affairs which existed before' (*Hansard*, 30 January 1948, p. 1417).

Secondly and partly arising from this point, for a variety of reasons water did not present itself as a priority candidate for nationalisation. In the 1940s the Left's thinking on public ownership was focusing increasingly upon coal and power, iron and steel and transport. Land nationalisation (a prominent call earlier in the century) was receiving less stress, which reflected recognition that this would imply enormous practical difficulties impinging upon property rights, some of which were in fact shared with extending state control in the water industry. On such criteria as urgency or suitability there were too many industries before water which appeared to possess stronger arguments for nationalisation, quite apart from specific historical or economic considerations which made early action paramount in particular cases.

Pragmatic considerations equally governed the exclusion of certain industries. The Ministry of Health, responsible for water, simply had its hands full with other concerns. Mikardo advised those who criticised the government's handling of water reform, that they were 'pushing at an open door' and implied that the Ministry of Health could only afford the time to be 'tinkering about' with the water industry, because of its preoccupations with the reforms of the health service and local government. When the politicians involved, he suggested, 'are a bit less busy with the doctors and local authorities and other problems which they have to deal with' they would surely set about addressing the question with vigour (*Hansard*, 30 January 1948, pp. 1409–15).

Both practicality and socialist doctrine played a part in determining what was included or excluded from the nationalisation programme. On the one hand, the case was made out for socialisation 'industry by industry, on the merits of each case' (Morrison, cited Chester 1975, p. 8). On the other hand, the ideological inspiration of proposed transfers of ownership was obvious. In a socialistic analysis undoubtedly a strong theoretical argument for nationalising the water industry could be made. On the grounds of expediency and practical necessity the case for it in 1945–7 seemed weak.

REFERENCES

PUBLIC RECORD OFFICE

PRO (1942), HLG/50/1882, Milne to Central Advisory Committee Members, November.
PRO (1943), CAB/117/18, Lord President's Committee on Water Supply, Report, 30 July.
PRO (1944), HLG/50/1876, Memo to Maude, 5 February.
PRO (1944), HLG/50/1884, G.H. Lovell to Ministry of Health, 21 April; British Waterworks Association, Memorandum, November.
PRO (1948), HLG/50/2274, 'Water: some notes on public ownership', 24 August; 'Water supply as a public service', Confidential Labour Party Paper, September; Young to Bevan, 13 November.
PRO (1950), CAB/124/234, 'Nationalisation of public water supply', A. Bevan, 10

March; Memorandum by the Lord Privy Seal, 'A National Water Supply Scheme', 11 May.
PRO (1951), CAB/124/234, 'Water', J.A.R. Pimlott, 14 February.
PRO (1951), HLG/68/104, Memorandum by the Minister of Local Government and Planning, July.

OFFICIAL SOURCES

Report from the Joint Select Committee on the Water Supplies (Protection) Bill [H.L.] (1910), together with the Proceedings of the Committee (226) vi.
Parliamentary Return (1914), *Return of Water Undertakings*, LXXXIX.
Board of Trade (1919, 1920), *Interim Report of the Water Power Resources Committee*, Cd. 79; *Second Interim Report*, Cd. 776.
Joint Committee on Water Resources and Supplies (1934–5), vol. II, minutes of evidence, appendix (121), vi.
Report from the Joint Committee on Water Resources and Supplies (1935–6), Proceedings of the Committee, minutes of evidence and appendix (159), vi.
Report by the Joint Committee of the House of Lords and the House of Commons appointed to consider the Water Undertakings Bill [H.L.] (1938–9), Proceedings of the Committee and minutes (130), viii.
Ministry of Health (1938–9), *Second Report of the Central Advisory Water Committee*, Cd. 5896.
Ministry of Health (1942–3), *Third Report of the Central Advisory Water Committee*, Cd. 6465.
Ministry of Health (1943–4), *A National Water Policy*, Cd. 6515.
Department of the Environment (1971), *The future management of water in England and Wales; A Report by the Central Advisory Committee*, London: HMSO.
Hansard, Parliamentary Debates, House of Commons.

PUBLISHED AND OTHER SOURCES

Chester, Sir Norman (1975), *The Nationalisation of British Industry 1945–51*, London: HMSO.
Dixon, F.J. (1920), 'Presidential Address', *Trans. of the Institution of Water Engineers*, 25: 6–22.
Gourley, H.J.F. (1935), 'Presidential Address', *Trans. of the Institution of Water Engineers*, 40: 12–23.
Gregg, P. (1967), *The Welfare State: An Economic and Social History of Great Britain from 1945 to the present day*, London: George G. Harrop.
Hassan, J.A. (1985), 'The Growth and Impact of the British Water Industry in the Nineteenth Century', *Economic History Review*, 38: 531–47.
Luckin, B. (1986), *Pollution and Control: A Social History of the Thames in the Nineteenth Century*, Bristol: Adam Hilger.
'Memorandum on the Final Report of the Water Power Resources Committee' (1922), *Water and Water Engineering*, 24: 241–5.
Millward, R. (1989), 'Privatisation in historical perspective: the UK water industry', in D. Cobham, R. Harrington and G. Zis (eds.), *Money, trade and*

payments: Essays in honour of D.J. Coppock, Manchester: Manchester University Press, pp. 188–209.

Municipal Yearbook (MYB).

Porter, E. (1978), *Water Management in England and Wales*, Cambridge University Press.

'Report of the Joint Conference of the Institution of Water Engineers, the British Waterworks Association, and the Water Companies Association on National Water Policy' (1935), appendix to *Trans. of the Institution of Water Engineers*, 40: 1–6.

Sheail, J. (1983), 'Planning, Water Supplies and Ministerial Power in inter-war Britain', *Public Administration*, 61: 386–95.

(1982), 'Underground water abstraction: indirect effects of urbanisation upon the countryside', *Journal of Historical Geography*, 8: 395–408.

Smith, K. (1972), *Water in Britain: A Study in Applied Hydrology and Resource Geography*, London: Macmillan.

Taylor, G.M.C. (1946), 'Presidential Address', *Trans. of the Institution of Water Engineers*, 51: 22–32.

'Water Supply Matters' (1922), *Municipal Journal*, p. 493.

10 Debating the nationalisation of the cotton industry 1918–50

John Singleton

1 Introduction

Given the dire problems faced by the British cotton industry during the twentieth century, it is not surprising that nationalisation became a significant issue. Institutionalist economic historians have suggested that Lancashire was put at a disadvantage because it had no visible hand to remould the cotton industry and coordinate its production and marketing strategies (Lazonick 1981a, 1983, 1986, Mass and Lazonick 1991). The visible hand that Lazonick has in mind is the Chandlerian business corporation, with its long-term strategy and its sophisticated management structure. Advocates of the public ownership of the mills believed that the visible hand of a British Cotton Corporation would have been equally efficacious.

Nationalisation had considerable support among the cotton workers during the 1930s and 1940s and the Labour Party was not unsympathetic to their aims. Previous studies have dismissed the operatives' support for public ownership as a tactical ploy to chivvy the government and employers into drawing up a scheme for rationalising the industry (Barry 1965, p. 340, Edgerton 1986, p. 270). While the war cry of nationalisation was never as popular in the mills as it was in the pits, it is misleading to suggest that the issue was not taken seriously by the operatives. State ownership was one of a number of options under consideration in Lancashire during the 1930s and 1940s. When Labour came to power in 1945, dark threats were made by ministers about what might happen to the masters if they failed to toe the socialist line. The 1946 Board of Trade Working Party report on cotton acknowledged that many employers saw nationalisation as a 'Sword of Damocles' hanging over Lancashire (Board of Trade 1946, p. 157).

This chapter explains and evaluates the debate over the nationalisation of the cotton industry. Section 2 provides a brief introduction to the problems confronting the cotton industry in the first half of the twentieth century. Section 3 examines the movement for nationalisation of the mills in the inter-war period, and section 4 considers the 1940s, when the campaign for nationalisation was rekindled and then fizzled out.

2   The condition of the cotton industry in Lancashire

There were a number of distinct processes in the production of cotton textiles. First, the raw cotton, which was imported in large bales, had to be untangled and its fibres combed out in a lengthy series of preparatory processes conducted in the cardroom. Spinning followed, in which cotton fibres were stretched and twisted into yarn of a certain fineness. Weaving involved the combination of vertical (warp) and horizontal (weft) yarn in order to make a piece of cloth. In many cases, yarn or cloth was dyed to make it more attractive. The bleaching of cloth and its printing with coloured patterns were common procedures. Dyeing, bleaching, and printing were grouped under the broad heading of finishing (Robson 1957, chapter 3).

In the British cotton industry, particularly after the mid nineteenth century, it was normal for spinning, weaving, and finishing to be carried out by separate firms. In 1939 only 23 per cent of spindles and 24 per cent of looms in the cotton industry were in vertically integrated (i.e., multi-process) firms (Jewkes and Jewkes 1966, p. 122). Several explanations have been offered for this high degree of specialisation. Farnie suggests that the availability of cheap land and labour encouraged the building of power-loom weaving sheds in north Lancashire, while spinning remained in the south of the county (Farnie 1979, pp. 296–7). Huberman (1990) argues that spinning and weaving became separated because it was easier to control a smaller workforce. Kenny (1982) maintains that the more capital-intensive spinning sector remained in the south because of its more sophisticated capital market.

Vertical integration is at the centre of the debate over Lancashire's reluctance to replace mule spindles with the reputedly superior ring spindles. Lazonick (1981b, 1987) states that ring-spun weft (unlike mule-spun weft) had to be rewound at considerable expense if it was taken to a separate weaving mill. For ring-spinning to be profitable, both spinning and weaving had to be conducted on the same site. Britain, argues Lazonick, ought to have emulated New England which was dominated by vertically integrated ring mills. Temin (1988), however, suggests that the prosperity of the New England cotton industry was not due to vertical integration but rather to the tariff against English competition. Vertical integration was an expedient to cope with New England's poor transport network and underdeveloped raw cotton and yarn markets. Marrison (1975) has shown that British cloth exports held up well against US competition in Latin America before 1914. On the eve of the First World War the British cotton industry supplied 70 per cent of the world's exports of cotton cloth, compared with the United States' 4.2 per cent and Japan's 1 per cent (Rose 1991, p. 3). Hence Lancashire's strategy and structure were appropriate before 1914.

The typical British cotton spinning or weaving firm was small. In 1911 the modal size of spinning firms in Lancashire was 90,000–100,000 spindles and the modal size of weaving firms was 500–600 looms, a minuscule proportion of industrial capacity in each case (Jewkes and Jewkes 1966, p. 120). But Britain also possessed some of the world's largest cotton textile producers. In 1913 the world's biggest cotton spinning company was Lancashire's Fine Spinners' and Doublers' Association. Its 2.8 million spindles made it three times the size of its largest New England competitor, and only marginally smaller than the entire Japanese factory spinning industry (Farnie and Yonekawa 1988, p. 174). Before 1914 Lancashire was a haven for small firms. Local markets for raw cotton, yarn, and cloth were highly efficient and transactions costs were low. While overall demand remained buoyant, small firms had little to fear from larger competitors.

After the First World War doubts were expressed about the structure of the cotton industry. The volume of British cotton cloth exports fell by 80 per cent between 1913 and 1938 and the output of cloth declined by approximately one half. A number of factors contributed to this crisis, including the overvaluation of sterling, falling incomes in underdeveloped countries, protectionism in Asia and the Middle East, the boycott of British goods in India, and the steady rise of foreign competition, particularly from Italy in the 1920s and Japan in the 1930s (Sandberg 1974, pp. 175–220, Shimizu 1986, Wolcott 1991). Most of these problems were beyond Lancashire's control. Given that world trade in cotton cloth declined by 25 per cent in the inter-war period, Lancashire could not have avoided hard times, regardless of the gradual shift in competitive advantage towards Asia.

Contemporary investigations into the cotton industry stressed the advantages of greater horizontal and vertical integration. It was argued that horizontal mergers and the closure of loss-making mills would enable the industry to overcome its financial weakness. Vertical mergers would lead to better coordination of decisions at different stages in the production and marketing process. Vertical integration would reduce the scope for middlemen and merchants to prey on the industry – they were accused of having a policy of divide and rule which involved refusing to place large orders with any one firm (Economic Advisory Council 1930, Clay 1931, Political and Economic Planning 1934, Kirby 1974).

Modest changes were made in the structure of the cotton industry in the inter-war period. During the speculative boom of 1919–20 many mills changed hands, but few new groups of any size were created. The Amalgamated Cotton Mills Trust was the most significant exception to this rule, acquiring fifteen spinning and weaving firms including the substantial vertically integrated Horrocks concern. But ACMT was a holding company of somewhat dubious financial provenance, and little advantage was taken of the opportunity to fully integrate the activities of the group (Porter 1974, Daniels and Jewkes 1928). The banks burnt their fingers in the post-war boom, making large loans to company promoters, which looked as though they would never be repaid. In 1929, at the prompting of the Bank of England, ninety-six of the poorest coarse spinners were herded into the giant 10,000,000 spindle Lancashire Cotton Corporation, which had as its immediate objective the scrapping of unwanted capacity and the protection of the banks' money (Bamberg 1988). Other defensive amalgamations were made at this time in the fine spinning and quilt weaving sections, but there was very little merger activity in the 1930s, and in 1939 the average cotton textile firm still possessed well under 1 per cent of the industry's capacity.

Greater horizontal and vertical integration did not guarantee success. In the early 1930s the horizontally integrated Lancashire Cotton Corporation accumulated huge losses, and its leaders suffered from an inability to curb the independence of managers in the individual mills. As the Cotton Board's head of statistics argued, even vertical integration was no panacea. Vertical firms were harder to manage: it was necessary for managers to have detailed knowledge of both spinning and weaving, and it was difficult for them to coordinate the activities of the spinning and weaving departments (Robson 1957, pp. 103–13). Poor quality managers would have aggravated these problems. John Maynard Keynes and Sir Stafford Cripps were scathing in their assessment of Lancashire's cotton masters (Singleton 1991, pp. 13–14, 36). Better managers would have helped the cotton industry, but could they have turned the tide which was running against Lancashire? As countries with low labour costs industrialised, the British cotton industry was destined to find it increasingly difficult to compete.

Lancashire's decline was brought forward in dramatic style by the crises of the 1920s and 1930s. These crises generated urgent calls for industrial reorganisation, but such restructuring would not have reversed the product cycle and the slow migration of cotton textile production from Lancashire to countries with warmer climates. Even in the 1930s this did not go unrecognised by Lancashire's more perceptive observers (Allen 1933, p. 225).

3   The nationalisation debate between the wars

In 1892 the Burnley Weavers' Association passed a resolution in favour of the '"socialization of the means of production, distribution, and exchange, to be controlled by a democratic State in the interests of the entire community"' (Howell 1983, p. 61). Yet, despite occasional rushes of enthusiasm, socialism appears to have been a minority sport in the Victorian and Edwardian cotton unions. Savage's work on Preston (1987) indicates that Liberalism and Toryism remained powerful forces in working-class politics throughout the decades leading up to the First World War. In some north Lancashire towns anti-socialist weavers' unions called Protection Societies were established during this period, and in 1899 a leading figure in the Operative Spinners' Amalgamation stood as a Conservative candidate in a parliamentary election in Oldham (White 1978, Trodd 1978, Bealey and Pelling 1958, p. 17). Prior to 1914 the cotton industry was in rude good health and its nationalisation was unthinkable to all but the most optimistic socialists.

At the close of the First World War there was a brief flowering of interest in the socialisation of the mills. These proposals originated at Nelson, among ancillary weaving operatives called beamers and twisters, who resented the large profits which textile firms had made during the war (Fowler and Fowler 1984, p. 89). At the 1919 annual conference of the United Textile Factory Workers' Association (UTFWA), the political umbrella organisation of the cotton unions, the beamers accused the employers of profiteering and argued that only nationalisation would enable the operatives to get their fair share of the spoils of war. Alongside loss-making industries like the railways, argued one delegate, Labour 'ought to nationalise those things that were making a profit. Nationalise the cotton industry and that would be one way of paying for the war' (*Cotton Factory Times* 1919). As it became clear that the UTFWA's leaders were not prepared to allow a vote on socialisation, the beamers accused the Stockport spinners of having a vested interest because they had invested union funds in cotton mill shares.

The feverish speculation of 1919–20 further encouraged the supporters of nationalisation to speak out. Big business and trustification appeared to be threatening Lancashire at this time. In *Chaos and Order in Industry*, G.D.H. Cole (1920) explained that the sole purpose of the financial reconstruction of the cotton industry by promoters was to increase the level of dividends to shareholders. Other things being equal, this would require downward pressure on wages in order to generate a greater surplus. Nationalising the cotton industry and putting it under democratic workers' control would save the operatives from this unpleasant fate. Cole did not believe that nationalisation would damage the competitiveness of Lancashire, and thought that operating a cotton mill was a routine affair. The only areas in which specialised business skills were necessary were raw cotton purchasing and cloth merchanting, and these sections might have to be left in private hands for the time being (Cole, pp. 159–71). Deploying a somewhat more colourful vocabulary, Zeph Hutchinson of the Independent Labour Party and the Nelson Weavers attacked the '"GREAT CAPITALIST VULTURES" . . . [who were] responsible for the bedlam-like stampede now taking place to grab hold of going concerns' (Hutchinson 1920, p. 24). Hutchinson's tract included a detailed guide to the activities of Lancashire's leading monopolists, and predicted that they would soon have the power to dictate terms to their unhappy operatives. Moreover, in the absence of serious overseas competition, the cotton 'trusts' would be free to exploit the impoverished consumers of the third world. Hutchinson called for the nationalisation of the mills under democratic control, quoting Ruskin: '"Workmen of England! Do you mean to go on for ever leaving your wealth to be consumed by the idler . . .?"', and repeated the accusation that union officials had shares in the trusts (Hutchinson 1920, pp. 29, 30).

Following the market's collapse in 1920, the problems of trustification and monopoly profits faded into the background. In the 1920s the most urgent issues were the organisation of short-time working and opposition to wage cuts. There was much hand-wringing about the responsibility of speculators for the industry's difficulties (UTFWA 1922). At first the slump in demand was not expected to be permanent, but as the decade wore on the unions became increasingly pessimistic. The Communist Party campaigned in 1924–5 for the nationalisation without compensation of the cotton industry, but they possessed neither influence nor credibility in Lancashire (Barry 1965, pp. 264–5). Cotton did not yet figure in the Labour Party's catalogue of industries to be nationalised. The Labour government of 1929–31 instituted a committee of enquiry into the cotton industry, but it did not consider public ownership to be a serious option (Economic Advisory Council 1930).

The unions were overwhelmed by the industry's difficulties and found it difficult to formulate a common strategy. Lancashire's network of cotton unions was highly decentralised and somewhat unruly. Each district had a separate union for each type of operative. While the unions combined into amalgamations at the county level to bargain over wages and conditions, each district retained a large measure of autonomy. Political and industrial attitudes were not uniform throughout the movement. Skilled workers such as mule spinners tended to be more conservative than less skilled workers such as weavers. Other things being equal, men tended to be more radical than women. There were many tensions within the mills between different groups of workers, for instance between mule spinners and their assistants called piecers, and between women weavers and their male foremen who were called overlookers (Turner 1962, Jowitt and McIvor 1988, chapters 1, 6, 11). Such a diverse constituency did not lend itself to the adoption of decisive policies. Many UTFWA conference debates were of a strongly adversarial nature.

The 1930 UTFWA conference recorded a contribution of a delegate of the warehousemen: 'He dared scarcely mention the word Socialism in such a meeting, but would it not be a good idea to begin to explore the advantages of public ownership?' (UTFWA 1930, p. 42). Intensification of the depression gave a new impetus to the search for a strategy which would save the industry. Before long the unions found themselves pursuing a belt and braces policy, seeking to cooperate with the employers in the formulation of rationalisation schemes, whilst at the same time calling for nationalisation.

Government policy in the 1930s was to encourage Lancashire to draw up its own plans for rationalisation and self-regulation. The state was unwilling to take direct responsibility for planning the cotton industry, but it was prepared to give statutory backing to proposals for reform which had the broad support of cotton folk. At the county level the Joint Committee of Cotton Trade Organisations acted as a bipartisan think-tank, considering the introduction of price maintenance schemes, output quotas, schemes for the scrapping of excess capacity, and proposals for industrial self government. Cooperation between the unions and the employers on the JCCTO took place on the strict understanding that this forum would not be used to air the nationalisation issue (Roberts 1984, Edgerton 1986, pp. 252–89).

Unemployment in cotton peaked at 38.5 per cent in 1931 (Jones 1987, p. 37). Further cuts in wages and the imposition of the hated more-looms system, which increased workloads for many weavers, served to encourage the radicals (Fowler and Fowler 1984, pp. 54–86). D.H. Macgregor, a leading academic economist, warned the spinning masters that left-wing pressure for nationalisation would surely grow if they failed to resolve Lancashire's structural problems (Macgregor 1934, p. 51). Zeph Hutchinson was waiting in the wings, and he told the 1933 UTFWA conference that it was a waste of time trying to reform capitalism in Lancashire:

They should direct their attention to the question of complete control . . . They would never get it by agreement. They would never root out the individualism that was inherent in the cotton trade; they could only brush it aside ruthlessly with the dictatorship of a Hitler. (UTFWA 1933, p. 63)

It was suggested by one of Mr Hutchinson's critics that he would be the ideal person to act as the Hitler of Lancashire. The UTFWA records for the 1930s and 1940s show that Hutchinson had a reasonable amount of support. There was a continuing debate within the unions about the benefits of nationalisation and its political prospects. Two major reports on the future of the industry also emerged from the union movement, the first advocating a corporatist compromise, and the second pleading for outright nationalisation.

The first of these proposals, appearing in 1933, called for an act of parliament to create a Cotton Control Board, similar to the First World War body of the same name. Members of the Board would be appointed by the President of the Board of Trade after consultation with the employers and trade unions. The CCB would restrict entry to the industry by means of a licensing scheme. Although the CCB would not interfere with collective bargaining between unions and employers about levels of wages, it would have the power to suspend the licences of firms which broke wage agreements. The main function of the CCB would be to devise reorganisation schemes for each section of the industry in consultation with interested parties. Parliament would be asked to give legal backing to these plans. Whilst it was hoped that the industry would have the good sense to cooperate, the CCB would have the authority to compel firms to amalgamate into larger groups, scrap redundant plant, and invest in new machinery. These measures would be funded out of a levy on firms continuing in the industry (TUC 1935a, pp. 29–31). This proposal was in line with current trends in corporatist thinking and fitted in well with the ethos of the JCCTO, although it did not satisfy Zeph Hutchinson and his followers (Carpenter 1976, Ritschel 1991).

The second scheme was more ambitious. In 1934 the leftists in the UTFWA took advantage of procedural confusion to force through a resolution asking the TUC to prepare a plan for the socialisation of the cotton industry. This TUC report argued with some justification that the rise of Japan was the underlying cause of Lancashire's difficulties. It added that the industry's problems had been aggravated by its atomistic structure, and its heavy indebtedness to the banks as a result of the 1919–20 speculative boom. Efficiency could be restored by nationalisation with fair compensation of the mills and the formation of a British Cotton Corporation. The BCC would be a Morrisonian public corporation, and board members would be appointed by the government. Operatives and unions would be consulted on appointments and on other matters through such bodies as works councils, but there would be no element of worker control of the mills. The BCC would coordinate the activities of sectional boards in spinning, weaving, and finishing, enabling

Lancashire to reap the advantages of vertical linkages, stable prices, good labour relations, and high quality strategic decision making (TUC 1935a, pp. 1–28).

In Labour Party circles similar ideas were under scrutiny, and a confidential report advocating nationalisation of the mills was produced by the New Fabian Research Bureau (Durbin 1985, p. 121). The TUC's socialisation plan was endorsed by the Labour Party and cotton nationalisation found its way into the 1935 general election manifesto. But no clear timetable for action was specified, and it was expected that there would be a transitional period of industrial self government, along the lines of the previous Cotton Control Board scheme, in order to reorganise the industry in preparation for nationalisation. Perhaps it was optimistic of the Labour Party to expect the employers to cooperate on these terms.

What did the unions really expect from nationalisation, and what chance was there of nationalisation in the 1930s? The TUC's socialisation programme stressed its beneficial effects for industrial efficiency, but the operatives were more interested in a living wage and security of employment. Indeed there was a danger that increased efficiency would lead to fewer rather than more long-term jobs. Many operatives doubted whether Lancashire could ever compete successfully with Asia. As one delegate of the beamers put it, the BCC could not restore Lancashire's pre-war competitiveness however hard it tried, and its main role should be to negotiate a global cartel to protect British jobs. He hoped that the BCC would:

put us in such a position, in our negotiations with other nations, that instead of the great and intense competition going on at the present time, we should be able to obtain agreements with the industries of other nations, and out of the chaos of the present system I believe we should bring some better form of order (TUC 1935b, p. 401).

In principle, a socialist BCC need not have been a toothless industrial dinosaur. If the British government had been prepared to threaten the Japanese cotton industry with total exclusion from colonial and dominion markets it is possible that the BCC could have negotiated an international cartel. But it is unlikely that a British government would have been either willing or able to force the colonies and dominions to follow this policy. Recent research indicates that the Lancashire lobby still wielded a good deal of influence over Indian import policy during the 1930s, but that there were limits to Lancashire's power of dictation (Chatterji 1992, Dupree 1990). The 1932 Ottawa Agreement, which instituted imperial preference, led to an increase in British cotton textile exports to Canada, Australia, and New Zealand, but it is doubtful whether these countries would have been willing to agree to even greater protection for Lancashire without major concessions in other areas (Sandberg 1974, pp. 203–4). Australia, following the Indian pattern, actually raised tariffs against Lancashire in the mid 1930s in order to protect its own mills, causing a boycott of Australian produce in some Lancashire towns (Copland and Janes 1937, pp. 354–8). By the 1930s the dominions had wills of their own in trade policy and could not easily have been dragooned into supporting the British Cotton Corporation. Their primary interest was in protecting their own infant industries, rather than in siding with Manchester against Osaka.

If attempts to hound Japan into a market sharing agreement proved to be unsuccessful, British cotton workers wanted the BCC to protect their jobs in other ways. Nationalisation was essential for:

guaranteeing a reasonable rate of wages and standard of working conditions for the operatives in the industry, either from the resources of the industry itself, or, if they are found to be inadequate to meet the cost of this necessary reform, then assistance should be provided from the pooled resources of the country (UTFWA 1936, p. 65)

Following nationalisation, it was argued, Lancashire's textile workers would be treated like civil servants, and could look forward to retiring on an excellent pension. Cotton operatives in the 1930s, like the miners in 1984–5, believed that they and their children had a right to secure and decently paid jobs. If, as seemed likely, the industry would never be fully competitive, the British housewife would have to pay more for her dresses, and the British taxpayer would have to subsidise the nationalised mills. Andrew Naesmith of the Amalgamated Weavers made no bones about this and declared that 'the British public are securing their cloth too cheaply' for the cotton industry to regain financial viability (TUC 1936, p. 450). Of course, there was nothing irrational about wanting full employment and good wages, and it was logical for the operatives to regard public ownership as a means to these ends. The question was whether the taxpayers of Britain and the consumers of the British Empire were prepared to foot the bill.

Outside Lancashire precious little interest was taken in the case for public ownership of the mills. The National government, which was dominated by Conservatives, was unlikely to be swayed by the TUC's rhetoric. Even within Lancashire the response of the electorate to the socialisation plan was disappointing. At the 1935 general election Labour candidates in the cotton towns were less successful than had been expected. Although there was a 9 per cent sub-regional swing from National to Labour between 1931 and 1935, Labour won only twelve of the forty-one seats in 'Eastern Lancastria' in 1935 (Stannage 1980, pp. 261, 264). Perhaps some supporters were put off by Labour's failure to give the unions their full backing during the more-looms dispute, or by mistrust of state intervention in the light of the 1934 act to enforce the new – and lower – wage lists in the weaving section.

In the late 1930s the TUC and the Labour Party withdrew from their commitment to nationalisation. In 1937 the TUC Economic Committee summoned UTFWA leaders to London to inform them that nationalisation was not politically feasible, and suggested that they devote their energies to cooperating with the employers in pressing for industrial self government (TUC 1937, p. 198, UTFWA 1937, pp. 19–25). The UTFWA took this advice and worked through the JCCTO to prepare the ground for the 1939 Cotton Industry (Reorganisation) Act (Joint Committee of Cotton Trade Organisations, 1937). The 1939 act made provision for the establishment of a Cotton Industry Board with powers to enforce schemes for the control of prices and output and the scrapping of surplus capacity. Such measures would be drawn up by sectional committees and submitted to the government for its approval. This corporatist arrangement bore a close resemblance to the earlier proposals for a new Cotton Control Board and the Conservative Research Department's 1937 scheme for a Cotton Industry Development Board (Edgerton 1986, p. 272). Given the political climate of the 1930s, this was the best the operatives could have expected.

4   The last throw of the dice: the 1940s

The coming of war delayed implementation of the 1939 act. Hitler provided Lancashire with six years in which to reconsider the arrangements to be made for its long-term survival. The sellers' market of 1945–50 gave Lancashire a further breathing space, but the end result was stalemate and the perpetuation of the atomistic industrial structure of the inter-war decades. As Labour romped to victory in 1945, some operatives expected that nationalisation would be restored to the political agenda, but the ambivalence of the unions and the Labour government, and the pressing nature of the export drive combined to ensure that public ownership of the mills remained a wistful aspiration.

Post-war planning was one of the main themes at the 1942 UTFWA conference. A delegate of the Preston Weavers' Association called for an enquiry to consider how the industry could be stabilised after the war. This gentleman pointed out that private enterprise was an affront to Catholic principles, particularly those relating to the family, and demanded that wages for men should be set at a level which would allow them to 'keep the women at home in comfort' (UTFWA 1942, p. 74). The Legislative Council of the UTFWA took up the challenge and in 1943 produced a report which concluded that the only way 'to meet foreign competition, satisfy the aspirations of the workers to a better life, and make the industry a national asset, is by Socialisation' (UTFWA 1943, p. 88). This plan was similar to that advanced by the TUC in 1935, and stressed that nationalisation would lead to greater horizontal and vertical coordination and a significant improvement in efficiency. Crucially, an International Board of Control for Textiles would be established to allocate world markets. Since this Board would be controlled by Britain and the USA, it would take a dim view of any misbehaviour by the Japanese and would have the authority to cut off their raw cotton imports. The report concluded that economic necessity had forced women to work in the mills 'and sacrifice time which could in many cases have been profitably spent in the care of the family and home'. Following nationalisation and the introduction of the global cartel, men would get better wages, and women would be free to return to their sinks (UTFWA 1943, p. 72).

At a special meeting of operatives to consider this report, a delegate of the overlookers praised it as the 'Magna Carta for the cotton industry', and Zeph Hutchinson said that it deserved their 'fanatical' support. Andrew Naesmith added that the rights to 'continuous employment' and a decent livelihood, which the Legislative Council's scheme was designed to guarantee, were fundamental principles of the Atlantic Charter. Scorn was poured on a *Manchester Guardian* article describing the report as the most 'defeatist' document ever to come out of Lancashire (LRO 1943). An early meeting was sought with government ministers and Lancashire MPs.

But the Churchill Coalition was not prepared to contemplate anything as drastic as nationalisation of the mills. They continued to plan for the reorganisation of the industry within the framework of private owner-ship. Raymond Streat, chairman of the Cotton Board, a tripartite organi-sation set up in 1939 to promote exports and research, collect statistics, and discuss industrial problems,[1] was in touch with right-wing ministers such a R.S. Hudson (Agriculture) and Lord Woolton (Reconstruction), and he echoed their views in speeches against the UTFWA's plan. Streat maintained that theoretical debates about nationalisation were beside the point:

We are faced with a critical condition, with the urgent problem of translating a vast industry from a war footing to a peace footing. That is no time to raise the highly contentious proposal of nationalisation and I suggest that members of all parties . . . should dismiss this matter from the present arena . . . Let us not delay work and progress by talking of things which are not practical politics. (PRO 1944a)

Hudson was delighted with Streat's intervention and wrote to Woolton that: 'Judging by what was said both by Labour MPs and Trade Union leaders in Manchester', he had persuaded them of the political impossibility of nationalisation for at least ten to fifteen years (PRO 1944b).

Meanwhile the unions had resumed their earlier belt and braces strategy, and were cooperating with Streat and the employers on the Cotton Board Committee to Enquire into Post-War Problems. This body did not even consider the option of nationalisation, and with bare-faced cheek suggested that protection and price maintenance were preconditions for reequipment (Cotton Board 1944). The Cotton Board's report met with a lukewarm response from the government. Hugh Dalton, the President of the Board of Trade, strongly opposed a textile price ring. Dalton believed that the creation of larger firms was essential before Lancashire could experience a revival and was not afraid to back a policy of compulsory mergers in spinning, although he was unable to persuade the cabinet to endorse such a radical proposal (Dupree 1992, p. 143, Singleton 1991, pp. 26–8).

Devotees of nationalisation believed that their chances would improve under a Labour government. But Labour's policy towards Lancashire in the 1940s was distinguished by muddle. Labour ministers did not know what to do for the best. Should they reject nationalisation outright, should they accept public ownership as a long-term objective, or should they merely use the threat of socialisation to whip the bosses into shape? Nationalisation of the mills was not included among Labour's manifesto pledges in 1945. Sir Stafford Cripps, the doyen of the pre-war left, remarked in 1944 that after the war there would be an export crisis and falling living standards, and '"you can't nationalise the cotton industry in the middle of that."' (Addison 1975, p. 262). But the overall impression given by Labour in 1945 was that nationalisation, whilst unlikely, could not be ruled out. George Tomlinson, the Labour MP for Farnworth and a former cotton operative, referred to cotton in an election broadcast, and called for 'more State initiative and enterprise' and the elimination of those 'parasites and gamblers' who had controlled the industry in the past to the detriment of 'industrious and God-fearing people' (Blackburn 1954, p. 148). These mysterious sayings can have done nothing to calm the nerves of the masters.

Streat was both alarmed by Labour's victory in 1945 and somewhat shocked to find Cripps at the Board of Trade: 'My mind has been anxious and restless . . . Can I conscientiously work for a conscientious socialist or ought I to resign? Can they apply socialism to an industry like cotton – certainly not if socialism means nationalisation' (Streat 1987, p. 267). Cripps wasted no time in asserting his authority, and warned the employers that extreme measures would be taken if they refused to cooperate with the government. When asked by J.S. Heaton, a spinning master, whether this meant nationalisation, Sir Stafford declined to give a straight answer (PRO 1945). Aneurin Bevan was eager to terrorise the spinners with threats of a state takeover, and Ellis Smith, a junior minister at the Board of Trade, resigned from the government in 1946, disgusted by Cripps's failure to nationalise the spinning mills (Singleton 1991, pp. 29–30).

Cripps had no shortage of advice on how to deal with the cotton industry. In addition to the UTFWA and Cotton Board reconstruction plans, the Fabian Research Group (1945) produced its blueprint for Lancashire. What was novel about the Fabian approach was its rejection of what it called 'muddled' corporatism in which it was unclear whether civil servants, the employers, or the unions were in charge. Instead, there should be a clear distinction between the provinces of private and state initiative. The state should establish organs for specific purposes, such as the removal of excess capacity, the purchasing of raw cotton, and the marketing of exports, but private enterprise would be left unfettered in other respects. Nationalisation was not anticipated for the time being, but at some stage it might be desirable to take finishing into public ownership, thereby suppressing monopolistic practices, and to socialise spinning in order to increase the pace of modernisation. An independent group of researchers, led by the economist J.R. Bellerby, advocated a scheme of partial nationalisation. State-owned mills would perform a stabilising function in the industry. In periods of high demand they would help to keep down prices by producing yarn and cloth in competition with private firms. During periods of weak demand the state mills would withdraw from competition with the private sector. Employment in the state mills would be maintained by bringing forward orders for public bodies such as the army, and some mills would be converted for use as training centres. Fluctuations in the level of stocks would be used as a guide to the policy of the nationalised sector (Bellerby 1943, pp. 225–39).

None of these schemes satisfied Cripps and he commissioned a tripartite Board of Trade Working Party to draw up a definitive plan which could be used by both government and industry as the basis for long-term policy. This initiative was unpopular. Employers feared that the Working Party would favour nationalisation, and the left regarded the whole exercise as a cynical attempt to head off support for public ownership. In the Working Party's final report there were calls for firms to amalgamate into larger groups and for statutory backing for schemes to facilitate the scrapping of redundant capacity and the purchase of new machinery. But it was unclear whether the amalgamations were to be voluntary or compulsory, and a minority of Working Party members wanted to let market forces determine the rate of investment. The report was a disappointment to Cripps, who had hoped for the emergence of a consensus within Lancashire (Board of Trade 1946, Allen 1946, Dupree 1992). Even the ghost of public ownership stalked the proceedings. A dissenting memorandum written by the union members of the enquiry pointed out that: 'according to our own faith, we should have preferred to work for a plan of complete socialisation of the industry' (Board of Trade, p. 241). In line with the Crippsian doctrine of tripartism, the Working Party recommended the establishment of a permanent central organisation to represent the industry's interests. There was an acrimonious dispute about whether this should be a separate body or a modified version of Streat's Cotton Board. By way of compromise, in 1948 the Cotton Board was redesignated a Development Council.

After considerable gnashing of teeth, Cripps decided to forge ahead with a scheme to subsidise the reequipment of the spinning mills. The investment subsidy was made conditional on the willingness of the unions to accept shift working, and the preparedness of the employers to merge into larger horizontal and vertical groups. However, the employers refused to take the bait and some of the unions were obstructive, so that the scheme was a flop. As this fiasco unfolded Cripps lost his patience and told Streat that perhaps: 'the unions would be more willing to make concessions in a nationalised industry'. Cripps thought that the employers were incorrigible, and Streat commented: 'It was alarming to see his mind turning to nationalisation – to anything that would rid him of these endlessly tiresome people' (Streat 1987, p. 398).

Labour's plans for the cotton industry were lost in the quagmire of industrial politics. Luckily for the employers, the long-term future of the cotton industry was of less immediate importance to ministers than Lancashire's contribution to the export drive. A decision by an angry cabinet to nationalise the mills, say in two years time, would have reduced any incentive for employers to cooperate with the state in meeting their crucial export targets (Singleton 1991, pp. 36–45). Dupree argues that Cripps ran into difficulties in 1945–8 because of his insensitivity to the industry's desire to conduct negotiations through the existing machinery of the Cotton Board. Once the Cotton Board had been promoted to the status of a Development Council, relations between the industry and the state were more cordial (Dupree 1992). But the establishment of friendly relations between the Cotton Board and the Board of Trade could not have saved Lancashire from the teeth of its overseas competitors. Only one issue really counted and that was the government's attitude towards protection. The Cotton Board lobbied ministers to grant the industry protection during the 1950s and met with a series of rebuffs until the eve of the 1959 election. If a nationalised cotton industry had been established in the 1940s, it too would have become a protectionist lobby within a couple of years.

Only one section of the industry, the purchasing of raw cotton, was taken into public ownership in the 1940s. During the war the statutory Cotton Control had been responsible for the importation of raw cotton. For several reasons, the Cotton Control's monopoly was allowed to continue in 1945. Large quantities of cotton came from the USA and the government was faced with a severe shortage of dollars. Moreover, the Labour Party was interested in the possibility of nationalising the Liverpool cotton market. Labour was opposed to what it regarded as gambling in raw cotton. It also thought that a state purchasing agency would be able to use its market power to get lower cotton prices for spinners and would achieve greater price stability by negotiating long-term contracts (Wiseman and Yamey 1956).

The Lord President's Economic Section was asked to report on the prospects for a state monopoly in raw cotton. James Meade was dismissive of the case for nationalisation. Raw cotton was a standardised commodity in a market in which there were many buyers and sellers: 'These are the classical conditions in which competition is likely to be in the social interest' (PRO 1946a). J.M. Fleming added that the Cotton Control had been lucky to be operating in the war during a period of rising cotton prices. In such circumstances it could not lose, but when prices started to fall there was a strong possibility that large losses would be made by a state buying agency (PRO 1946b). Both the Liverpool merchants and the spinning masters objected to nationalisation. Even the socialist Lord Mayor of Liverpool, Alderman Luke Hogan, objected to: 'the very fabric [i.e., cotton] upon which the port is built being torn away bit by bit . . . our businesses going, and our unemployment growing' (PRO 1946c). Labour chose to ignore this advice and another state monopoly in the form of a Raw Cotton Commission duly came into being at the start of 1948.

The performance of the RCC was unimpressive. It failed to prevent frequent changes in raw cotton prices, despite the fact that this had been one of its main objectives. Spinners complained that the RCC was unable to supply them with cotton of a consistently good quality. The bureaucrats of the Commission lacked the expertise of the private cotton traders, few of whom were prepared to offer their services to the state sector for relatively low salaries. Although the Commission succeeded in concluding long-term deals at fixed prices with colonial governments, this resulted in losses when the free market price of cotton fell (*Manchester Guardian* 1949, pp. 16–24, Leubuscher 1956, pp. 53–66). Harold Wilson, who replaced Cripps as President of the Board of Trade, admitted that there had been difficulties with the personnel, but thought that private traders would have done no better than the RCC at a time of grave dollar shortage (PRO 1949).

Labour's thoughts turned in 1948 to the question of which industries should be nationalised during their second term of office. The Labour Research Department produced a report which put the cotton industry under the microscope. It began by berating the employers: 'Repeated efforts to awaken the industry's sense of responsibility have too often met with only a momentary response . . . the industry is suffering from an inferiority complex which does not permit it to engage in modernisation' (Labour Party 1948a, p. 20). The administrative complexity of nationalising hundreds of small firms, especially in weaving, would be immense, but there were strong grounds for taking the spinning section into public ownership. In the light of recent policy failures in spinning, the Research Department believed that nationalisation offered the best hope of re-equipping the spinning mills. The nationalisation of some, or indeed all, of the textile machinery industry would render such a strategy foolproof (Labour Party 1948a, pp. 21–2).

Ernest Thornton, secretary of the UTFWA, was asked to comment on these findings. He said that the mood in the unions was shifting against nationalisation. Elderly male spinnners were afraid that public ownership would lead to a higher level of investment. Thus, mules operated by men would be scrapped and replaced by rings operated by women. The optimal solution, argued Thornton, would be to delay nationalisation until most of the mule spinners had retired and could no longer complain (Labour Party 1948b, Higgins 1993, p. 355). Needless to say the Labour Party did not bother to include cotton in its manifesto of 1950.

Douglas Jay floated a rather different approach in 1948. Why should the state not set up in competition with private firms, as it did in the munitions industry during wartime?

In industries like cotton spinning today, what is really needed is the building of several large-scale modern efficient new mills in the area – e.g., Merseyside – where labour is available. Only this can break the double impasse of labour shortage and inertia inside an industry . . . Why not start Government production right away if there is a need for it? (NMLH 1948)

Jay hoped that the demonstration effect of these modern state-owned mills would lead to an improvement in the performance of the industry as a whole. Harold Wilson also favoured a mixture of private and public enterprise in the 1950s, when he was commissioned by the UTFWA to revise their 1943 strategy. Wilson held that the spinning industry was in the grip of monopolistic forces. The state should purchase a controlling interest in the large combines to ensure that they acted in the public interest, pursued a vigorous programme of reequipment, and refrained from bullying independent spinners and weavers (UTFWA 1957). But neither Jay's nor Wilson's ideas were likely to be implemented under the Conservative governments which ruled Britain after 1951.

5   Conclusion

This chapter has sought to dispel the illusion that the campaign for the nationalisation of the cotton industry was no more than a passing fad of union officials in the mid 1930s. Nationalisation was an issue which generated a heated debate in the industry during the 1930s and 1940s. This debate was conducted on several levels. On the one hand, supporters of nationalisation stressed the benefits to be gained from better coordination of raw material purchasing, spinning, weaving, finishing, and marketing. Technical economies of scale were not expected to be large in textile production, but it was asserted that nationalisation would lead to substantial managerial economies. On the other hand, many union officials admitted that these savings would not be sufficient to restore Lancashire to its former competitive position. They arged that nationalisation would have to be accompanied by cartel agreements with foreign producers, government subsidies of textile workers' wages, and higher cloth prices. Their objective was the straightforward – and in many respects quite admirable – one of preserving the jobs and incomes of their members and of future generations of operatives.

The Labour Party did not consider nationalisation of the cotton industry to be out of the question on either political or economic grounds. During the 1930s and 1940s a policy of socialising the cotton mills fluttered on the fringes of the manifesto. But cotton remained in limbo for three sets of reasons. Firstly, cotton was not an essential industry: it had no strategic importance and it was not a vital public service. The cotton industry was expendable, unlike coal, electricity, the railways, steel, and gas. Secondly, nationalising the cotton industry would not have secured its export markets. Additional measures would have been necessary in order to protect Lancashire's overseas markets. Such measures would have included the coercion of Commonwealth textile consumers and Japanese and Asian textile producers. Thirdly, unlike the miners, the cotton operatives found it difficult to formulate and stick to a clear long-term policy. Only nationalisation would satisfy the miners, but the cotton unions were willing to compromise.

NOTES

I am particularly grateful to Marguerite Dupree, Douglas Farnie, Alan Fowler, and John King for their helpful comments on an earlier draft.
1 During the course of the war the Cotton Board was also responsible for administering the concentration scheme in finishing, looking after closed mills, and the Utility Scheme.

REFERENCES

Addison, P. (1975), *The Road to 1945: British Politics and the Second World War*, London: Jonathan Cape.
Allen, G.C. (1933), *British Industries and their Organisation*, London: Longman.
　(1946), 'The report of the Working Party on the cotton industry', *Manchester School*, 14: 60–73.
Bamberg, J.H. (1988), 'The rationalization of the British cotton industry in the interwar period', *Textile History*, 19: 83–101.
Barry, E.E. (1965), *Nationalisation in British Politics: The Historical Background*, London: Jonathan Cape.
Bealey, F. and Pelling, H. (1958), *Labour and Politics, 1900–1906: A History of the Labour Representation Committee*, London: Macmillan.
Bellerby, J.R. (1943), *Economic Reconstruction: A Study of Post-war Problems*, vol. 1, London: Macmillan.
Blackburn, F. (1954), *George Tomlinson*, London: Heinemann.
Board of Trade (1946), *Working Party Reports: Cotton*, London: HMSO.
Carpenter, L.P. (1976), 'Corporatism in Britain, 1930–45', *Journal of Contemporary History*, 11: 3–25.
Chatterji, B. (1992), *Trade, Tariffs and Empire: Lancashire and British Policy in India 1919–1939*, Delhi: Oxford University Press.
Clay, H. (1931), *Report on the Position of the English Cotton Industry*, London: Securities Management Trust.
Cole, G.D.H. (1920), *Chaos and Order in Industry*, London: Methuen.
Copland, D.B. and Janes, C.V. (eds.), (1937), *Australian Trade Policy: A Book of Documents, 1932–1937*, Sydney: Angus & Robertson.
Cotton Board (1944), *Report of the Cotton Board Committee to Enquire into Post-war Problems*, Manchester: Cotton Board.
Cotton Factory Times (1919), 35, 5 September, p. 3.
Daniels, G.W. and Jewkes, J. (1928), 'The post-war depression in the Lancashire cotton industry', *Journal of the Royal Statistical Society*, 91: 153–92.
Dupree, M. (1990), 'Fighting against fate: the cotton industry and the government during the 1930s', *Textile History*, 21: 101–17.
　(1992), 'The cotton industry: a middle way between nationalisation and self-government?', in H. Mercer, N. Rollings and J. Tomlinson (eds.) *Labour Governments and Private Industry: The Experience of 1945–1951*, Edinburgh: Edinburgh University Press, pp. 137–61.
Durbin, E. (1985), *New Jerusalems: The Labour Party and the Economics of Democratic Socialism*, London: Routledge & Kegan Paul.
Economic Advisory Council (1930), 'Report of the Committee on the Cotton Industry', Cmd. 3615.

Edgerton, D.E.H. (1986), 'State intervention in British manufacturing industry, 1931–1951: a comparative study of policy for the military aircraft and cotton textile industries', University of London Ph.D. thesis.

Fabian Research Group (1945), *Cotton: A Working Policy*, London: Victor Gollancz.

Farnie, D.A. (1979), *The English Cotton Industry and the World Market, 1815–1896*, Oxford: Clarendon Press.

Farnie, D.A. and Yonekawa, S. (1988), 'The emergence of the large firm in the cotton spinning industries of the world, 1883–1938', *Textile History*, 19: 171–210.

Fowler, A. and Fowler, L. (1984), *The History of the Nelson Weavers' Association*, Nelson: Burnley Textile Workers Union.

Higgins, D.M. (1993), 'Rings, mules, and structural constraints in the Lancashire textile industry, c. 1945–c. 1965', *Economic History Review*, second ser., 46: 342–62.

Howell, D. (1983), *British Workers and the Independent Labour Party, 1888–1906*, Manchester: Manchester University Press.

Huberman, M. (1990), 'Vertical disintegration in Lancashire: a comment on Temin', *Journal of Economic History*, 50: 683–90.

Hutchinson, Z. (1920), *The Trusts Grip Cotton*, London: Independent Labour Party.

Jewkes, J. and Jewkes, S. (1966), 'A hundred years of change in the structure of the cotton industry', *Journal of Law and Economics*, 9: 115–34.

Joint Committee of Cotton Trade Organisations (1937), *Lancashire's Remedy*, Manchester: Joint Committee of Cotton Trade Organisations.

Jones, S. (1987), 'Work, leisure, and the political economy of the cotton districts between the wars', *Textile History*, 18: 3–58.

Jowitt, J. and McIvor, A. (eds.) (1988), *Employers and Labour in the English Textile Industries, 1850–1939*, London: Routledge.

Kenny, S. (1982), 'Sub-regional specialization in the Lancashire cotton industry, 1884–1914: a study in organizational and locational change', *Journal of Historical Geography*, 8: 41–63.

Kirby, M.W. (1974), 'The Lancashire cotton industry in the inter-war years: a study in organizational change', *Business History*, 16: 145–59.

Labour Party [Labour Party Library, London] (1948a), Research Department, report on the cotton industry (R.D. 178).

   (1948b), Research Department, text of interview with Ernest Thornton (R.D. 179).

Lazonick, W. (1981a), 'Competition, specialization and industrial decline', *Journal of Economic History*, 41: 31–8.

   (1981b), 'Factor costs and the diffusion of ring spinning in Britain before World War One', *Quarterly Journal of Economics*, 96: 89–109.

   (1983), 'Industrial organization and technological change: the decline of the British cotton industry', *Business History Review*, 57: 195–236.

   (1986), 'The cotton industry', in *The Decline of the British Economy*, B. Elbaum and W. Lazonick (eds.), Oxford University Press.

   (1987), 'Stubborn mules: some comments', *Economic History Review*, second ser., 40: 80–6.

Leubuscher, C. (1956), *Bulk Buying from the Colonies: A Study of the Bulk*

Purchase of Colonial Commodities by the United Kingdom Government, London: Oxford University Press.

LRO [Lancashire Record Office, Preston] (1943), UTFWA, Report of the Special General Council Meeting to Consider the Legislative Council's Report (DDX1274/15/5).

Macgregor, D.H. (1934), *Enterprise, Purpose, and Profit: Essays on Industry* Oxford: Clarendon Press.

Manchester Guardian (1949), *A Manchester Guardian Survey: The Government and the Cotton Trade*, Manchester: Manchester Guardian.

Marrison, A.J. (1975), 'Great Britain and her rivals in the Latin American cotton piece goods markets, 1880–1914', in B.M. Ratcliffe (ed.), *Great Britain and Her World, 1750–1914: Essays in Honour of W.O. Henderson*, Manchester: Manchester University Press.

Mass, W. and Lazonick, W. (1991), 'The British cotton industry and international competitive advantage: the state of the debates', in M.B. Rose (ed.), *International Competition and Strategic Response in the Textile Industries since 1870*, London: Frank Cass.

NMLH [National Museum of Labour History, Manchester] (1948), Labour Party, Research Department, report by Douglas Jay on the future of nationalisation policy (R.D. 161).

Political and Economic Planning (1934), *Report on the British Cotton Industry*, London: Political and Economic Planning.

Porter, J.H. (1974), 'The commercial banks and the financial problems of the English cotton industry, 1919–39', *Revue Internationale d'Histoire de la Banque*, 9: 1–16.

PRO (1944a), Cotton Board Minutes, 115th meeting, 6 June 1944, speech by Sir Raymond Streat to the Lancashire MPs (BT175/3).

(1944b), Ministry of Reconstruction, file on the cotton industry, letter from R.S. Hudson to Lord Woolton, 8 September 1944 (CAB124/336).

(1945), Board of Trade, file on cotton industry reconstruction, notes of a meeting between Sir Stafford Cripps and the Federation of Master Cotton Spinners, 11August, 1945 (BT64/980).

(1946a), Ministry of Reconstruction, file on bulk purchasing of cotton, memorandum by James Meade, 7 March 1946 (CAB124/337).

(1946b), Ministry of Reconstruction, file on bulk purchasing of cotton, memorandum by J.M. Fleming, 7 March 1946 (CAB124/337).

(1946c), Ministry of Reconstruction, file on bulk purchasing of cotton, speech of the Lord Mayor of Liverpool, 26 March 1946 (CAB124/338).

(1949), Cabinet Committee on Socialisation of Industries, report on the Raw Cotton Commission by Harold Wilson, 28 June 1949 (CAB134/690).

Ritschel, D. (1991), 'A corporatist economy in Britain? Capitalist planning for industrial self-government in the 1930s', *English Historical Review*, 106: 41–65.

Roberts, R. (1984), 'The administrative origins of industrial diplomacy: an aspect of government – industry relations, 1929–1935', in J. Turner (ed.), *Businessmen and Politics: Studies of Business Activity in British Politics, 1900–1945*, London: Heinemann.

Robson, R. (1957), *The Cotton Industry in Britain* London: Macmillan.

Rose, M.B. (1991), 'Introduction', in M.B. Rose (ed.), *International Competition and Strategic Response in the Textile Industries since 1870*, London: Frank Cass.

Sandberg, L.G. (1974), *Lancashire in Decline: A Study in Entrepreneurship, Technology, and International Trade*, Columbus: Ohio State University Press.

Savage, M. (1987), *The Dynamics of Working Class Politics: The Labour Movement in Preston, 1900–1940*, Cambridge University Press.

Shimizu, H. (1986), *Anglo-Japanese Trade Rivalry in the Middle East in the Interwar Period*, London: Ithaca.

Singleton, J. (1991), *Lancashire on the Scrapheap: The Cotton Industry, 1945–1970*, Oxford University Press.

Stannage, T. (1980), *Baldwin Thwarts the Opposition: The British General Election of 1935*, London: Croom Helm.

Streat, E.R. (1987), *Lancashire and Whitehall: The Diaries of Sir Raymond Streat, 1931–57*, vol. 2, ed. M. Dupree, Manchester: Manchester University Press.

Temin, P. (1988), 'Product quality and vertical integration in the early cotton textile industry', *Journal of Economic History*, 48: 891–907.

Trodd, G. (1978), 'Political change and the working class in Blackburn and Burnley, 1880–1914', University of Lancaster Ph.D. thesis.

TUC [Trades Union Congress] (1935a), *Cotton: The T.U.C. Plan of Socialisation*, London: Trades Union Congress General Council.

  (1935b), Annual conference report, 1935.

  (1936), Annual conference report, 1936.

  (1937), Annual conference report, 1937.

Turner, H.A. (1962), *Trade union growth, structure and policy: a study of the cotton unions*, London: Allen & Unwin.

UTFWA [United Textile Factory Workers Association] (1922), *Inquiry into the Cotton Industry*, Accrington: United Textile Factory Workers Association.

  (1930), Annual conference report, 1930.

  (1933), Annual conference report, 1933.

  (1936), Annual conference report, 1936.

  (1937), Annual conference report, 1937.

  (1942), Annual conference report, 1942.

  (1943), *Report of the Legislative Council on Ways and Means of Improving the Economic Stability of the Cotton Textile Industry*, Rochdale: United Textile Factory Workers Association.

  (1957), *Plan for Cotton*, Ashton: United Textile Factory Workers Asociation.

White, J.L. (1978), *The Limits of Trade Union Militancy: The Lancashire Textile Workers, 1910–1914*, Westport, Conn: Greenwood.

Wiseman, J. and Yamey, B.S. (1956), 'The Raw Cotton Commission, 1948–52', *Oxford Economic Papers*, 1: 1–34.

Wolcott, S. (1991), 'British myopia and the collapse of Indian textile demand', *Journal of Economic History*, 51: 367–84.

III

Government and the process of industrial change in the 1940s

11 'The Thin End of the Wedge?': nationalisation and industrial structure during the Second World War

Peter Howlett

1 Introduction

In the British economy in the Second World War state intervention reached unprecedented heights as government extended its control over both product and factor markets. It was argued that this extension of state power was necessary in order to mobilise resources to meet the strategic and economic strains the war would impose and that it was merely a temporary phenomenon which would be reversed with the onset of peace. Although business in general supported the temporary centralisation of economic power in the hands of the state, this did not prevent it from being concerned that the extension of state power would itself be permanent or that it might have potentially important implications for industrial management, control and structure (Howlett 1994b). Such fears found their most obvious focus in those cases where the state took control of private companies and, in particular, where it nationalised private companies. Three firms were nationalised during the war: the airframe manufacturers Short Brothers; S.G. Brown Ltd., makers of precision instruments; and Power Jets Ltd, who made jet propulsion engines (Tivey 1973, p. 40, Edgerton 1984).

Of these, the case of Short Brothers attracted most attention. In a debate on its nationalisation in the House of Lords in April 1943 the government attempted to allay the concerns of the business community by stating: 'there is no need to fear that this is the thin end of the wedge' (PRO 1943d). This chapter will address both the thin end of the wedge, the nationalisation of Short Brothers, and the wedge itself, that is the more general issue raised by the nationalisation of Shorts. In particular did the distortion of the market during the war have any long-term impact on the industrial structure of the economy? Thus, sections 2 and 3 will examine why Shorts was nationalised (was it the result of ideology or the outcome of the strategic necessities of wartime?) and what impact state control had on its performance. Section 4 takes a broader view of the effect of state intervention during the war on industrial structure by analysing the ways in which its wartime powers could affect industrial structure and how industrial structure changed in this period.

2   Government and the aircraft industry

The roots of the nationalisation of Short Brothers can be traced back to the inter-war years. The Air Ministry had argued in the late 1930s that, as a major supplier of capital to the aircraft firms, it should have a greater influence in their management; in 1938 they even went as far as to argue for representation on the Boards of aircraft firms (Edgerton 1984, pp. 258–9, PRO 1935). This partly reflected their view that most aircraft firms were badly managed; indeed an Air Ministry survey of 1936 came to the conclusion that only three firms had the potential to deal successfully with large-scale production programmes (Hayward 1989, p. 21). It is probable that the procurement policy of the Ministry contributed to the problems of aircraft manufacturers in the inter-war period but the greater burden of guilt rested with the firms themselves, some of whom were reluctant to produce aircraft designed by others. In this period the Ministry did use its market power to bring about changes in management practice and personnel, in companies such as the airframe producers Blackburn and even in a powerful concern like Vickers, and to encourage takeovers and mergers (Hayward 1989, Edgerton 1991, pp. 78–9). However, they had no legal power to force changes and, for example, were unsuccessful in removing the car manufacturers Rootes from the management of a shadow factory (Edgerton 1984, pp. 258–9).

The war saw a great expansion in the contracts placed by government firms and in the capital provided by the state to firms producing for it. Table 11.1 shows just how extensive this capital assistance was in the aircraft industry: by 1945 the state had provided over £400 million of capital to aircraft factories, 66 per cent of it to works extensions and 34 per cent to shadow factories; in terms of broad categories of usage, 45 per cent was spent on building and air-raid precautions and 55 per cent on providing new plant and machinery. The core aircraft manufacturers, the producers of airframes and engines, received more than half of this capital (split almost evenly between the two) and their share was much larger than the various metal manufacturers who received the next largest shares. Given the size of this capital assistance it is not surprising that the state become more actively involved in firms where it felt there were problems, particularly in the cases of airframe and engine producers, and its directives to firms now also had greater legal weight.

This power was best encapsulated in the government standing order SRO 196. This allowed the state to intervene in a company to which it had

Table 11.1. *Estimated capital assistance to aircraft industry July 1939–September 1945*

Total assistance (£)	425,597,468

as percentage of total	
(a) by recipient	
Shadow factories	34
Works extensions	66
(b) by general use	
Building and air raid precautions	45
Plants and machine tools	55
(c) by specific use, selected items	
Engines	26
Airframes	25
Fabricated light metal	7
Aluminium (including bauxite)	6
Aviation fuel and allied products	4
Propellers	4
Magnesium	3
Aircraft equipment	1

Source: calculated from (PRO undated-a).

provided substantial financial support if the company was deemed to be inefficient. In such circumstances the state could appoint its own company directors to enable the company to run more efficiently. The aircraft industry was particularly wary of these state powers and the appointment as the Minister of Aircraft Production in November 1942 of the 'strongly socialist' Sir Stafford Cripps (who had advocated nationalisation in the inter-war years) led to a panic among manufacturers (see Edgerton this volume). They thought Cripps would exploit the political potential of SRO 196 and use it as an excuse for nationalisation (FBI 1943a, FBI 1943b, FBI 1943c). It was also felt that 'extreme labour people' would deliberately sabotage a firm so that a government director with strong labour sympathies would be appointed and he would then be used as the focal point for labour discontent (FBI 1943b). Here paranoia set in and it was claimed that incidents like this would quickly multiply and spread throughout industry causing massive disruption.

The nationalisation of Short Brothers appeared to confirm the manufacturers worst fears. However, when seen against the background of how the Ministry of Aircraft Production (MAP) usually dealt with inefficient manufacturers, and in the context of the unusual circumstances at Shorts, it appears not so much as a blueprint for a sweeping programme of state ownership of industry but as a final response to a unique problem.

By 1942 the system of investigating problem firms had become formalised in the shape of the Industrial Advisory Panel of the Ministry of Production. If a department, or any government organ, felt that there were problems in any particular firm (either because the workers or the management had informed it of alleged difficulties or because its own officials had become concerned) it would request the Panel to send a team (usually consisting of two members) to investigate the firm. Thus, for example, in July 1942 the Panel investigated Citroen Cars for the Ministry of Supply who were concerned that 40 per cent of the shell rings produced by the company were rejects. The Panel team reported that this reflected bad tooling by the company which in turn reflected the fact that the management had no engineering experience. Thus, a production engineer was appointed and the production of rejects fell to only 0.2 per cent (PRO 1942c). In another case, a team was sent to investigate the Scottish Motor Traction Company (SMT) in April 1943 as, among other things, their output of Hurricane wings and labour productivity showed very large monthly variations. MAP had initially attempted to deal with one of the more important factories run by the firm by placing it under the management of Hawker but apparently to no avail. In this case the team recommended rationalising the payments systems both for contracts to the firm and to employees within the firm (PRO 1943e).

Table 11.2 provides a summary of Industrial Panel investigations carried out between July 1942 and April 1943. Investigations into individual companies (as opposed to investigations into more general issues such as the use of labour in the shipyards or the usefulness of the Capacity Allocation Register 392) accounted for nearly three out of every four investigations. MAP initiated by far the most investigations (thirteen out of the total of thirty in this period) and these were dominated by investigations into individual firms (accounting for a third of the total). Despite this, it is important to note that aircraft firms were not unique in having problems during the war and despite the fact that nine different aircraft firms were investigated in this period (Short Brothers being investigated twice – see below) only one of them was actually nationalised.

The preference of MAP was to persuade the management, and often the workers as well, to accept their recommended changes in personnel or production systems or in payments systems. A good example of this was that of Fairey's, the London based airframe producer, which, in December 1942, became the first firm to have a government Controller appointed under the Defence Regulations. However, the Controller was appointed with the active support of the existing management and Cripps

Table 11.2. *Summary of Industrial Panel investigations by topic, July 1942–April 1944*

Initiating department	Topic		Total
	General issues	Individual companies	
MAP	3	10	13
Ministry of Supply	1	5	6
Admiralty	1	3	4
Others	3	4	7
Total	8	22	30

Source: calculated from various reports in (PRO 1942a, PRO 1942b).

visited the factory in early 1943 to win the support of the workforce (PRO (undated-b), pp. 465–70). Why then did the state resort to nationalisation in the case of Short Brothers?

3   The nationalisation of Short Brothers

Short Brothers set up the first aircraft factory in the world in Kent in 1909, producing aircraft designed by the Wright brothers and by their own staff.[1] Its reputation in the inter-war years was as a designer and producer of seaplanes but the 1920s were lean years in which they produced only thirty-six aircraft and survived by producing buses for companies such as Thomas Tilling and London General Omnibus and Midland Red. The rearmament drive improved their situation greatly and indeed it became obvious that their Kent plant would not be able to meet the much greater orders that the war would bring. Thus, with encouragement from the Air Ministry they joined with Harland and Woolf to create a new joint company, Short Bros and Harland Ltd (of which Short Brothers owned 60 per cent of the shares) in June 1936.[2] The Short and Harland shadow factory was built in 1938 and they delivered their first aircraft, a Bristol Bombay, the following year. During the war Short Harland would build the Bombay, the short-lived Hereford medium bomber and, with Short Brothers, the Sunderland flying boat. However, the most important contribution of the Shorts Group to the war effort was the production of the Stirling heavy bomber.

The first Stirling prototype flew in May 1939 and the first production model exactly one year later. Shorts acted as the parent company for the Stirling which was also produced by Austins. However, the Stirling was not a success. It was twice as costly to produce in terms of man hours as the Lancaster and the latter also only needed about 75 per cent of the materials required to make the Stirling: as late as mid 1943 it was estimated that after flow production had been attained it took 141,000 man hours to produce the Stirling III ('from the raw materials upwards') compared to only 86,000 man hours for the Lancaster IV and V (PRO 1943g). Also, the Shorts Group was failing abjectly to produce the number of Stirlings required of it: in 1941 it produced less than 50 per cent of the planned output and in 1942 it produced only 60 per cent (PRO 1933, PRO 1941).

Even allowing for the tendency of MAP to inflate its production targets and the general difficulties encountered with the heavy bomber programme this was an abysmal performance. In part this reflected serious design problems, which were revealed in a letter to the Industrial Panel in early 1943:

The fact that trouble has been experienced with Stirlings made elsewhere than at Short's Rochester, reflects no credit on Short's. The basic reason for the trouble is that Short's . . . has allowed the development of the Stirling to undermine its flying qualities to the stage when it became aero-dynamically critical. Short's got away with it by their technical skill in nursing each individual aircraft until aero-dynamic balance was obtained; a clever practice which nevertheless killed their own production and misled other producers (PRO 1943b)

This was followed by a visit to Shorts by an Industrial Panel team who reported on 18 January 1943 (PRO 1943a). The team found that the management at Shorts simply could not cope with the much greater demands placed on them by the war (including the massive expansion of production, the increased turnover, the managing of a multi-plant operation, and so on), despite help they had received from MAP (Edgerton 1984, p. 260). It also felt there was a more serious, deep-seated problem with the way the management viewed production:

[Their inter-war] training, and indeed the tradition of the Company, were such as to militate against an easy acceptance of flow production, which has been rendered still more difficult by the large number of comparatively small and widely separated factories which the company now has to operate.

This was less of a problem in Belfast where the factory was suited to flow production but Short Harland had serious labour problems. The team recommended that a new management team was required to strengthen the firm: a new Chairman, a new Director of Production and a new Personnel Manager. Also steps needed to be taken to improve labour relations in Belfast.

Oswald Short (one of the three original brothers who founded the firm) resigned four days later and the Board appointed a new chairman, Sir Frederick Heaton (Chairman and Managing Director of Thomas Tilling). Heaton then set about trying to ring the changes but his plans were vehemently opposed by other board members who even went as far as to lobby government ministers to intervene on their behalf (PRO 1943c). Heaton appealed to Cripps who, as he had done with Fairey's, appointed an Authorised Controller (Mr Layton Bennett). However, at Fairey's the Controller had been appointed with the support of the management but this was not the case at Shorts. Heaton as Chairman had little success in reorganising the company and it is therefore difficult to see how an outsider imposed on the same recalcitrant board could hope to do better. Cripps recognised the inevitable and on 23 March 1943 nationalised Short Brothers by buying its share capital for £447,493.

Cripps and his Ministry did not escape lightly from this. Cripps was attacked in the Commons and, more vigorously, in the debate on the nationalisation of Short Brothers in the House of Lords (PRO 1943d), during which opponents of the nationalisation raised the spectre of Cripps the ideologue orchestrating unprecedented and unwarranted state intervention in the market. Despite this the debate is informative because it made clear that there were two issues involved. The first was the right of the government to intervene in the management of firms whose work was an important contribution to the war effort but which were deemed to be inefficient. This was relatively uncontroversial. Indeed, by 1943, the state controlled and intervened in so many aspects of economic life it would have appeared either perverse or the actions of the hopelessly optimistic to have strongly opposed such actions. They were, after all, fairly common and the Industrial Panel was a formal mechanism for ensuring that the state only intervened where necessary.

The more controversial aspect was the imposition of state ownership. It was argued in the case of Short Bros that this was necessary because the responsibility to appoint directors lay with the shareholders and in such a hostile atmosphere this was the only way the state could ensure that its nominees were appointed or that its appointees or supporters plans were carried through. In particular, the reforms of working methods and the very generous payments system (under which, according to investigators, workers could get high bonuses without earning them through pro- duction or productivity increases) required, could, and did, encounter strong opposition from the workforce (PRO 1943h, PRO 1943i). It was also argued, rather lamely, that it would be unfair to make private shareholders bear the cost of the reorganisation of the company that was needed.

An alternative to state ownership would have been to sack the entire board of directors but it was feared that this would have resulted in the immediate breaking up of the design team which the original investigation had urged should be safeguarded. It might be thought that such a safeguard was unnecessary given the poor job the design team had done on the Stirling. However, design teams in this strategically important area were scarce and the team at Short Brothers had a good track record and were an important reserve of acquired skills and knowledge. Further, as Edgerton (this volume) argues the state was keen on protecting aircraft design teams and promoting competition between them in the belief that this was strategically and economically sensible.

In the circumstances, therefore, Cripps had little alternative: Shorts was an important producer of airframes and particularly of what was viewed by Churchill and others as the key strategic weapon, the heavy bomber, and MAP was keen that Stirling capacity could be switched to producing the more economical and successful Lancaster. Furthermore, 1943 saw the economy reaching the limits of its manpower constraint and it was vital that a company whose various activities were responsible for the employment of 45,597 workers (of whom, 20,047 were directly employed by Short Brothers, including 4,314 in Swindon, and 19,911 by Short Harland) should be as productive as possible; given the scarcity of capacity, nor could the 3.5 million square feet of factory space controlled by Shorts be ignored (PRO 1943h, PRO 1945).

What impact did the nationalisation of Shorts have on its production? One of the original reasons why MAP had been concerned about the management at Shorts was that they had refused to switch to Lancaster production. By the time state ownership was imposed on the company, however, it had been decided not to switch production at Shorts to the Lancaster but to continue to produce the Stirling (which even if it was not effective as a heavy bomber could be used as a paratroop transport aircraft and a glider tug). Therefore we must assess the impact of nationalisation of Shorts by asking two questions: did nationalisation result in an increase in production?; did nationalisation lead to an improvement in meeting its production programme targets set by the state? Since the Stirling heavy bomber was the most strategically important aircraft produced by the company the analysis will focus on its production.

In terms of physical production the state was claiming one year after the nationalisation that it had been a great success. The production of Stirling aircraft, based on financial years, rose thus (PRO 1944a):

	1942/3	1943/4	Percentage increase
Short Brothers	175	239	37
Short Harland	191	418	119
Shorts Group	366	657	80

In parliament Cripps claimed that production at Shorts had risen by 69 per cent compared to the previous year and that labour productivity had also risen substantially (PRO 1944b). However, although the increases were impressive Cripps omitted two important pieces of information: first, aircraft production during the war followed a well-known and documented upward 'production curve' and thus such increases over time were not unusual; secondly, a major problem at Shorts had been its woeful inability to meet its production targets but Cripps did not say if this had improved (Devons 1950, pp. 10, 31, 208–9, PRO 1943f). Furthermore, the comments by Cripps, and similar comments at the time by his colleagues, give no indication of the very different performances of the two halves of the Shorts Group that is shown by the above figures: from a rough parity of Stirling production in 1942/3, Short Harland was producing 75 per cent more Stirling aircraft than Short Brothers a year later; also, Short Harland managed to increase their production of Sunderland aircraft by a much larger percentage, albeit from a much lower base figure.

Table 11.3 provides more detailed information about the production of Stirling heavy bombers by Shorts: it was calculated from the Weekly Statistical Bulletin of MAP and shows the average weekly output per month from November 1941 to December 1943. The gradual upward trend in output at both Short Brothers and Short Harland does suggest that it did follow a typical 'production curve' (production peaked in early 1944 and was deliberately run down thereafter). Shorts was nationalised at the end of March 1943 but, given the 'production curve', it is not obvious from table 11.3 that this had any marked impact on the trend of production. Comparing the peak weekly average production figures before and after nationalisation lends some support to the view that it was beneficial for Short Harland: at Short Brothers these figures were, respectively, 4.75 and 5.6, representing a relatively modest 18 per cent increase; at Short Harland, however, the pre-nationalisation peak was 5.25 in March 1943 and the post-nationalisation peak was 9.0, representing a 72 per cent increase.

Figure 11.1 shows the total monthly output figures as a percentage of their production programme targets and thus allows us to assess whether state ownership improved this aspect of the performance of Shorts. This evidence does suggest that state ownership did improve the performances of both Short Brothers and Short Harland. Short Harland had performed abysmally in 1942, reaching a nadir in January 1943 when it produced less than one-third of its target output, but after nationalisation it showed a marked improvement in meeting or exceeding its monthly targets; although it failed to maintain this initial high standard in the second half of the year its performance was still far superior to that of the previous

Table 11.3. *Shorts Group output of Stirling bombers: average weekly output per month November 1941–December 1943*

		Short Brothers	Short Harland
1941	November	1.50	1.75
	December	1.25	2.00
1942	January	1.40	2.00
	February	1.00	2.75
	March	1.50	2.50
	April	2.00	2.50
	May	3.40	3.00
	June	2.50	4.50
	July	2.75	2.75
	August	3.00	4.60
	September	4.00	4.75
	October	2.80	3.80
	November	3.00	4.25
	December	4.75	2.75
1943	January	3.40	2.40
	February	4.75	4.50
	March	4.75	5.25
	April	3.00	6.75
	May	4.00	6.60
	June	4.75	8.75
	July	4.80	5.20
	August	5.00	9.00
	September	4.50	9.00
	October	5.60	8.80
	November	5.00	7.75
	December	4.00	8.67

Source: calculated from (PRO 1941).

year. In the case of Short Brothers the initial impact of nationalisation was a sudden fall in its target completion rate (in April 1943 it produced only two-thirds of its output target) but thereafter it recovered to maintain a completion rate of 85 per cent or above; the striking feature of Figure 11.1 for Short Brothers is the relative stability after June 1943 compared to the period before March 1943.

Despite the claims of the state there is no conclusive evidence that nationalisation led to a marked improvement in the performance of Shorts. What evidence there is suggests that state ownership was possibly more beneficial in the case of Short Harland. This in turn probably reflected the potential of the two companies: Short Brothers plant had traditionally relied on relatively small-scale batch production and had

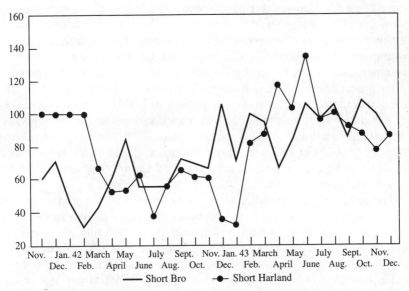

11.1 Stirling bomber output as percentage of programme.
Source: Calculated from (PRO, 1941).

resisted flow production techniques, which in any case were impractical because of its size, whereas Short Harland had originally been created to deal with much larger orders and had been set up to operate on flow production lines and therefore it had a greater potential output. State intervention may have helped Short Harland by creating better and more frequent contact between it and its parent company and by fostering better labour relations (for example, it helped to set up a Joint Production Committee). The situation was summed up by a committee set up in 1944 to consider the future of the Shorts Group (PRO 1945). It concluded that the: 'Belfast group of factories are much more up to date, compact and efficient . . . than those at Rochester'.

It recommended that the Kent operations be moved to Belfast. This was rejected at the time but it was inevitable; the Kent factory finally closed in June 1948.

4   The state and industrial structure during the War

The state did not use its extended powers during the war to promote a programme of nationalisation. The case of Short Brothers demonstrates that nationalisation was a last resort and it is not mere coincidence that all three firms nationalised during the war had some strategic importance. However, the actions of the state during the war could have had a long-term impact on the overall structure of industry and on the structure within specific industries (as is suggested by several studies in this volume). The extent of state influence on the economy during the war cannot be underestimated: it controlled both prices and quantities in many markets during the war through both its legislative powers and the power gained by it becoming the dominant consumer in the economy. It introduced new taxes (most notably the Excess Profits Tax), controlled the supply of labour and other scarce resources, placed direct and indirect restrictions on capital and severely curtailed exports and decided what could be imported (Howlett 1994b).

The nature of the war meant that the state had to take control of the supply of scarce resources in the economy and this is why it introduced restrictions on the use of many raw materials and centrally allocated the more important ones (Howlett 1994a). Many of these controls extended into the post-war years to help control inflation and to maintain external balance (Cairncross 1985, pp. 344–51). Thus, in 1946, 94 per cent of all industrial raw materials were controlled by the state but even as late as 1951 this figure stood at 41 per cent (Tomlinson 1993, p. 11). The way the controls operated, their extent, and the timing of their removal must have had important implications for the market and therefore must have influenced industrial structure. They did encourage new entry in some industries (such as biscuits), exit in other industries (bread and flour confectionery), and the use of a system of quotas and allocations invited mergers and acquisitions to occur (Evely and Little 1960, p. 180). However, in terms of business history and industrial structure the period 1939–55 remains under a shroud and our knowledge of the long-term effects of these controls remains vague.

This section will consider how the wartime role of the state could have potentially affected industrial structure, in particular what effect it had on industrial concentration and on employment patterns in manufacturing. The issue of industrial concentration will be examined by considering the state policy known as the Concentration of Production Drive. This was initiated to rationalise resources in industries deemed less essential to the war effort, typically consumer goods industries, in order to release labour and capacity to the munitions industries.

The degree of industrial concentration in an industry, or economy, is the most common statistical method used to measure changes in industrial organisation. It is far from an ideal measure, and there are theoretical and empirical problems associated with it, but there is no ready alternative other than in depth studies of individual industries (Hannah 1983, pp. 179–84, Curry and George 1983, pp. 203–25). There is no study of changes in industrial concentration during the war but there are several studies which span the war years. These studies show that there was a strong trend towards increased industrial concentration in Britain in the twentieth century. However, one period which bucks the trend is 1935 to 1955, which most studies suggest witnessed no significant change in industrial concentration, and Prais has even argued that it decreased (Hannah 1983, pp. 123–42, Prais 1974, p. 4). Concentration may have fallen in the war because conditions favoured small firms compared to large firms:

Quotas of production, restrictions on capital investment etc., may have hindered the growth of large firms and kept alive some small firms, which had been given a quota, when otherwise they might have died. It is also possible small firms were able to adapt more quickly (Curry and George 1983, p. 228)

Merger activity has also been cited as an important factor for increased concentration but such activity was minimal in this period (Curry and George 1983, p. 228).

The Concentration of Production Drive (henceforth CPD) was, in effect, a process of rationalisation, albeit a temporary one, forced on the predominantly consumer goods industries by the state. This suggests, contrary to the trend identified by Prais, that in those industries affected concentration increased during the war. Further, resources in these industries were placed under the control of 'nucleus firms' and it does not seem unreasonable to suggest that in the immediate post-war years this, if anything, would again encourage increased concentration since the war years may have revealed the benefits of merger of acquisition to the nucleus firm. In practice it is difficult to measure the impact of the CPD because there is no detailed information about the structure of individual industries in 1939 or 1945. The second-best solution is to use the study by Evely and Little (1960), based on Census of Production data (but excluding nationalised industries), which compares changes in industrial structure between 1935 and 1951. This poses many problems, the most obvious being that observed changes between 1935 and 1951 may not be related to the war in general or the CPD in particular, and so at best can only give a tentative and broad suggestion as to what happened. The Evely and Little data will be contrasted with the results of a Federation of British Industry (FBI) survey on the effects of the CPD. This poses another problem in that the definition of an industry or trade given by the FBI survey may not coincide with the carefully constructed definitions given by Evely and Little.

In Appendix K of their book Evely and Little give a list of twenty-seven trades which experienced increased concentration in industrial structure between 1935 and 1951 and fourteen trades which experienced decreased concentration and provide information that allows employment and the number of establishments in those trades to be calculated; the FBI survey provides data for twenty-seven industries on the number of establishments closed and labour released due to the CPD (Evely and Little 1960, p. 340, Howlett 1994b, p. 144). However, the overlap between the two sets of data amounts to only four industries. The evidence related to these four industries is presented in table 11.4.

Table 11.4 shows that of the four industries, toilet preparations suffered most in terms of employment and establishments lost during the CPD compared to the 1935 levels, the industry saw half of its establishments closed and it lost a quarter of its workforce. The table also shows that the CPD was aimed primarily at establishments employing considerably less workers than the average size of establishment in 1935; toilet preparations is noticeable as the only one of the four industries where the average establishment closed employed more than half of the number of workers employed on average in 1935. In comparing the situation in 1951 with 1935, toilet preparations again stands out in that employment in 1951 was 50 per cent greater than in 1935 and, given that the number of establishments was virtually the same, the average number of employees per establishment had also increased by a similar margin. Further, of these four industries toilet preparations was the only one classified by Evely and Little as experiencing increased concentration between 1935 and 1951. This suggests that the CPD was important in the case of toilet preparations in bringing about a long-term change in its industrial structure.

Evely and Little, however, argue that the CPD had an important impact in only three, or possibly four, trades (building bricks, tinplate, textile finishing and possibly carpets), although, surprisingly given their general caution, they produce no substantive quantitative evidence to support this claim (Evely and Little 1960, p. 179). More significantly, their work implies that the CPD was relatively unimportant compared to other factors increasing long-term changes: thus, whereas building bricks and tinplate are identified as trades experiencing increased concentration between 1935 and 1951, textile finishing and carpets experienced decreased concentration (Evely and Little 1960, p. 340). Elsewhere it has also been argued that the direct effects of the CPD on industrial concentration were probably minimal because the scheme was implemented on the understanding that it was a temporary arrangement that would be reversed at the end of the war (Howlett 1994b, p. 143).

Evely and Little do not offer any reason to explain why increased

Table 11.4. *The impacts of the Concentration of Production Drive on four industries*

	(1) Employment	(2) No. of establishments	(3) (1)/(2)
CPD as % of 1935			
Toilet preparations	26	49	54
Linoleum	4	16	25
Gloves	5	25	20
Boots and shoes	12	36	33
1951 as % of 1935			
Toilet preparations	150	99	151
Linoleum	108	87	124
Gloves	107	131	82
Boots and shoes	98	115	85

Note: CPD is the loss due to the Concentration of Production Drive.
Sources: The figures for 1935 and 1951 were calculated from Evely and Little (1960), p. 340, the CPD figures are from Howlett (1994b, p. 144).

concentration occurred in toilet preparations between 1935 and 1951 but merely point out that it was a trade that witnessed mergers and acquisitions (Evely and Little 1960, p. 23). However, it is likely that wartime concentration, by forcing firms to temporarily integrate and pool resources, did help to pave the way for such mergers and acquisitions in the post-war years. If this was so it suggests that it was the indirect effects of the CPD rather than its direct effects that were more important in potentially affecting industrial structure in the long term.

Turning to employment, it is no surprise that the Second World War brought about a marked change in the structure of the working population: civil employment was squeezed from 92 per cent of the working population in 1939 to 75 per cent in 1945 as the armed forces expanded (from 2 per cent to 24 per cent). Within civil employment there was also marked changes as the munitions and related industries (centred on engineering, metals, vehicles and chemicals) increased and the consumer goods industries experienced a sharp decline, from 49 per cent of the working population in 1939 to 29 per cent in 1945 (Howlett 1994a, table 7). Changes in the manufacturing sector were obviously driven by the strategic objectives of the state in wartime. How did this affect the long-term pattern of employment within the sector?

There is no consistent series for employment within the manufacturing sector that includes the war years. Feinstein has produced a series that

Table 11.5. *Change in share of manufacturing employment (by percentage point) 1924–38, 1938–45 and 1948–55*

	1924–38	1938–45	1948–55
Food, drink, tobacco	+ 1	− 2	0
Chemicals	0	+ 3	+ 1
Iron and steel	− 1	0	− 1
Engineering and shipbuilding	+ 2	+ 11	+ 1
Vehicles	+ 2	+ 6	+ 1
Other metal industries	+ 1	+ 1	0
Textiles	− 7	− 5	− 1
Clothing	− 1	− 4	− 1
Bricks, pottery, glass, cement	0	− 2	0
Timber, furniture	+ 1	− 1	0
Paper, printing, publishing	0	− 3	0
Leather and other manufacturing	0	− 2	0

Sources: 1924–38 and 1948–55 calculated from Feinstein (1972), T129–30; 1938–45 calculated from Central Statistical Office (1951), pp. 8, 17–23, 27–8; see text.

covers the period preceding and succeeding the war years (ending in 1938 and starting again in 1948) and this was used in conjunction with the official statistics for the war years (henceforth CSO) to produce table 11.5. The employment categories used by CSO for the war years do not match those used by Feinstein.[3] Further, the classification used by Feinstein changed in 1948 so that the pre-war and post-war figures he gives are not consistent. However, our interest is not with the levels of employment in individual industries but in the relative shifts between them and this makes the classification issue less of a problem. Thus, with one exception the share of each individual industrial category in total manufacturing employment in 1938 given by the Feinstein data is very close (within one percentage point) to that given by the CSO data. The one exception is the category I have called engineering and shipbuilding; for 1938 Feinstein gives this category a 17 per cent share of total manufacturing employment whereas CSO gives it a 21 per cent share.[4]

Table 11.5 attempts to examine how important the war was in bringing about changes in the pattern of manufacturing employment compared to the peacetime years of the inter-war period (1924–38) and the immediate post-war years (1948–55). It shows how the share of each manufacturing category in total manufacturing employment changed over each of the three sub-periods. The change shown is not the percentage change but the percentage point change; thus, in 1924 the iron and steel industry accounted for 6 per cent of manufacturing employment but by 1938 it had fallen to 5 per cent, a change of −1 percentage point.

The impact of the war is startling: between 1948 and 1955 no category saw its share of manufacturing employment change by more than one percentage point and in the inter-war period no category, except for textiles, saw its share change by more than two percentage points; during the war, however, no fewer than six of the twelve categories witnessed a change of three percentage points or more, with engineering and ship-building increasing its share by a massive eleven percentage points. The figures for the post-war period also demonstrate that the dramatic shifts of the war years were not simply reversed on the ending of the war and that the war therefore brought about some permanent changes in the relative importance of different manufacturing industries. It could be argued, however, that the war merely acted as a catalyst since (with the exceptions of food, drink and tobacco, and timber and furniture) the wartime shifts were in the same direction as industries had experienced in the inter-war years.

5   Conclusion

The nationalisation of Shorts did not represent the thin end of the wedge, it was not part of a plan of widespread nationalisation in the aircraft industry or of other private industries. Cripps, in nationalising the company, was not grinding an ideological axe but was merely responding to strategic and political pressures associated with the high profile heavy bomber programme, pressures to which the management of the company seemed impervious. Shorts was nationalised because its management, unlike those at other companies which encountered problems and which the state took a more active role in, refused to cooperate with attempts to strengthen its organisation and improve its efficiency. Cripps would have been negligent if he had allowed the situation to continue. At best, it provides more evidence for the view that there was some support for the idea of nationalising, or taking under more direct state control, the design end of the aircraft industry (Edgerton 1984). Thus, despite the chaotic state of affairs at Shorts, including serious design failings, the original Industrial Panel team emphasised the need to keep the valuable experience and expertise of its design team (headed by Arthur Gouge) together. Unfortunately, Gouge was one of those opposed to managerial change and he eventually left and joined Saunders Roe.

The issue of the impact of the war on industrial structure raises more questions than it answers. The importance of the war to the structure of business is recognised by the scholars of the USA and Japan but research on this topic for the British economy is limited (Chandler 1977, pp. 476–83, Sakudo and Shiba 1994). It has been suggested above that the Concentration of Production Drive may have had important indirect consequences in certain industries and that state controls on raw materials did have direct consequences for market structure (although these have yet to be quantified). This is not a minor point. The issue of 'the role of the market environment', which in the period 1935–55 pivoted on state policies and state-business relations, has been recently raised as potentially one of the most important factors in explaining the productivity gap between Britain and the USA and thus in explaining the relative decline of the British economy (Broadberry and Crafts 1992). Thus, if we are to improve our understanding of the relative decline of the British economy since 1945 further research on this issue is required.

NOTES

1 The general material on Shorts is drawn from Barnes (1967) and Preston (1978).
2 To keep matters simple, in the text Short Brothers will refer to the original company (mainly based at Rochester in Kent but during the war it also had other sites, for example in Swindon and at Windermere), Short Harland to the jointly owned company (based in Belfast) and Shorts Group will refer to both. Details of the structure of the Short Group in early 1943 are given in (PRO 1943a) and its structure towards the end of the war was detailed in (PRO 1945).
3 For example, in 1938 Feinstein gives employment in the food, drink and tobacco industries as 767,000 whereas CSO gives it as 640,000; Feinstein gives total manufacturing employment as 6.97 million and CSO gives it as 6.36 million.
4 The official series has a large category which it calls metals, engineering, vehicles and shipbuilding. Feinstein, on the other hand, provides separate categories for iron and steel, electrical engineering, mechanical engineering and shipbuilding, vehicles, and other metal industries. CSO does provide more disaggregated data on its category but this is presented in an unhelpful manner which makes it impossible to derive consistent sub-categories. Data was given on employment in iron and steel and vehicles; also the other metal industries category was derived by summing together employment data on non-ferrous metal manufacture, bolts etc., and scientific instruments etc. (although given the vagueness of the CSO definitions these should be treated with caution). It was not possible to disaggregate the CSO data further and thus the residual from metals, engineering, vehicles and shipbuilding was placed into the engineering and shipbuilding category.

REFERENCES

Barnes, C.H. (1967), *Shorts Aircraft Since 1900*, London: Putnam.
Broadberry, S.N. and Crafts, N.F.R. (1992), 'Britain's Productivity Gap in the 1930s: Some Neglected Factors', *Journal of Economic History*, 52.
Cairncross, A. (1985), *Years of Recovery*, London: Methuen.
Central Statistics Office (1951), *Statistical Digest of the War*, London: HMSO.
Chandler, A.D. Jr. (1977), *The Visible Hand*, Cambridge, Massachusetts: Harvard University Press.

Curry, B. and George, K.D. (1983), 'Industrial Concentration: a Survey', *Journal of Industrial Economics*, 31.

Devons, E. (1950), *Planning in Practice. Essays in Aircraft Planning in Wartime*, Cambridge University Press.

Edgerton, D. (1984), 'Technical innovation, industrial capacity and efficiency: public ownership and the British military aircraft industry, 1935–1948', *Business History*, 26.

(1991), *England and the Aeroplane: an Essay on a Militant and Technological Nation*, London: Macmillan.

Evely, R. and Little, I.M.D. (1960), *Concentration in British Industry*, Cambridge University Press.

FBI (Modern Records Centre, University of Warwick, Federation of British Industry Files) (1943a), MSS.200/F/3/S2/15/140, letter from the Chairman of English Electric Company Limited to Locock, 21 February 1943.

FBI (1943b), MSS.200/F/3/S2/15/34, Joint Advisory Committee debate on SRO 196, 22 February 1943.

FBI (1943c), MSS.200/F/3/S2/15/34, extract from *Hansard*, 31 March 1943.

Feinstein, C.H. (1972), *National Income, Expenditure and Output of the United Kingdom 1855–1965*, Cambridge University Press.

Hannah, L. (1983), *The Rise of the Corporate Economy* (second edition), London: Methuen.

Howlett, P. (1994a), 'The Wartime Economy, 1939–1945', in R. Floud and D. McCloskey (eds.), *The Economic History of Britain Since 1700. Volume 3*, Cambridge University Press.

Howlett, P. (1994b), 'British Business and the State During the Second World War', in Sakudo and Shiba (eds.) (1994).

Hayward, K. (1989), *The British Aircraft Industry*, Manchester: Manchester University Press.

Prais, S.J. (1974), 'A New Look at the Growth of Industrial Concentration', *Oxford Economic Papers*, 26.

Preston, J.M. (1978), *A Short History of Short Brothers Aircraft Activities in Kent, 1908–1964*, Rochester: North Kent Books.

PRO (1933), AIR19/524 (1933–1945. Aircraft: delivery, import and export figures), table on planned and actual production by Shorts.

PRO (1935), AIR19/143 (1935. Aircraft industry and current problems), memorandum by C.L. Bullock (Permanent Under Secretary of State for Air), 19 November 1943.

PRO (1941), AVIA10/315–318 (Ministry of Aircraft Production Weekly Statistical Bulletins. Nos. 1–111. 8/11/41–18/12/43).

PRO (1942a), BT28/420/IC/114 (1942 May–1943 August. Industrial Advisory Panel: investigations into companies not giving complete satisfaction).

PRO (1942b), BT28/421/IC/114a (1942 July–September. Industrial Advisory Panel: reports of factory investigations).

PRO (1942c), BT28/420/IC/114 , Industrial Panel report, 8 July 1942.

PRO (1943a), BT28/426/IC/114/6 (1942 December–1944 April. Short Bros. Ltd.: enquiry into the efficiency of the firm and its associated concerns), Report by Sir George Schuster and R. Barlow on Short Bros. Ltd. and Short Harland Ltd., 18 January 1943.

PRO (1943b), BT28/426/IC/114/6 letter to the Secretary of the Industrial Panel, 8 February 1943.

PRO (1943c), BT28/426/IC/114/6, letter from MAP to Lyttleton (Minister of Production), 23 February 1943.

PRO (1943d), BT28/426/IC/114/6, extract from *Hansard*, House of Lords, cols. 151–69, 13 April 1943.

PRO (1943e), BT228/432/IC/114/11 (1943 April–May. Scottish Motor Tractor Co. Ltd.: investigations into company affairs in order to recommend methods for achieving maximum production), Interim Report by the Industrial Panel team investigating the Scottish Motor Traction Company, April 1943; Final Report by the Industrial Panel team investigating the Scottish Motor Traction Company, July 1943.

PRO (1943f), PREM3/36/2 (Correspondence on aircraft programmes), letter from Cripps to Churchill, 7 June 1943.

PRO (1943g), AVIA9/61 (1943–1944. Labour requirements for aircraft production), letter by E.B. Bowyer, 10 June 1943.

PRO (1943h), BT28/1191/MISC 135 (1943 June–December. Short Bros (Rochester and Bedford) Ltd.: Review, 1943), 'A General Review', 25 November 1943.

PRO (1943i), BT28/447/IC/114/26, Report of the Industrial Panel into Short Brothers works in the Medway area, 23 December 1943.

PRO (1944a), BT28/426/IC/114/6, letters from Nigel Campbell to the Minister of Production, 6 and 9 April 1944.

PRO (1944b), BT28/426/IC/114/6, extract from *Hansard*, Parliamentary Questions, col. 756, 26 April 1944.

PRO (1945), AVIA15/2175 (1944–1949. Board of Short Bros. Rochester and Bedford Ltd.: Post-war reorganisation), Report of Committee on the Future of Short Brothers (Rochester and Bedford) Ltd., 5 January 1945.

PROa (undated-a), (Public Records Office, Kew), CAB102/274 ('Aircraft Production and Factories', unsigned), 1 and 4.

PROb (undated-b), PREM4/34/5.

Sakudo, J. and Shiba, T. (eds.) (1994), *World War II and the Transformation of Business Systems*, Tokyo: Tokyo University Press.

Tivey, L. (1973), *Nationalisation in British Industry* (revised edition), London: Cape.

Tomlinson, J. (1993), 'Mr. Attlee's Supply-side Socialism', *Economic History Review*, 46.

12   The political economy of nationalisation: the electricity industry

Martin Chick

> I am sure that the power of vested interests is vastly exaggerated compared with the gradual encroachment of ideas. Not, indeed, immediately, but after a certain interval; for in the field of economic and political philosophy there are not many who are influenced by new theories after they are twenty-five or thirty years of age, so that the ideas which civil servants and politicians and even agitators apply to current events are not likely to be the newest. But soon or late, it is ideas, not vested interests, which are dangerous for good or evil.
>
> John Maynard Keynes, *The General Theory of Employment, Interest and Money*

These closing lines of Keynes's *General Theory*, published in February 1936, provide a neat summary of the main theme of this chapter on the long prelude to the nationalisation of the electricity industry in April 1948. The decision of the Attlee government to transfer the industry from municipal and private hands into public ownership was a last exasperated, culminating conclusion to a prolonged struggle to effect the reorganisation of the structure of the industry, in particular on its distribution side. The oft-made remark that the nationalisation programme contained few long-considered practical proposals for the management of the newly nationalised industries is largely correct, and also, not that surprising, if the nationalisation programme is viewed as the end of a long process rather than the initiation of a new one. Similarly, the observation that nationalisation grouped together a motley and sometimes inconsistent collection of ideas, aims and aspirations reflects its origins. What began largely as a technical case for the reorganisation of the electricity industry came to acquire wider and vaguer social ambitions. The irony was that, in the end, the original technical case for reorganisation, which was probably always overstated, came to be overtaken by the later *arriviste* social ideas of extending supply and controlling and equalising prices.

1   The case for reorganisation

Technical demands for the reorganisation of the electricity industry were long standing. In the generating section of the industry dissatisfaction with the inefficient structure, foregone economies of scale and high prices came to a head in the mid 1920s. Pressure from industrial users pushed the Conservative Baldwin government in to appointing the Weir Committee, whose main recommendation for the establishment of a Central Electricity Board (CEB) was enacted in 1926. In what is now a familiar tale to economic and business historians (Hannah 1977, pp. 207–26), the CEB, by purchasing electricity from selected stations and planning new power station capacity, was able to initiate a process of productivity improvement, such that, from generating 443 units of electricity per ton of coal in 1914 and 631 units in 1920, output had risen to 1,566 units per ton by 1939. Despite taking inputs of cartelised coal prices, the cost of electricity 'at the busbars' (the point at which electricity entered the transmission or distribution system) was reduced from 1.098d. per unit in 1923 to an average of 0.34d. per unit in 1939 and 0.39d. per unit in 1940 (Hannah 1977, p. 223).

Although concern with the structure of the generating section of the industry dominated discussions of the industry during the 1920s, dissatisfaction with the structure of distribution continued to rumble on in the background. Parliamentary Acts in 1919 and 1922 had provided for the determination of Electricity Districts and the establishment of Joint Electricity Authorities in cases where the Commissioners considered that the organisation should be improved. In 1926, while considering generation, the Weir Committee recommended that new distribution franchises should be established, each with a tenure of fifty years, and the Commissioners, empowered by Section 39 of the 1926 Electricity (Supply) Act, did establish twenty large undertakings during the next ten years. However, powers to amalgamate existing undertakings or prevent municipalities establishing new franchised undertakings were not given, one consequence being a proliferation of new undertakings, with 126 additional franchises being granted between 1921 and 1932 (Hannah 1979, p. 237). These nestled uneasily among older-established franchises, many of which were approaching maturity. The imminent maturation of these franchises, during the 1930s and 1940s, forced discussion of distribution to the fore. A succession of abortive legislation, quiet meetings and reports to the Minister in 1931, 1934 and 1935 occupied a half decade of underachievement which closed with the appointment of the McGowan Committee in July 1935 charged with reviewing the organisation of the distribution of electricity and suggesting improvements. Reflecting on a

Table 12.1. *Total costs of distributions per unit of electricity sold 1933–4*

Annual sales of undertakings	d. per unit
0 to 1 million units	2.48
1 to 5 million units	1.49
5 to 10 million units	1.14
10 to 25 million units	0.89
25 to 50 million units	0.77
50 and over 50 million units	0.59

Source: PRO 1937, para. 4.

distribution system which it dubbed as 'chaotic', the Committee made many suggestions for greater standardisation within the industry (PRO 1937, para. 5). In what were essentially observations on the need for some 'tidying-up', attention was drawn to the coexistence of two different types of current. At the end of 1933–4, seventy-seven undertakings were supplying direct current only, 282 undertakings were supplying alternating current only, and 283 undertakings were supplying both (PRO 1936a, para. 303). In addition, nineteen principal voltages existed in the industry, although the large bulk of 407 undertakings were supplying consumers at the standard voltages, namely 230 volts (for lighting) and 400 volts (for power and industrial purposes). The variety of voltages not only inconvenienced consumers who moved to a different district only to find that their portable electric appliances would not work, but also produced situations, most usually in large cities, where there were different systems and different voltages on opposite sides of the street (PRO 1936a, para. 4).

As for the structure of the industry itself, there were 625 separate authorised undertakers operating 635 undertakings (PRO 1937, para. 4). Of the 635 separate undertakings in existence at the end of 1933–4, some 400 were selling less than 10 million units per annum. The aggregate sales of these 400 undertakings was less than 10 per cent of the sales of all 635 undertakings (PRO 1937, para. 4). The total costs of distribution for undertakings selling 50 million units and over per annum was under one quarter of the cost for undertakings selling 1 million units or less, only two-fifths of that for undertakings selling from 1 to 5 millions and about one-half of that for undertakings selling from 5 to 10 millions.

The implication was that the larger units were better able to exploit available economies of scale, although consideration of the apparent advantages enjoyed by large undertakings over medium-sized ones was clouded by differences in the nature of the area served and local demand elasticities (Hannah 1979, p. 244). Nonetheless, there was a tendency to believe that what had worked in generation would also work, even if not to the same extent, in distribution. Implied argument through comparison was employed. As the McGowan Committee noted, while across the country as a whole, the average cost of generation had fallen from 0.9675d. per unit sold in 1924–5 to 0.5231d. in 1933–4, representing a reduction of 46 per cent in what may be termed the wholesale cost, in contrast the cost of electrical energy attributable to local distribution had risen from 0.7573d. per unit sold in 1924–5 to 0.8278d. in 1931–2. There had been some slight reduction in the two succeeding years, but the cost in 1933–4 at 0.7664d. per unit sold was higher than the cost in 1924–5 (PRO 19365a, para. 420). Alluding to the assumed benefits of standardisation and larger units, the McGowan Committee stated that its initial aim was to reduce the existing total of some 635 undertakings to about 250 (PRO 1937, para. 5).

2   Private persuasion or public compulsion?

In urging this mix of standardisation and restructuring, the McGowan Committee was not saying anything particularly new. What was new was that the need for reorganisation was being stated in public and based on the collated presentation of evidence. Yet, the persistent problem was how to effect such reorganisation. There appeared to be a growing realisation that, left to itself, the market was unlikely to resolve the problem and, if left to themselves, the Local Authorities were likely to act so as to accelerate and exacerbate the disintegration of the industry. The forty-two year franchises provided in the Electric Lighting Act of 1888 were beginning to fall due, and the fear was that if local authorities exercised their rights of purchase, 'disintegration' rather than consolidation might beset the industry, with 100 of the undertakings existing in 1937 being split up into 344 undertakings (PRO 1937, para. 4). Changes to local government boundaries had only made matters potentially worse, since, as the areas of undertakings no longer bore a tight relation to political divisions, the number of local authorities able to purchase parts of company undertakings had increased (Hannah 1979, p. 238).

Given the necessity of acting to prevent disintegration and the apparent desirability of securing consolidation, attention focused on the means of compelling change. On this, the McGowan Committee was a little diffident. It did recognise that the state would in some way have to achieve the restructuring that the market could not. It was recognised that 'any attempt to carry through a scheme of reorganisation on a voluntary basis was bound to fail and legislation must confer definite and adequate compulsory powers' (PRO 1936d, para. 471). In this view, the McGowan Committee received strong support from the succeeding Cabinet Committee on Electricity Distribution in February 1937 (PRO 1937, para. 18) which confirmed that 'existing powers are inadequate to secure a proper grouping of areas' (PRO 1937, para. 4). Such views were based on past experience, much of it in generation in the years preceding the establishment of the CEB in 1926. Early attempts, as in the Electricity (Supply) Act of 1919 to secure the voluntary establishment of joint electricity authorities, whose duty it would have been to reorganise the supply of electricity in their districts, were subsequently held to have been fatally flawed by the absence of compulsory powers (PRO 1937, para. 4). Draft legislation produced by the Electric Power Supply Committee which provided for the compulsory transfer of generating stations and main transmission lines to District Authorities, and for the establishment of the Electricity Commissioners to carry the proposals into effect, was 'emasculated' at a late stage by the exclusion of the proposed compulsory powers. The verdict of the Weir Committee, as quoted by the McGowan Report, on the outcome of the 1919 Act was one of frustration and increasing impatience:

Five years of patient and capable effort have been unavailing. Co-ordination has not been achieved. The advisory bodies created under the Act have agreed on technical schemes, but local interests have prevented the carrying out of those schemes. Delay and procrastination are widespread, and the policy of suasion can only be written down as failure. (PRO 1936a, para. 45)

Nor had a 'policy of suasion' enjoyed any more success in promoting the reorganisation of the distribution side of the electricity industry. Once it was accepted that persuasion had failed and that compulsion was required, there was still a variety of opinions on the form and pace of any process of compulsory reform. McGowan, impressed with the informed behind-the-scenes work of the Electricity Commissioners in the run-up to the establishment of the CEB, turned to the Commissioners again in preparing the way for any compulsory reorganisation (PRO 1936a, paras. 46–9). As a facilitating prologue to eventual compulsory reorganisation, the Electricity Commissioners were to divide the country into convenient areas within which any necessary consolidation could occur (PRO 1937, para. 6). Surveying the industry, the Electricity Commissioners anticipated that the process of reorganisation, involving the preparation of just under 100 schemes, would take a minimum of five years from the enactment of the necessary legislation (PRO 1937, para. 6).

The McGowan Report's proposed use of the Electricity Commissioners was viewed as a stage in a process by which all undertakings, including those not then subject to purchase by local authorities, might be taken into public ownership. While the McGowan Report was important as a public statement of the need for reorganisation by compulsion, the response to the Report also highlighted differences of opinion on the pace of this reorganisation. While the McGowan Committee saw no reasons to recommend any departure from the general principle laid down by Parliament of eventual public ownership (PRO 1936a, para. 188) (indeed they saw themselves as extending this principle) they did lengthen the time-span of this process, envisaging 'ultimate public ownership' as likely to take not more than fifty years (PRO 1937, para. 10).

McGowan's approach of progress by stealth was in sharp opposition to alternative, more rapid strategies being advanced by Herbert Morrison. As the Labour government's Minister of Transport in 1929, Morrison had established a departmental committee to consider the problems of the electricity industry, the committee delivering its report to Morrison on 31 March 1931 (Hannah 1979, p. 239). The report offered two major options. One was the reorganisation of all the existing undertakings under regional, publicly owned distribution boards supplying large areas. The other was to reorganise around the existing large undertakings, with smaller undertakings being taken over by their larger neighbours (Hannah 1979, p. 239). The first option held most appeal for Morrison, and formed the basis for a strategy of reorganisation which became closely identified with him long after the collapse of the Labour government in August 1931 had consigned the committee's report to the growing heap of unused reformist strategies. Morrison's subsequent experience of the workings of the London Joint Electricity Authority simply confirmed his belief that the conflicts of interest inherent in divided ownership could only be resolved by the extension of more effective and publicly owned boards, appointed by the Minister, based on the CEB model which Morrison increasingly admired. Morrison's thinking which was steadily consolidating itself into a firm strategy from the late 1920s, was given vent during the House of Commons debate on the McGowan Report on 25 November 1936. Recapitulating on former proposals, Morrison's suggestion was for the abolition of the 600 or so electricity supply undertakings, the CEB and the Electricity Commissioners, and the transfer of the generating and distributing undertakings to a national corporation, under which would be arranged regional boards subject to the policy of the national board (PRO 1937, para. 13). Morrison was advocating not only a much sharper turn of pace, but also a much more prominent and immediate assumption of public ownership. He offered an alternative way of reorganising electricity distribution by eliminating all existing undertakings and substituting regional boards under public control as an alternative to McGowan's solution of retaining the larger and more efficient undertakings and allowing them to absorb the smaller and less efficient (PRO 1936, p. 8). The McGowan Committee's response was to reject such ideas for an 'immediate and complete reorganisation on a regional basis under public control by the setting up of regional boards which would buy out all existing undertakings' (PRO 1936d, para. 2).

The rejection of Morrison's proposals by both the McGowan Committee and the Cabinet Committee on Electricity Distribution involved the mixing of objections to both the proposed pace of change and the proposed organisational structure of any reformed electricity industry. The main arguments deployed against Morrison were that his reforms would cause an 'unnecessary dislocation of many well-managed undertakings which have proved to be economic distribution units' (PRO 1937, para. 13). Concern was also expressed that there would be uncertainty about the amount of compensation to be paid, since there was no existing statutory or accepted basis for the purchase of power companies with rights in perpetuity. Strong opposition from these and other companies, as well as from local authorities, was also expected (PRO 1937, para. 13). Moreover, while Morrison spoke of the need for 'technical people' and of the proposed national corporation as 'a business concern' (PRO 1937, para. 13), the McGowan Committee as reported by Sir John Snell emphasised more that the industry itself was generally in a 'flourishing and efficient' condition, even if the rate of progress was uneven, and that, in general, they did not see grounds for the wholesale replacement of all existing undertakings at a time 'when industry generally is improving' (PRO 1936b, p. 8). The statistics of expansion were easy to cite. Sales of electricity to consumers for all purposes had risen from 3,512 million units in 1920–1 to 11,467 million units in 1933–4; the charges for electricity as measured by the average revenue received per unit of electricity sold to all classes of consumers, including public lighting and traction (but excluding bulk supplies), had fallen from 2.48d. per unit in 1921–2 to 1.26d. in 1933–4; and the number of consumers connected had increased from 2.6 million in 1927–8 to 6,109,000 by the end of 1933–4 (PRO 1936a, para. 94). However these statistics were prefaced with the remark that this had been achieved by the electricity supply industry 'notwithstanding its complicated and, in many cases, uneconomic structure' (PRO 1936a, para. 93).

Thus, by 1937, almost all of the technical and economic arguments for the reorganisation of electricity distribution had been rehearsed, there was common agreement that reorganisation would require compulsion, and an expectation that at some point in the future the industry would be in public ownership. Differences in opinion clearly existed over the form and structure of public ownership, but the main area of conflict was on how quickly and how aggressively any compulsory reorganisation should be pursued and implemented. Thus much of the interest of the decade preceding nationalisation lies not in the technical reasons advanced for nationalisation, but in how the pace and assumptions of the argument changed such that, within eleven years of the publication of the McGowan Report's somewhat hesitant suggestions, legislation for the nationalisation of the electricity industry was making its way through Parliament.

3   Vested interests and the extension of supply

What then explains this shift in opinion? Part of the immediate explanation lies in the fate of the McGowan Report itself. Supported by government in parliamentary debates (PRO 1937, paras. 3 and 13), there was a widespread and natural expectation that the Report's main recommendations would enjoy rapid legislative enactment. That the Report's recommendatons should be enacted was urged by the Cabinet Committee on Electricity Distribution, while the need for speed was emphasized by many, including the McGowan Committee. With much technical opinion in the industry supporting the Report's main proposals, McGowan urged that the moment should be seized, any delays only adding to the cost of any eventual process of standardisation and, with purchase rights maturing, affording opportunities for further 'actual disintegration' of the industry's structure (PRO 1937, para. 137).

Yet, in place of any anticipated zymotic fermentation of ideas and capturing of the moment, came procrastination, prevarication and delay. A decade of underachievement culminated in glorious parliamentary torpor. The doomed legislative process started well enough. The recommendations of the McGowan Committee and the Cabinet Committee were made known to the representative Associations of the electricity industry in April 1937. Written representations and deputations from the Associations were received until February 1938, Parliamentary Counsel produced a preliminary draft Bill in January 1938, and discussions on the more important clauses proceeded until October 1938. However, other bills then came to have priority and, in fact, no final bill was ever produced by the responsible Parliamentary Counsel. In March 1938, the Prime Minister announced that, given a heavy legislative programme, he saw no prospect of proceeding with the Bill, an announcement that was repeated in November 1938. A mix of procrastination and neglect followed until 12 February 1941, when the Minister of Transport, in reply to a Question, stated that it would not be practicable to undertake the large reorganisation of the industry during the war (PRO 1942b, Appendix II).

The failure to enact the McGowan Report's recommendations was further evidence of the failure of a political economy to effect what many within it recognised as being necessary. This was but the latest in a line of failed legislative attempts to implement change. The failure of previous legislative reform had formed the background to the establishment of the McGowan Committee itself. In October 1933, a draft Bill was ready which provided for eighty large undertakings to absorb the 420 (8 per cent of the total capital of the industry) smallest undertakings. Yet, this attempt to tackle the issue of legislative compulsion was subject to dilution within the civil service and ultimately fell foul of a row between John Kennedy, a full-time Commissioner, and the new Minister of Transport, Hore-Belisha. This instance of diluting and aborting potential legislation not only itself had a notable precedent (see Electricity (Supply) Act 1919), but it also had counterparts in other industries. The attempt to introduce compulsory reorganisation in the coalmining industry, through the use of the Coal Mines Reorganisation Commission, had been stopped by the activities of powerful parliamentary interests within Parliament.

Securing compulsion in a parliamentary democracy encountered two main problems. Firstly, given the time which it took for industries to develop and establish the wealth and influence that is reflected and represented in their power within institutions like Parliament, there was always a lag between the current economic importance of an industry and its political clout. In general, declining industries with a previous history of economic strength could fight a sustained, rearguard action against attempts to expose them to further competition by means of their lagged power within institutions. This was as true of coalminers within the TUC as it was of coal owners within Parliament. Vice versa, just as this lagged influence slowed down any process of 'exit', it also obstructed 'entry' by new industries and groups who had not yet developed and nursed the necessary strength within institutions. The lag noted by Keynes, in the quotation heading this chapter, concerning the pervading of ideas is related in part to this lag.

The second problem dogging attempts to achieve compulsory reorganisation concerned democracy itself. So long as property rights formed the rockbed of legal and parliamentary assumptions and principles, it would always be difficult legislatively to facilitate the taking of property by one interest group from another. At the very least, an appeal procedure would have to be admitted, not least because the lobby power of threatened vested interests would see this as a powerful instrument of obstruction and delay. In electricity reform, it was clear that any reorganisation proposals were likely to encounter opposition from the small undertakings. In part, their arguments had some merit in that some undertakings did have lower costs and lower prices than their larger and more conservative neighbours (Political and Economic Planning 1936, p. 128). Hearing appeals from resistant undertakings would inevitably take time and slow down moves towards reorganisation. Sir John Snell's estimate was that if Special Order procedure were applied in all cases, it might take some seven or eight years to complete the reorganisation.

By the late 1930s, attempts to achieve reorganisation within electricity distribution had moved from frustrated suasion, through obstructed compulsion and on to a consideration of national ownership. In part, this reflected a diminishing faith in the ability to achieve reorganisation by means of negotiation with vested interests. As has been seen, Keynes had noted this contemporary concern with the power of vested interests in the final lines of *The General Theory*. Yet, as Keynes had also observed earlier in 1930, accompanying any growing preoccupation with vested interests was also a changing attitude towards businessmen as a species:

In short, the average businessman is no longer envisaged as the feverishly active and alert figure of the classical economists, who never missed a chance of making a penny if it was humanly possible, and was always in a state of stimulus up to the limit of his capacity. The new view of him seems to be that he is a fellow who is easy-going and content with a given income and does not bestir himself unduly to increase it to what would be for him the maximum attainable. (Keynes, 1930 pp. 5–6)

However, an explanation of a move towards nationalisation bedded simply in arguments concerning dissatisfaction would be incomplete. The existence of dissatisfaction with a system will not necessarily provide sufficient reason or volition for change. The objection made will be to 'change for its own sake'. What was important was that positive benefits could be envisaged as emanating from a new system; that, in short, something better could be put in place of the existing structure. It was in this context that the belief in exploiting economies of scale was important, even if partly illusory. Veracity has little to do with strength of belief. Yet faith in potential economies of scale had, as has been seen, not been in itself sufficient to effect the sought after reorganisation. What was required to overcome the medley of resistance from vested interests and misgivings concerning property transfers on the part of democratic and legal concerns, was a wider 'public interest' argument which could clearly demonstrate the 'greater good' which the forcible transfer of property rights would make possible. References to the 'public interest' are inevitably loose and vague allusions which embrace a clutter of aspirations. As such, they are elusive and distasteful to academics. The argument of the rest of this chapter, however, is that it was this very width and looseness of invocations of the 'public interest', with all of its internal inconsistencies, which helps in large part to explain why a move was made fairly quickly to legislating for nationalisation within a parliamentary democracy.

The extension of supply to rural areas and sections of urban conurbations which the market was less willing to supply, became an increasingly powerful theme in discussions of the industry during the 1930s and the Second World War. In part, these discussions had some technical basis, the argument being that an extension of supply, which would involve a mixing of rural and urban loads, might result in improved load factors. The McGowan Committee advocated the judicious amalgamation of urban and rural areas so as to vary the type of supply and so increase the 'load factor' (PRO 1936b). The figures of load factor and load per head of population for the year 1933–4 showed that no less than 271 out of 635 undertakings had a load factor of less than 25 per cent, and that 299 out of 603 undertakings, including many which had a comparatively long franchise, were selling less than 100 units per head of population (PRO 1936a, para. 360). By increasing the size of undertakings, the McGowan Committee hoped to improve the diversity of load, thereby improving load factor (PRO 1936a, paras. 104–5). Such amalgamations as McGowan proposed had already been effected successfully in a number of cases where an urban undertaking (as at Aylesbury, Chester, Colchester, Norwich) had assumed responsibility for the development of adjacent rural areas (PRO 1936c). Yet, there was also a good deal of confusion in the debate about the savings likely to emerge from improved load factors. Real gains were only likely to come where the relationship between the CEB and the undertakings was renegotiated (Hannah 1979, p. 246).

Extension of supply also drew support from engineers in the industry (Hannah 1979, pp. 224, 243), as well as being a *leitmotif* for McGowan's vision for the future role of the Commissioners. While the McGowan Committee was not prepared to give the Electricity Commissioners compulsory powers to require further amalgamations or transfers if a scheme was not considered to be working satisfactorily, they were prepared to give the Electricity Commissioners powers to require undertakers to submit and to carry out approved schemes of extensions from time to time for any underdeveloped parts of their area where there was a reasonable prospect of an economic return (PRO 1936a). Electricity supply was to be extended both within urban areas, and, in particular, to rural areas. At the end of 1934, in urban areas alone, one-fifth of the total mileage of streets had not been laid with distributing mains (PRO 1936a, para. 359), and in rural areas there were constant calls for cheaper and more extensive supply of electricity.

Allied to the call for extension of supply, were growing suggestions that a greater uniformity of tariffs and prices should exist between undertakings and areas. One of the arguments for forming large undertakings enjoying improved load factors and economies of scale was to make any benefits from increased efficiency available to more people. As the McGowan Report noted:

we feel bound to endorse the view expressed by the Electric Power Supply Committee in 1918 that the object to be kept in view is not merely to have exceptionally low costs in a few small and specially favoured areas, but rather to have the same or lower costs available over wider areas. (PRO 1936a, para. 122)

McGowan's proposed scheme of consolidation in larger areas aimed to secure the adoption of uniform methods of charging throughout the consolidated area and, as far as possible, actual uniformity of charges (PRO 1936a, para. 197). This objective drew support from government and also from the industry which recommended price pooling as one means of achieving this. Pooling so as to secure uniform prices drew support from representatives of the Power Companies Association (PRO 1937, Appendix C).

4   The impatience of war

This cocktail of dissatisfaction, optimistic hopes of improved technical efficiency, and rising expectations all combined during the war to transfuse the series of discussions on the post-war organisation of the electricity industry. Having initially used the disturbance of war to suspend discussion of the industry's future, by 1942 the subject was back on the agenda and being discussed in a markedly changed manner. Notable was the report by Sir William Jowitt, the Paymaster General, who was asked to take charge of reconstruction questions in March 1942 and who, by August of the same year, had completed his report on the electricity industry (PRO 1942b). Reflecting and encapsulating a growing sentiment, not least in a memorandum by the Electricity Commissioners on the comprehensive reorganisation of the electricity supply industry (PRO 1942a), Jowitt's report marked a shift away from the 'evolutionary' scheme of the McGowan Committee (PRO 1942c). Jowitt's report reminded its readers of the McGowan Report's stress on the need for reorganisation and, besides up-dating the McGowan Report's statistics on the size and structure of the industry, regarded the case for reorganisation as being so self apparent as to require no further 'commission or fact-finding enquiry to take place'. Equally, as Jowitt emphasised, 'it is quite obvious that it is useless to rely on any voluntary system of reorganisation' (PRO 1942b, para. 9). Jowitt urged that the alternative option rejected by the McGowan Committee now be taken up:

I have come to the conclusion that in the six years that have passed since the McGowan Report was produced it has become obsolete, and I recommend the solution stated in paragraph 88(i) of that Report, namely a complete reorganisation on a regional basis under public control by the setting up of regional boards which would buy out all existing undertakings. It is very possible, indeed, that if the McGowan Commission were sitting after three years of war they would have come to the same conclusion. (PRO 1942b, para. 14)

Jowitt's view that it was now useless to rely on any voluntary system of reorganisation was confirmed by the War Cabinet Sub-Committee on the Future of the Electricity Industry which considered his report. A last moment of speculation on the part of Ralph Assheton (Financial Secretary, Treasury) on whether voluntary reorganisation might occur, if it was made clear that in the event of failure compulsion would be applied, was crushed by Sir Cyril Hurcomb (Electricity Commission) and H. Hobson (CEB). Hurcomb and Hobson were of the view that the history of the industry during the previous twenty years showed that 'any such hope was bound to be frustrated; the divergent interests within the Industry were irreconcilable' (PRO 1943a). Vested interests and particular exceptions to the general technical slogan of 'small bad, big good' combined to compound latent tendencies to deadlock. By 1943, the McGowan strategy of avoiding political difficulties by gradually allowing large undertakings to absorb neighbouring small undertakings in an 'evolutionary process' (PRO 1943b, para. 14), had simply seized up. As the Sub-Committee noted:

In the event . . . the difficulties of deciding which undertaking should absorb which proved to be formidable; this was due partly to the cleavage of interests between the Local Authority and the Company groups of undertakings, and partly to the difficulty of ruling that undertakings which were in themselves efficient should be absorbed by other undertakings simply because they were small. (PRO 1943b, para. 14)

The Sub-Committee also supported Jowitt in his dissension from McGowan's concern with the 'unnecessary dislocation' likely to be caused by large-scale changes. As Jowitt had remarked: 'I am by no means certain that a really drastic reform such as I have indicated may not be easier to get through than a partial and piecemeal reform such as was indicated in those proposals' (PRO 1942b, para. 23).

In the 1943 meetings of the War Cabinet Sub Committee on the Future of the Electricity Industry, not only was there further and final disregard of any voluntary system of reorganisation, but the fears of 'unnecessary dislocation' of the supply industry, caused by a scheme of complete reorganisation on a regional basis, were being talked down. Echoing Jowitt, Hobson of the Central Electricity Board argued that, while any reorganisation was bound to cause some disruption, in his view the smaller the number of distribution units, and the simpler (though more drastic) and more definite the plan of reorganisation, the smaller would any dislocation be. If anything, the McGowan Committee's espousal of the 'ultimate public ownership' was now regarded as likely to perpetuate dislocation (PRO 1943a). In short:

we are forced to the conclusion that the McGowan Committee's scheme no longer meets the case. While this scheme aims at an evolutionary solution, it entails, nevertheless, a large number of transfers of small (mainly municipal) undertakings to their larger neighbours (both municipal and Company) and is likely to be highly controversial. At the same time, even after regrouping was complete, it woud leave such a large number of separate undertakings that it would be unlikely to achieve the objects of reorganisation on a scale commensurate with the disturbance which it would cause. (PRO 1943b, para. 3)

As striking as the conclusions of Jowitt and the Sub-Committee, were the manner, pace and vocabulary of their delivery. Allusions to the perceived pervasive obstacles represented by vested interests were widespread and the impossibility of persuading vested interests to amalgamate into substantial units now appeared to be a matter of common wisdom. Increasingly, discussions which took cognisance of vested interests were likely to end in impasse. In 1943, in preparing their Report on the Future of the Electricity Industry, the Sub-Committee were charged with confidentiality and were precluded from consultation with representatives of the industry (PRO 1943b, para. 2). The overwhelming sense of the correspondence, minutes and reports during 1942–3 was that the time for major changes had arrived. Typical was the reflection of Jowitt (PRO 1942b, para. 24):

my own reading of the political situation makes me think that we should not hesitate to embark on bold measures of reconstruction which will appeal to the imagination of the public. There surely comes a time in the history of a nation when he who tinkers is lost. (PRO 1942b, para. 24)

In part, this sense of there being no alternative simply arose from a frustrated derision for the alternative strategies which had been attempted and recommended. Yet, the shift in pace and tone was also based on the maturing of inter-war ideas into firm convictions. One such conviction was that electricity was not a luxury for higher-income and urban groups, but a basic necessity: 'The Public have increasingly come to regard electricity as a necessity and not a mere luxury: and it should be regarded from the same point of view as sewerage or water' (PRO 1942b, para. 20).

The move to this view also enabled Morrison's long-held views on price uniformity to gain further ground. As before, this involved a mixing of arguments concerning industrial structure and more socio-political notions of equity. Regarding structure, whereas the McGowan Committee (PRO 1936c, para. 12) had not prepared a detailed plan of the appropriate grouping of undertakings, and the scheme prepared by the Minister of Transport in 1937 had contemplated the possibility of 123 separate groups, the Sub-Committee on the Future of the Electricity Industry were 'satisfied that the number of distribution undertakings should be reduced to a much lower figure than this' (PRO 1943b, para. 15). By 1943, the Sub-Committee on the Future of the Electricity Industry was proposing that the 580 distribution undertakings should be replaced by fourteen Regional Distribution Boards (PRO 1943c, para. 17). This proposed structure was now much closer to that advocated by Morrison in 1936 (PRO 1937, para. 13). Not only did this shift in thinking on the appropriate size of regional units reflect a different attitude towards 'compulsion', 'dislocation' and the inadequacies of 'evolution', but it also reflected a greater willingness to move towards accepting some of the wider social aims which Morrison had been pursuing in his advocacy of fewer and larger units. By 1943, the advantage afforded by large regional units in facilitating a 'close approach to uniformity of price' was being emphasised (PRO 1943c, para. 33).

Size of undertaking, extension of supply and uniformity of pricing were now beginning to come together in a manner advocated by Morrison as long ago as 1932:

As things are, it is impossible to secure throughout the country as a whole any reasonable uniformity of charges, or the necessary development of difficult areas, or a real pushing sales policy, or a sufficient service organisation. (Morrison 1932)

To jump ahead, Morrison, as Lord President in the Attlee government, was to take his arguments further and to run into arguments with Shinwell (Minister of Fuel and Power) over the appropriate balance between central and regional organisation, and also with economists concerning the very issue of pricing. The meetings of the Committee for Socialised Industries were notable for revealing how far Morrison wanted to go, how far opinion seemed to have come, and for setting up the basis for many arguments to come. Typical is the following long exposition from Morrison, when arguing in favour of giving the control of distribution to a single national authority:

The fundamental purpose of nationalisation was . . . to secure greater efficiency in the industry . . . to reduce costs and provide surplus funds which could be used to extend the benefits of cheap electricity to rural areas where . . . electricity was either not available or unreasonably expensive . . . Ultimately, he would like to see a standard charge for electricity throughout the whole country, the tariff varying according to the purposes for which the electricity was being used, and the industry being at liberty to make special arrangements with individual interests . . . He realised that this system of postalisation had its opponents among some of the economists, but he did not find the arguments which they advanced convincing. The argument that each consumer should pay the precise cost incurred in bringing electricity to his premises would, if followed to its logical conclusion, prevent even a small municipality from adopting a system of standard charges within its own boundaries. (PRO 1946)

5   Towards nationalisation

The nationalisation of the electricity industry in 1948 involved the transfer of the generating side of the industry, as well as that of distribution. The technical, efficiency motives for this are less easy to discern, since, as has been seen, the operation of the CEB had secured much of the sought productivity improvements. Again, as with distribution, there were some untidy and increasingly complicated arrangements within the generating side of the industry which required sorting out. As with distribution, any reorganisation of generating pricing structures was likely to have to accommodate the pressures of a greater move towards equalisation of prices. Again, Jowitt was clear on this:

It is clear that one of the objects at which we should aim is that of bringing about a much greater unification of the wholesale price of electricity, that is the price at which the Central Electricity Board sells to its customers. It may be impossible, and perhaps undesirable to obtain complete equality, for adjustments may have to be made between the north and south, but the Central Electricity Board should acquire as owners all such stations as are required for generation and should no longer have to rely on the giving of directions to various owners as to the manner in which their stations should be worked. (PRO 1942b)

Given the need to reorganise relations between the CEB and many owners, the push for greater uniformity of prices, and the interface of generation with the public corporation of the CEB, to move the entire generation side of the industry into public ownership did not appear so large a step. Earlier, the issue of ownership had been cleverly side-stepped by the Weir Committee in recommending the establishment of the CEB. As was argued with tact and ingenuity:

we propose not a change in ownership, but the partial subordination of vested interests in generation to that of a new authority for the benefit of all, and this only under proper safeguards, and in a manner which will preserve the value of the incentive of private enterprise. (Hannah 1977, p. 210)

By 1942–3, such elision had disappeared to be replaced by the more direct recommendations of Jowitt.

The Electricity Supply Act, 1926, which established the Central Electricity Board has undoubtedly proved most beneficial. At the same time, that Act cannot be regarded as constituting a complete and final solution of the problems of generation. The separation of responsibility between the Central Electricity Board on the one hand and the authorities operating the generating stations on the other hand was a compromise solution, and the time has now come to complete central responsibility. (PRO 1942b)

While recommending either that the functions of the CEB be extended or that a new national authority be constituted, Jowitt 'did not anticipate that this reform would excite any considerable political controversy' (PRO 1942b, paras. 6–7). Jowitt's views were supported by the Sub-Committee on the Future of the Electricity Industry who argued that there was 'a strong case for centralising in the hands of a single generating authority the ownership, and not merely the control, of the stations generating for public supply' (PRO 1943c, para. 3).

The main theme of this chapter has been that while the pursuit of economies of scale, improved load factors and other sources of efficiency improvements were important in providing much of the technical case for the restructuring of the electricity industry, they do not by themselves provide a full explanation of why the electricity industry was nationalised in 1948. In addition, a wide mix of dissatisfaction, frustration and shifting attitudes towards availability and price of output all combined to make a case for the achievement of reorganisation by means of public ownership. That in explaining the shift to public ownership, the jumble of ideas that formed the 'public interest' provided an important basis for legitimating this forcible transfer of property. The medley of arguments in favour of public ownership appear to have merged and gathered pace and bite in the decade preceding nationalisation, and in particular during the war years from 1942. The impact of the war in terms of shifting expectations and moving personnel has not been discussed explicitly in this chapter, but may well be worthy of closer examination. When, following the election of the Attlee Government in 1945, the nationalisation of the electricity industry was effected, there was something of an air of inevitability about it. Whether the election of a Conservative government in 1945 would have made much difference is difficult to say, but it is not easy to see what alternative options, especially in distribution, were available. It did appear by 1945 that, as Keynes had suggested, vested interests were in the end unable to stop the implementation of an idea whose time had come.

REFERENCES

Hannah, L. (1977), 'A pioneer of public enterprise: the Central Electricity Board and the National Grid, 1927–1940' in B. Supple, *Essays in British Business History*, Oxford: Clarendon Press.

(1979), *Electricity Before Nationalisation*, London: Macmillan.

Keynes, J.M. (1930) 'The question of high wages', *The Political Quarterly*, January–March, in D. Moggridge (ed.) (1981), *The Collected Writings of John Maynard Keynes*, vol. XX, *Activities 1929–31*, Cambridge.

(1974), *The General Theory of Employment, Interest and Money*, pb edn, London: Macmillan.

Morrison, H.M. (1932), 'Reorganisation of Electricity', Labour Party Archives, Policy No. 56, June.

Political and Economic Planning (1936), *Report on the Supply of Electricity in Great Britain*, London.

PRO (1936a), CAB 27/617, Report of the Committee on Electricity Distribution, May.

(1936b), CAB 27/617, E.D.(36)1st meeting, Cabinet: Committee on Electricity Distribution, Minutes, 8 July.

(1936c), CAB 27/617, E.D.(362), Cabinet: Committee on Electricity Distribution, Memorandum by the Minister of Transport, L. Hore-Belisha, 15 July.

(1936d), CAB 27/617, C.P. 288(36) Cabinet: Committee on Electricity Distribution, Interim Report, 27 October.

(1937), CAB 27/617, CP(64)37, Cabinet: Committee on Electricity Distribution, Second Report, 17 February.

(1942a), CAB 87/105, Memorandum, 'Electricity Commission: Post-War Reorganisation of Electricity Supply', August.

(1942b), CAB 87/4, R.P.(42)37, War Cabinet: Committee on Reconstruction Problems; Report on the Electricity Industry by the Paymaster General', 7 August.

(1942c), CAB 87/105, Letter to Paymaster General from the Chairman of the Electricity Commission, 4 September.

(1943a), CAB 87/4, R.P.(E.S.)(43)5th Meeting, War Cabinet, Sub-Committee on the Future of the Electricity Industry, Minutes of a meeting, 16 June.

(1943b), CAB 87/4, R.P.(E.S.)(43)36, Final, War Cabinet, Reconstruction Committee, Report of the Sub-Committee on the Future of the Electricity Industry, 20 December.

(1943c), CAB 87/4, R.P.(E.S.)(43)36/46, (Final), War Cabinet, Reconstruction Committee, Report of the Sub-Committee on the Future of the Electricity Industry, 30 December.

(1946), CAB 21/2208, Lord President's Office, Extract from Minutes of (S.I.M.)(46)9th meeting, 22 May.

13 Partners and enemies: the government's decision to nationalise steel 1944–8

Ruggero Ranieri

My aim is to discuss some of the issues arising out of the attempt by the first post-war Labour government to nationalise the steel industry. An important part in the process was played by the government's relationship with the industry's powerful trade association, the BISF. In fact, it will be argued that the government's initial hope was that nationalisation could be somehow carried out by consent with the industry. In the spring and summer of 1947 this led to protracted talks between Ministers and the leadership of the BISF on a possible compromise short of nationalisation.

Broadly the records confirm that nationalisation of steel was highly controversial inside the Attlee government and that the leadership would have probably dropped it, had they not been under pressure from members of the left both inside the Cabinet, among Labour backbenchers and in the trade unions. The difficulties in reaching a compromise, however, were not only of a political nature. Civil servants too found themselves at a loss when asked to consider alternatives such as extensive government shareholding, or a strong board capable of projecting a technocratic dimension. When the decision to proceed to full nationalisation was taken, the practical solutions to be adopted were again a subject of much discussion, given the complexity of the industry's structure.

1 Articulating the strategies: planners, corporatists, liberals

The discussion on the future of the steel industry gathered pace in the course of 1944, when the government's attention was being increasingly turned away from the day-to-day management of the war economy towards planning ahead for the post-war world (Hargreaves and Gowing 1952, chapter 23). The steel industry had been tightly fitted into the machinery of the war economy, and there was some recognition that its performance had been at least creditable. Criticism of the industry, however, persisted, some accusations – such as that of charging high prices and reaping exaggerated profits – harking back to the thirties.[1]

Three main bodies of opinion on the industry can be detected at this time. One was what one might call the modernising, rationalising or planning view. Perhaps its most prominent spokesman was the President of the Board of Trade, Hugh Dalton, and he had the support of many both in the trade union movement and amongst academic and technical wartime recruits to the Civil Service. The modernisers shared a pessimistic outlook of the industry's competitiveness and they had in mind a vast programme of restructuring to be achieved through a combination of state investment and direct controls (Morgan 1984, p. 24, Pimlott 1985, pp. 440f., Vaizey 1974, pp. 108–10).

A second view was forcefully expressed by the Minister of Supply, Andrew Duncan, and, not surprisingly given the role which he had played inside the industry since 1934, it reflected the point of view of the Federation. According to this body of opinion the best course after the war was to have, just as in the thirties, a cartel acting under the loose supervision of a governmental body modelled on the IDAC (Tolliday 1987, chapter 13).

Finally there was a liberal view, according to which the industry was overprotected and needed more competition on the free market. It was held by most members of the Economic Section, who frequently couched their arguments in the language of macroeconomic management (Cairncross and Watts 1989, chapter 5). The implications of their views for the steel industry, however, were unmistakably of a free trade, *laissez-faire* nature.

Each of these three points of view could overlap at certain points with the others, but they were fundamentally distinct, at least in the initial stages. At one point, however, this distinction became blurred, for, building on the intimate government–industry cooperation achieved during the war, the point of view of the planners fell into line with that of the corporatists, who in turn seemed prepared to recognise the need for investment and rationalisation. The remaining differences between the two approaches on prices, cartels and the degree of protection were either not brought out into the open, or fudged (Burn 1961, p. 109). The liberals, on the other hand, because of their reluctance to measure up to the real problems of the industry, were increasingly marginalised and were not able to make any significant contribution.

Finally there was nationalisation. This was an issue confined to the internal debate of the Labour Party, and it did not emerge in the open until Labour's unexpected election victory in July 1945 (Burn 1961, pp. 112–25, Ross 1965, pp. 36–40, Jay 1989, p. 124, Dalton 1957, pp. 423–3, pp. 443–6). Clearly a number of the modernisers believed that nationalisation would help them achieve their ends, but others were less sure. It has been pointed out that the decision taken by Labour in 1945 to include steel among the industries to be nationalised was a reaction of the 'fundamentalists' against the more pragmatic attitudes over the economy which were emerging in at least part of the leadership (Brooke 1989). This might explain why the matter was invested of a kind of symbolism, which was effectively to restrict the government's room for manoeuvre.

Mainstream Labour politicians and economists were part of a wider body of opinion that had come to believe in the virtues of modernisation, increased government controls and investment (Morgan 1984, pp. 99, 130). Increasingly moreover, in the steel industry as well as elsewhere, modernisation was seen as something that could be achieved by strengthening cooperation with the industry. After July 1945, therefore, Ministers followed the most logical course: they tried to graft their party's agenda for public ownership upon the wider existing consensus over planning and cooperation. Nationalisation was hence presented as a reasonable step intended to develop what had already been agreed upon.

Although it is not possible to follow in any detail the debate that was carried out over the steel industry in 1944–5, it is important to recall that the initiative for an independent enquiry into the industry had come from the modernisers. In the course of 1944 the Board of Trade had embarked upon a detailed review of the prospects of manufacturing and, as far as the steel industry was concerned, it had reached the conclusion that capital equipment was out of date, prices were too high, and too much reliance had been placed upon cartels and protection (PRO 1944a). If prospects were to be improved, much investment and restructuring needed to be carried out, and in a hurry. Such an approach, however, was not congenial to Duncan. He did not believe that the industry was in need of a radical reappraisal and appeared more than happy with the way it had conducted itself since the mid thirties. Perhaps some adjustments might prove necessary but on the whole the arrangements that were in force deserved to be maintained (PRO 1944b).

Duncan's opinions were influential enough to prevent the launching of an independent enquiry and it was decided instead that there should be an internal examination of the industry conducted jointly by the Ministry of Supply and the Board of Trade. This resulted in a long report (PRO 1945a) drafted under the supervision of Oliver Franks, then Permanent Secretary of the Ministry of Supply and of Norman Chester, a member of the Economic Section who had been very close to Beveridge's entourage.

A few weeks after the report's conclusion Chester told his colleagues at the Economic Section that 'The policy chapters . . . had tried to steer a reasonable course between nationalization and unrestricted private enterprise'. There was no realistic possibility, he observed somewhat defensively, of disenfranchising the strong trade association, especially since the impression was

that the leaders of the iron and steel industry were much keener on developing the efficiency of their industry than were the leaders of say the coal and cotton industry. The present president of the Iron and Steel Federation who . . . was the head of Stewart's and Lloyds, Macdiarmid, one of the most efficient steel firms in the world, had succeeded in getting the leading firms a long way towards formulating individual plans for modernisation.

Hopefully therefore a moderate amount of government assistance could go a long way towards modernisation. 'If this important basic industry could be tackled vigorously then in five or six year's time the whole of British industrial prospects would be correspondingly improved' (PRO 1945b, p. 1), Chester concluded.

The keynote here, clearly, was a belief in a joint effort, rather than in the government providing the industry with a blueprint for modernisation. What had happened to so effectively blend the approaches of the planners and the corporatists? Probably the decisive factor had indeed been as Chester pointed out, the effort made by the Federation to move some way in meeting the concerns of some of its critics. In its preliminary report to the Ministry of Supply issued in December 1944 one detects a skilful mixture of continuity and novelty: on one side, the traditional corporatist stress on self government, the need for protection, subsidies and cartelisation, on the other, a strong emphasis on new investment and on the need for government supervision (BISF 1944b).

Indications are that at this stage the larger, more modern, firms had taken the upper hand in formulating the Federation's policy and were prepared to recognise that future investment was to be something more than a patching-up operation. Radical programmes were to be given the go ahead, with the Federation taking the lead, and if necessary putting forward its own plans. The wartime experience, moreover, had given words like planning and government supervision a less daunting ring and even the most reluctant inside the industry were convinced by the sheer weight of evidence, that some form of control was there to stay and that one might just as well try to make the best of it (Burn 1961, p. 69, Vaizey 1974, pp. 104–6).

Much of the Franks–Chester report was also devoted to modernisation. Its premise was that the industry had become uncompetitive so that reequipment was to take absolute priority. A number of investment plans were spelled out: in particular there was to be replacement and expansion of blast furnace capacity and concentration on those finished products, such as sheet and tinplate, which were bound to play a major role in the export trade. Underlying all this there was to be a switch to mass-producing methods and better exploitation of economies of scale.

About protection, cartels, price fixing and the nature of government powers, the report, however, took a much more cautious line. First of all it acknowledged that the industry pending its reorganisation should be granted a five-year period of protection and this by itself went a long way in meeting the Federation's demands. Equally important was that, by not producing anything new on the issue of prices and subsidies it effectively endorsed the continuation of the current system of centrally fixed, flat prices across the industry, bolstered by an array of levies designed to equalise costs among different firms (PRO 1945a, chapter 7). This was the hub of the corporatist pattern of management and its preservation was at the heart of the Federation's strategy. Nor were the vague noises made about the need for a governmental body with more teeth than the pre-war IDAC enough to counter this fundamental concession.

When the Economic Section examined the report they were immediately suspicious of it. The bulk of opinion was quite unanimous, with Robbins, Tress, Meade, Jewkes, Dennison, all extremely critical. Muddled corporatist solutions were rejected as was microeconomic intervention.

It was unwise, it was remarked, to commit resources to any particular programme of expansion, for it might not be economically sound or justified. Moreover looking at one industry at a time bred pessimism and the 'all or nothing' approach adopted by the modernisers, meaning that if the industry didn't rapidly reequip it was doomed, was also considered a fallacy. There would always be the efficient firm which could meet competition by pricing at marginal cost. Needless to say price fixing was considered a mistake. Promises of protection to the industry were equally misguided, Robbins sentenced, and it was dangerous to promise 'certain industries a special claim on resources *irrespective of their size*, rather than relying on the marginal principle to determine what size was desirable'. Nor was it thought proper to launch a post-war investment programme, since capital costs would be high, inflation mounting and therefore there would be a need to keep government expenditure down. The industry, in fact, should be told to concentrate on a few export-earning schemes. Possibly the most caustic prescription was proffered by Mr Tress:

Costs – he said – and the price of the product compared with that produced overseas are important, not the technical efficiency of the industry . . . in general we want to discourage investment during the transition (PRO 1945b, p. 4)

Clearly comments such as these could exercise very little influence upon the future of steel. Above all they revealed limited understanding of features such as economies of scale, gains from vertical integration or oligopolistic constraints on prices. It seems that this was a missed opportunity, for there was much that could have been constructively said from a liberal point of view against the kind of autarchic, rigid regulation of the steel market that the Federation was advocating and the Franks–Chester report only mildly resisting. An open market allowing for imports, a price policy designed to foster rather than stymie competition, a better testing of investment criteria might have provided the kind of guidelines needed for state-led modernisation of a more liberal kind.[2]

Whatever chances there were in 1945, or indeed in the next few years, for such an exercise, they were missed. The discussion on steel was wound up by the Reconstruction Committee of the War Cabinet on 30 April 1945 (PRO 1945c). The Franks–Chester report's main recommendation that the industry should be requested to draw up a detailed plan for modernisation within the next six months was fully endorsed by the Cabinet. Differences emerged over nationalisation and, as a result of the Economic Section's remarks, some noises were made by the Chancellor of the Exchequer, Sir John Anderson, against granting the industry unqualified protection. On the whole, however, the alliance between the modernisers and the corporatists dominated the proceedings. Dalton spoke in favour of the report and said that he felt that the industry was entitled to a considerable amount of government assistance in carrying out its Five Year Plan. Statutory controls on prices should stay and protection would be necessary, given that 'rigorous control of imports was in any event likely to be required', in order to defend the balance of payments position after the war. Duncan agreed that modernisation should be encouraged. He too favoured price controls and acknowledged the need for a measure of government supervision.

2   1946: Attempting nationalisation by consent

In the aftermath of the war controls over every aspect of steel production continued very much according to the wartime pattern. Imports of raw materials and semi-finished goods were centralised and a strict system of quotas imposed, while the need to provide for an increasing quantity of exports of engineering goods meant that a system of allocation, even if less stringent and detailed than the one enacted during the war, was maintained. Prices remained fixed with much pressure to keep them as low as possible in a period of latent inflation. As a result government subsidies directed to compensate for higher prices of foreign ore, scrap and semi-finished goods were kept in force. The extraordinary powers which wartime legislation had conferred to the government were allowed to continue by way of the Supplies and Services Act, and in fact additional powers over new building and issuing of export licenses were granted (Ranieri 1993, pp. 129–33).

Franks talked of how in the Ministry of Supply it was difficult to 'be sure where the Department ended and the Iron and Steel Federation began' (PRO 1946d, Franks 1947). The Iron and Steel Control remained in being through 1946, but its staff – which at the peak of the war effort had numbered up to 750 – were leaving it by the day to return to their home firms. As a consequence, considering that it had been the Control which had kept in touch with the producers, the government's operative capacity was severely weakened, whereas the Federation's hand was strengthened.

The main operative centres at Steel House were two: there was a large statistical section, headed by Robert Shone, which reviewed the costs of the firms thereby determining the details of the price structure, and there was the so-called planning section, headed by John Duncanson, which was responsible for allocations, quotas and imports and distribution of raw materials. In addition there was a section responsible for the development proposals (later passed on to the Iron and Steel Board) and a commercial division (BISC), which arranged the shipment and transfer of imports, the collection of levies, the payment of subsidies and certain export business. It would be wrong to view this machine as simply performing the functions of a large private cartel. It was in many fields – such as for imports, prices and subsidies – carrying out policies, for which official responsibility lay with the government (PRO 1947i).

The Five-Year Plan presented in December 1945 by the BISF was intended as the lasting fruit of the meeting of minds sealed by the Franks–Chester report. In many ways it was a remarkable achievement (BISF 1946). Here was an industry, it was noted, that had been criticised just a few years earlier as a 'decadent survivor from the spacious days of the nineteenth century', which was proposing to embark on a massive renewal programme, which would entail the replacement of 40 per cent of its existing capacity over the next few years (PRO 1946b).

The total cost of the programme was put at £168 million over seven and a half years, which meant an annual charge of about £22.5 million compared with £6.5 in the late thirties. Big new developments and rationalisation were contemplated in each of the main steel producing regions: there was to be a large new hot strip mill at Port Talbot, a new broad-flange beam mill and increased specialisation in the north-east, a complete reorganisation of rail production in Lancashire, and new large-scale development both in the midlands and in Scotland. The plan, on the other hand, rested firmly on the main assumptions of the corporatist tradition. It was, in fact, predicated on a thinly disguised bargain offering reequipment against continued protection and financial assistance from the state. It said that the steel firms would be able to secure about half of the funds they needed from their own resources and implied that most of the rest would have to be somehow raised by the public sector. Much of the share which the companies were prepared to raise, moreover, also appeared to depend on government allowances: namely it was to come out of special depreciation provisions and out of compensation for the arrears of repairs accumulated during the war (PRO 1946h).

The Ministry of Supply applauded the plan enthusiastically. In fact a small committee of officials and experts – some of them, it must be added, closer to the Federation than they were to the government itself – endeavoured to provide a kind of official guidebook to it, dwelling on its main attractions, underlying its difficulties, spelling out a number of first steps which needed immediate attention (PRO 1946a).

The politicians liked the plan just as much as their officials. Yet they had been elected on a clear mandate to nationalise the steel industry and there was no getting away from the fact that the sheer announcement of nationalisation was likely to damage relations with the Federation. John Wilmot, the Minister of Supply, clearly understood the complexities of the issue as early as in the autumn of 1945. Firstly he saw that nationalisation was technically very difficult to implement: the industry was a motley collection of firms (up to 2,500 if all the small jobbers and iron foundries were counted) a few of them large, most of them very small, engaged in the most disparate activities. It was very difficult, for example, to draw a line between the steel industry and engineering. Furthermore, in order to draw up the appropriate legislation, one needed an enormous amount of information which it would be very difficult for the government to assemble without the assistance of the industry (PRO 1945d).

There were other question marks. It was difficult to present a convincing case for nationalisation when one approved so wholeheartedly of how the industry was managed. It was also likely that, once nationalisation was announced, the Five Year Plan would encounter delays – and that became a near certainty once Attlee had announced in April 1946 that the legislation on steel would have to wait until the third session of Parliament (PRO 1946e). Finally day-to-day cooperation might be threatened at a time of frequent shortages of steel. Because, however, nationalisation could not be dropped, and because, as the following events were to prove, any half-way solution was politically fraught with risk, Ministers faced some very unpalatable choices. Of course everything would be put right if nationalisation were to be carried out without confrontation, in other words if the Federation could be coaxed into accepting it, or at least into tolerating it.

Morrison at this stage was expressing support for nationalisation. It was, he said at the Ministerial Committee for the Socialisation of Industries held on 14 March 1946, part of the Labour manifesto and, if one were to reject it, it should be shown to be against the national interest. His remarks, none the less, betrayed a certain awe of the Federation. The required overhaul of the industry – he said – could not be safely left by the government to what he called an 'unregulated' private monopoly, however great its influence, for this would mean that private owners would still be able to command the best technical advice. By implication the government, according to Morrison, knew very little about the industry and could do very little to influence it in the short term (PRO 1946c).

Dalton used a more strident tone. Speaking in a parliamentary debate held in May 1946, he started by praising the Federation's independent Chairman, Andrew Duncan, for the work he had done in organising the cartel. He called him a 'great Socialist Executive', who had welded the steel firms

together into a single, regulated, disciplined, monopolistic combination. He led this industry into a situation . . . in which nationalisation became inevitable. He took the industry a long step along the road to Socialism . . . We intend to finish the work which he began. If we left half way – as the Iron and Steel Federation now propose – we should only have achieved the Corporative State, the same people . . . operating in the morning as the Iron and Steel Federation outside the Ministry and in the afternoon as the Iron and Steel Control inside the Ministry. And both the workers in the industry and the users – the motor manufacturers and the rest – left outside on the mat. (PRO 1946i, Chester 1975, p. 158)

Undoubtedly the last part of Dalton's analysis was perceptive but one suspects that he was partly trying to convince himself, when he described the steel cartel as a stepping stone on the road to nationalisation. The clever, obstinate, ultimately bitter opposition that Duncan and his team were to put up over the following months would prove the contrary to him.

Bevin tried to work out a practical solution. He put forward the idea of a Board, appointed by the government, which would keep the relationship with the Federation alive, follow up on the Plan and also deal with the practical problems of nationalisation. He told his colleagues that he 'had talked to quite a number of people' and that one suggestion that had come up was to let the Board 'take over firms piecemeal' (PRO 1946g). There was, indeed, a general recognition that a new body would have to be appointed to supervise the industry, to replace the fading Steel Control – but what Bevin had in mind was not simply a technical replacement. He was thinking of a panel on which the top figures of the Federation would sit and which would function as a kind of general staff on the government's behalf. In return the government would offer a kind of nationalisation *à la carte*, whereby the Federation itself would be allowed to define the boundaries of the public sector (PRO 1946g).

Bevin's ideas were endorsed by the Cabinet with the result that there was much talk in the months leading up to the late summer of 1946 of a public basic sector existing side by side with a private finishing sector. Very little background work was done, however, to give such a partition practical meaning. The important thing was that the two overriding concerns of the government, modernisation and a public Board, should somehow be kept together, discussed in the same room by the same people, possibly with some trade off involved and with the Federation doing all the practical work.

The Federation, however, refused to play. Their view on nationalisation was much less subtle, both owners and managers regarding it with unconcealed chagrin. They also felt betrayed since, after having lived up to the government's planning requirements, they were now being told that they could not be trusted to carry out the plan under private ownership. Nor did they take kindly to a Board designed to carve up the industry, such as the government was proposing (Vaizey 1974, pp. 123–4). Any industrialist who would accept to serve on such a Board, said the Federation, would be branded as a 'quisling'. One year later, as we shall see, their attitude would change, but in the summer of 1946 they were quite adamant: the only Board they could conceive of was a mild reenactment of the Steel Control, which would avoid duplicating the Federation's technical staff and steer well clear of nationalisation (PRO 1946j).

Since all the leading figures in the industry stood by the Federation and the government wanted the Board to include a number of influential industrialists, the government had little choice but to give in. The Iron and Steel Board that was appointed in September 1946 was a weak technical body, which had very little to do with what the Cabinet had proposed in the spring. Although it was entrusted with monitoring the development of the Plan, it was perfectly apparent that Steel House would retain the final say (Burn 1961, pp. 191–3, Ross 1965, pp. 57–8). Two out of six members of the Board, moreover, were members of the Federation and they were soon to make their mark as among the most outspoken opponents of nationalisation. What was more, the government had to acknowledge that it could not use the Board for drawing up a feasible plan for transferring the industry to the public sector. This task was entrusted, instead, to a team of civil servants, who were openly prevented by the Federation from having any contact whatsoever with the industry (PRO 1946k).

3   1947: Compromise rejected

A first nationalisation scheme was put together in Whitehall between the autumn of 1946 and the spring of 1947. The Cabinet endorsed it in the early spring of 1947 on the understanding that it would be turned into a bill in the next few months. There were, however, quite a few Ministers who expressed their reservations, while others went further and spoke out against what they considered a totally misguided venture. In particular Lord Jowitt, the Lord Chancellor, thought that the state should buy a stake of up to 51 per cent in the existing steel companies and exercise control with the help of a strong Board, which should also be made responsible for all new developments. This was the way, he added, both to save an enormous amount of public expenditure and to promote efficiency (PRO 1947f, Dalton 1962, pp. 248).

Such proposals were not new. As early as December 1945 Douglas Jay, acting in his capacity as Attlee's advisor, had put forward a short brief along similar lines (PRO 1945e). In the following July plans for partial ownership had been tabled by the chief of the South African Steel Corporation, Henrik Van der Bijl, who had been brought in by the government in a vain attempt to assuage the Federation.[3] Nothing practical, however, had emerged from such exercises, owing to a large extent, as will be shown, to the prejudices surrounding mixed ownership both among the civil servants and in the Labour Party. On the other hand, if the policy of nationalisation by consent was to stand any practical chance, it was precisely ideas such as a strong Board and minority or majority state share holdings which needed to be explored. It was, therefore, a clever tactical move on the part of the Federation to take them up and present them to the government as the basis for an eleventh-hour amicable solution (Keeling and Wright 1964, pp. 167–70). Between the end of May and mid July of 1947 a number of meetings ensued between Duncan, Ellis Hunter (president of the BISF), Morrison, Wilmot and Attlee.

An important background factor to those talks was the coal crisis which had broken out during the previous winter, which had cost the country around 750,000 tons of steel and had strained the supply of inputs into important industries such as shipbuilding and engineering as well as affecting exports programmes and housing reconstruction. This made it all the more important for the government to maintain a good working relationship with the steel industry for there was an urgent need to lift output again and to allocate more steel to the sectors in need (PRO 1947h).

A crucial meeting took place on 21 May, on Duncan's request. His case was that the Federation, having heard about the latest government proposals on nationalisation, wanted to meet the Prime Minister to find an acceptable alternative. The session, as we learn from a set of carefully drawn verbatim minutes, was very long, sometimes tense (PRO 1947g). It is quite clear that neither Morrison, nor Attlee understood much about the industry; Wilmot doing just slightly better. Duncan, on the other hand, with the discreet backing Hunter, made a number of powerful and compelling statements, taking firm hold of the discussion.

Duncan did not present the Federation's case merely as a plea to avoid nationalisation. It was, he said, a proposal for a lasting cooperation with the government which would, among other things, set a model for other industries and open the way for improved planning and efficiency.[4] He was prepared, he said, to see a permanent Board endowed with powers to carry out effective policy control, and 'to acquire or to participate in shareholdings in cases where they felt it was necessary in order to facil-itate and effect the best ultimate organisation'. He clarified this point further:

it may well be – he said – that there will be circumstances where, as the Minister of Supply said to us, there is a philosophical doubt as to whether it is right and proper to knock people about without being prepared to stand the financial racket, and there may be, in the evolution of the plan, occasions when the Board or the Minister thought the only proper thing to do was to take a participation or even an acquisition or property. (PRO 1947g, p. 4)

Duncan's reference to the south Wales strip mill development was but thinly disguised and it was taken up by Wilmot. Was he thinking, Wilmot asked, of the possibility of the state owning the strategic sectors of the industry, in order to carry out a process of concentration and reorgani-sation? Duncan did not confirm, but neither did he deny, stressing that he preferred to see the state involved through participation, rather than by taking overall control.

The fact that the new continuous hot strip mill should have been brought up in this way was not really surprising, given that it was by far the most ambitious of the projects contained in the Five Year Plan and that it depended on the state for a substantial part of its finance. The Steel Company of Wales, which had just been set up as a joint operation concern between RTB (Richard Thomas and Baldwins), GKN (Guest Keen and Nettlefolds) and a number of smaller tinplate companies, was about to install the new mill at Margam, Port Talbot and to match it with two cold reduction mills at Llanally and Swansea, for the production of tinplate, sheet and light plates. In July 1947 the Finance Corporation for Industry, a body designed to assist large capital projects which acted under government sponsorship and with the backing of the Bank of England and of major banks and institutions (Groove 1962, pp. 247–8), agreed to cover the costs of the operation by advancing a loan of 35 million pounds, equal to more than half of the final estimated cost, for which the stock raised by the Company on the market would provide the collateral (PRO 1947m). State involvement, albeit of an indirect nature, therefore, was more than just hypothetical.

The Ministers, however, had yet to make their pitch for full nationalisation. They presented their case in terms of efficiency and rationalisation. Morrison said that the Federation should not think that the government was proceeding on 'doctrinaire' motives; the truth was that he considered nationalisation 'swifter, cleaner and likely to be more efficient'. There would be no discussions, no profits or losses to be shared, added Attlee, if the government took a clean sweep.

Duncan answered in two ways. He first pointed out the inconsistency of nationalising not an industry, but a number of manufacturing firms, some of which were not primarily engaged in steel. Doesn't the government realise that they will be seen as wishing to take over 'the whole industrial world'? He then pointed out that this would have a great 'psychological' impact, and jeopardise future relations. Why break up the 'complete' harmony that had been established during the last fourteen years in 'the most public minded industry we have got in the country'. An industry which – he added – had produced a plan. 'I cheered it very loudly when it came – interjected Wilmot, who together with Morrison was becoming increasingly sympathetic towards the Federation's case (PRO 1947g, p. 11).

Wilmot tried one last argument: would not, he asked, a Board, such as Duncan was proposing, create uncertainty by its very powers to acquire companies? 'The best schoolmaster – replied Hunter – does not use the cane' (PRO 1947g, p. 21).

After this remarkable session the Ministers were left to make sense of what they had heard and turn it, if possible, into a practical scheme, which could be sold to the Cabinet and, more importantly, to Parliament. The truth of the matter was that they had been found wanting on their own ground and the shallowness of their understanding about what the state wanted to achieve and about how it could be achieved had been exposed.

There was further evidence that nobody in the Cabinet had any great regard for the full-blown nationalisation scheme – a 'technical nightmare' as it was referred to. But would a strong Board be politically feasible? One Minister pointed out that it would lose the support of the backbenchers; another that 'selective acquisition would create great discontent as between one constituency and another'. Perhaps it could be presented as an intermediate solution, a first step which in due course, perhaps in the next Parliament, would be followed by a complete takeover. Perhaps the

Federation itself could be pushed further, and made to accept nationalisation from the start. Wilmot, for example, optimistically observed that
Duncan's attitude suggested 'what had hitherto seemed impossible, that it
might be possible to attain the Government's objectives in agreement'
(PRO 1947j, p. 1).

New talks with the Federation were held in July by Morrison and
Wilmot (PRO 1947k). The scheme upon which they were finally able to
reach a general understanding came short of a government takeover, but
it did include what seemed to be significant concessions on the part of the
industry. A new central Board would be created, endowed with statutory
wide-ranging powers and enjoying direct access to the firms and by
agreement it would take over the Federation's organisational machine.
Duncan, perhaps with a touch of irony, pointed to the fact that it was only
natural for the government to want to reappropriate itself of some of the
functions which it had hitherto so happily farmed out.

The government would be also granted some new powers in carrying
out acquisitions although on how far these should go views differed.
Morrison asked for something like a blank cheque, whereby there would
be a negotiated, piecemeal takeover over a number of years, whereas the
Federation agreed only to acquisitions on an *ad hoc* basis, in the case of
new developments, or in those cases in which private enterprise should
show itself unwilling. They also said, this time, that they did not like the
idea of the state acquiring full ownership of the south Wales development
and that, in any case, they wanted each acquisition to be subject to
Parliamentary scrutiny. Any transfer of ownership should be the responsibility of the new Board, or, at any rate, should be subject to its appeal.

Although the fine print of the agreement was never spelled out, it
appeared, therefore, that the government would have had to be content
with a limited amount of state ownership. Morrison openly recognised as
much when he presented the outlines of the agreement to the Cabinet at
the end of July (PRO 1947l). He said, somewhat pessimistically, that it
looked as if the state would enter in possession only of the less efficient
units in the industry. There was nothing, however, under the conditions
that were thought acceptable by the Federation to stop the government
from advancing a positive agenda of its own. Indeed, as was shown, some
of the best plant being developed was already strongly affected by state-
sponsored investment.

It is interesting briefly to consider why the Federation went as far as it
did. Granted that the firms were prepared to go to any length to avoid a
takeover by the state, there would have been a danger in a 'strong' Board
if the State were to use it to interfere in the affairs of the industry. There
was no sign, however, that the government had any intention of doing so:
the meeting of minds over the industry's management was complete. To

ensure that it would remain so, not far from Duncan's Board would still lie the encompassing network of the Federation. The opponents of the compromise were quick to point this out in Cabinet: moving the staff would not deprive the Federation of its upper hand; its strength resided in its close connection with the firms.

The failure by Ministers to insist on the south Wales scheme is truly striking and it was a reminder of the fact that the government had lost the initiative the year before, when it had, in all but name, surrendered the development plan to the Federation. Many of the schemes that Duncan and Hunter were trumpeting as great achievements of the industry were being, in those very months, postponed, even cancelled; it is doubtful whether the Ministers fully knew about them. The Board that was being proposed would have allowed the government to vet all investment schemes, to fix prices, to acquire shares in companies, to force amalgamation and concentration, to allocate raw materials and production quotas. It would have been an authority far more powerful than the High Authority of the ECSC or than the Board set up in 1953. Such considerations, however, are pointless: the government already possessed most of the powers and chose to exercise them by proxy.

It is well known that Morrison's and Wilmot's compromise was rejected by Cabinet between late July and early August 1947 (PRO 1947n). The government decided instead to proceed, in due time but within the current legislature, with the full takeover of the industry. The episode, which occupies no small part in the legend of the Attlee government, has been analysed at length so that it will be sufficient here to look at it briefly from the angle of steel policy (Pelling 1984, pp. 84–5, Morrison 1960, p. 296, Dalton 1962, pp. 251–3, Wilson 1962, p. 25).

The first thing to note is that no strong case was made in defence of the compromise solution; its supporters, of which there were many, saw it mainly as a way to avoid nationalisation, which they considered an unfortunate muddle. It would allow, they said, cooperation with the industry to continue very much as before. Little else emerged to its credit.

The most vocal opponents of the compromise, led by Bevan, were few in number, but they could point to sentiments which were being expressed outside the Cabinet, especially in the Parliamentary Party. There was much talk of a government sell-out, of shady back room deals with the Federation (Williams-Thompson 1951, p. 46). There is also evidence that opinion in the trade unions was hardening in the same direction.[5] Not that this side had much offer in terms of practical solutions: simply, as Dalton was to say about Bevan, it was a question of 'nailing' one's 'colours to the mast' (Dalton 1962, p. 251).

The majority of the Ministers, comprising most of the top figures in the

Cabinet such as Dalton, Cripps and Bevin – and also Attlee, although he spoke very little – were all believers in some form of nationalisation by consent. They regarded what they were being offered by Morrison as consent without nationalisation, but with the prospect, instead, of a damaging fight with a large and vocal part of their supporters. Not seeing any particular merit in it, equally sceptical about nationalisation, they decided to press on with the previous policy, whatever that might have been. How indecisive was their choice is perhaps best revealed by the fact that a few months later, in the spring of 1948, when a second draft of the Steel Bill came to Cabinet, the Ministers were prepared to consider the question all over again. Once more they reached the conclusion that Morrison's compromise scheme was politically intractable (PRO 1948c).

4   1948: Drafting the bill

The first scheme for nationalisation was the work of a team of officials headed by Frank Lee, who had been moved in from the Treasury to take charge of the newly formed Iron and Steel Division of the Ministry of Supply. While this first exercise proved to be both extensive and useful, the final drafting of the Bill was accomplished roughly one year later under the direction of S. Wilson, after George Strauss had taken the place of the disgraced Wilmot.[6]

No help was forthcoming, as was said, from the Federation, nor from the Board, so that the officials had to draw mainly upon their own knowledge of the industry and upon the records they had available. They were called upon to demarcate the firms and plants to be nationalised and to collect information about their capital structure, in order to be able to gauge, among other things, the amount of compensation to be paid. They also had to map out the attributions of the new public central authority – the Iron and Steel Corporation as it came to be called – in which the companies' shares were to be vested.

Part of the blame for the uncertainty surrounding nationalisation was subsequently attached to the civil servants (Williams-Thompson 1951, p. 41, Dalton 1962, p. 137), but the records show that their contribution was technically proficient, especially if one considers how inconsistent their mandate was. They were, in fact, being asked at the same time not to antagonise the industry and to steer away from anything that might expose the government to allegations of weakness on the part of the radical wing of the Labour movement. The inevitable result was that they oscillated between a market-oriented, flexible model and a rigidly central-ised one.

The most obvious market-oriented solution was to envisage government partial ownership through shareholdings in the companies. This, however, was rejected not only because of the fear that it might elicit criticism of a political nature, but also because there was very little faith that it could be made to work. It was thought that mixed ownership would give rise to conflicting loyalties that would impair the work of the managers, and that even a minority private interest might be able to restrict the operations of the public sector: 'the tail might wag the dog' as it was put (PRO 1947a, p. 26).

Yet there was at least one example that might have proved otherwise. The Air Division of the Ministry of Supply, it emerged, had inherited from the Board of Trade a commanding share of 60 per cent, in Shorts Bros Ltd, the aircraft manufacturers, and they reported that 'we find we have no difficulty in getting our way with Shorts on everything that matters, although we leave to the company the maximum freedom of action and endeavour to treat them in the same way as we treat the other members of the industry'. There was no indication, moreover, that state control had made the venture less attractive, given that the shipbuilders Harland and Wolff seemed willing to go to any length to keep a minority interest in it (PRO 1947d).

What was lacking was an accepted philosophy of government share-holding. This was clearly revealed when the steel team asked the Treasury about their majority participation in Anglo-Iranian Oil Co. They received the answer that there were no guidelines either on appointments or on management supervision: everything was done by rule of thumb and it was extremely difficult even to put the evidence together (PRO 1946l).

The search for a more flexible arrangement designed in particular to appease the industry's management, produced what, at one point, was called a 'federal solution'. It rested on the fact that the government would acquire the shares of each steel company, rather than choosing to buy the steel assets from the companies as had been done in the case of coal. Individual companies, thereafter, would retain their identity and continue to function as separate units, with substantial freedom in their day-to-day management, under loose central supervision (PRO 1947a, p. 13, PRO 1947c, doc E. 37a). Gradually, however, as the Bill acquired its final shape, a much more centralised pattern asserted itself: the central board was given more and more power and although the companies were maintained they were in fact deprived of any real autonomy.

The failure to draw attention to the practical advantages of competition and market flexibility was again largely a consequence of choosing not to challenge the tightly cartelised structure of the industry. A meek attempt to introduce some liberalisation in foreign trade allowing users of steel goods to buy freely on the market, subject to import licenses, was rejected

Table 13.1. *Concentration in the steel industry: selected indicators 1951–3*

Percentage shares held by:	big 6	2nd 7	3rd 8	50 others
Employment 1952	54	22	12	12
Sales 52/53	54	21	9	16
Ingot output 1953	60	24	8	8
Average profits 51/3	54	24	7	10
Capital expenditure 52/53	59	27	8	7

Notes:
Big Six: Stewarts and Lloyds, United Steel, Dorman Long, Richard Thomas and Baldwins, Steel Company of Wales, Colvilles.
Second Seven: English Steel Corporation, Summers, John and Sons, South Durham Steel and Iron, The Lancashire Steel Company, Guest Keen Baldwin, Consett, Firth Browns.
Third Eight: Hadfields, Beardmore, Staveley, Park Gate, Firth-Vickers, John Lysaght, Brown Bayleys, Briton Ferry.
Source: PRO 1960, p. 3 (blue).

by Ministers: centralised buying not only of raw materials but also of steel and alloys was to be encouraged, they said, either by the public industry's board or by some other government agency (PRO 1947e).

One of the most controversial issues proved to be the scope of acquisition. The fairly high degree of concentration inside the industry, of which table 13.1 gives some indication, prompted schemes to limit nationalisation to a few large firms. The first such scheme was considered in 1947 and it would have covered twenty-five companies, each producing more than 1 per cent of the total steel or 1.5 per cent of alloy steel (PRO 1947b). One year later a similar proposal was considered by Strauss (Chester 1975, pp. 172f; PRO 1960, pp. 9–11). Clearly either scheme would have made nationalisation a much swifter, less cumbersome operation. On the other hand, both would have entailed a measure of interaction between the public and the private sectors, which was open to allegations of compromise on political grounds, and technically was considered muddled and difficult to handle. Prices would have to be negotiated, the officials remarked; there might be margins for competition, embarrassing assurances about raw materials might have to be extended.

If a strong case for extended public ownership could be made, it was on the grounds that it would eventually facilitate reorganisation of the industry. This was indeed the thrust of the first blueprint drawn up in 1947, covering 105 companies all the way from iron ore, to pig iron, steel down to finished products, including many independent re-rollers. The aim was to eventually bring about more vertical integration, in particular between steelmakers and re-rollers, in order to achieve economies in transport and heating (PRO 1947a, section 5; PRO 1947c, doc E39).

Large independent re-rollers claimed an important share of the market for light rail, merchant bar, rods, hoop and strip, amounting to 35 per cent of final output and their existence could well be regarded as breeding inefficiency, especially in the case of standard products which could be mass produced. The line was therefore drawn in order to leave out of the public sector only the smaller jobbers, whose mills turned out specified products in small lots. Furthermore, in the tinplate trade, in order to facilitate concentration in the new large south Wales mills it was proposed that all small independent producers should also be nationalised, eventually to be merged or disposed of. The argument for concentration, however, was soon lost in the midst of other considerations and the scheme which finally emerged although fairly comprehensive, by setting fixed output ceilings beneath which companies would escape takeover, left out all the small tinplate producers.[7]

The acquisition of steel companies carried with it two problems, the importance of which was already evident in the preparatory stage: one was whether hiving off of non-steel interests was to be allowed, and the other was the relationship with the Federation.

The extent to which the state, by choosing to acquire the whole of the steel companies, would get involved in a number of diverse manufacturing activities, especially engineering and chemicals, became apparent as the drafting of the scheme proceeded. Taking only the biggest six firms, 17 per cent of their sales and 19 per cent of their workforce were outside the iron and steel sector, whereas for the next seven firms in order of size both shares were above 20 per cent (PRO 1960, pp. 18–19). In the months leading to the implementation of the Bill the government, therefore, made a number of sympathetic noises, to the extent that it would not stand in the way of companies planning to split up in order to 'hive off' their non-steel assets. In the most important case, however, that of Dorman Long, the decision fell against the company (Chester 1975, pp. 187–8).

Dorman Long had proposed to split in two, with one company carrying out the firm's chemical and structural engineering work. The latter was particularly important, accounting for about one quarter of the country's entire capacity. Although it was conceded that technically the operation was viable, the Minister of Supply opposed it on 'social and economic' grounds and the Cabinet endorsed his views in October 1949. Two arguments stood out: firstly, it was said that the best technicians and administrators, had they been offered the chance, would have opted for the company remaining in the private sector; secondly, it was claimed that the hived-off company would cease to use British steel. A third argument was never brought out in the open but it was probably just as influential, namely that structural engineering was by far the most profitable part of Dorman Long.

A subject fraught with ambiguity was the future of the Federation. It was said that the Corporation's aim should be to replace it, by an orderly and negotiated takeover of its functions (PRO 1947a, pp. 92, 230–6). Preferably one would have nationalised it but, given that it represented numerous small firms which were to remain private, this would have implied tabling a hybrid bill, that is one affecting private as opposed to a general class of interests (Ross 1965, pp. 92–3, Burn 1961, pp. 309–11). Because such Bills were subject to a lengthy procedure, involving petitions from the interests concerned, it would have delayed things considerably.

In the end the Bill said very little about the Federation, and in view of the obstructive tactics which its leaders were to employ against the Iron and Steel Corporation in the course of 1951, this proved an unfortunate decision. The most obvious solution of allowing the nationalised sector to participate in the cartel, possibly with a commanding voice, seems never to have been considered. Yet about 350 companies were to escape takeover and although they accounted for barely 10 per cent of steel production, for some finished products their share was much higher, reaching 80 per cent (Keeling and Wright 1964, p. 174). This would clearly enable the leaders of Steel House to exercise at least some influence.

How should the Corporation manage the industry and relate to the nationalised firms? Should it be conceived as a holding company, or should it be a large company in its own right, with the powers to engage directly in manufacturing? If the latter choice were made, given that the Memoranda of Association of the companies were drafted in the widest possible terms, covering rights in areas ranging from banking to shipbuilding, it followed that the Corporation would have to be given a very wide scope indeed. This was no less true if it were decided to limit the Corporation to those activities which the companies were actually carrying out at the takeover date (PRO 1948a).

The case for a holding company appeared, therefore, to be fairly strong. As a holding company the Corporation did not need any powers of its own, it would simply carry out its mandate through the companies. Moreover it would not be open to the charge of wanting to meddle in commercial activities. At one point such a prospect elicited a flurry of enquiries into matters of industrial organisation: Wilmot compared the new structure to ICI, a combine taking over a subsidiary. The combine would, he said, lay down the broad policy and the subsidiaries would engage in day-to-day administration (PRO 1947e).

This exercise, however, was both superficial and short lived, and in 1948 Strauss was arguing already against any decentralisation, both on political and technical grounds. He observed that 'a holding company . . . would appear to many of our supporters to smack too much of City financial methods' and said that, anyway, he wanted the Corporation to carry out certain functions, such as centralised purchase of materials and centralised selling, directly (PRO 1948d, p. 2).

In its final shape, therefore, the Corporation retained the name of a holding company, but such were the powers with which it was endowed, that it looked much more like a monocratic and manipulative conglomerate (Chester 1975, pp. 446–50). It could take over or create new companies in any area of manufacturing in which its controlled companies happened to be engaged as well as engaging itself directly in production. The companies, on the other hand, had no statutory independence, nor any financial autonomy, since the Corporation would be judged from the financial results of the entire industry. To further increase the scope for central interference the Bill contained a number of departures from standard Company Law, allowing, for example, the Corporation to remove any company director from his post. While, therefore, the original intention of keeping to a 'federal' structure had succeeded in ruling out any reorganisation of the industry according to functional or regional criteria, it had been subsequently overshadowed by fears of granting the companies any effective independence. Indeed, it was remarked, that centralisation in the case of steel was much more pronounced than in coal or gas, which had been at least divided into regional units.

Bestowing large powers on the Corporation was a poor substitute for an industrial strategy and this became apparent when the role of the Minister was considered. The importance of this issue fully emerged once it was realised by the Cabinet, in the summer of 1948, that the whole case for nationalisation rested on very shaky ground.

This discussion was sparked off by Morrison, who was still convinced that his compromise offered a better alternative.

If we leave the company structure and most of the company directors, but deprive them of the profits motive, are we not still dependent to some extent – particularly in the short run – on the goodwill of a small body of industrialists, while at the same time arousing the bitter hostility of some of them by the action we are taking? (PRO 1948b, p. 2)

Bevin reminded him that the alternative to public ownership was the continuance of a powerful private cartel which might act against the national interest (PRO 1948c). He then went on to say that the industry's capacity was inadequate, and that under private ownership it was unlikely to reach the needed 20 million tons. Other Ministers seemed to like this argument and interjected that the industry had failed both to modernise and to expand. Because, however, this implied a fundamental departure from the government's previous endorsement of the industry's plan, an official reexamination was called for. One month later it produced a brief to be used by the Ministers in the ensuing parliamentary debate, in which the merits of expansion under public ownership were conveniently stressed (PRO 1948e).

Whatever the merits of Bevin's case, to turn it, at just one remove from the introduction of the Bill, into the official justification for nationalising the industry showed a remarkable degree of improvisation.[8] The industry could, moreover, easily prove that it was one step ahead. In the course of 1948 its 1945 Plan was revised upward, on the basis of the increases in demand which had been registered since late 1947.[9]

One result of this new emphasis on planning was to prompt a request for new Ministerial powers (Chester 1975, pp. 906f.). It was pointed out that too narrow a definition of such powers might mean that there would be less scope for planning than if the industry had remained under private ownership and that if the Minister of Supply was expected to influence the pattern and volume of production he needed to be able to give the appropriate directions to the Corporation. In particular specific powers were requested over the industry's capacity ceilings, over location of new plants and over types, qualities and sizes of finished products. They would have made the steel industry unique, since in other nationalised industries Ministers were merely empowered to issue general directives to the Boards and to approve of their capital programmes, much of their influence resting upon informal contact.

In support of his request Strauss pointed out that, if the Minister wanted the Corporation to change the location of a new plant, he was powerless: the only constraint for the Corporation were the negative powers of the Board of Trade under the Town and Country Planning Act.

Extensive, detailed powers called, however, for the staff to man them and the backing of adequate financial resources. Carrying the previous example further, were the Corporation to object to the new proposed location on commercial grounds, given that it was responsible for its own budget, it was up to the Minister to meet the eventual extra costs.

It appeared, however, that a planning budget was not to the Treasury's liking and, equally important, that the emergence of similar concepts had never been part of the general ethos of the nationalisation programme (Cairncross 1985, pp. 477, 488–9). Strauss's demands were, therefore, rejected and their strongest opponent, not surprisingly, turned out to be Morrison. He pointed out that the new powers were 'contrary to the hitherto accepted doctrine that socialised boards could be trusted to act, by and large, in the national interest and need not be subjected to the same degree of control as private industry' (PRO 1948g, p. 32).

The crucial role assigned to the 'Board', as opposed to any possible machinery for government planning, was a reflection of how deeply the whole exercise had been influenced by the corporatist philosophy. The hope seemed to be that, above and beyond the conflict over the dispossession of private owners, the industry could go on happily cooperating with the state. Firms were kept intact in the name of continuity, but, more importantly, a strong central Board provided the best guarantee of an enduring monopoly.

Little room was made for the views either of the planners or of the liberals. A few of the planners, such as Norman Chester, had taken a hand in drafting the tedious technicalities of the Steel Bill. Most others, to the extent that they were still active in the industry, must have been employed by the Federation. Had they been able to make any useful contribution?

The evidence suggests that the Federation failed to carry out the brave ideas that it had mapped out in 1945. Many small plants which initially had been thought of as inefficient and needing replacement were, on the contrary, allowed to develop. Blast furnace reequipment was delayed with the result that average size remained well below international standards. The three major integrated developments which were to be initiated in Scotland, in the north-east and in the midlands were cancelled. Economies of scale were not exploited, vertical integration remained insufficient (Burn 1958, p. 290, Vaizey 1974, pp. 146–9).

The failure was blamed on the persistent boom and the attendant shortages, which had encouraged full use of existing plant. Nevertheless the costs of the industry as a whole were not brought down, although this was disguised by equalisation schemes and government subsidies. Moreover, although overall investment was high, amounting to £400 million in 1952 prices for the period 1946–52, against a forecast of £340 million (£168 million in 1946 prices), a much larger share of it than expected was devoted to patching-up operations. The evidence, therefore, points to a serious lack of purpose on the Federation's side. Possibly the uncertainty about impending nationalisation also took its toll. That the government failed to focus on the relevant issues must be, however, more than a conjecture.

5   The state and steel in France and Italy: comparative perspectives

Because there are many points in common between the British, the French and Italian experience of relations between the state and the steel industry in the immediate post-war years, a few comparative remarks might be useful to put the experience of nationalisation in better perspective. The three viewpoints about the industry which we discussed – the corporatist, the modernising and the liberal – were also articulated in France and Italy, although the people that articulated them and the balance between them was different in each case. Also day-to-day management of the industry was much the same, in that a close collaboration was established between the relevant ministries and the professional steel associations, although perhaps not in quite as tightly knit a way as in Britain.

Both in France and in Italy nationalisation proposals were advanced, but did not materialise. More importantly they were not entertained by the same groups eventually to emerge at the helm of planning. This might not have been the case in France if, in late 1944, Mendès-France had been allowed to implement his programme, in which the iron and steel industry featured as part of the priority heavy industrial sector, which the state was supposed to nationalise. Further plans for nationalisation were tabled separately in 1945 and 1946 by the Socialist and Communist Party, the latter producing a very detailed scheme, calling for the industry to be regrouped into four regional corporations, under strict guidance from the controlling Ministry (Fontaine 1950, pp. 152–5, Andrieu 1987, p. 262).

In Italy calls for extensive state ownership came in 1945 from the CGIL – the trade union confederation – and from elements of the much divided Socialist Party. They were however somewhat blunted by the fact that IRI, the state corporation created in 1933, owned majority shareholdings of a number of important steel companies, which it had regrouped in 1937 in its subsidiary holding company, Finsider. A few in the Left were extremely uneasy about Finsider, considering it little more than an emanation of private industry, but many others greeted it as a useful substitute for state ownership, or at least as a first step towards it.

Fears of a possible takeover by the state lingered on among steel industrialists in both countries, but by the time the debate over modernisation was joined they had receded into the background. In France the modernising thrust was provided by the team of planners of the Commissariat au Plan, headed by Jean Monnet. Steel was one of the six sectors in which they concentrated their efforts (Mioche 1986). In Italy the modernisers gathered around Oscar Sinigaglia, Finsider's chief executive. Their programme, launched in 1947, was called the Sinigaglia plan and it called for the concentration of production in a few big state-owned integrated coastal plants, of which the most important was Cornigliano, where a new continuous strip mill was to be located (Sinigaglia 1948). Also the Monnet plan envisaged installation of two hot strip continuous mills – one in the north-east and one in Lorraine.

The distinctive feature both of the Italian and the French experience, and one lacking in Britain, was that the modernisers were able to over-come the resistance of the industry's cartel by a mixture of arm twisting and forceful state intervention and that they were assisted in doing so by a clear insight into the industry's problems and operations. The Commissariat au Plan came closest to a technocratic description and it acted in two ways: by advising government departments over allocations of raw materials and other controls, and by controlling investment, especially after the ERP Counterpart Funds accruing to the French government had been allotted to the Fonds de Modernisation (Mioche 1993, Kuisel 1981, pp. 239f). As the Schuman Plan was to show, it was also able to bring to bear on the industry international considerations, such as the problems of access to German coal and the future of the Ruhr (Lynch 1984, Milward 1984, pp. 128f).

In Italy Finsider, being itself part of the industry, had the ability to undermine the private firms' cartel by competitive pricing, or by striking alliances with corporations such as Fiat who were particularly interested at that stage in expanding the market for coils. Finsider also enjoyed privileged links with the government which helped it obtain a disproportionately large share of investment funds, and to steer tariff policies according to its priorities (Ranieri 1993, pp. 120f).

6   Conclusion

Clearly the modernisation drive was not an unqualified success in either of the two countries, but it did allow the modernisers to disentangle themselves from the stifling embrace of the steel cartel. In Britain this, on the contrary, was rendered very difficult by the principle of industrial self government, on which the partnership between government and industry was based. The British steel industry offers perhaps one of the best examples of a strong trade association, whose existence was brought about, and then nurtured by the government's choice of handing over to it the operation of a number of key controls (Rogow 1955, pp. 52, 60f).

During the last period of the war, as was seen, there had been a renewed interest in planning of which the Franks–Chester report bore the mark. Soon however it appeared that the corporatist bias, together with an undue concentration of everybody's minds on the issue of nationalisation were watering down the planning agenda. Possibly, however, the root of the problem lay deeper.

Steven Tolliday has blamed the government in the thirties for lacking 'both . . . the bureaucratic apparatus and expertise to proffer technocratic solutions'. 'There were no significant advocates in government circles of the view that the government could run industry better than industrialists', he writes (Tolliday 1987, pp. 335–6). Essentially the same situation obtained after 1945, and possibly it is explained by the persistence of a deep-seated *laissez faire* prejudice, sometimes cloaked under the mantle of doctrinaire 'all or nothing' beliefs. In this respect both the Italian and the French experiences are instructive, because they point to the wide scope of state intervention in a modern mixed economy.

In Britain there was much departmental tinkering with the industry: the Treasury had some powers, so did the Board of Trade and the Ministry of Supply, but there seems to have been very little coordination. Many powers, moreover, were farmed out to the Federation, others to the Board. Nobody seems to have taken up the responsibility of fashioning a distinct governmental viewpoint. In the meantime the politicians were tearing themselves apart over nationalisation and in the end could do no better than to hope that disinterested managers under state ownership would bring about the much needed modernisation.

NOTES

1 In the autumn of 1944 Mr G.W. Lucas, president of the Motor Agent's Association, complained that the price of British steel was 50 per cent higher than world prices, and he blamed the industry for being overprotected and cartelised. Although he seems to have overstated the price difference, it was true that high grade sheet for automobiles was much more expensive than in the US, a fact which could be linked to the problems met in implanting the new strip mill technology in Britain. In the view of many, moreover, this was but part of a more general pattern of poor management, and low productivity (BISF 1944a, Burn 1961, pp. 41f., Vaizey 1974, pp. 97–9).

2 The need for market-oriented planning was articulated among others by Duncan Burn, who served during the war as a temporary civil servant in the Ministry of Supply and later, as industrial correspondent to *The Times*, kept in close touch with the industry. 'Nationalisation', he wrote in 1946 in a draft of a letter he subsequently sent to Morrison, 'cannot work effectively either if the central government interferes in day to day decisions or if it fails to perform its proper functions – of giving nationalised industries a broad indication of objective, a remit, as the Americans would say, and of proscribing the specific activities which in a particular industry will amount to monopolist exploitation. Investments should clearly be selected where they promise the lowest ultimate costs. Development should be encouraged only in branches where a British product can be made at least as cheaply as an overseas product can be supplied ... A flat price for steel – such as the present type of uniform delivered price – is a characteristic monopoly device which has serious economic disadvantages, and has stood in the way of advance; it is the kind of thing which should be proscribed by central government, and some system of zonal pricing is required ... The functions [of the central public agency] will be narrow in scope but crucial in importance; they will require only a small staff but high powered' (see Burn Papers 1946).

3 South Africa's ISCOR had been set up in 1934, and 90 per cent of its capital belonged to the state. During the war capacity for crude steel had risen to 600,000 tons and the Corporation had distinguished itself in supplying spares to the Allied troops in North Africa. It did not run a monopoly, however, given that it worked alongside two smaller private companies. Van der Bijl had been marshalled to London by the government in July 1946, but after having spoken with both the Ministers and the BISF he seems to have declined the offer of becoming permanent chairman of the new Board. The gist of his proposals is reported in PRO (1947a, p. 20). He wanted the government to control the industry but also to extend a pledge to the Federation that 'some measure' of private ownership would be maintained. The government would participate in the new companies that were to be financed as a result of the development plant, thereby acquiring a minority stake in the industry.

4 This was in keeping with the role he had exercised since the mid thirties in the steel industry as a kind of 'national conciliator', a 'national interest' figure, as Tolliday calls him, 'somewhere between business and politics, capable of mediating between government interests and the constituency of industrialists' (Tolliday 1987, p. 336).

5 In the literature the evidence on the attitude of the trade unions towards the compromise is mixed. Lincoln Evans, General Secretary of the Iron and Steel Trades Confederation, claimed that he had wanted a compromise (Donoughue and Jones 1973, p. 403). But the evidence of the records points in a different direction: the Executive Council of the Iron and Trades Confederation told Attlee that they were 'perturbed' by the 'hesitant' policy of the government and that not only did they want immediate nationalisation, but also Wilmot should be sacked and a more decisive Minister appointed. This in fact is what happened just a few weeks later (PRO 1947o).

6 The best inside story of the tribulations surrounding the drafting of the Bill is to be found in a long note drawn up between 1949 and 1952 by Mr Wilson himself, see PRO (1952). Details of the workings inside the Ministry of Supply are provided in Williams-Thompson (1951), pp. 35f.

7 A lower limit was set, whereby only companies producing or hot rolling over 20,000 tons of steel or producing over 20,000 tons of pig iron, or 50,000 tons of iron ore would be nationalised. A further exception was made for companies engaged in motor vehicle production, which also ran steel mills (Keeling and Wright 1964, p. 171). Later as a further concession to the smaller companies, it was decided that if a company due for nationalisation had less than 15 per cent of its labour force engaged in the Bill's scheduled activities it would escape takeover (Chester 1975, pp. 180–1).

8 Bevin's ideas rested on the advice he was getting from the trade unions. As he wrote to Morrison: 'Regarding greater production I find in talking to people in the trade that they regard the present position of fifteen million tons or thereabouts as being the likely figure which private enterprise could carry . . . They will, immediately a recession sets in begin restrictions.' On the other hand, 'If Western Union is to be maintained then ultimately our proportion in this country – if we have regard for the demand for specialised steel, for capital goods for the Colonies and overseas generally – cannot be allowed to be less than 20 million tons.' He went on to say that in the pre-war period had the

government been 'wise' in directing the industry and thinking ahead about future balance of payments problems it would have encouraged the building of a further 5 million tons of capacity. Bevin also pointed to the extremely long and divisive arguments that preceded the installation of the strip mills. 'Those strip mills should have been in before the war, and, had they been in 1945, then our tinplate position would have been such that we could have altered the whole food situation in this country' (PRO 1948f).

9 The target for steel output had hence been set at 17.5 million tons (for 1953–4), against the previous 16 million (for 1952–3) (Burn 1961, pp. 243–4).

REFERENCES

Andrieu, C., Le Van, L. and Prost, A. (eds.) (1987), *Le Nationalisations de la Libération – De l'utopie au compromis*, Paris: Presse de la Fondation Nationale de S.P.

BISF (1944a), British Iron and Steel Federation, *Steel prices and costs*, November.
    (1944b), *Report by the British Iron and Steel Federation to the Ministry of Supply*, December, 63 pp. (unpublished) (PRO, CAB 124/789).
    (1946), *Iron and Steel Industry*, Reports by the British Iron and Steel Federation and the Joint Iron Council, Cmd. 6811.

Brooke, S. (1989), 'Revisionists and Fundamentalists: The Labour Party and Economic Policy During the Second World War', *The Historical Journal*, 32(1): 157–75.

Burn, D.L. (1961), *The Steel Industry 1939–1959 – A Study in Competition and Planning*, London: Cambridge University Press.
    (1958), 'Steel', in D.L. Burn (ed.), *The Structure of British Industry*, vol. I, London: Cambridge University Press: 260–308.

Burn Papers (1946), *Papers of D.L. Burn* (British Library of Political and Economic Science, LSE) 6/30 (87), Draft copy of a letter by D.L. Burn (*The Times*) to the Right Hon. H. Morrison, June 1946.

Cairncross, A. (1985), *Years of Recovery – British Economic Policy 1945–1951*, London: Methuen.

Cairncross, A. and Watts, N. (1989), *The Economic Section 1939–1961 – A Study in Economic Advising*, London: Routledge.

Chester, N. (1975), *The Nationalisation of British Industry 1945–1951*, London: HMSO.

Dalton, H. (1957), *The Fateful Years – Memoirs 1931–1945*, London: Frederick Muller.
    (1962), *High Tide and After – Memoirs 1945–1960*, London: Frederick Muller.

Donoughue, B. and Jones, G.W. (1973), *Herbert Morrison – Portrait of a Politician*, London: Weidenfeld and Nicolson.

Fontaine, M. (1950), *L'industrie sidérurgique dans le monde et son évolution économique depuis la seconde guerre mondiale*, Paris: PUF.

Franks, O. (1947), *Central Planning and Control in War and Peace*, London: LSE.

Groove, J.W. (1962), *Government and Industry in Britain*, London: Longmans.

Hargreaves, E.L. and Gowing, M.M. (1952), *Civil industry and trade*, London: HMSO. [History of the Second World War, UK Civil Series].

Jay, D. (1989), *Change and Fortune – A political record*, London: Hutchinson.

Keeling, B.S. and Wright, A.E.G. (1964), *The Development of the Modern British Steel Industry*, London: Longmans.

Kuisel, R. (1981), *Capitalism and the state in modern France – Renovation and economic management in the twentieth century*, Cambridge University Press.

Lynch, F. (1984), 'Resolving the Paradox of the Monnet Plan: National and International Planning in French Reconstruction', *Economic History Review*, 229–43.

Milward, A.S. (1984), *The Reconstruction of Western Europe 1945–51*, London: Methuen.

Mioche, P. (1986), 'Les plans et la sidérurgie: du soutien mitigé à l'effacement possible (1946–1960)', in H. Rousso (ed.), *De Monnet à Massé*, Paris: Editions du CNRS, pp. 127–37.

(1993), 'Le Plan Marshall et la sidérurgie française' in Ministère de l'Economie des Finances et du Budget, *Le Plan Marshall et le relèvement économique de L'Europe*, Paris: CHEFF, pp. 303–18.

Morgan, K. (1984), *Labour in Power 1945–1951*, Oxford: Clarendon Press.

Morrison, H. (1960), *An Autobiography by Lord Morrison of Lambeth*, London: Odhams Press.

Pelling, H. (1984), *The Labour Governments 1945–1951*, London: Macmillan.

Pimlott, B. (1985), *Hugh Dalton*, London: Macmillan.

PRO (1944a), R (44) 150, War Cabinet, Reconstruction Committee, Memorandum by the President of the Board of Trade, September 2 1944 (CAB 124/789).

(1944b), R (44) 166, War Cabinet, Reconstruction Committee, Memorandum by the Minister of Supply, September 26 1944 (CAB 124/789).

(1945a), R (45) 36, War Cabinet, Reconstruction Committee, 'Iron and Steel', Joint Memorandum by the Minister of Supply and the President of the Board of Trade, April 6 1945 (CAB 124/789).

(1945b), E.C.(S) (45) 8, Economic Section of the War Cabinet Committee Secretariat, 'The Iron and Steel Industry', Minutes of a Staff meeting held on the 17th of April to discuss the Report on the Iron and Steel Industry, 24 April 1945 (CAB 124/789).

(1945c), R. (45), 17th meeting, War Cabinet, Reconstruction Committee, Minute 2, 30 April 1945 (CAB 124/789).

(1945d), L.P. (45) 228, Reconstruction by the Ministry of Supply, 'Future of the Iron and Steel Industry', 7 November 1945 (CAB 71/19).

(1945e), Lord President of the Council, Memo by D. Jay (Prime Minister's Office) 'Iron and Steel Industry', 31 December 1945 (CAB 124/790).

(1946a), Lord President of the Council, Memorandum by the Ministry of Supply, 'Iron and Steel', 4 March 1946 (CAB 124/790).

(1946b), S.I.(M) 46, 45 Meeting, 14 March 1946 (CAB 134/687).

(1946c), S.I.(M) (46) 9, Economic Section of the Cabinet, 'Capital Development and Future Organization in the Iron and Steel Industry', 25 March 1946 (CAB 134/687).

(1946d), Lord President of the Council, Memo by A. Johnston (Lord President's Office), 26 March 1946 (CAB 124/790).

(1946e), C.M. (46), Minute 3, 4 April 1946 (CAB 128/5).

(1946f), MM 650/pt. i, Minute 'Iron and Steel', 11 April 1946 (BT 231/28).

(1946g), C.P.(46) 152, Memorandum by the Secretary of State for Foreign Affairs, 'Future of the Iron and Steel Industry', 11 April 1946 (CAB 129/9).

(1946h), TI 11/01, 'Iron and Steel Debate: Finance of Industry Plan', memo, May 1946 (T 228/74).

(1946i), TI 11/01, Notes of H. Dalton's speech, 28 May 1946 (T 228/74).

(1946j), MM 650/38, Ellis Hunter (Bisf) to John Wilmot (Minister of Supply), 4 July 1947, doc. 81 (BT 231/32).

(1946k), MM 650/33 Pt. 1, Minute from U.S. (S. Pl), 'Iron and Steel Preparation of Plans for Public Ownership', 13 September 1946, doc. E 2a (BT 231/30).

(1946l), TI 3/109/01, Treasury minute, 15 November 1946 (T 228/24).

(1947a), MM 650/33 Pt. 1, 'Scheme for Public Ownership of Sections of the Iron and Steel Industry' and 'A Note on Timing and Tactics', January 1947, doc. E. 15 (BT 231/30).

(1947b), MM 650/33 Pt. 1, 'Public ownership of the Iron and Steel Industry' by F.G. Lee (US/IS), 31 January 1947, doc. E. 15c (BT 231/30).

(1947c), MM 650/33 Pt. 1, 'Notes of Meetings with the Minister to discuss the Report', 11–26 February 1947, documents E 37a to E 44 (BT 231/30).

(1947d), MM 650/33 Pt. 1, Minute by US (Air) 'Public Ownership of Sections of the Iron and Steel Industry' 18 February 1947, doc. E. 46 (BT 231/30).

(1947e), S.I.(M) (47), 2nd Meeting, Minute 1, March 25, 1947 and 3rd Meeting, Minute 2, 27 March 1947 (CAB 134/688).

(1947f), C.M. (47) 40th Conclusions, Minute 2, 28 April 1947 (CAB 128/9).

(1947g), Lord President of the Council, 'Notes of a Meeting held on Wednesday 21st May, 1947 10 Downing Street S.W.1' (CAB 124/791).

(1947h), MM 650/33 pt. 1, Note to Mr. Wilson (Ministry of Supply) from U.S./I.S: 'Notes for Minister's opening statement at S.I.(M) Committee', 13 June 1947, doc. E. 99a (BT 231/30).

(1947i), MM 650/33 Pt. 1, Minute to Mr Bailey (Ministry of Supply) from U.S/I.S. 're the executive functions and staff which would be taken over from the Iron and Steel Federation', 17 June 1947, doc. E 100a (BT 231/30).

(1947j), S.I.(M) (47), 6th Meeting, 18 June 1947 (CAB 134/688).

(1947k), Ministry of Supply, Iron and Steel Divison, 'Note of a Meeting held in the Lord President's Room, n.11 Downing Street, on Wednesday 16th of July at 5.15 p.m' (BT 255/103).

(1947l), C.P. (47) 212, 'Reorganisation of the Iron and Steel Industry: Joint Memorandum by the Lord President of the Council and the Minister of Supply', 21 July 1947 (CAB 129/20).

(1947m), Iron and Steel Division, Ministry of Supply 'Selected Companies – Issues of Fresh Capital of exchange or conversion of capital since 16th July 1945', July 1947 (BT 255/263).

(1947n), C.M. (47), 64th conclusions, Minute 2, 24 July 1947; C.M. (47), 66th conclusions, Minute 4, 31 July 1947; C.M. (47), 70th conclusions, Minute 6, 7 August 1947 (CAB 128/10).

(1947o), Prime Minister's Office, Harry Douglass (Iron and Steel Trades Confederation) to Right Hon. C.R. Attlee, 23 August 1947 (PREM 8/1489, pt. i).

(1948a), C.P. (48) 123, 'Iron and Steel Bill', Memorandum by the Minister of Supply, 20 May 1948 (CAB 129/27).

(1948b), C.P. (48) 136, 'Iron and Steel Bill', Memorandum by the Lord President of the Council, 2 June 1948 (CAB 129/27).

(1948c), C.M. (48), 36th Conclusions, Minute 4, 7 June 1948 (CAB 128/12).

(1948d), C.P. (48), 157, Memorandum by Minister of Supply, 'Iron and Steel Bill', 22 June 1948 (CAB 129/28).

(1948e), C.P. (48), 181, Iron and Steel Bill, Review of Arguments, 15 July 1948 (CAB 129/28).

(1948f), Prime Minister's Office, E. Bevin to H. Morrison, 17 July 1948 (PREM 8/1489, pt. ii).

(1948g), C.M. (48), 63rd Conclusions, Minute 4, 15 October 1948 (CAB 128/13).

(1952), Iron and Steel Nationalisation Papers, S.S. Wilson's Personal Notes, 1949–1952 (BT 231/30).

(1960), Iron and Steel Nationalisation Papers, Ministry of Power, 'Iron and Steel Industry Nationalisation and Denationalisation', Notes by S.S. Wilson, 12 February 1960 (BT 231/1).

Ranieri, R. (1993), 'Inside or outside the magic circle: the Italian and British Steel industries face to face with the Schuman Plan and the European Coal and Steel Community', in A.S. Milward, F. Lynch, R. Ranieri, F. Romero, V. Sorensen, *The Frontier of National Sovereignty – History and Theory 1945–1992*, London: Routledge, pp. 117–54.

Rogow, A.A. (1955), *The Labour Government and British Industry 1945–1951*, Oxford: Basil Blackwell.

Ross, G. (1965), *The Nationalization of Steel – One Step Forward, Two Steps Back?*, London: Macgibbon and Koe.

Sinigaglia, O. (1948), 'The Future of the Italian Iron and Steel Industry', *Banca Nazionale del Lavoro Quarterly Review*, n. 4, pp. 240–5.

Tolliday, S. (1987), *Business, Banking and Politics – The Case of Steel 1918–1939*, Cambridge, Mass: Harvard University Press.

Vaizey, J. (1974), *A History of British Steel*, London: Weidenfeld and Nicholson.

Williams-Thompson, R.B. (1951), *Was I Really Necessary*, London: World's Press News Publishing Co.

Wilson, C. (1962), *A Man and His Times – A memoir of Sir Ellis Hunter*, Middlesbrough: Newman Neame.

IV

Review and conclusions

14 The ownership of British industry in the post-war era: an explanation

Robert Millward and John Singleton

By the end of the 1940s the boundary between public and private economic activities in Britain had shifted decisively. One half of annual capital expenditure in the UK was undertaken in the public sector of which some 40 per cent was accounted for by the nationalised industries. This was the pattern for the next thirty years. The Conservative government which came to power in 1951 denationalised iron and steel along with road haulage. Later, in the 1960s and 1970s, airports and parts of the motor vehicle industry – Rolls-Royce, British Leyland – were brought into public ownership whilst iron and steel were renationalised. But the rest was untouched and the boundary had therefore remained unchallenged. Not until the 1980s did matters change. How then can we explain the particular constellation of private and public industry at the end of the 1940s? How can we resolve the puzzles left over from chapter 1? James Meade, argued in a memorandum for the Lord President's Economic Section that grounds for nationalisation were market concentration, capital intensity, senility (Howsen, vol. II, pp. 52–3): how close was this to the experience of the following five years?

To start with, let us underline the key factors influencing government industrial policies over the thirty years 1920–50. In the inter-war period the high unemployment levels and the falling value of the currency reflected the decline of the staple industries and the general loss of business to Germany, Spain, the USA and the new industrial competitors in Eastern Europe and Asia. These then were the key issues for coal, cotton, steel, shipbuilding and other parts of manufacturing but they also affected new export orientated service industries like airlines which were straggling behind KLM and Lufthansa let alone the American airline companies (chapter 4 above, Lyth). In the domestic infrastructure the four railway companies – the value of whose capital stock was almost as big as the whole of manufacturing industry – faced constant complaints from business users whilst experiencing severe financial problems from the loss of freight staples traffic and from the growing competition from road transport. By 1932 some £260 million of railway capital carried no dividend for shareholders (chapter 6, Crompton). Finally gas and electricity distribution networks were a motley collection of small municipal and private undertakings resisting all pressures to form larger business units (chapter 7, Wilson, chapter 12, Chick).

The Second World War of course then made production capacity an issue of national defence. For our purposes the significance of this lies firstly in the fact that the pressure on armaments and aircraft production started in the 1930s and was a factor in the Air Ministry launching in 1936 the government-owned, contractor-operated Shadow Factory schemes for engines and air frames, supplemented in 1938 by the 'extension' factories operated by aircraft firms. This backward vertical integration by the Defence Ministries meant that, in conjunction with the Royal Ordnance Factories and Naval Dockyards, the state's involvement in the manufacturing sector was rising rapidly, albeit in products which were purchased by the state (cf. chapter 8, Edgerton).

After the war the question was how the continuing demand for aircraft and other armaments was to be met. By that stage there were two other large problems facing the government. One was the reconstruction needs of the economy with its attendant shortages, rationing and fuel crises as resources were reallocated to civil employment. The other was the dollar shortage and the imperative of boosting exports. This was to be a key consideration for many manufacturing industries; how to get labour back to the mills in Lancashire, given the memories of low wages and unemployment in cotton in the inter-war years; how to ensure there was enough steel to allow industries to meet their export targets – 75 per cent of sales for motor cars.

These then were the immediate problems of the day. The industrial structure which emerged by 1951 may be summed up in the following way:

a) The infrastructure and extractive industries were 100 per cent publicly owned (excepting small parts of road transport, mining, quarrying and water supply).

b) Manufacturing and distribution, including aircraft production, were left in private ownership (excepting steel and small undertakings like Shorts Brothers and the Raw Cotton Commission and some of the manufacture of armaments for the state).

c) Public enterprises were owned by central government, accountable to Parliament, centrally run and organised (with Local Authority water supply and bus services the main exceptions).

d) A battery of physical controls on commodity supplies was retained after the war, reduced in scope in the late 1940s but then reinforced during the Korean War and even in 1954 they still existed for some key raw materials like coal, jute and scrap iron whilst controls on company borrowing and share issues did not disappear until the end of the 1950s.

As a starting point a political historian, digging in heels, might argue that the 'cause' of this set of institutional arrangements was the election of a Labour government in 1945. In particular, without Labour, the large-scale nationalisations would not have occurred. However the Conservative Party throughout this period had no clear strategy on these issues. In the depressed economic conditions of the inter-war period they could not reject public ownership out of hand especially given their role in the creation of the Central Electricity Board, the London Passenger Transport Board and British Overseas Airways Corporation and in the National government's initiative in Ordnance Factories. The 'etatist' wing of the Party was barely distinguishable on many issues from the Morrisonian wing of the Labour Party and in 1938 Harold Macmillan described Labour's programme for the nationalisation of the Bank of England, coalmining, power, land and transport as mild compared with his own plan (chapter 2, Singleton). The Conservatives' Industrial Charter of 1947 opposed nationalisation and direct planning in principle but fudged privatisation outside one or two small sectors in road and air transport, claiming that privatising the large public corporations would be too disruptive.

Moreover a large body of professional opinion by the late 1930s and 1940s was canvassing a more interventionist government stance in industrial matters. The McGowan Committee on electricity supply (1936) and the Cadman Report on civil aviation (1938) were advocating a major streamlining of their respective industries. E.H.E. Woodward, General Engineer and Manager of the North-Eastern Electricity Supply Company saw ownership as irrelevant and advocated the establishment of regional public electricity boards (Hannah 1979, chapter 10). By 1945 the Reid Committee, made up mainly of mining engineers from the private companies, was all but recommending nationalisation (cf. Beacham 1945) whilst in the same year the Heyworth Report on gas supply crossed the line and advocated the establishment of regional public boards.

Indeed industrial policy involving mere arms-length regulation had been discredited by the 1940s. The coal-owners' image had been dented as early as the 1920s (Supple 1986). During the Second World War their 'solution' for the industry was a Central Board comprising representatives of the management and owners but no miners or customers and yet supposedly acting as trustees for the industry in dealings with Parliament (Kirby 1977, p. 194). Similar 'corporatist' solutions forwarded by the Joint Committee of Electricity Supply Associations and, for airlines, by the various shipping and railway undertakings with shares in airline companies were not well received (Hannah 1979, p. 342, Lyth 1990, p. 2).

Hence the election of a Labour government was the opportunity for, rather than the underlying cause of, the nationalisations. There was a broad political consensus for government intervention, which increasingly focused on the ownership issue. None of which is to deny that, as we shall argue, the presence of a Labour government affected the form and scale of public ownership.

Another line of argument is that the industrial structure of the late 1940s reflected in part the success of administrative planning during the war. In fact all the evidence suggests that during the war government policy towards the ownership of industry was essentially pragmatic. The state invested in chemicals and engineering without taking the companies into public ownership. Short Brothers Ltd. was nationalised in 1943 only after a series of unsuccessful attempts to enforce standards. The manner in which the company developed the Stirling heavy bomber militated against flow production though the design team was good and was retained. The only other manufacturing companies brought into public ownership during the war were also in strategically sensitive areas: S.G. Brown Ltd, makers of precision instruments, and Power Jets Ltd, designers of jet propulsion engines. The Short Brothers case was indeed therefore, as the government claimed, not the thin edge of the wedge (chapter 11, Howlett). In fact the wartime experience with armaments had very different consequences. In the 1920s and early 1930s those advocating nationalisation of armaments production were aiming to socialise the 'merchants of death'. By the end of the inter-war period and following a Royal Commission report of 1936 the argument had shifted to considering nationalisation as a means of raising efficiency. In the event much armament production was left in the private sector and by creating new scientific weapons during the war the companies emerged with great credit and with no strong pressure to be brought up to scratch (chapter 8, Edgerton).

There were sectors where the war revealed or caused problems; in particular coal and railways which emerged from the war with 'a poor bag of assets' (Cairncross 1985, p. 471). Relief for the railway companies' struggles during the inter-war period with a declining freight staples traffic and with road competition did not come until 1941 from which date they were guaranteed a fixed annual payment of £43.5 million. Thereafter however fares and tariffs were frozen. The capital stock, including locos and other rolling stock, was not replenished, whilst over the period 1938–46 passenger mileage rose by 10 per cent and freight net ton miles by 27 per cent (Aldcroft 1968, p. 99). Coal production declined in part because of the initial loss of manpower to the armed forces but output per man fell from 300 tons in 1931 to 248 tons in 1945. Greasley (chapter 3 above) argues that this was not due to reduced effort. Nor does he invoke the resentment felt at the 1941 Essential Work Order (Kirby 1977, pp. 171–4). The industry was simply operating at full capacity and any significant increase in output would have to come from investment in new equipment.

Both the structure and the degree of concentration of British industry were affected by the war but it seems at most to have accentuated or reinforced trends that can be observed before 1939 and after 1945. Over the twenty years from 1935 there was actually little change in the concentration of industry and Howlett (chapter 11) suggests that the impact of the Concentration of Production Drive was at best delayed and indirect. There were significant changes in industrial structure with the output of chemicals, engineering and vehicles rising substantially and the shares of textiles, clothing, leather and paper falling. But these trends had emerged before the war and they were to continue afterwards. The war had simply speeded up the whole process.

Our explanation of the pattern of industrial ownership which emerged by 1950 is that the decisions of the Labour government on industrial policy and public ownership were affected by three things. First the need to meet export targets was central. Second there was a commitment to public ownership and economic planning in some areas but only a poorly articulated philosophy of how to cope with what remained in the private sector. Thirdly it had, like all governments, to respond first to areas where the problems appeared greatest; that is, it had to set priorities.

In that context, taking the *infrastructure* into public ownership had two clear merits. It provided the opportunity for exploiting the scale economies which many observers claimed existed: in the distribution networks and in the marketing and finance of electricity and gas; in the generation of electricity supply, high tension transmission already being in public ownership; in the merger of local water undertakings, drainage authorities and sewage works into integrated river basin systems; in the merger of the four railway companies. Secondly, it offered the prospect of eliminating the excess profits which were available for the private undertakings with *de facto* monoplies 'in the field' or which would have been available if private firms had been amalgamated into new large business units. Of course public ownership was not theoretically needed to achieve this since there was always the option of arms-length regulation. It was the perceived failure of inter-war regulation in airlines, gas and water supply, retail electricity supply and railways which enhanced the case for an alternative form of industrial intervention. The litany of failed regulation is to be found in the stream of government enquiries: the 1931 Boscawen Report on transport, the 1936 McGowan Report on electricity, the 1930s reports of the Joint Committee on Water Resources and Supplies, the 1938 Cadman Report on civil aviation and the 1945 Heyworth Report on gas. This is then sufficient to explain the emergence in the 1940s of the publicly owned area gas and electricity boards, the Railway Executive, British Overseas Airways Corporation, British European Airways Corporation and the concentration of generation and transmission in the new British Electricity Authority.

The priorities of the Labour government were of course determined by the severity of the problems they faced and the ease with which they could be resolved. This is particularly germane to understanding inaction in the whole field of water resource development. Water supply had all the classic features of utilities in early twentieth-century Britain. In 1944 there were still 1,196 separate undertakings. Arguments for nationalisation had been advanced since the turn of the century. A plan for nationalisation was adopted in 1948 by the Cabinet's Industries for Nationalisation Sub-Committee but was buried under other events. There were three underlying elements in this outcome. First was the absence of any chronic supply crisis: demand was growing at 1.6 per cent per annum 1900–50, much less than subsequently and less, so far as we can gather, than in the nineteenth century (chapter 9, Hassan). Although the physical infrastructure of land drainage and sewage works was neglected there was nothing like the collapse of underground networks which occurred later. At the same time the range of interested parties in the industry and the range of interested government departments were much larger than in gas and electricity. The suppliers of services included private water companies, local authority water supply undertakings, drainage authorities, local authority sewage authorities and river conservancy bodies. Property rights in land and water were held by all the above institutions together with riparian interests, landowners and industrialists. Within Whitehall they had a fertile field for lobbying amongst the various government departments involved: Ministry of Health, Board of Trade, Ministry of Agriculture and Fisheries, Department of Scientific and Industrial Research. The hurdles to be surmounted in any reorganisation of the industry were formidable (chapter 9, Hassan).

Coal is not usually thought of as part of the infrastructure. We cannot invoke the previous line of argument to explain its transfer to public ownership. It had, that is, all the features of a classic competitive industry. The presence of economies of scale in mining has always been disputed and in any case the size is not likely to generate natural monopoly problems. So why was coal brought into public ownership? The economic issue in coal was really about output levels and capacity. The production technology for all practical purposes involved constant returns to scale but of course all factors of production could not be varied. The massive expansion in the second half of the nineteenth century used more and more labour to work a given set of coal deposits. Technical improvements in cutting and hauling did take place but it was essentially a low productivity, albeit profitable, expansion. By the 1940s the scope for raising output, even by reallocating labour across districts, was limited. Yet coal was a major strategic commodity both in the war and in the late 1940s.

It is Greasley's thesis (chapter 3) that the owners cannot really be criticised for how they responded to changes in demand; from 1870 through to the Second World War, the response was economically efficient. Yet as his story indicates the coal owners had been discredited in the public perception by the 1940s. Coalmining was of course dangerous, dirty, highly regionalised and a potent setting for a disgruntled labour force. By the twentieth century the miners had significant political clout and accounted for nearly half of union sponsored Members of Parliament in 1935 (chapter 2, Singleton). Paradoxically, although nationalisation has often been more strongly associated with coalmining than other industries it was not typical of the rest of the industries which were nationalised in 1945–50. By 1945 there was a severe problem about achieving target output levels. All the technical advice to the government was that the industry needed reorganising. The owners were discredited whilst the workers, well represented in Parliament, wanted nationalisation and that is what they got.

Union support for public ownership in other industries was much more qualified and the rent-seeking model which might explain nationalisation in terms of unions has little relevance in the British context outside mining where it was as much a touchstone of British politics (chapter 2, Singleton). Thus unions in the infrastructure industries, in motor vehicles, cotton and some other parts of manufacturing and distribution might advance the cases for public ownership, but they had little influence. Indeed close examination of manufacturing suggests that in the late 1940s the export drive was the prime consideration. The merits of public ownership in terms of capturing scale economies and eliminating monopoly profits were not so obvious. The production technology in these industries was much more conducive to competition both domestically and from exports than the infrastructure industries. The need to promote larger business units and raise technical progress and capital intensity was recognised but these were long-term problems and in any case the Labour government, as we shall see, had no well-articulated philosophy for intervention in these areas and 'much policy towards private industry was evolved while the government was in power' (Mercer, Rollings and Tomlinson 1992, p. 4).

The export objective necessitated short-term solutions; essentially enough labour and raw materials to raise output with current technologies. Cotton was in 'the front line of a battle for the balance of payments' (Stafford Cripps, quoted in Singleton 1990). Production of yarn and cloth had halved between 1937 and 1945 and exports had fallen even more. The government pressed firms to improve the wage structure and working conditions to induce young people and former munition workers, especially women operatives, to return to the mills. In this atmosphere the millowners were safe as long as they met the export targets and the only part of the industry to be brought into public ownership was the raw cotton exchange; the Raw Cotton Commission would ease the export drive by negotiating long-term contracts with colonial governments for the price of raw cotton. The long-term regeneration of the industry was of secondary importance (chapter 10, Singleton). In motor vehicles the underlying long-term problems were even further from the government's gaze. The industry had undergone some rationalisation in the inter-war period with the number of firms falling from 113 in 1914 to forty-one in 1929 and to thirty-three by 1938 (chapter 5, Bowden). By the end of the 1940s UK output was double that of France, four times that of Germany and eight times that of Italy: the UK was the second highest car-producing country in the world. The prime issue was exports, the target for which was set at 50 per cent of production in 1946, raised to 75 per cent in 1947. Continuing physical controls allowed the government to give the industry priority for fuel, steel and other raw materials; indeed the allocations could be reduced were the industry to fail to meet the export targets. In 1948 the Labour Party's Sub-Committee on Nationalisation accepted the arguments and declared that the motor industry was unsuitable for nationalisation.

The longer-term problems of these industries were those of raising capital intensity, technical progress and productivity. The Labour Party was uncertain how best to harness the concept of public ownership to these needs of the manufacturing sector, regardless of whether the industries under consideration were relatively atomistic, as in cotton, or oligopolistic, as in steel and motor vehicles. The hand-wringing over steel in the years 1944–8 illustrates the issues vividly. Ranieri (chapter 13) identifies, for these purposes, three groups within Whitehall towards the end of the war. The 'modernisers' envisaged a vast programme of restructuring, to be achieved through a combination of state investment and direct controls. The 'corporatists' wanted a return to arms-length regulation with high tariffs, a cartel and an important role for the employers' organisation, the British Steel Federation. Finally there were the 'liberals' promoting competition and the elimination of protection and all other forms of government intervention. This last view was well represented in the Lord President's Economic Section who argued that the commitment of resources to particular sectors was special pleading; the market could do most of the things the modernisers seemed to want, echoing James Meade's dismissal of the case for a state monopoly of raw cotton where the classical conditions existed in which competition was likely to be in the public interest (chapter 10, Singleton).

The 1944 Plan for steel was a corporatist solution giving the British Steel Federation much of what it wanted. The Labour Party's position was nearest to the modernisers but the unevenness of the Labour Ministers' commitment to nationalisation reflected an uncertainty about how to intervene in a capital intensive, oligopolistic industry. In their dealings with the motor vehicle industry they were much more circumspect. Introducing new models was costly and risky; better the shareholder bear this risk than the taxpayer. The Labour Party was in fact remarkably clear that design, performance and style in the production of cars would stagnate without competition and competition could be stimulated only under private ownership (chapter 5, Bowden). In steel there had been a long-term movement for nationalisation. Its importance as a strategic commodity was underlined in the fuel crisis of 1946–7 and the associated balance of payments problems which led to the abandonment of sterling convertibility in August 1947. The fuel crisis had cost the country some 750,000 tons of steel, straining supplies to important industries like shipbuilding and engineering and denting the programmes for exports and housing (chapter 13, Ranieri). The Labour government had been elected in 1945 on a clear mandate to nationalise steel. But the industry was made up of a very disparate set of firms and neither the civil servants nor the politicians had the detailed knowledge to plan the industry.

In the 1947 discussions about an Iron and Steel Board, Ministers were outmanoeuvred by the Federation's leaders. When it came to drafting the nationalisation bill in 1948 various options including partial public ownership were in the wind. But there were no ready formulae for guiding a policy of, say, government shareholdings in private companies. There was no philosophy of interaction between private and state sectors on which to draw. The Iron and Steel Corporation which emerged in 1951 was a highly centralised organisation with little differentiation from the public corporation structures which had been agreed on for the infrastructure industries.

This brings us back to the four features of the industrial structure in 1951 set out earlier in this chapter. The incidence of public and private ownership across industries has been explained. What remains is the form of public ownership in the coal and infrastructure sectors and specifically the essentially 'national' and centralised basis of the new institutions. In the coal industry regional public boards, perhaps based on coalfields, would have been consistent with an optimistic view of the size of scale economies. But allowing such boards to operate independently in the coal market would have flown against all the history of the miners' battles against interregional competition in wages and prices. In the case of railways the realisation of scale economies on a national scale had been on the agenda since the Royal Commission report of 1931 and the emergence of the Railway Executive operating all the country's railway assets was a natural consequence. However the National Coal Board was established to do rather more than simply minimise interregional competition and the Railway Executive was but one arm of a larger transport organisation, the new British Transport Commission. Similarly, as we noted in chapter 1, the new gas industry structure was not simply a set of area boards. There was a British Gas Council acting as an overarching supervisory body and the British Electricity Authority had a similar role *vis-à-vis* the Area Electricity Boards quite apart from its position as the sole generator and transmitter. These bodies were uniformly expected to develop programmes for investment and training for this was essentially a reconstruction programme: an upgrading of the stock of physical and human capital to which all post-war governments were committed. The Labour government was to do this through physical planning rather than using the price system. In the case of transport, coordination between different modes was to be an aspect of planning rather than left to the market. Hence it was the British Transport Commission – vested with the assets of its five Executives for Railways, Road Transport, London Transport, Hotels, Docks and Inland Waterways – which had responsibility for providing an integrated transport system.

The new corporations were then clearly expected to develop investment and training programmes and to participate in the administrative apparatus of transport. These responsibilities were mirrored in the specific objectives laid on them to promote the 'public interest' in the production of coal, promote the efficient supply of cheap gas and electricity and provide an efficient, adequate, economic and fully integrated transport system – to paraphrase the Acts of Parliaments. These dimensions of the new public enterprises were to prove troublesome throughout the post-war period. Electricity, for example, was increasingly being seen, in some parts of the Labour Party, as a 'basic necessity' to be offered at a uniform price (chapter 12, Chick). How the new corporations were to do that whilst developing a commercial ambience and an independence of government departments became the major issue in the next thirty years.

In summary, we should first recognise that, in view of the success of large firms in the United States, and perceptions of the disorder and waste caused by excessive competition at home, there was a growing conviction in informed circles between 1920 and 1950 that giant enterprises were inherently more efficient than smaller firms. The superiority of large planned enterprises was in some degree an article of faith rather than a scientifically proven fact (just as in the 1980s privatisation was held by many to be the only solution to the problems of industries in the public sector). Although there were clear opportunities for large technical economies of scale in, for example, steel and electricity generation, these economies had not been unequivocally demonstrated in some other industries such as coal and air transport. Moreover, it was simply assumed that the bigger the enterprise, particularly if it was liberated from family control, the better would be the performance of its management. When the existing owners of firms refused to cooperate in the restructuring of their industries in order to create giant units, and where private enterprise could not be trusted to run the reorganised industries in the public interest, it was but a short step to the advocacy of nationalisation.

Public ownership was thought to be most urgent in transport and power utilities and industries such as coal and steel which supplied intermediate products. If these sectors could be made more efficient, the economy as a whole would benefit from lower costs and prices. The nationalisation of consumer goods industries such as cars and cotton textiles was another matter. Not only did the government already have enough on its plate between 1945 and 1950, but it doubted whether the potential gains in efficiency from public ownership would outweigh the short-run disruption in exports during the transition. In any case, the microeconomic implications of nationalising these industries had not been fully worked out, and there were strong reservations even in left-wing circles about the advantages of state ownership of industries which needed to be flexible and design-conscious in the quest for success in international markets.

REFERENCES

Aldcroft, D.H. (1968), *British Railways in Transition*, Macmillan.
Beacham, A.J. (1945), 'Efficiency and Organisation of the British Coal Industry', *Economic Journal*, Vol. 55, June–September.
Boscawen Report (1931), *Final Report*, Royal Commission on Transport, Command 3420.
Cadman Report (1938), *Report of the Committee of Inquiry into Civil Aviation*, Command 5685, March.
Cairncross, A. (1985), *Years of Recovery: British Economic Policy 1945–51*, Methuen.
Hannah, L. (1979), *Electricity Before Nationalisation*, Macmillan.
Heyworth Report (1945), *Report of the Committee of Inquiry into the Gas Industry 1945*, Command 6699.

Howson, S. (Ed.) (1989/90), *The Collected Papers of James Meade*, London: Unwin Hyman.

Kirby, M.W. (1977), *The British Coal Mining Industry 1870–1946*, Macmillan.

Lyth, P. (1990), 'A Multiplicity of Instruments: The 1946 Decision to Create a Separate British European Airline and its Effects on Airline Productivity', *Journal of Transport History*, Vol. 11, No. 2.

Mcgowan Report (1936), *Report of the Committee on Electricity Distribution*, Ministry of Transport, May.

Mercer, H., Rollings, N. and Tomlinson, J.D. (1992), *Labour Governments and Private Industry: The Experience of 1945–1951*, Edinburgh: Edinburgh University Press.

Reid Report (1945), *Report of the Technical Advisory Committee on Coal Mining*, Command 6610.

Singleton, J. (1990), 'Planning for Cotton 1945–51', *Economic History Review*, vol. XLIII, No. 1, pp. 62–78.

Supple, B. (1986), 'Ideology or Pragmatism?: The Nationalisation of Coal 1916–46', in N. Mckendrick and R.B. Outhwaite (ed.), *Business Life and Public Policy: Essays in Honour of D.C. Coleman*, Cambridge University Press.

Index

accidents, 4
air transport
  air services in early 1920s, 67–70
  British European Airways Corporation,
    5, 73, 78–85, 314
  British Overseas Airways Corporation,
    5, 65, 73, 77–85, 311, 314
  British South American Airways, 73,
    78–9, 81
  Cadman Report 1938, 7, 75–6, 311, 313
  Civil Aviation Act 1946, 80–1
  Civil Aviation Authority, 7
  economics of air transport, 82–4
  foreign competition, 67–76
  Hambling Report 1923, 69–70
  Imperial Airways, 70–1, 72, 74–6
  labour relations, 75
  Maybury Report 1935, 71–2
  motives for state intervention, 65–7
  nationalisation 1939, 76–7
  Railway Air Services, 71, 74
  subsidies to private firms, 70–6
  Swinton Plan 1945, 77–80
Alchian, A. A., 4
Anderson, Sir J., 280
armaments industry
  aircraft production in Second World
    War, 238–41
  defence R&D, 174–7
  development of armaments industry,
    166–70
  Power Jets, 165, 176, 237, 312
  Royal Commission on the Private
    Manufacture of and Trading in Arms
    1936, 170, 175, 312
  Royal Dockyards, 8, 164, 178–83, 310
  Royal Ordnance Factories, 20, 164, 173,
    178–83, 310, 311
  state production of arms in 1930s and
    1940s, 177–82
  structure of industry 1950, 182–3
  union attitudes, 172–3, 180–1
Ashworth, W., 164, 180

Assheton, R., 269
Atomic Energy Authority, 177, 184
Attlee, C. R., 17, 23–4, 208, 282, 285, 290
Australia, nationalisation in, 19

bakeries, proposed nationalisation of, 19
Baldwin, S., 17
Balfour Committee, 120
Bank of England, 5, 6, 18, 19, 21, 22, 23,
    215, 286, 311
banking system, proposed nationalisation
    of, 15, 16, 19–20
Beacham, A., 52
Beaverbrook, Lord, 110
Bellerby, J. J., 225
Bevan, A., 14, 23, 24, 25, 202, 207, 208, 225
Beveridge, W., 277
Bevin, E., 16, 27, 283–4, 290
Birkenhead, Lord, 50
Brady, R., 28
British Broadcasting Corporation, 5, 9, 18
British Leyland, 309
British Transport Commission, 4, 5, 8,
    107–9, 318
Brooke, S., 21
Brown Ltd, S. G., 237, 312
Bulgaria, nationalisation in, 19
Butler, R. A., 22
Butterfield, P., 139

Cairncross, Sir A., 145
canals, nationalisation of, 15, 16
Cecil, Lord H., 19
cement industry, proposed nationalisation
    of, 16, 25
Chadwick, E., 189
Chandler, A. D., 212
Chantler, P., 150, 153–8
chemical industry, proposed
    nationalisation of, 15, 16, 25
Chester, N., 277–8, 297
Christian socialism, 14
Churchill, Sir W. S., 23, 68, 110, 244

coal industry
  coal industry before 1939, 46–50
  Coal Mines Act 1930, 6, 38–9, 49, 52, 55,
    56, 61
  Coal Mines Reorganisation
    Commission, 37, 52, 61
  development of public policy, 59–62
  National Coal Board, 4, 5, 7, 9, 26, 37,
    60, 318
  nationalisation 1947, 37
  problems in World War Two, 39–46
  proposed nationalisation of coal
    distribution, 18
  Reid Committee 1945, 38, 50–4, 311
  Royal Commission on Coal Supplies
    1903–5, 59
  Samuel Commission 1925, 9, 51–2, 53,
    55, 56, 60
  Sankey Commission 1919, 51, 60
  under private ownership, 50–9
Cole, G. D. H., 216
commercial objectives of nationalised
  industries, 18–19
communism, 16, 217
compensation, 9, 26
Concentration of Production Drive,
  248–51, 253–4, 313
Conservative Party
  attitude to nationalisation before 1939,
    17–20
  attitude to nationalisation 1939–45, 20–2
  attitude to nationalisation 1945–51, 22–7
  air transport, 76–80
  coal industry, 38
  cotton industry, 23
  gas industry, 22, 158
  Industrial Charter 1947, 22–3, 311
  management of nationalised industries,
    26
  privatisation, 4, 22–3, 26, 309
  steel industry, 24
consumer councils, 23
cotton industry
  Board of Trade Working Party Report
    1946, 212, 225–6
  British Cotton Corporation, 219
  Cotton Board, 223, 224, 226
  Cotton Control, 227
  Cotton Control Board, 219
  Cotton Industry (Reorganisation Act)
    1939, 222
  development of cotton industry, 213–15
  Joint Committee of Cotton Trade
    Organisations, 218
  Legislative Council Report 1943, 222–4
  Liverpool cotton market, 23, 227

  Raw Cotton Commission, 227–8, 310,
    316
  unions and nationalisation, 216–29
  women workers, 223, 228
Cripps, Sir R. S., 20, 23, 80, 176, 215,
  224–6, 228, 239–41, 243–5, 253, 290
Cube, Mr, 25

Dalton, H., 23, 24, 26, 202, 208, 224, 276
  283, 289–90
de Havilland, G., 67
Demsetz, H., 4
Dennison, S. R., 279
depressed regions, 5
Devons, E., 182
discount houses, proposed nationalisation
  of, 25
drink industry, proposed nationalisation
  of, 15
Drucker, P., 15
Duncan, A., 276–7, 280, 283, 285–9
Duncanson, J., 281
Dupree, M., 226
Durbin, E., 21

economics of politics, 26–9
Edwards, J., 206
electricity
  Area Electricity Boards, 5, 318
  British Electricity Authority, 5, 8, 314,
    318
  Central Electricity Board, 5, 7, 9, 17,
    126, 146, 258, 261–2, 270, 272–3, 311
  Electricity Commissioners, 261–2, 267,
    268
  Electricity (Supply) Act 1926, 258, 261,
    273
  industrial structure, 258–60
  McGowan Committee, 7, 258–70, 311,
    313
  Power Companies Association, 268
  Weir Committee, 258, 261, 272
  World War Two, 268–72
Evely, R., 249–50
externalities, 6, 8

Fabian Research Group, 225
Farnie, D. A., 213
Feinstein, C. H., 252
Ferguson, Senator H., 24
Finance Corporation for Industry, 286
financial performance of nationalised
  industries, 19
Fleming, J. M., 227
food distribution, proposed nationalisation
  of, 19

Ford, H., 104
Foreman-Peck, J., 95
Franks, O, 277–8
Freeman, J., 173
Freeman, Sir W., 176
French steel industry, 297–9

Gamble, A. M., 15, 21
Gaitskell, H., 17
gas industry
    Area Gas Boards, 5, 159
    British Commercial Gas Association,
        147, 158
    British Gas Council, 5, 8, 157, 158, 318
    British Gas Federation, 153, 158, 160
    development of gas industry, 145–7
    economics of gas supply, 147–50
    Gas Legislation Committee 1933, 151
    Gas Regulation Act 1920, 152–3, 154
    Gas Undertakings Act 1932, 151
    Heyworth Report 1945, 7, 149–59, 160,
        161, 206, 311, 314
    in World War Two, 155–6
    National Fuel and Power Committee
        1928, 154, 155–6
    National Gas Authority, 154
    National Gas Council, 153
    PEP Report 1939, 149–59
    proposed regional integration, 150–4
    union atitudes, 158–9
Geddes, Sir E., 70, 117
Glyn, Sir R., 131
Gowers, E., 52
Grimethorpe colliery, 26
Guild Socialism, 9

Harris, N., 17
Harrod, Sir R., 54
Heaton, Sir F., 243
Henderson, A., 171
Hilton-Young, Sir E., 194
Hobson, H., 269–70
Hogg, Q., 21
Holt, G., 67
Hore-Belisha, L., 265
Hornby, W., 180
Huberman, M., 213
Hudson, R. S., 223–4
Hunter, E., 285–7
Hurcomb, Sir C., 269
Hutchinson, Z., 217, 218–19, 223

Imperial Chemical Industries, 5, 25, 179,
    182, 294
industrial self-government, 17–19
Italian steel industry, 297–9

Jay, D., 21, 228–9, 285
Jewkes, J., 279
Jowitt, Sir W., 268–70, 273, 285

Kelf-Cohen, R., 145, 159
Kem, Senator J.P., 24
Kenny, S., 213
Keynes, J. M., 215, 257, 265–6, 273
Keynesianism, 15–16, 21, 22
Knollys, Lord, 78

Labour Party
    air transport, 80–1
    armaments industry, 171–3, 182
    Clause Four, 14–15
    coal industry, 27, 37–9
    cotton industry, 212, 217, 220–2, 224–9
    election manifesto 1945, 20–2
    gas industry, 157–61
    influence of unions, 27–9
    motor vehicles, 88–9, 94–111
    nationalisation plans before 1939,
        14–17
    nationalisation policy 1945–51, 22–6,
        311–19
    public corporation, 16–17
    railways, 132, 140–1
    steel, 276–7, 282–97
    water supply, 192, 200–2, 206–9
Lancaster, Colonel C. G., 26
land, proposed nationalisation of, 15, 16,
    18, 25
Lazonick, W., 213
Liberal Party, 14, 15
life assurance, proposed nationalisation of,
    15, 18, 25
Little, I. M. D., 249–50
Londonderry, Lord, 68
London Passenger Transport Board, 5, 9,
    10, 18, 138–9, 311
Lord, L., 91, 112 n. 5
Lord President's Economic Section, 227,
    277, 279, 309, 316–17
Lyttleton, O., 21

McCloskey, D. N., 13
MacDonald, J. R., 16
McKinnon Wood, R., 175
Macmillan, H., 17–19
machine tool industry, proposed
    nationalisation of, 25
management, 9, 18, 21, 23, 25, 38–9
Marrison, A. J., 213–14
Masefield, Sir P., 82
Maude, Sir J., 197, 317
Meade, J., 227, 279, 309

meat supply, proposed nationalisation of, 16, 25
Metropolitan Water Board, 5, 9
Mikardo, I., 207, 209
Miliband, R., 20
milk distribution, proposed nationalisation of, 18
Milne-Watson, Sir D., 159
minerals, proposed nationalisation of, 16, 25
miners, 19, 20, 26, 27–8, 37, 40–4
ministerial interference, 21, 23
Money, Sir L. C., 14
Moore-Brabazon, J. T. C., 179
Morgan, K. O., 144–5, 159
Morrison, H., 9, 16–17, 23, 24, 26, 79–80, 123–4, 132–3, 140, 201–2, 262–3, 271, 285–9
motor vehicle industry
    development of the industry, 89–94
    European comparisons, 101–4
    financial position, 97–100
    Labour Party rejects nationalisation, 88–9
    performance of the industry, 95–109
    pricing, 100
    rationalisation, 94–6
    schemes for partial nationalisation, 101–9
    standardisation, 96–7
    Transport Act 1947, 107–9
    US multinationals in Britain, 104–7
Municipal Corporations Association, 200–1

Naesmith, A., 221, 223
National Health Service, 14
National Transport Trust, 121
natural monopoly, 6
New Fabian Research Bureau, 218
Next Five Years Group, 18, 122, 133, 171
Noel Baker, P., 172
North of Scotland Hydro-Electric Board, 5, 164
Nuffield Industrial Conferences, 21

Olson, M., 27
Ottawa Agreement, 220

Perkins, R., 75
pollution, 7
Porsche, Dr, 102
Port of London Authority, 5, 9
Post Office, 8
Prais, S. J., 249
prohibition of alcohol, 20

property rights, 4
public corporation model, 8, 9, 16–17, 18
public opinion, 21–2, 25
public service objectives, 19

railways
    electrification, 125–31
    financial position, 117–19, 124–5, 131–6
    Gore-Browne Report 1942, 139–40
    internal organisation of companies, 136–8
    in World War One, 116
    Railway Executive, 7, 314, 318
    Railways Act 1921, 117
    Royal Commission on Transport (Boscawen Commission) 1931, 120–1, 122–3, 124, 125–6, 138, 313, 318
    union attitudes, 140
    Weir Committee 1931, 126–8, 138
Reith, Sir J., 75
rent-seeking, 27–9
road transport, 6, 8, 22, 26
Robbins, L., 279
Rogow, A. A., 26
Runciman, W., 20

Salter, W. E. G., 54
Scott, J. D., 175
Sheail, J., 194, 197
Shinwell, E., 9, 157, 161, 271
shipbuilding, proposed nationalisation of, 25
shipping, proposed nationalisation of, 15, 19
Shone, R., 281
Shore, P., 26
Short Brothers, 20, 164, 165, 237, 239–47, 253, 291, 310, 312
Smith, E., 207, 225
Society of Motor Manufacturers and Traders, 108
Stamp, Sir J., 129, 132–5, 136
steel industry
    British Iron and Steel Federation, 275, 278–94, 316–17
    Five Year Plan, 280–2, 296
    Franks-Chester Report, 278–9, 280, 281, 299
    Iron and Steel Corporation of Great Britain, 3, 5, 290–7, 317
    Iron and Steel Trades Confederation, 27
    proposed partial nationalisation, 285–90
    Steel Bill, 290–7
stock ownership, 9
Strachey, J., 9
Strauss, G., 290, 295, 296

Streat, Sir E. R., 223., 224, 226
strikes, 26
sugar refining, proposed nationalisation of, 16, 25
Swinton, Viscount, 77–9
Sylvester, A. E., 157
syndicalism, 9
Szlumper, G., 117

Tate & Lyle, 25
Tawney, R. H., 14
Temin, P., 213
Thompson, Lord, 174
Thornton, E., 228
Tizard, Sir H., 176
Tolliday, S., 299–300
Tomlinson, G., 224
Tomlinson, J., 15
Trade Union Congress, 9, 219–20, 221
transport coordination, 122–4
Tress, R., 279
tripartism, 226

Union of Postal Workers, 9
union-sponsored MPs, 27–8
US aid and nationalisation, 24

Van der Bijl, H., 285

Walkland, S. A., 15

Water supply
    Association of Waterworks Engineers, 202, 203
    Advisory Committee on Water, 194, 203
    British Waterworks Association, 198, 202, 203
    Central Advisory Committee (Milne Committee), 195, 196, 198, 201, 203, 204
    comparison with electricity and gas policies, 204–6
    development of water supplies, 189–96
    Joint Committee on Water Resources 1935–6, 201
    Land Drainage Act 1930, 191
    Water Act 1945, 196–200, 203, 207
Weir, Lord, 175
Whitelaw, W., 139
Whittle, F., 176
wholesale trade, proposed nationalisation of, 25
Wilmot, J., 23, 282, 285–9, 294
Wilson, H., 228–9
Winster, Lord, 80
Withers, H., 19, 20
Wood, Sir K., 76–7, 78
Woods Humphrey, G., 70, 75
Woodward, E. H. E., 311
Woolton, Lord, 25–6, 223–4
worker control, 9, 14–15, 16–17, 20, 21
worker representatives, 9, 16–17
Wormsley, B. H., 149, 155

DATE DUE

GAYLORD   PRINTED IN U.S.A.